Horace G. Wadlin

Relation of the liquor traffic to pauperism, crime, and insanity

Horace G. Wadlin

Relation of the liquor traffic to pauperism, crime, and insanity

ISBN/EAN: 9783743417458

Manufactured in Europe, USA, Canada, Australia, Japa

Cover: Foto ©Suzi / pixelio.de

Manufactured and distributed by brebook publishing software (www.brebook.com)

Horace G. Wadlin

Relation of the liquor traffic to pauperism, crime, and insanity

RELATION

OF THE

LIQUOR TRAFFIC

TO

PAUPERISM, CRIME, AND INSANITY.

[FROM THE TWENTY-SIXTH ANNUAL REPORT OF THE
MASSACHUSETTS BUREAU OF STATISTICS
OF LABOR, pp. 1–416.]

BY

HORACE G. WADLIN,

CHIEF OF THE BUREAU OF STATISTICS OF LABOR.

BOSTON:
WRIGHT & POTTER PRINTING CO., STATE PRINTERS,
18 POST OFFICE SQUARE.
1896.

RELATION

OF THE

LIQUOR TRAFFIC

TO

PAUPERISM, CRIME, AND INSANITY.

[FROM THE TWENTY–SIXTH ANNUAL REPORT OF THE
MASSACHUSETTS BUREAU OF STATISTICS
OF LABOR, pp. 1–416.]

BY

HORACE G. WADLIN

CHIEF OF THE BUREAU OF STATISTICS OF LABOR.

BOSTON:
WRIGHT & POTTER PRINTING CO., STATE PRINTERS,
18 POST OFFICE SQUARE.
1896.

CONTENTS.

CONTENTS.

RELATION

OF THE

LIQUOR TRAFFIC

TO

PAUPERISM, CRIME, AND INSANITY.

Relation of the Liquor Traffic

TO

Pauperism, Crime, and Insanity.

The information contained in this Part has been collected
and is presented under the authority of Chapter 332 of the
Acts of 1894, the first and principal Section of which is as
follows :

"The bureau of statistics of labor is hereby directed to ascertain, from
all sources available, facts and statistics showing the number of commitments to all institutions, penal and charitable, resulting from the use or
abuse of intoxicating liquors, the number of crimes committed by persons
while under the influence of intoxicating liquors, the number of crimes of
each class thus committed, the number of paupers whose present condition
can be traced to the use or abuse of intoxicating liquors by themselves or
by their parents, guardians or others ; the number of persons who have
been pronounced insane and whose condition can be traced to the use or
abuse of intoxicating liquors by themselves, their ancestors or by others,
and in general such other data as will tend to show the relation of the
liquor traffic to crime, pauperism and insanity in this Commonwealth : and
the period of time to be covered by this investigation shall include not less
than twelve successive months."

While the investigation thus rests upon legislative mandate,
it falls properly within the province of a Bureau whose prime
duty, under the Act creating it, is the presentation of statistical details, " especially in relation to the commercial, industrial, social, educational, and sanitary condition of the laboring
classes, and to the permanent prosperity of the productive
industries of the Commonwealth." The permanent prosperity

of the industries of the Commonwealth and the industrial condition of the laboring classes is without question seriously affected by the presence of pauperism, crime, and other disorganizing social influences. Any facts relating to these evils, or any data which may throw light upon the relation of intemperance thereto, are of importance in the study of industrial conditions. For these reasons the Bureau in previous reports has canvassed certain phases of the general subject, particularly in the Report for 1877, Part V, "Pauperism and Crime;" the Report for 1879, Part VI, "Statistics of Drunkenness and Liquor Selling, 1874 and 1877;" the Report for 1880, Part III, "Statistics of Crime, 1860–1879;" and the Report for 1881, Part II, "Statistics of Drunkenness and Liquor Selling, 1870–1879."

Under the terms of the Act authorizing the present investigation, the collection of information occupied twelve successive months, the period closing August 20, 1895. It has been prosecuted through the different State institutions for the reception of paupers and the insane, and through the prisons and courts of the Commonwealth. All persons committed to these institutions, or passing through the courts for criminal offences, have been directly interviewed by the agents of the Bureau and their testimony taken concerning their habits with respect to the use of intoxicating liquors, and as to the habits of their parents, guardians, or others who may have exerted a direct influence upon them. The results of the investigation thus rest upon the direct testimony of those immediately concerned, except in the case of the insane, who, for obvious reasons, were incapable of giving direct information themselves. Respecting the insane, therefore, the testimony of others has been taken, and no effort has been spared to bring out full and reliable data covering the special points of inquiry respecting each of the classes referred to. The inquiries were carefully formulated before beginning the investigation, and the work has been carried out by agents of the Bureau especially selected for the purpose.

The report covers 3,230 returns as to pauperism, 26,672 as to crime, and 1,836 as to insanity. The evidence condensed in the tables, therefore, rests upon personal interviews with respect to 31,738 cases of pauperism, crime, and insanity, and comprises the largest amount of direct information, that is to say, information secured by direct personal interviews with the persons immediately concerned, that has ever been obtained; and while the results may be compressed into a comparatively few pages, it will be readily understood that the work of investigation has required the utmost care in order to secure trustworthy and reliable data, and has called for extraordinary tact and patience on the part of those who have prosecuted the inquiries, and who have had intimate personal relations with the large number of individuals contributing to the fund of information.

The returns relating to crime are more complete and trustworthy than those respecting pauperism and insanity, owing to the fact that a more complete record exists relating to the persons committed for different offences in the courts, and the record itself in many cases afforded conclusive evidence upon a special point of the inquiry. For example, if a person had been committed a number of times during a series of years for drunkenness, this of itself threw light upon his habits as to the use of intoxicating liquor. Whenever a person is convicted of an offence in the courts, the conviction becomes a matter of record, and the criminal history of a person may be traced through successive years if he has been before the courts at different times. Concerning the paupers and the insane no such definite record covering a series of years exists.

Besides this, the prisoners as a class are much more intelligent than the paupers, and better capable of giving valuable evidence. Many of the paupers whose history enters into the present investigation are of comparatively low intelligence. Frequently they have no knowledge concerning their fathers and mothers, and are therefore incapable of giving testimony as to their parents' habits, and being State paupers, without legal settlement in the towns or cities from whence they were committed to the institutions in which they were found, it is extremely difficult to secure information upon this point. This difficulty is increased by the fact that in a very large number of cases, as will appear from the tables, the parents were of foreign birth.

The question at once arises how far can the information given by those belonging to the defective classes, either paupers or criminals, be considered free from falsehood. In other words, is it probable that these persons have given truthful answers when catechised as to their personal habits concerning the use of intoxicating liquors, and are their statements trustworthy respecting the effect which such use may have had on their present condition? In reply, it must be said that the experience of the Bureau leads to the belief that their statements are trustworthy, and that in its general results the evidence presented in the tables may be taken as conclusive. Opinions to the contrary previously held by some who have had personal relations with the defective classes, have been modified by the results secured as the investigation has progressed.

It might be suspected that the percentage of untruthful answers would be largest among the criminal classes, but it has been found that nearly all the prisoners, if properly approached, would give faithful testimony respecting their habits in the use of liquor and as to the habits of their parents. This is unqualifiedly true with regard to the intelligent prisoners, who in general attempted no concealment of facts in their answers. Naturally, the lower the grade of the person replying, the greater the difficulty experienced in obtaining answers, and a larger proportion of the women than of the men to whom the inquiries were put endeavored to conceal their delinquencies. As a rule, personal short-comings were acknowledged rather more freely than those of parents, and the defects of fathers reported more readily than those of mothers. The vagrants and tramps constituted the most unsatisfactory persons from whom to obtain information in regard to themselves or their parents, many of them at first claiming to be total abstainers, and also asserting the same virtue for their fathers and mothers. In the majority of cases, however, as soon as the persons who were questioned understood the object of the inquiries they endeavored to answer honestly; and whenever concealment or evasion was attempted at first, it was soon found that the disposition to avoid the questions or to mis-state the facts could easily be detected and counteracted. In general, therefore, there is no ground for asserting that those who have replied to the questions of our agents have done other than state the exact facts so far as it was possible for them to do so. The exceptions to the rule are not sufficient in number to vitiate the results of the investigation. It is not necessary to enlarge upon this point, but simply to state, as we have already done, that we believe the results of the tables may be accepted as trustworthy and reliable.

While it has been necessary, in prosecuting the investigation to depend mainly upon the replies obtained by close questioning of persons committed, this has been supplemented by an examination of all the records having a bearing upon the case, as well as by visits to the police stations or to other places where information could possibly be obtained. Where the same person has been questioned more than once, as frequently occurred, notably in appealed cases from the criminal courts, the answers obtained at the different times have been compared, with the result that, generally, the replies have been found to agree very closely.

The total number of cases of pauperism, crime, and insanity covered by the returns does not absolutely indicate the number of individuals committed to the different institutions, but the total number of cases or commitments irrespective of individuals. In analyzing the tables hereafter, we shall frequently allude to the cases reported in personal terms; for example, we speak of them as if they related to entirely different individuals. While it has been impossible to avoid this entirely, it should be understood that certain individuals are duplicated in the returns, for the reason that the same person may have been committed several times during the period covered by the investigation to one institution, or to different institutions, criminal, reformatory, or insane, on different charges. The duplications due to this cause are, however, not very numerous among the paupers and insane, being greatest in number among those criminals who have been committed during the year for minor offences, among which the distinctly liquor offences predominate. Each separate commitment has been noted, however, as each had its specific cause, and the object to be attained by it varied in the different institutions.

Every available source of information has been canvassed. In numerous cases where prisoners had paid fines and were released before they could be interviewed, the agent of the Bureau was obliged to visit the courts where the prisoners were convicted, perhaps finding it necessary to go to the police station, to communicate with the officers who made the arrests, or to make inquiries in the immediate neighborhood of the prisoners' homes before the facts could be accurately determined. This, of itself, involved a large amount of work, but contributed, of course, to the accuracy of the results.

Information relating to the insane, and especially as to the bearing which heredity has upon the subjects covered by the inquiries concerning the insane, was found more difficult to obtain than with respect to the other two classes, the individual members of which were capable of giving direct testimony. So far as the resources at our command permit, the inquiries as to the insane have been thoroughly made, but while the results are indicative, they are less exhaustive than with respect to the paupers and criminals. In the case of paupers and insane persons, the records of the Board of Lunacy and Charity have been canvassed to verify, as far as possible, the information relating to the patients of the insane asylums and hospitals, and the inmates of the institutions at Tewksbury and Bridgewater. The prisoners and paupers who were interrogated, with scarcely an exception, were very civil and obliging to the agents of the Bureau, and their per-

Pauperism; Sex and Political Condition: By Age Periods.

	SEX AND POLITICAL CONDITION.	AGE PERIODS				
		Under 1	1-4	5-9	10-14	15-19
1	*Males.*	78	42	38	47	60
2	Citizen born, . . .	77	37	27	35	22
3	Naturalized, . . .	–	–	–	–	–
4	Alien, ...	1	4	11	12	38
5	Unknown, . . . ' . .	–	1	–	–	–
6	*Females.*	68	28	27	24	66
7	Citizen born, . . .	67	26	20	19	30
8	Alien, . . . ' . .	1	2	7	5	36
9	Unknown, ...	–	–	–	–	–

sonal knowledge as to the liquor habits of other inmates of the institutions was frequently of great advantage in obtaining correct information. The officers of the institutions were uniformly courteous and obliging, and they have rendered the Bureau aid in every possible way in prosecuting the investigation. In the correctional institutions, officers who were acquainted with the character of the prisoners were detailed to assist the Special Agents of the Bureau, and their experience has been of material assistance.

Under the terms of the Act, the investigation naturally divides itself into three sections. Although the facts relating to crime would naturally precede the others, if the order fixed in the Act were followed, the plan of tabulation pursued renders it more convenient to first present the tables relating to pauperism, each table being followed by a brief summary in text of its leading points.

PAUPERISM.

It should be noted at the outset that the facts presented in the tables relate to all the paupers in the institutions canvassed by the Bureau, without discrimination as to age. For the purpose, however, of showing the ages, political condition, nativity, and parent nativity of the paupers, we insert two tables before introducing those which particularly relate to the use of intoxicating liquors.

The first table shows the sex and political condition of the paupers and their ages by periods.

Pauperism ; Sex and Political Condition : By Age Periods.

AGE PERIODS							Totals	
20-29	30-39	40-49	50-59	60-79	80 +	Unknown		
548	675	553	343	231	18	–	2,633	1
142	183	137	59	37	5	–	761	2
28	62	90	73	59	8	–	320	3
374	422	323	208	132	5	–	1,530	4
4	8	3	3	3	–	–	22	5
184	88	55	27	27	3	–	597	6
52	20	12	5	6	1	–	258	7
131	68	42	22	21	2	–	337	8
1	–	1	–	–	–	–	2	9

Pauperism; Sex and Political Condition: By Age Periods — Concluded.

	SEX AND POLITICAL CONDITION.	AGE PERIODS				
		Under 1	1-4	5-9	10-14	15-19
1	BOTH SEXES.	146	70	65	71	126
2	Citizen born, . . .	144	63	47	54	52
3	Naturalized, . . .	–	–	–	–	–
4	Alien, ...	2	6	18	17	74
5	Unknown, ...	–	1	–	–	–

It will be seen from the table that 3,230 pauper commitments are included. Of these, 2,633 relate to males and 597 to females. Of the paupers covered by these commitments, 1,867 were alien, 1,019 citizen born, and 320 naturalized, while the political condition of 24 was unknown.

With respect to ages, considering aggregates only, 146 were under one year of age, 70 from 1 to 4, 65 from 5 to 9, 71

Pauperism; Parent Nativity: By Sex and Political Condition.

	PARENT NATIVITY.	MALES				
		Citizen Born	Natural-ized	Alien	Unknown	Totals
1	Both parents *native,* . . .	217	4	4	1	226
2	Both parents *foreign,* . . .	414	261	1,511	13	2,199
3	Both parents *unknown,* . . .	36	–	7	8	51
4	Father *native,* mother *foreign,* .	40	2	4	–	46
5	Father *foreign,* mother *native,* .	32	1	–	–	33
6	Father *native,* mother *unknown,* .	–	–	–	–	–
7	Father *foreign,* mother *unknown,* .	–	52	4	–	56
8	Father *unknown,* mother *native,* .	12	–	–	–	12
9	Father *unknown,* mother *foreign,* .	10	–	–	–	10
10	TOTALS, ...	761	320	1,530	22	2,633

Referring only to the totals for both sexes, we note that 305 paupers had both parents native, while 2,652 had both parents foreign. The relative proportions by sexes are as follows: males with both parents native, 8.58 per cent; females with both parents native, 13.23 per cent; males with both parents foreign, 83.52 per cent; females with both parents foreign, 75.88 per cent. The nativity of parents was unknown for 68

Pauperism; Sex and Political Condition: By Age Periods — Concluded.

| AGE PERIODS | | | | | | | Totals | |
20-29	30-39	40-49	50-59	60-79	80 +	Unknown		
732	763	608	370	258	21	-	3,230	1
194	203	149	64	43	6	-	1,019	2
28	62	90	73	59	8	-	320	3
505	490	365	230	153	7	-	1,867	4
5	8	4	3	3	-	-	24	5

from 10 to 14, 126 from 15 to 19, 732 from 20 to 29, 763 from 30 to 39, 608 from 40 to 49, 370 from 50 to 59, 258 from 60 to 79, while 21 were 80 years of age or over. The larger number, it will be seen, was between 20 and 60 years of age, and this statement is true both for males and females.

The next table shows the parent nativity of the paupers.

Pauperism; Parent Nativity: By Sex and Political Condition.

| FEMALES | | | | BOTH SEXES | | | | | |
Citizen Born	Alien	Unknown	Totals	Citizen Born	Naturalized	Alien	Unknown	Totals	
77	2	-	79	294	4	6	1	305	1
123	328	2	453	537	261	1,839	15	2,652	2
14	3	-	17	50	-	10	8	68	3
21	1	-	22	61	2	5	-	68	4
5	3	-	8	37	1	3	-	41	5
2	-	-	2	2	-	-	-	2	6
2	-	-	2	2	52	4	-	58	7
7	-	-	7	19	-	-	-	19	8
7	-	-	7	17	-	-	-	17	9
258	337	2	597	1,019	320	1,867	24	3,230	10

paupers only. Of the others, 68 had native fathers but foreign mothers; 41, foreign fathers but native mothers; 2, fathers native but mothers unknown; 58, fathers foreign but mothers unknown; 19, fathers unknown but mothers native; and 17, fathers unknown, mothers foreign. The preceding tables taken together show very clearly the foreign influence among the paupers. While, as shown by the first table, 1,019 were actually born in this country, it will be seen, from the second table, that only 305 had both parents native born.

The next table bears directly upon the influence of the use of intoxicating liquor and exhibits the liquor habits of the paupers, males and females being presented separately, and also shows the town or city from which the paupers were sent to the institutions in which they were found.

Town or City from which Sent, and Liquor Habits of Paupers.

COUNTIES, CITIES, TOWNS, AND SEX.	Excessive Drinkers	Other Drinkers	Unknown	Total Abstainers	Number of Paupers
BARNSTABLE.	–	5	1	1	7
Barnstable,	–	–	1	–	1
Males,	–	–	–	–	–
Females,	–	–	1	–	1
Harwich,	–	2	–	–	2
Males,	–	2	–	–	2
Females,	–	–	–	–	–
Provincetown,	–	2	–	1	3
Males,	–	2	–	1	3
Females,	–	–	–	–	–
Sandwich,	–	1	–	–	1
Males,	–	1	–	–	1
Females,	–	–	–	–	–
BERKSHIRE.	–	8	–	6	14
Dalton,	–	1	–	1	2
Males,	–	–	–	–	–
Females,	–	1	–	1	2
New Marlborough,	–	–	–	4	4
Males,	–	–	–	1	1
Females,	–	–	–	3	3
NORTH ADAMS,	–	4	–	1	5
Males,	–	3	–	–	3
Females,	–	1	–	1	2
PITTSFIELD,	–	1	–	–	1
Males,	–	1	–	–	1
Females,	–	–	–	–	–
Sandisfield,	–	1	–	–	1
Males,	–	1	–	–	1
Females,	–	–	–	–	–
Savoy,	–	1	–	–	1
Males,	–	1	–	–	1
Females,	–	–	–	–	–

Town or City from which Sent, and Liquor Habits of Paupers — Continued.

COUNTIES, CITIES, TOWNS, AND SEX.	Excessive Drinkers	Other Drinkers	Unknown	Total Abstainers	Number of Paupers
BRISTOL.	10	67	13	55	145
Attleborough, ...	-	1	-	1	2
Males, ...	-	1	-	1	2
Females, ...	-	-	-	-	-
Dighton, ...	-	-	-	1	1
Males, ...	-	-	-	1	1
Females, ...	-	-	-	-	-
Easton, ...	-	1	-	-	1
Males, ...	-	1	-	-	1
Females, ...	-	-	-	-	-
Fairhaven, ...	-	-	-	1	1
Males, ...	-	-	-	1	1
Females, ...	-	-	-	-	-
FALL RIVER, ...	7	31	11	24	73
Males, ...	6	27	6	14	53
Females, ...	1	4	5	10	20
NEW BEDFORD, . . .	2	26	2	25	55
Males, ...	1	22	-	17	40
Females, ...	1	4	2	8	15
Norton, ...	-	1	-	-	1
Males, ...	-	1	-	-	1
Females, ...	-	-	-	-	-
TAUNTON, ...	1	7	-	3	11
Males, ...	1	7	-	2	10
Females, ...	-	-	-	1	1
ESSEX.	19	82	18	48	167
Andover, ...	-	1	-	-	1
Males, ...	-	1	-	-	1
Females, ...	-	-	-	-	-
BEVERLY, ...	-	1	-	1	2
Males, ...	-	1	-	-	1
Females, ...	-	-	-	1	1
Danvers, ...	-	-	1	-	1
Males, ...	-	-	1	-	1
Females, ...	-	-	-	-	-
GLOUCESTER, ...	-	3	4	3	10
Males, ...	-	3	2	1	6
Females, ...	-	-	2	2	4
HAVERHILL, ...	3	10	1	7	21
Males, ...	3	8	1	3	15
Females, ...	-	2	-	4	6

Town or City from which Sent, and Liquor Habits of Paupers — Continued.

COUNTIES, CITIES, TOWNS, AND SEX.	Excessive Drinkers	Other Drinkers	Unknown	Total Abstainers	Number of Paupers
ESSEX — Con.					
LAWRENCE,	11	42	10	24	87
Males,	10	38	9	14	71
Females,	1	4	1	10	16
LYNN,	2	7	-	11	20
Males,	2	6	-	3	11
Females,	-	1	-	8	9
NEWBURYPORT,	-	2	-	1	3
Males,	-	2	-	1	3
Females,	-	-	-	-	-
North Andover,	1	-	-	-	1
Males,	1	-	-	-	1
Females,	-	-	-	-	-
Peabody,	-	2	-	-	2
Males,	-	2	-	-	2
Females,	-	-	-	-	-
Rockport,	-	4	-	1	5
Males,	-	4	-	-	4
Females,	-	-	-	1	1
SALEM,	2	10	2	-	14
Males,	2	8	1	-	11
Females,	-	2	1	-	3
FRANKLIN.	-	3	-	12	15
Montague,	-	-	-	4	4
Males,	-	-	-	2	2
Females,	-	-	-	2	2
New Salem,	-	1	-	-	1
Males,	-	1	-	-	1
Females,	-	-	-	-	-
Northfield,	-	1	-	-	1
Males,	-	1	-	-	1
Females,	-	-	-	-	-
Orange,	-	1	-	3	4
Males,	-	1	-	1	2
Females,	-	-	-	2	2
Wendell,	-	-	-	5	5
Males,	-	-	-	5	5
Females,	-	-	-	-	-
HAMPDEN.	1	13	2	15	31
CHICOPEE,	-	5	-	3	8
Males,	-	5	-	1	6
Females,	-	-	-	2	2

Town or City from which Sent, and Liquor Habits of Paupers — Continued.

COUNTIES, CITIES, TOWNS, AND SEX.	Excessive Drinkers	Other Drinkers	Unknown	Total Abstainers	Number of Paupers
HAMPDEN — Con.					
HOLYOKE,	–	2	–	3	5
Males,	–	2	–	3	5
Females,	–	–	–	–	–
Ludlow,	–	1	–	–	1
Males,	–	1	–	–	1
Females,	–	–	–	–	–
Monson,	–	–	–	2	2
Males,	–	–	–	2	2
Females,	–	–	–	–	–
Palmer,	–	–	2	2	4
Males,	–	–	2	1	3
Females,	–	–	–	1	1
SPRINGFIELD,	–	2	–	4	6
Males,	–	2	–	–	2
Females,	–	–	–	4	4
Westfield,	1	3	–	1	5
Males,	1	3	–	1	5
Females,	–	–	–	–	–
HAMPSHIRE.	1	6	2	6	15
Easthampton,	–	1	–	3	4
Males,	–	1	–	–	1
Females,	–	–	–	3	3
Goshen,	–	–	–	1	1
Males,	–	–	–	–	–
Females,	–	–	–	1	1
Hatfield,	–	–	–	1	1
Males,	–	–	–	–	–
Females,	–	–	–	1	1
Huntington,	–	–	–	1	1
Males,	–	–	–	1	1
Females,	–	–	–	–	–
NORTHAMPTON,	–	1	2	–	3
Males,	–	1	2	–	3
Females,	–	–	–	–	–
Ware,	1	4	–	–	5
Males,	1	4	–	–	5
Females,	–	–	–	–	–
MIDDLESEX.	145	399	83	243	870
Bedford,	–	1	1	–	2
Males,	–	1	1	–	2
Females,	–	–	–	–	–

Town or City from which Sent, and Liquor Habits of Paupers — Continued.

COUNTIES, CITIES, TOWNS, AND SEX.	Excessive Drinkers	Other Drinkers	Unknown	Total Abstainers	Number of Paupers
MIDDLESEX — Con.					
Billerica, ...	-	1	-	4	5
Males, ...	-	1	-	2	3
Females, ...	-	-	-	2	2
CAMBRIDGE, ...	3	15	4	18	40
Males, ...	3	11	1	6	21
Females, ...	-	4	3	12	19
Chelmsford, ...	-	2	-	-	2
Males, ...	-	2	-	-	2
Females, ...	-	-	-	-	-
Dracut, ...	1	1	1	1	4
Males, ...	1	1	1	1	4
Females, ...	-	-	-	-	-
Dunstable, ...	-	1	-	-	1
Males, ...	-	1	-	-	1
Females, ...	-	-	-	-	-
EVERETT, ...	-	2	-	2	4
Males, ...	-	2	-	1	3
Females, ...	-	-	-	1	1
Framingham, ...	2	2	-	1	5
Males, ...	2	2	-	1	5
Females, ...	-	-	-	-	-
Hudson, ...	-	-	2	-	2
Males, ...	-	-	1	-	1
Females, ...	-	-	1	-	1
Lexington, ...	-	-	-	1	1
Males, ...	-	-	-	1	1
Females, ...	-	-	-	-	-
LOWELL, ...	12	64	5	58	139
Males, ...	11	56	4	25	96
Females, ...	1	8	1	33	43
MALDEN, ...	1	1	1	-	3
Males, ...	1	1	1	-	3
Females, ...	-	-	-	-	-
MARLBOROUGH, . . .	1	1	1	3	6
Males, ...	1	1	1	1	4
Females, ...	-	-	-	2	2
Maynard, ...	-	2	-	3	5
Males, ...	-	1	-	2	3
Females, ...	-	1	-	1	2
MEDFORD, ...	-	1	-	4	5
Males, ...	-	1	-	-	1
Females, ...	-	-	-	4	4

Town or City from which Sent, and Liquor Habits of Paupers — Continued.

COUNTIES, CITIES, TOWNS, AND SEX.	Excessive Drinkers	Other Drinkers	Unknown	Total Abstainers	Number of Paupers
MIDDLESEX — Con.					
Melrose,	-	5	-	-	5
Males,	-	5	-	-	5
Females,	-	-	-	-	-
NEWTON,	-	2	-	4	6
Males,	-	2	-	3	5
Females,	-	-	-	1	1
North Reading,	-	1	-	-	1
Males,	-	1	-	-	1
Females,	-	-	-	-	-
Reading,	-	-	-	1	1
Males,	-	-	-	-	-
Females,	-	-	-	1	1
Sherborn,	1	1	-	-	2
Males,	1	1	-	-	2
Females,	-	-	-	-	-
Shirley,	-	1	-	-	1
Males,	-	1	-	-	1
Females,	-	-	-	-	-
SOMERVILLE,	4	1	-	2	7
Males,	3	1	-	2	6
Females,	1	-	-	-	1
Stoneham,	-	-	-	1	1
Males,	-	-	-	1	1
Females,	-	-	-	-	-
Tewksbury,	116	261	64	132	573
Males,	114	260	64	95	533
Females,	2	1	-	37	40
Townsend,	-	-	-	1	1
Males,	-	-	-	1	1
Females,	-	-	-	-	-
Wakefield,	-	2	-	1	3
Males,	-	-	-	1	1
Females,	-	2	-	-	2
WALTHAM,	2	5	-	-	7
Males,	2	5	-	-	7
Females,	-	-	-	-	-
Watertown,	-	-	2	-	2
Males,	-	-	2	-	2
Females,	-	-	-	-	-
Wayland,	-	1	-	-	1
Males,	-	1	-	-	1
Females,	-	-	-	-	-

Town or City from which Sent, and Liquor Habits of Paupers— Continued.

COUNTIES, CITIES, TOWNS, AND SEX.	Excessive Drinkers	Other Drinkers	Unknown	Total Abstainers	Number of Paupers
MIDDLESEX — Con.					
Westford, ...	-	-	-	1	1
Males, ...	-	-	-	-	-
Females, . . .	-	-	-	1	1
Weston, ...	-	1	-	1	2
Males, ...	-	1	-	-	1
Females, . . .	-	-	-	1	1
Wilmington, . . .	-	2	-	-	2
Males, ...	-	2	-	-	2
Females, . . .	-	-	-	-	-
Winchester, . . .	-	1	-	-	1
Males, . . .	-	-	-	-	-
Females, . . .	-	1	-	-	1
WOBURN, ...	2	21	2	4	29
Males, ...	1	20	2	2	25
Females, . . .	1	1	-	2	4
NORFOLK.	2	4	3	9	18
Braintree, ...	-	2	-	1	3
Males, ...	-	1	-	-	1
Females, ...	-	1	-	1	2
Dedham, ...	1	1	-	1	3
Males, ...	1	1	-	-	2
Females, . . .	-	-	-	1	1
Hyde Park, . . .	-	-	1	3	4
Males, ...	-	-	1	1	2
Females, . . .	-	-	-	2	2
Medfield, ...	-	1	1	-	2
Males, ...	-	1	1	-	2
Females, . . .	-	-	-	-	-
Norwood, ...	1	-	-	1	2
Males, ...	1	-	-	1	2
Females, . . .	-	-	-	-	-
QUINCY, ...	-	-	1	2	3
Males, ...	-	-	1	2	3
Females, . . .	-	-	-	-	-
Wellesley, ...	-	-	-	1	1
Males, ...	-	-	-	1	1
Females, . . .	-	-	-	-	-
PLYMOUTH.	8	14	1	4	27
Abington, ...	-	2	-	1	3
Males, . . .	-	2	-	1	3
Females, . . .	-	-	-	-	-

Town or City from which Sent, and Liquor Habits of Paupers — Continued

COUNTIES, CITIES, TOWNS, AND SEX.	Excessive Drinkers	Other Drinkers	Unknown	Total Abstainers	Number of Paupers
PLYMOUTH — Con.					
Bridgewater, ...	5	5	1	–	11
Males, ...	5	5	–	–	10
Females, ...	–	–	1	–	1
BROCKTON, ...	3	1	–	1	5
Males, ...	3	1	–	–	4
Females, ...	–	–	–	1	1
East Bridgewater, . . .	–	1	–	–	1
Males, ...	–	1	–	–	1
Females, ...	–	–	–	–	–
Hingham, ...	–	–	–	1	1
Males, ...	–	–	–	–	–
Females, ...	–	–	–	1	1
Norwell, ...	–	1	–	–	1
Males, ...	–	1	–	–	1
Females, ...	–	–	–	–	–
Plymouth, ...	–	1	–	1	2
Males, ...	–	1	–	–	1
Females, ...	–	–	–	1	1
Rochester, ...	–	1	–	–	1
Males, ...	–	1	–	–	1
Females, ...	–	–	–	–	–
Rockland, ...	–	1	–	–	1
Males, ...	–	1	–	–	1
Females, ...	–	–	–	–	–
West Bridgewater, . . .	–	1	–	–	1
Males, ...	–	1	–	–	1
Females, ...	–	–	–	–	–
SUFFOLK.	309	958	119	426	1,812
BOSTON, ...	308	956	118	423	1,805
Males, . . .	288	883	101	202	1,474
Females, . .	20	73	17	221	331
CHELSEA, . . .	1	2	1	3	7
Males, . . .	1	2	1	1	5
Females, . .	–	–	–	2	2
WORCESTER.	9	43	13	41	106
Athol, ...	–	1	–	–	1
Males, ...	–	1	–	–	1
Females, ...	–	–	–	–	–
Charlton, ...	–	–	1	–	1
Males, ...	–	–	1	–	1
Females, ...	–	–	–	–	–

Town or City from which Sent, and Liquor Habits of Paupers — Continued.

COUNTIES, CITIES, TOWNS, AND SEX.	Excessive Drinkers	Other Drinkers	Unknown	Total Abstainers	Number of Paupers
WORCESTER — Con.					
Clinton, ...	–	1	–	–	1
Males, ...	–	–	–	–	–
Females, ...	–	1	–	–	1
Douglas, ...	–	1	–	1	2
Males, ...	–	1	–	1	2
Females, ...	–	–	–	–	–
Dudley, ...	–	2	–	–	2
Males, ...	–	2	–	–	2
Females, ...	–	–	–	–	–
FITCHBURG, ...	–	2	–	1	3
Males, ...	–	1	–	1	2
Females, ...	–	1	–	–	1
Gardner, ...	1	3	1	2	7
Males, ...	1	3	1	1	6
Females, ...	–	–	–	1	1
Grafton, ...	1	–	–	–	1
Males, ...	1	–	–	–	1
Females, ...	–	–	–	–	–
Hardwick, ...	–	2	–	–	2
Males, ...	–	2	–	–	2
Females, ...	–	–	–	–	–
Leominster, ...	–	–	–	1	1
Males, ...	–	–	–	–	–
Females, ...	–	–	–	1	1
Milford, ...	–	–	1	–	1
Males, ...	–	–	1	–	1
Females, ...	–	–	–	–	–
Southborough, ...	1	–	–	–	1
Males, ...	1	–	–	–	1
Females, ...	–	–	–	–	–
Spencer, ...	1	1	–	–	2
Males, ...	1	1	–	–	2
Females, ...	–	–	–	–	–
Sterling, ...	–	1	–	–	1
Males, ...	–	1	–	–	1
Females, ...	–	–	–	–	–
Sturbridge, ...	–	–	–	5	5
Males, ...	–	–	–	2	2
Females, ...	–	–	–	3	3
Sutton, ...	–	1	–	–	1
Males, ...	–	1	–	–	1
Females, ...	–	–	–	–	–

Town or City from which Sent, and Liquor Habits of Paupers — Concluded.

COUNTIES, CITIES, TOWNS, AND SEX.	Excessive Drinkers	Other Drinkers	Unknown	Total Abstainers	Number of Paupers
WORCESTER — Con.					
Warren, ...	-	-	2	-	2
Males, ...	-	-	2	-	2
Females, ...	-	-	-	-	-
Webster, ...	1	2	-	3	6
Males, ...	1	2	-	2	5
Females, ...	-	-	-	1	1
West Boylston, ...	-	-	-	1	1
Males, ...	-	-	-	-	-
Females, ...	-	-	-	1	1
Winchendon, ...	-	1	-	-	1
Males, ...	-	1	-	-	1
Females, ...	-	-	-	-	-
WORCESTER, ...	4	25	8	27	64
Males, ...	4	25	5	11	45
Females, ...	-	-	3	16	19
Not Given, ...	1	1	1	-	3
Males, ...	1	1	-	-	2
Females, ...	-	-	1	-	1

RECAPITULATION.

COUNTIES, SEX, AND THE STATE.	Excessive Drinkers	Other Drinkers	Unknown	Total Abstainers	Number of Paupers
BARNSTABLE.	-	5	1	1	7
Males, . . .	-	5	-	1	6
Females, . . .	-	-	1	-	1
BERKSHIRE.	-	8	-	6	14
Males, ...	-	6	-	1	7
Females, ...	-	2	-	5	7
BRISTOL.	10	67	13	55	145
Males, . . .	8	59	6	36	109
Females, . . .	2	8	7	19	36
ESSEX.	19	82	18	48	167
Males, ...	18	73	14	22	127
Females, ...	1	9	4	26	40

RECAPITULATION — Concluded.

Counties, Sex, and The State.	Excessive Drinkers	Other Drinkers	Unknown	Total Abstainers	Number of Paupers
FRANKLIN.	-	3	-	12	15
Males,	-	3	-	8	11
Females,	-	-	-	4	4
HAMPDEN.	1	13	2	15	31
Males,	1	13	2	8	24
Females,	-	-	-	7	7
HAMPSHIRE.	1	6	2	6	15
Males,	1	6	2	1	10
Females,	-	-	-	5	5
MIDDLESEX.	145	399	83	243	870
Males,	140	381	78	145	744
Females,	5	18	5	98	126
NORFOLK.	2	4	3	9	18
Males,	2	3	3	5	13
Females,	-	1	-	4	5
PLYMOUTH.	8	14	1	4	27
Males,	8	14	-	1	23
Females,	-	-	1	3	4
SUFFOLK.	309	958	119	426	1,812
Males,	289	885	102	203	1,479
Females,	20	73	17	223	333
WORCESTER.	9	43	13	41	106
Males,	9	41	10	18	78
Females,	-	2	3	23	28
NOT GIVEN.	1	1	1	-	3
Males,	1	1	-	-	2
Females,	-	-	1	-	1
THE STATE.	505	1,603	256	866	3,230
Males,	477	1,490	217	449	2,633
Females,	28	113	39	417	597

In analyzing this table we shall refer chiefly to the recapitulation, it being obvious that the facts for any particular city or town are shown in detail. For the State as a whole, out

of the 3,230 paupers, only 505 were found to be excessive
drinkers; of these, 477 were males and 28 females.   Drinkers
of other degrees, than that termed excessive, numbered 1,603,
of whom 1,490 were males and 113 females.   On the other
hand, 866 paupers were total abstainers, the numbers for the
sexes being practically equal, the males numbering 449 and
the females 417.   From a table hereinafter presented, showing the habits of the paupers in detail, by age periods, it will
appear, however, that the total abstainers were principally
children or persons under fifteen years of age.   The total
abstainers include 449 males, out of a total of 2,633, or
17.05 per cent, and 417 females, out of a total of 597, or
69.85 per cent.   Only 256 paupers remained unclassified as
to liquor habit, of whom 217 were males and 39 females.
More than 50 per cent of the paupers were returned from the
county of Suffolk, the total being 1,812.   Of these, 309 were
excessive drinkers, the males being largely in preponderance,
while 958 were classed as "Other Drinkers," that is, not
excessive, the males in this class being far more numerous
than the females.   It will be seen that substantially two-thirds
of the total number of the paupers returned from Suffolk
County belonged to one or the other of these classes, the proportions as compared with the total number being slightly
larger than was found in the State as a whole.   The proportion of excessive drinkers, about one-sixth of the total number, is about the same in Suffolk County as in the State as
a whole.   Suffolk County contains the city of Boston.   It
may be interesting to note the facts in the counties which
include the agricultural districts of the State, for instance,
Berkshire and Franklin.   A comparatively small number of
paupers are accredited to these counties, there being but 14
returned from Berkshire County, of whom only eight were
subject to the drink habit, none being classed as excessive
drinkers.   There were but 15 reported from Franklin County,
of whom only three were addicted to drink, none being excessive drinkers.

Referring again to the recapitulation, we note that the
number of total abstainers largely exceeds the number of
excessive drinkers, and in terms of percentages may summarize the facts as follows: 15.63 per cent of the total

number of paupers were reported as excessive drinkers ; 49.63 per cent, as addicted to the drinking habit, but not excessively ; 26.81 per cent, total abstainers, chiefly young persons, as will hereinafter appear ; and 7.93 per cent, habit unknown. The drinking habit, either excessive or other, is thus found to affect 65.26 per cent of the whole number.

An unduly large number of commitments from the town of Tewksbury will be noted in this and subsequent tables. This is due to the fact that, for the purpose of obtaining shelter or food, tramps and vagrants desiring admission to the State Almshouse located there, go to the town officers and obtain commitment papers to this institution, although not actual residents of the town. The number returned as from Tewksbury in the table is 573, nearly all of whom are males. Of the males, 114 report themselves as excessive drinkers while 260 others are reported as victims of the drinking habit, but not excessive drinkers. Only 95 are credited with being total abstainers.

The next table pushes the inquiry back so as to show the drinking habits of the parents of the paupers, presented by sexes, and exhibiting also the cities and towns to which the pauper is accredited.

Town or City from which Sent, and Liquor Habits of Parents of Paupers.

COUNTIES, CITIES, TOWNS, AND SEX.	One or Both Parents Intemperate	One or Both Parents Total Abstainers	Liquor Habits of Both Parents Unknown	Number of Paupers
BARNSTABLE.	2	2	3	7
Barnstable, ...	–	–	1	1
Males, ...	–	–	–	–
Females, ...	–	–	1	1
Harwich, ...	1	–	1	2
Males, ...	1	–	1	2
Females, ...	–	–	–	–
Provincetown, ...	1	2	–	3
Males, ...	1	2	–	3
Females, ...	–	–	–	–
Sandwich, ...	–	–	1	1
Males, ...	–	–	1	1
Females, ...	–	–	–	–

Town or City from which Sent, and Liquor Habits of Parents of Paupers
— Continued

Counties, Cities, Towns, and Sex.	One or Both Parents Intemperate	One or Both Parents Total Abstainers	Liquor Habits of Both Parents Unknown	Number of Paupers
BERKSHIRE.	12	2	-	14
Dalton,	2	-	-	2
Males,	-	-	-	-
Females,	2	-	-	2
New Marlborough,	4	-	-	4
Males,	1	-	-	1
Females,	3	-	-	3
NORTH ADAMS,	4	1	-	5
Males,	2	1	-	3
Females,	2	-	-	2
PITTSFIELD,	1	-	-	1
Males,	1	-	-	1
Females,	-	-	-	-
Sandisfield,	1	-	-	1
Males,	1	-	-	1
Females,	-	-	-	-
Savoy,	-	1	-	1
Males,	-	1	-	1
Females,	-	-	-	-
BRISTOL.	78	30	37	145
Attleborough,	2	-	-	2
Males,	2	-	-	2
Females,	-	-	-	-
Dighton,	1	-	-	1
Males,	1	-	-	1
Females,	-	-	-	-
Easton,	-	1	-	1
Males,	-	1	-	1
Females,	-	-	-	-
Fairhaven,	1	-	-	1
Males,	1	-	-	1
Females,	-	-	-	-
FALL RIVER,	28	18	27	73
Males,	21	14	18	53
Females,	7	4	9	20
NEW BEDFORD,	38	8	9	55
Males,	30	6	4	40
Females,	8	2	5	15
Norton,	1	-	-	1
Males,	1	-	-	1
Females,	-	-	-	-

Town or City from which Sent, and Liquor Habits of Parents of Paupers — Continued.

COUNTIES, CITIES, TOWNS, AND SEX.	One or Both Parents Intemperate	One or Both Parents Total Abstainers	Liquor Habits of Both Parents Unknown	Number of Paupers
BRISTOL — Con.				
Taunton, ...	7	3	1	11
Males, ...	7	2	1	10
Females, ...	-	1	-	1
ESSEX.	84	38	45	167
Andover, ...	1	-	-	1
Males, ...	1	-	-	1
Females, ...	-	-	-	-
BEVERLY, ...	-	1	1	2
Males, ...	-	-	1	1
Females, ...	-	1	-	1
Danvers, ...	-	-	1	1
Males, ...	-	-	1	1
Females, ...	-	-	-	-
GLOUCESTER, ...	4	1	5	10
Males, ...	3	-	3	6
Females, ...	1	1	2	4
HAVERHILL, ...	10	7	4	21
Males, ...	6	5	4	15
Females, ...	4	2	-	6
LAWRENCE, ...	48	18	21	87
Males, ...	38	15	18	71
Females, ...	10	3	3	16
LYNN, ...	11	6	3	20
Males, ...	6	3	2	11
Females, ...	5	3	1	9
NEWBURYPORT, ...	-	2	1	3
Males, ...	-	2	1	3
Females, ...	-	-	-	-
North Andover, ...	-	-	1	1
Males, ...	-	-	1	1
Females, ...	-	-	-	-
Peabody, ...	1	1	-	2
Males, ...	1	1	-	2
Females, ...	-	-	-	-
Rockport, ...	2	1	2	5
Males, ...	2	-	2	4
Females, ...	-	1	-	1
SALEM, ...	7	1	6	14
Males, ...	7	1	3	11
Females, ...	-	-	3	3

Town or City from which Sent, and Liquor Habits of Parents of Paupers — Continued.

COUNTIES, CITIES, TOWNS, AND SEX.	One or Both Parents Intemperate	One or Both Parents Total Abstainers	Liquor Habits of Both Parents Unknown	Number of Paupers
FRANKLIN.	7	8	–	15
Montague, ...	–	4	–	4
Males, ...	–	2	–	2
Females, ...	–	2	–	2
New Salem, ...	1	–	–	1
Males, ...	1	–	–	1
Females, ...	–	–	–	–
Northfield, ...	1	–	–	1
Males, ...	1	–	–	1
Females, ...	–	–	–	–
Orange, ...	4	–	–	4
Males, ...	2	–	–	2
Females, ...	2	–	–	2
Wendell, ...	1	4	–	5
Males, ...	1	4	–	5
Females, ...	–	–	–	–
HAMPDEN.	13	12	6	31
CHICOPEE, ...	6	1	1	8
Males, ...	4	1	1	6
Females, ...	2	–	–	2
HOLYOKE, ...	1	4	–	5
Males, ...	1	4	–	5
Females, ...	–	–	–	–
Ludlow, ...	–	–	1	1
Males, ...	–	–	1	1
Females, ...	–	–	–	–
Monson, ...	–	–	2	2
Males, ...	–	–	2	2
Females, ...	–	–	–	–
Palmer, ...	1	1	2	4
Males, ...	1	–	2	3
Females, ...	–	1	–	1
SPRINGFIELD, ...	2	4	–	6
Males, ...	1	1	–	2
Females, ...	1	3	–	4
Westfield, ...	3	2	–	5
Males, ...	3	2	–	5
Females, ...	–	–	–	–

Town or City from which Sent, and Liquor Habits of Parents of Paupers
— Continued.

COUNTIES, CITIES, TOWNS, AND SEX.	One or Both Parents Intemperate	One or Both Parents Total Abstainers	Liquor Habits of Both Parents Unknown	Number of Paupers
HAMPSHIRE.	8	3	4	15
Easthampton, . . .	3	1	–	4
Males, . . .	1	–	–	1
Females, . . .	2	1	–	3
Goshen, ...	–	–	1	1
Males, . . .	–	–	–	–
Females, . . .	–	–	1	1
Hatfield, . . .	–	–	1	1
Males, . . .	–	–	–	–
Females, . . .	–	–	1	1
Huntington, . . .	–	1	–	1
Males, . . .	–	1	–	1
Females, . . .	–	–	–	–
NORTHAMPTON, . .	–	1	2	3
Males, . . .	–	1	2	3
Females, . . .	–	–	–	–
Ware, ...	5	–	–	5
Males, . . .	5	–	–	5
Females, . . .	–	–	–	–
MIDDLESEX.	411	255	204	870
Bedford, ...	1	–	1	2
Males, ...	1	–	1	2
Females, ...	–	–	–	–
Billerica, ...	3	2	–	5
Males, ...	2	1	–	3
Females, ...	1	1	–	2
CAMBRIDGE, . . .	21	9	10	40
Males, ...	13	1	7	21
Females, ...	8	8	3	19
Chelmsford, . . .	–	2	–	2
Males, ...	–	2	–	2
Females, ...	–	–	–	–
Dracut, ...	2	–	2	4
Males, ...	2	–	2	4
Females, ...	–	–	–	–
Dunstable, . . .	1	–	–	1
Males, ...	1	–	–	1
Females, ...	–	–	–	–
EVERETT, ...	2	2	–	4
Males, ...	1	2	–	3
Females, ...	1	–	–	1

Town or City from which Sent, and Liquor Habits of Parents of Paupers
— Continued.

COUNTIES. CITIES, TOWNS, AND SEX.	One or Both Parents Intemperate	One or Both Parents Total Abstainers	Liquor Habits of Both Parents Unknown	Number of Paupers
MIDDLESEX — Con.				
Framingham, ...	3	1	1	5
Males, ...	3	1	1	5
Females, ...	-	-	-	-
Hudson, ...	-	-	2	2
Males, ...	-	-	1	1
Females, ...	-	-	1	1
Lexington, ...	-	1	-	1
Males, ...	-	1	-	1
Females, ...	-	-	-	-
LOWELL, ...	78	36	25	139
Males, ...	52	22	22	96
Females, ...	26	14	3	43
MALDEN, ...	-	1	2	3
Males, ...	-	1	2	3
Females, ...	-	-	-	-
MARLBOROUGH, ...	1	4	1	6
Males, ...	1	2	1	4
Females, ...	-	2	-	2
Maynard, ...	-	4	1	5
Males, ...	-	3	-	3
Females, ...	-	1	1	2
MEDFORD, ...	1	4	-	5
Males, ...	1	-	-	1
Females, ...	-	4	-	4
Melrose, ...	2	2	1	5
Males, ...	2	2	1	5
Females, ...	-	-	-	-
NEWTON, ...	3	1	2	6
Males, ...	2	1	2	5
Females, ...	1	-	-	1
North Reading, ...	1	-	-	1
Males, ...	1	-	-	1
Females, ...	-	-	-	-
Reading, ...	-	-	1	1
Males, ...	-	-	-	-
Females, ...	-	-	1	1
Sherborn, ...	1	1	-	2
Males, ...	1	1	-	2
Females, ...	-	-	-	-

Town or City from which Sent, and Liquor Habits of Parents of Paupers — Continued.

COUNTIES, CITIES, TOWNS, AND SEX.	One or Both Parents Intemperate	One or Both Parents Total Abstainers	Liquor Habits of Both Parents Unknown	Number of Paupers
MIDDLESEX — Con.				
Shirley, ...	-	1	-	1
Males, ...	-	1	-	1
Females, ...	-	-	-	-
SOMERVILLE, ...	4	2	1	7
Males, ...	4	2	-	6
Females, ...	-	-	1	1
Stoneham, ...	-	1	-	1
Males, ...	-	1	-	1
Females, ...	-	-	-	-
Tewksbury, ...	268	161	144	573
Males, ...	249	145	139	533
Females, ...	19	16	5	40
Townsend, ...	1	-	-	1
Males, ...	1	-	-	1
Females, ...	-	-	-	-
Wakefield, ...	3	-	-	3
Males, ...	1	-	-	1
Females, ...	2	-	-	2
WALTHAM, ...	3	1	3	7
Males, ...	3	1	3	7
Females, ...	-	-	-	-
Watertown, ...	-	-	2	2
Males, ...	-	-	2	2
Females, ...	-	-	-	-
Wayland, ...	1	-	-	1
Males, ...	1	-	-	1
Females, ...	-	-	-	-
Westford, ...	-	1	-	1
Males, ...	-	-	-	-
Females, ...	-	1	-	1
Weston, ...	2	-	-	2
Males, ...	1	-	-	1
Females, ...	1	-	-	1
Wilmington, ...	2	-	-	2
Males, ...	2	-	-	2
Females, ...	-	-	-	-
Winchester, ...	1	-	-	1
Males, ...	-	-	-	-
Females, ...	1	-	-	1

Town or City from which Sent, and Liquor Habits of Parents of Paupers
— Continued.

COUNTIES, CITIES, TOWNS, AND SEX.	One or Both Parents Intemperate	One or Both Parents Total Abstainers	Liquor Habits of Both Parents Unknown	Number of Paupers
MIDDLESEX — Con.				
WOBURN, ...	6	18	5	29
Males, ...	6	14	5	25
Females, ...	-	4	-	4
NORFOLK.	7	4	7	18
Braintree, ...	2	-	1	3
Males, ...	-	-	1	1
Females, ...	2	-	-	2
Dedham, ...	2	-	1	3
Males, ...	2	-	-	2
Females, ...	-	-	1	1
Hyde Park, ...	-	2	2	4
Males, ...	-	1	1	2
Females, ...	-	1	1	2
Medfield, ...	1	-	1	2
Males, ...	1	-	1	2
Females, ...	-	-	-	-
Norwood, ...	-	1	1	2
Males, ...	-	1	1	2
Females, ...	-	-	-	-
QUINCY, ...	1	1	1	3
Males, ...	1	1	1	3
Females, ...	-	-	-	-
Wellesley, ...	1	-	-	1
Males, ...	1	-	-	1
Females, ...	-	-	-	-
PLYMOUTH.	13	4	10	27
Abington, ...	1	1	1	3
Males, ...	1	1	1	3
Females, ...	-	-	-	-
Bridgewater, ...	5	2	4	11
Males, ...	5	2	3	10
Females, ...	-	-	1	1
BROCKTON, ...	-	1	4	5
Males, ...	-	-	4	4
Females, ...	-	1	-	1
East Bridgewater, . . .	1	-	-	1
Males, ...	1	-	-	1
Females, ...	-	-	-	-

Town or City from which Sent, and Liquor Habits of Parents of Paupers
— Continued.

COUNTIES, CITIES, TOWNS, AND SEX.	One or Both Parents Intemperate	One or Both Parents Total Abstainers	Liquor Habits of Both Parents Unknown	Number of Paupers
PLYMOUTH — Con.				
Hingham, ...	1	-	-	1
Males, ...	-	-	-	-
Females, ...	1	-	-	1
Norwell, ...	1	-	-	1
Males, ...	1	-	-	1
Females, ...	-	-	-	-
Plymouth, ...	2	-	-	2
Males, ...	1	-	-	1
Females, ...	1	-	-	1
Rochester, ...	-	-	1	1
Males, ...	-	-	1	1
Females, ...	-	-	-	-
Rockland, ...	1	-	-	1
Males, ...	1	-	-	1
Females, ...	-	-	-	-
West Bridgewater, . . .	1	-	-	1
Males, ...	1	-	-	1
Females, ...	-	-	-	-
SUFFOLK.	860	448	504	1,812
BOSTON, ...	857	445	503	1,805
Males, ...	695	347	432	1,474
Females, ...	162	98	71	331
CHELSEA, ...	3	3	1	7
Males, ...	2	2	1	5
Females, ...	1	1	-	2
WORCESTER.	45	31	30	106
Athol, ...	1	-	-	1
Males, ...	1	-	-	1
Females, ...	-	-	-	-
Charlton, ...	-	-	1	1
Males, ...	-	-	1	1
Females, ...	-	-	-	-
Clinton, ...	1	-	-	1
Males, ...	-	-	-	-
Females, ...	1	-	-	1
Douglas, ...	-	2	-	2
Males, ...	-	2	-	2
Females, ...	-	-	-	-

Town or City from which Sent, and Liquor Habits of Parents of Paupers
— Continued.

COUNTIES, CITIES, TOWNS, AND SEX.	One or Both Parents Intemperate	One or Both Parents Total Abstainers	Liquor Habits of Both Parents Unknown	Number of Paupers
WORCESTER — Con.				
Dudley,	2	-	-	2
Males,	2	-	-	2
Females,	-	-	-	-
FITCHBURG,	2	1	-	3
Males,	1	1	-	2
Females,	1	-	-	1
Gardner,	3	2	2	7
Males,	2	2	2	6
Females,	1	-	-	1
Grafton,	-	1	-	1
Males,	-	1	-	1
Females,	-	-	-	-
Hardwick,	1	1	-	2
Males,	1	1	-	2
Females,	-	-	-	-
Leominster,	-	1	-	1
Males,	-	-	-	-
Females,	-	1	-	1
Milford,	-	-	1	1
Males,	-	-	1	1
Females,	-	-	-	-
Southborough,	1	-	-	1
Males,	1	-	-	1
Females,	-	-	-	-
Spencer,	1	-	1	2
Males,	1	-	1	2
Females,	-	-	-	-
Sterling,	1	-	-	1
Males,	1	-	-	1
Females,	-	-	-	-
Sturbridge,	4	1	-	5
Males,	2	-	-	2
Females,	2	1	-	3
Sutton,	1	-	-	1
Males,	1	-	-	1
Females,	-	-	-	-
Warren,	-	-	2	2
Males,	-	-	2	2
Females,	-	-	-	-

Town or City from which Sent, and Liquor Habits of Parents of Paupers
— Concluded.

COUNTIES, CITIES, TOWNS, AND SEX.	One or Both Parents Intemperate	One or Both Parents Total Abstainers	Liquor Habits of Both Parents Unknown	Number of Paupers
WORCESTER — Con.				
Webster, ...	3	3	–	6
Males, ...	2	3	–	5
Females, ...	1	–	–	1
West Boylston, . . .	–	1	–	1
Males, ...	–	–	–	–
Females, ...	–	1	–	1
Winchendon, . . .	–	1	–	1
Males, ...	–	1	–	1
Females, ...	–	–	–	–
WORCESTER, ...	24	17	23	64
Males, ...	15	12	18	45
Females, ...	9	5	5	19
NOT GIVEN.	2	–	1	3
Males, ...	2	–	–	2
Females, ...	–	–	1	1

RECAPITULATION.

COUNTIES, SEX, AND THE STATE.	One or Both Parents Intemperate	One or Both Parents Total Abstainers	Liquor Habits of Both Parents Unknown	Number of Paupers
BARNSTABLE.	2	2	3	7
Males, . . .	2	2	2	6
Females, . .	–	–	1	1
BERKSHIRE.	12	2	–	14
Males, ...	5	2	–	7
Females, ...	7	–	–	7
BRISTOL.	78	30	37	145
Males, ...	63	23	23	109
Females, . . .	15	7	14	36
ESSEX.	84	38	45	167
Males, . . .	64	27	36	127
Females, . .	20	11	9	40
FRANKLIN.	7	8	–	15
Males, ...	5	6	–	11
Females, ...	2	2	–	4

RECAPITULATION — Concluded.

COUNTIES, SEX, AND THE STATE.	One or Both Parents Intemperate	One or Both Parents Total Abstainers	Liquor Habits of Both Parents Unknown	Number of Paupers
HAMPDEN.	13	12	6	31
Males, .	10	8	6	24
Females,	3	4	–	7
HAMPSHIRE.	8	3	4	15
Males, .	6	2	2	10
Females,	2	1	2	5
MIDDLESEX	411	255	204	870
Males, .	351	204	189	744
Females,	60	51	15	126
NORFOLK.	7	4	7	18
Males, .	5	3	5	13
Females,	2	1	2	5
PLYMOUTH.	13	4	10	27
Males, .	11	3	9	23
Females,	2	1	1	4
SUFFOLK.	860	448	504	1,812
Males, .	697	349	433	1,479
Females,	163	99	71	333
WORCESTER.	45	31	30	106
Males, .	30	23	25	78
Females,	15	8	5	28
NOT GIVEN.	2	–	1	3
Males, ...	2	–	–	2
Females, ...	–	–	1	1
THE STATE.	1,542	837	851	3,230
Males, ...	1,251	652	730	2,633
Females, ...	291	185	121	597

Confining our analysis as before to the recapitulation, we find that of the 3,230 paupers, 1,542 report one or both parents intemperate, while 837 report that either one or both

parents were total abstainers. If only one parent was reported
as intemperate or a total abstainer, he is included with those
having both parents intemperate or total abstainers, respectively. For 851, the facts as to the liquor habits of both of
the parents were not obtainable, and are therefore reported as
unknown. Expressed in terms of percentages, the results may
be summarized as follows : of the total number, 47.74 per cent
had one or both parents intemperate, while one or both parents
were abstainers in the case of 25.91 per cent, the facts being
unknown for 26.35 per cent. The proportions which each of
these classes bear to the grand total are substantially the same
as are found in the county of Suffolk, for which county the
figures are as follows : one or both parents intemperate, 860 ;
one or both parents abstainers, 448 : unknown, 504.

The two tables thus presented exhibit the facts as to the
liquor habits of the paupers and of the parents of the paupers.
These facts- being admitted, it does not of course follow that
the pauperism of the person was due either to his own use or
abuse of intoxicating liquors, or to the intemperate habits of
his parents. For the purpose of determining whether or not
these habits led to the present condition of pauperism, the
facts contained in the following tables are presented, the first
of which contains the replies to the question " Is the person's
present condition of pauperism due to the use or abuse of
intoxicating liquors."

*Is the Person's present Condition of Pauperism due to the Use or Abuse of
Intoxicating Liquors.*

SEX AND POLITICAL CONDITION.	Yes	No	Not Ascertained	Totals
Males.	1,217	1,011	375	2,633
Citizen born, .	288	273	200	761
Naturalized, .	148	155	17	320
Alien, . .	776	610	144	1,530
Unknown, .	5	3	14	22
Females.	57	386	154	597
Citizen born, .	14	130	114	258
Alien, . .	43	256	38	337
Unknown, .	–	–	2	2

Is the Person's present Condition of Pauperism due to the Use or Abuse of Intoxicating Liquors — Concluded.

Sex and Political Condition.	Yes	No	Not Ascertained	Totals
BOTH SEXES.	1,274	1,427	529	3,230
Citizen born, ...	302	403	314	1,019
Naturalized, ...	148	155	17	320
Alien, ...	819	866	182	1,867
Unknown, ...	5	3	16	24

For the State as a whole, 1,274 persons replied "Yes," 1,427, "No," while for 529 persons the information was not ascertained. The proportions of the different sexes with respect to the replies to this question vary, as, of the males, 1,217, nearly one-half of the total number, considered their present condition of pauperism due to the liquor habit, while of the females, only 57, less than one-tenth of the total number, were of this class.

The next table contains the replies received to the question : "Did the intemperate habits of one or both parents lead to the pauperism of the person considered."

Did the Intemperate Habits of one or both Parents lead to the Pauperism of the Person Considered.

Sex and Political Condition.	Yes	No	Not Ascertained	Totals
Males.	96	2,273	264	2,633
Citizen born, .	61	593	107	761
Naturalized, .	1	309	10	320
Alien, . .	34	1,364	132	1,530
Unknown, .	–	7	15	22
Females.	60	461	76	597
Citizen born, .	49	175	34	258
Alien, . .	11	286	40	337
Unknown, .	–	–	2	2
BOTH SEXES.	156	2,734	340	3,230
Citizen born, ...	110	768	141	1,019
Naturalized, ...	1	309	10	320
Alien, ...	45	1,650	172	1,867
Unknown, ...	–	7	17	24

As shown in the table, only 156 persons out of the 3,230 replied "Yes" to this question, while for 2,734 the answer was unequivocally "No." For 340 persons the question remained unanswered. Summarizing the results exhibited in the two tables, we find that while nearly one-half the total number of paupers had parents one or both of whom were intemperate, only 156, or less than five per cent, considered that the intemperate habits of their parents led to their present condition of pauperism, while 1,274, or 39.44 per cent, admitted that their own habits, as to the use of intoxicating liquors, were the immediate cause of their pauperism. Of course, the answers in the tables relate to the direct influence of the parents' habits, and do not take into account the possible effect upon the person of inherited appetite.

The next table contains the replies received to the question "Did the intemperate habits of the legal guardians of the person, other than parents, lead to his (or her) state of pauperism."

Did the Intemperate Habits of the Legal Guardians of the Person, other than Parents, lead to his (or her) state of Pauperism.

SEX AND POLITICAL CONDITION.	Yes	No	Not Ascertained	Totals
Males.	7	2,368	258	2,633
Citizen born, .	5	657	99	761
Naturalized, .	–	310	10	320
Alien, .	2	1,394	134	1,530
Unknown, .	–	7	15	22
Females.	40	488	69	597
Citizen born, .	16	211	31	258
Alien, . .	24	277	36	337
Unknown, .	–	–	2	2
BOTH SEXES.	47	2,856	327	3,230
Citizen born, .	21	868	130	1,019
Naturalized, .	–	310	10	320
Alien, . .	26	1,671	170	1,867
Unknown, .	–	7	17	24

Of course, a comparatively small number of paupers would be of the class which would be affected by the habits of their legal guardians, other than their parents, and, as will be seen from the table, only 47 of the whole number replied "Yes" to this question. The negative replies numbered 2,856, the number concerning whom this point could not be ascertained being only 327.

The final table bearing upon this phase of the question contains the answers to the question "Did the intemperate habits of others (not parents or guardians) lead to the pauperism of the person considered."

Did the Intemperate Habits of Others (not Parents or Guardians) lead to the Pauperism of the Person Considered.

Sex and Political Condition.	Yes	No	Not Ascertained	Totals
Males.	96	2,269	268	2,633
Citizen born,.	19	636	106	761
Naturalized,.	11	298	11	320
Alien, ...	66	1,328	136	1,530
Unknown, ...	–	7	15	22
Females.	3	515	79	597
Citizen born,.	2	218	38	258
Alien, ...	1	297	39	337
Unknown, ...	–	–	2	2
Both Sexes.	99	2,784	347	3,230
Citizen born,.	21	854	144	1,019
Naturalized,.	11	298	11	320
Alien, ...	67	1,625	175	1,867
Unknown, ...	–	7	17	24

Of this class, there are a comparatively small number, namely, 99, who answered "Yes." The number who replied "No" was 2,784; while in 347 cases this point was not ascertained. Summarizing the answers as to the effect upon the pauperism of the individual of the intemperate habits of those who were his natural or legal guardians, we find that of the 3,230 persons considered, 156 attributed their pauperism to the intemperate habits of one or both parents, 47, to the intemperate habits of their legal guardians (not parents), and 99, to intemperate habits of others. That is to say, out of the total number, 302, or slightly less than 10 per cent, attributed their present condition of pauperism to the in-

temperate habits of others upon whose care they were more
or less dependent, while we may again note that 1,274 persons out of the total number, or about 40 per cent, attributed
their present condition of pauperism to their own intemperate
habits.

The mere statement that a person is addicted to the use of
intoxicating liquor does not disclose the extent to which the
habit has acquired ascendency over him. Nevertheless, it is
a well known fact that there are very great differences of
habit among drinkers. Some are confirmed sots and so entirely
slaves of appetite that the will has become destroyed and the
victim cannot control his desire for intoxicants; others drink
only at intervals, possibly only under the influence of comrades,
or under what may be called a social influence. The liquor
traffic affects these drinkers in different ways, and those who
propose remedies for its evil effects must necessarily recognize
these differences of habit. Any given remedy will not prove
effective in all cases. Just as there must be discrimination in
dealing with the evil of intemperance, there should also be a
distinction made between the different kinds of drinkers, who
through the use of liquor have become paupers, criminals, or
who are found among the insane.

In a general way this difference of habit has been recognized
in the preceding tables, in which the number of excessive
drinkers is tabulated separately from drinkers of other degree.
The next series of tables, however, is intended to exhibit in
detail the habits of the paupers and of their fathers and
mothers as to the use of liquor. In these tables the paupers
are classified as citizen born, naturalized, and alien; by sex,
and by age periods. In collecting the data an effort was
made to discriminate as to the particular manner in which
liquor was used by those addicted to drinking. The tables,
for example, first show the number addicted to the use of
liquor, and these are afterwards classified under five different
heads, namely, excessive drinkers, social drinkers, home
drinkers, periodical drinkers, and occasional drinkers. In
grading the individuals in this manner, it frequently occurred that the same person might properly be classed
under more than one head. Thus it follows that the number

reported of what may be termed "drinking conditions" is in excess of the number of individual drinkers. Thus, taking the total number of persons addicted to the use of intoxicating liquors who are represented in the first table, namely, 2,108, it was found that 4,533 drinking conditions were represented among these 2,108 individual cases, or an average of 2.15 drinking conditions to each person. This explanation will enable the table to be readily understood.

The method of grading the cases under the five heads named requires some explanation however. The term "excessive drinkers" includes all who are completely under the influence of the drinking habit, — who are, in fact, common drunkards. The "social drinkers," on the other hand, are those who rarely drink except with others, and who are led to drink principally under the prevailing custom of "treating." This class is fitly represented by one who remarked "I would not touch it during the week at all, but when Saturday came, and I got my wages, I used to go out with the boys and get full." This class, in combination with others, is perhaps the most numerous, and is the class from which the periodical drinkers and the excessive drinkers are principally recruited. The "home drinkers" include those who seldom drink at saloons, confining their use of intoxicants almost exclusively to the family circle. Those who are classed as "periodical drinkers," have sprees at periodically recurring intervals, separated by weeks or months during which they do not touch liquor at all. Closely allied to these are the "occasional drinkers," who are addicted to the solitary drinking habit. They drink occasionally, and almost entirely by themselves.

Of course, as we have said, many drinkers belong to more than one class, and the classification is more or less arbitrary. That these differences of habit exist must be recognized, and the reader can no doubt recall, within his experience, individual types of each of the classes named. Many combinations occur and have been noted by our agents and followed in tabulating the data. There are, for instance, occasional drinkers who also have periodical sprees, and, more numerous than these, the social drinkers, who have periodical sprees. There are home drinkers who drink socially and may at times have prolonged periods of debauch; and it is, of course, true that the excessive drinkers are also, in most cases, social drinkers, periodical " spreers," and home drinkers. Their habit of drinking is not confined to any particular form. They drink whenever and wherever they can obtain liquor. The first table relates entirely to the paupers individually.

Pauperism; Sex, Political Condition, and Liquor Habits of Paupers: By Age Periods.

AGE PERIOD: Under 10.

SEX AND PO-LITICAL CONDITION.	Number addicted to the Use of Intoxicating Liquors	Excessive Drinkers	Social Drinkers	Home Drinkers	Periodical Drinkers	Occasional Drinkers	Aggregate Number of Drinking Conditions	Average Number of Drinking Conditions	Liquor Habits Unknown	Total Abstainers
Males.	–	–	–	–	–	–	–	–	–	158
Citizen born,	–	–	–	–	–	–	–	–	–	141
Alien, . .	–	–	–	–	–	–	–	–	–	16
Unknown, .	–	–	–	–	–	–	–	–	–	1
Females.	–	–	–	–	–	–	–	–	–	123
Citizen born,	–	–	–	–	–	–	–	–.	–	113
Alien, . .	–	–	–	–	–	–	–	–	–	10
BOTH SEXES.	–	–	–	–	–	–	–	–	–	281
Citizen born,	–	–	–	–	–	–	–	–	–	254
Alien, . .	–	–	–	–	–	–	–	–	–	26
Unknown, .	–	–	–	–	–	–	–	–	–	1

AGE PERIOD: 10–14.

Males.	1	–	–	–	–	1	1	1.00	6	40
Citizen born,	1	–	–	–	–	1	1	1.00	6	28
Alien, . .	–	–	–	–	–	–	–	–	–	12
Females.	1	–	1	–	–	1	2	2.00	1	22
Citizen born,	–	–	–	–	–	–	–	–	–	19
Alien, . .	1	–	1	–	–	1	2	2.00	1	3
BOTH SEXES.	2	–	1	–	–	2	3	1.50	7	62
Citizen born,	1	–	–	–	–	1	1	1.00	6	47
Alien, . .	1	–	1	–	–	1	2	2.00	1	15

Pauperism; Sex, Political Condition, and Liquor Habits of Paupers: By Age Periods — Continued.

AGE PERIOD: 15–19.

SEX AND POLITICAL CONDITION.	Number addicted to the Use of Intoxicating Liquors	Excessive Drinkers	Social Drinkers	Home Drinkers	Periodical Drinkers	Occasional Drinkers	Aggregate Number of Drinking Conditions	Average Number of Drinking Conditions	Liquor Habits Unknown	Total Abstainers
Males.	22	1	17	11	1	20	50	2.27	6	32
Citizen born,	7	–	5	2	1	6	14	2.00	2	13
Alien, . .	15	1	12	9	–	14	36	2.40	4	19
Females.	7	–	6	4	–	7	17	2.43	5	54
Citizen born,	3	–	2	1	–	3	6	2.00	1	26
Alien, . .	4	–	4	3	–	4	11	2.75	4	28
BOTH SEXES.	29	1	23	15	1	27	67	2.31	11	86
Citizen born,	10	–	7	3	1	9	20	2.00	3	39
Alien. . .	19	1	16	12	–	18	47	2.47	8	47

AGE PERIOD: 20–29.

Males.	413	102	240	141	121	251	855	2.07	54	81
Citizen born, .	102	22	51	26	40	62	201	1.97	12	28
Naturalized, .	21	4	16	11	7	16	54	2.57	2	5
Alien, . .	289	76	172	104	74	173	599	2.07	37	48
Unknown, .	1	–	1	–	–	–	1	1.00	3	–
Females.	48	6	37	33	10	40	126	2.63	11	125
Citizen born, .	11	2	9	8	2	9	30	2.73	3	38
Alien, . .	37	4	28	25	8	31	96	2.59	7	87
Unknown, .	–	–	–	–	–	–	–	–	1	–
BOTH SEXES.	461	108	277	174	131	291	981	2.11	65	206
Citizen born, .	113	24	60	34	42	71	231	2.04	15	66
Naturalized, .	21	4	16	11	7	16	54	2.57	2	5
Alien, . .	326	80	200	129	82	204	695	2.11	44	135
Unknown, .	1	–	1	–	–	–	1	1.00	4	–

AGE PERIOD: 30–39.

Males.	566	150	317	197	177	318	1,159	2.05	65	44
Citizen born, .	154	35	78	43	61	79	296	1.92	19	10
Naturalized, .	55	14	32	15	18	31	110	2.00	1	6
Alien, . .	356	100	207	139	98	208	752	2.11	38	28
Unknown, .	1	1	–	–	–	–	1	1.00	7	–

Pauperism; Sex, Political Condition, and Liquor Habits of Paupers: By Age Periods — Continued.

AGE PERIOD: 30-39 — Concluded.

SEX AND POLITICAL CONDITION.	Number addicted to the Use of Intoxicating Liquors	Excessive Drinkers	Social Drinkers	Home Drinkers	Periodical Drinkers	Occasional Drinkers	Aggregate Number of Drinking Conditions	Average Number of Drinking Conditions	Liquor Habits Unknown	Total Abstainers
Females.	35	9	22	22	4	25	82	2.34	9	44
Citizen born, .	7	3	3	3	1	3	13	1.86	3	10
Alien, . .	28	6	19	19	3	22	69	2.46	6	34
BOTH SEXES.	601	159	339	219	181	343	1,241	2.06	74	88
Citizen born, .	161	38	81	46	62	82	309	1.92	22	20
Naturalized, .	55	14	32	15	18	31	110	2.00	1	6
Alien, . .	384	106	226	158	101	230	821	2.14	44	62
Unknown, .	1	1	–	–	–	–	1	1.00	7	–

AGE PERIOD: 40-49.

Males.	465	115	262	197	162	260	996	2.14	54	34
Citizen born,	117	33	55	39	41	56	224	1.91	10	10
Naturalized, .	77	15	49	31	25	50	170	2.21	6	7
Alien, . .	270	67	157	126	95	153	598	2.21	36	17
Unknown, .	1	–	1	1	1	1	4	4.00	2	–
Females.	30	9	17	20	4	18	68	2.27	4	21
Citizen born,	5	1	2	3	1	2	9	1.80	–	7
Alien, . .	25	8	15	17	3	16	59	2.36	3	14
Unknown, .	–	–	–	–	–	–	–	–	1	–
BOTH SEXES.	495	124	279	217	166	278	1,064	2.15	58	55
Citizen born,	122	34	57	42	42	58	233	1.91	10	17
Naturalized, .	77	15	49	31	25	50	170	2.21	6	7
Alien, . .	295	75	172	143	98	169	657	2.23	39	31
Unknown, .	1	–	1	1	1	1	4	4.00	3	–

AGE PERIOD: 50-59.

Males.	297	63	191	146	88	190	678	2.28	21	25
Citizen born,	42	6	29	19	19	28	101	2.40	7	10
Naturalized, .	65	10	49	35	15	49	158	2.43	3	5
Alien, . .	189	47	112	91	54	112	416	2.20	9	10
Unknown, .	1	–	1	1	–	1	3	3.00	2	–
Females.	10	1	7	8	3	7	26	2.60	4	13
Citizen born,	–	–	–	–	–	–	–	–	1	4
Alien, . .	10	1	7	8	3	7	26	2.60	3	9

Pauperism: Sex, Political Condition, and Liquor Habits of Paupers: By Age Periods— Concluded.

AGE PERIOD: 50-59 — Concluded.

Sex and Political Condition.	Number addicted to the Use of Intoxicating Liquors	Excessive Drinkers	Social Drinkers	Home Drinkers	Periodical Drinkers	Occasional Drinkers	Aggregate Number of Drinking Conditions	Average Number of Drinking Conditions	Liquor Habits Unknown	Total Abstainers
Both Sexes.	307	64	198	154	91	197	704	2.29	25	38
Citizen born,	42	6	29	19	19	28	101	2.60	8	14
Naturalized, .	65	10	49	35	15	49	158	2.43	3	5
Alien, . .	199	48	119	99	57	119	442	2.22	12	19
Unknown, .	1	–	1	1	–	1	3	3.00	2	–

AGE PERIOD: 60-79.

Males.	194	45	128	94	35	134	436	2.25	9	28
Citizen born,	31	7	22	11	4	22	66	2.13	1	5
Naturalized, .	47	9	31	26	6	35	107	2.28	1	11
Alien, . .	113	27	74	56	25	76	258	2.28	7	12
Unknown, .	3	2	1	1	–	1	5	1.67	–	–
Females.	10	3	5	4	1	6	19	1.90	5	12
Citizen born,	1	–	–	–	–	1	1	1.00	1	4
Alien, . .	9	3	5	4	1	5	18	2.00	4	8
Both Sexes.	204	48	133	98	36	140	455	2.23	14	40
Citizen born,	32	7	22	11	4	23	67	2.09	2	9
Naturalized, .	47	9	31	26	6	35	107	2.28	1	11
Alien, . .	122	30	79	60	26	81	276	2.26	11	20
Unknown, .	3	2	1	1	–	1	5	1.67	–	–

AGE PERIOD: 80 +.

Males.	9	1	6	2	2	7	18	2.00	2	7
Citizen born,	2	–	2	–	–	2	4	2.00	–	3
Naturalized, .	4	1	2	1	1	2	7	1.75	2	2
Alien, . .	3	–	2	1	1	3	7	2.33	–	2
Females.	–	–	–	–	–	–	–	–	–	3
Citizen born,	–	–	–	–	–	–	–	–	–	1
Alien, . .	–	–	–	–	–	–	–	–	–	2
Both Sexes.	9	1	6	2	2	7	18	2.00	2	10
Citizen born,	2	–	2	–	–	2	4	2.00	–	4
Naturalized, .	4	1	2	1	1	2	7	1.75	2	2
Alien, . .	3	–	2	1	1	3	7	2.33	–	4

RECAPITULATION.

SEX AND POLITICAL CONDITION.	Number addicted to the Use of Intoxicating Liquors	Excessive Drinkers	Social Drinkers	Home Drinkers	Periodical Drinkers	Occasional Drinkers	Aggregate Number of Drinking Conditions	Average Number of Drinking Conditions	Liquor Habits Unknown	Total Abstainers
Males.	1,967	477	1,161	788	586	1,161	4,193	2.13	217	449
Citizen born,	456	103	242	140	166	256	907	1.99	57	248
Naturalized, .	269	53	179	119	72	183	606	2.25	15	36
Alien, . .	1,235	318	736	526	347	739	2,666	2.16	131	164
Unknown, .	7	3	4	3	1	3	14	2.00	14	1
Females.	141	28	95	91	22	104	340	2.41	39	417
Citizen born,	27	6	16	15	4	18	59	2.19	9	222
Alien, . .	114	22	79	76	18	86	281	2.46	28	195
Unknown, .	-	-	-	-	-	-	-	-	2	-
BOTH SEXES.	2,108	505	1,256	879	608	1,285	4,533	2.15	256	866
Citizen born,	483	109	258	155	170	274	966	2.00	66	470
Naturalized, .	269	53	179	119	72	183	606	2.25	15	36
Alien, . .	1,349	340	815	602	365	825	2,947	2.18	159	359
Unknown, .	7	3	4	3	1	3	14	2.00	16	1

RECAPITULATION: BY AGE PERIODS.

SEX AND AGE PERIODS.	Number addicted to the Use of Intoxicating Liquors	Excessive Drinkers	Social Drinkers	Home Drinkers	Periodical Drinkers	Occasional Drinkers	Aggregate Number of Drinking Conditions	Average Number of Drinking Conditions	Liquor Habits Unknown	Total Abstainers
Males.	1,967	477	1,161	788	586	1,181	4,193	2.13	217	449
Under 10, .	-	-	-	-	-	-	-	-	-	158
10-14,	1	-	-	-	-	1	1	1.00	6	40
15-19,	22	1	17	11	1	20	50	2.27	6	32
20-29,	413	102	240	141	121	251	855	2.07	54	81
30-39,	566	150	317	197	177	318	1,159	2.05	65	44
40-49,	465	115	262	197	162	260	996	2.14	54	34
50-59,	297	63	191	146	88	190	678	2.28	21	25
60-79,	194	45	128	94	35	134	436	2.25	9	28
80+,	9	1	6	2	2	7	18	2.00	2	7
Females.	141	28	95	91	22	104	340	2.41	39	417
Under 10, .	-	-	-	-	-	-	-	-	-	123
10-14,	1	-	1	-	-	1	2	2.00	1	22
15-19,	7	-	6	4	-	7	17	2.43	5	54
20-29,	48	6	37	33	10	40	126	2.63	11	125

RECAPITULATION: BY AGE PERIODS — Concluded.

SEX AND AGE PERIODS.	Number addicted to the Use of Intoxicating Liquors	Excessive Drinkers	Social Drinkers	Home Drinkers	Periodical Drinkers	Occasional Drinkers	Aggregate Number of Drinking Conditions	Average Number of Drinking Conditions	Liquor Habits Unknown	Total Abstainers
*Females-*Con.										
30–39,	35	9	22	22	4	25	82	2.34	9	44
40–49,	30	9	17	20	4	18	68	2.27	4	21
50–59,	10	1	7	8	3	7	26	2.60	4	13
60–79,	10	3	5	4	1	6	19	1.90	5	12
80+,	–	–	–	–	–	–	–	–	–	3
BOTH SEXES.	2,108	505	1,256	879	608	1,285	4,533	2.15	256	866
Under 10,	–	–	–	–	–	–	–	–	–	281
10–14,	2	–	1	–	–	2	3	1.50	7	62
15–19,	29	1	23	15	1	27	67	2.31	11	86
20–29,	461	108	277	174	131	291	981	2.13	65	206
30–39,	601	159	339	219	181	343	1,241	2.06	74	88
40–49,	495	124	279	217	166	278	1,064	2.16	58	55
50–59,	307	64	198	154	91	197	704	2.29	25	38
60–79,	204	48	133	98	36	140	455	2.23	14	40
80+,	9	1	6	2	2	7	18	2.00	2	10

Referring to the recapitulation of the table, it will be found that drinking habits for 2,108 cases are reported, including both sexes and all ages. Among these, there are represented 505 instances of excessive drinkers; 1,256, social drinkers; 879, home drinkers; 608, periodical drinkers; and 1,285, occasional drinkers; the aggregate number of drinking conditions actually represented among the 2,108 individual cases being 4,533, or an average of 2.15 per person; that is to say, on an average, each individual case falls under at least two of the heads mentioned in the table. In 256 cases the particular form of the drinking habit is unreported, and the number of total abstainers, brought forward from the tables previously presented, is 866. The number of cases reported among the males addicted to the use of liquor is 1,967, and among the females 141. Of the females there are only 28 instances of excessive drinkers reported, as against 477 among the males. The number of instances of social drinkers reported among the males is 1,161, and among the females 95. By scanning the classification of ages, it will be seen that very few, either males or females, under the age of 20 years, are reported as addicted to the use of intoxicating liquors, and none appear under the age of 10 years. In the age period 20 to 29, 413 cases appear among the males, and 48 among the females. Of these, among the males, there appear 102 instances of excessive drinkers, and among the females, six. The number reported as addicted to the use of intoxicating liquors in each decennial age period above the age of 20 and below the age of 50 ranges from 75 to 84 per cent for males, and from 26 to 54 per cent for females, and about the same proportion of the whole number are excessive drinkers in each age period, this proportion being about 25 per cent among the males, and from 12.50 to 25 per cent among the females. The progress of the drinking habit is very clearly indicated by the classification by ages in this table. The next table exhibits the same line of facts for the fathers of paupers.

Pauperism ; Sex, Political Condition, and Liquor Habits of Fathers of Paupers: By Age Periods.

AGE PERIOD: Under 1.

SEX AND POLITICAL CONDITION.	Number addicted to the Use of Intoxicating Liquors	Excessive Drinkers	Social Drinkers	Home Drinkers	Periodical Drinkers	Occasional Drinkers	Aggregate Number of Drinking Conditions	Average Number of Drinking Conditions	Liquor Habits Unknown	Total Abstainers
Males.	39	14	23	10	11	23	81	2.08	28	11
Citizen born,	38	14	22	9	11	22	78	2.05	28	11
Alien, . .	1	–	1	1	–	1	3	3.00	–	–
Females.	30	10	18	10	8	18	64	2.10	19	19
Citizen born,	29	9	18	10	8	18	63	2.17	19	19
Alien, . .	1	1	–	–	–	–	1	1.00	–	–
BOTH SEXES.	69	24	41	20	19	41	145	2.10	47	30
Citizen born,	67	23	40	19	19	40	141	2.10	47	30
Alien, . .	2	1	1	1	–	1	4	2.00	–	–

AGE PERIOD: 1-4.

Males.	23	7	13	9	4	13	46	2.00	16	3
Citizen born,	21	6	12	9	4	12	43	2.05	13	3
Alien, . .	2	1	1	–	–	1	3	1.50	2	–
Unknown, .	–	–	–	–	–	–	–	–	1	–

Pauperism; Sex, Political Condition, and Liquor Habits of Fathers of Paupers: By Age Periods — Continued.

AGE PERIOD: 1–4 — Concluded.

SEX AND POLITICAL CONDITION.	Number addicted to the Use of Intoxicating Liquors	Excessive Drinkers	Social Drinkers	Home Drinkers	Periodical Drinkers	Occasional Drinkers	Aggregate Number of Drinking Conditions	Average Number of Drinking Conditions	Liquor Habits Unknown	Total Abstainers
Females.	12	6	7	2	2	6	23	1.92	10	6
Citizen born,	12	6	7	2	2	6	23	1.92	9	5
Alien, . .	-	-	-	-	-	-	-	-	1	1
BOTH SEXES.	35	13	20	11	6	19	69	1.97	26	9
Citizen born,	33	12	19	11	6	18	66	2.00	22	8
Alien, . .	2	1	1	-	-	1	3	1.50	3	1
Unknown, .	-	-	-	-	-	-	-	-	1	-

AGE PERIOD: 5–9.

Males.	14	6	6	6	3	6	27	1.93	19	5
Citizen born,	8	4	2	3	2	2	13	1.63	16	3
Alien, . .	6	2	4	3	1	4	14	2.33	3	2
Females.	14	8	5	3	3	5	24	1.71	11	2
Citizen born,	10	6	3	2	3	3	17	1.70	9	1
Alien, . .	4	2	2	1	-	2	7	1.75	2	1
BOTH SEXES.	28	14	11	9	6	11	51	1.82	30	7
Citizen born,	18	10	5	5	5	5	30	1.66	25	4
Alien, . .	10	4	6	4	1	6	21	2.10	5	3

AGE PERIOD: 10–14.

Males.	16	5	8	4	6	9	32	2.00	25	6
Citizen born,	7	1	5	3	4	5	18	2.57	23	5
Alien, . .	9	4	3	1	2	4	14	1.56	2	1
Females.	7	5	3	1	2	2	13	1.67	6	11
Citizen born,	5	3	1	1	2	1	8	1.60	3	11
Alien, . .	2	2	2	-	-	1	5	2.50	3	-
BOTH SEXES.	23	10	11	5	8	11	45	1.96	31	17
Citizen born,	12	4	6	4	6	6	26	2.17	26	16
Alien, . .	11	6	5	1	2	5	19	1.73	5	1

Pauperism; Sex, Political Condition, and Liquor Habits of Fathers of Paupers: By Age Periods — Continued.

AGE PERIOD: 15-19.

SEX AND POLITICAL CONDITION.	Number addicted to the Use of Intoxicating Liquors	Excessive Drinkers	Social Drinkers	Home Drinkers	Periodical Drinkers	Occasional Drinkers	Aggregate Number of Drinking Conditions	Average Number of Drinking Conditions	Liquor Habits Unknown	Total Abstainers
Males.	31	4	25	17	4	25	75	2.42	18	11
Citizen born,	9	2	7	6	3	7	25	2.78	9	4
Alien, . .	22	2	18	11	1	18	50	2.27	9	7
Females.	24	6	15	12	3	15	51	2.13	23	19
Citizen born,	10	4	5	3	1	5	18	1.80	10	10
Alien, . .	14	2	10	9	2	10	33	2.36	13	9
BOTH SEXES.	55	10	40	29	7	40	126	2.29	41	30
Citizen born,	19	6	12	9	4	12	43	2.26	19	14
Alien, . .	36	4	28	20	3	28	83	2.31	22	16

AGE PERIOD: 20-29.

Males.	283	21	249	172	24	249	715	2.53	140	125
Citizen born,	64	7	53	32	8	53	153	2.39	35	43
Naturalized, .	18	-	17	8	2	17	44	2.44	4	6
Alien, . .	201	14	179	132	14	179	518	2.58	97	76
Unknown, .	-	-	-	-	-	-	-	-	4	-
Females.	99	21	80	59	15	77	252	2.55	40	45
Citizen born,	22	7	16	12	4	16	55	2.50	13	17
Alien, . .	77	14	64	47	11	61	197	2.56	26	28
Unknown, .	-	-	-	-	-	-	-	-	1	-
BOTH SEXES.	382	42	329	231	39	326	967	2.53	180	170
Citizen born,	86	14	69	44	12	69	208	2.42	48	60
Naturalized, .	18	-	17	8	2	17	44	2.44	4	6
Alien, . .	278	28	243	179	25	240	715	2.57	123	104
Unknown, .	-	-	-	-	-	-	-	-	5	-

AGE PERIOD: 30-39.

Males.	319	20	284	177	23	285	789	2.47	219	137
Citizen born,	87	10	69	41	6	71	197	2.26	56	40
Naturalized, .	28	-	28	13	1	28	70	2.50	18	16
Alien, . .	203	10	186	122	16	185	519	2.56	138	81
Unknown, .	1	-	1	1	-	1	3	3.00	7	-

Pauperism; Sex, Political Condition, and Liquor Habits of Fathers of Paupers: By Age Periods — Continued.

AGE PERIOD: 30-39 — Concluded.

SEX AND POLITICAL CONDITION.	Number addicted to the Use of Intoxicating Liquors	Excessive Drinkers	Social Drinkers	Home Drinkers	Periodical Drinkers	Occasional Drinkers	Aggregate Number of Drinking Conditions	Average Number of Drinking Conditions	Liquor Habits Unknown	Total Abstainers
Females.	43	15	29	25	3	29	101	2.35	21	24
Citizen born,	7	3	4	3	-	4	14	2.00	8	5
Alien, . .	36	12	25	22	3	25	87	2.42	13	19
BOTH SEXES.	362	35	313	202	26	314	890	2.46	240	161
Citizen born,	94	13	73	44	6	75	211	2.24	64	45
Naturalized, .	28	-	28	13	1	28	70	2.50	18	16
Alien, . .	239	22	211	144	19	210	606	2.54	151	100
Unknown, .	1	-	1	1	-	1	3	3.00	7	-

AGE PERIOD: 40-49.

Males.	239	11	203	145	19	214	592	2.48	185	129
Citizen born,	55	5	43	23	9	45	125	2.27	39	43
Naturalized, .	48	2	45	31	3	44	125	2.60	23	19
Alien, . .	135	4	114	90	7	124	339	2.51	121	67
Unknown, .	1	-	1	1	-	1	3	3.00	2	-
Females.	24	4	19	13	3	17	56	2.33	17	14
Citizen born,	5	1	3	2	1	3	10	2.00	4	3
Alien, . .	19	3	16	11	2	14	46	2.42	12	11
Unknown, .	-	-	-	-	-	-	-	-	1	-
BOTH SEXES.	263	15	222	158	22	231	648	2.46	202	143
Citizen born,	60	6	46	25	10	48	135	2.25	43	46
Naturalized, .	48	2	45	31	3	44	125	2.60	23	19
Alien, . .	154	7	130	101	9	138	385	2.50	133	78
Unknown, .	1	-	1	1	-	1	3	3.00	3	-

AGE PERIOD: 50-59.

Males.	150	4	138	97	13	138	390	2.60	110	83
Citizen born,	20	1	18	8	5	18	50	2.50	18	21
Naturalized, .	27	-	25	20	2	25	72	2.67	28	18
Alien, . .	102	3	94	68	6	94	265	2.60	62	44
Unknown, .	1	-	1	1	-	1	3	3.00	2	-

Pauperism; Sex, Political Condition, and Liquor Habits of Fathers of Paupers: By Age Periods — Continued.

AGE PERIOD: 50-59 — Concluded.

SEX AND POLITICAL CONDITION.	Number addicted to the Use of Intoxicating Liquors	Excessive Drinkers	Social Drinkers	Home Drinkers	Periodical Drinkers	Occasional Drinkers	Aggregate Number of Drinking Conditions	Average Number of Drinking Conditions	Liquor Habits Unknown	Total Abstainers
Females.	12	1	7	5	1	9	23	1.92	13	2
Citizen born,	3	-	1	1	1	2	5	1.67	2	-
Alien, . .	9	1	6	4	-	7	18	2.00	11	2
BOTH SEXES.	162	5	145	102	14	147	413	2.55	123	85
Citizen born,	23	1	19	9	6	20	55	2.39	20	21
Naturalized, .	27	-	25	20	2	25	72	2.67	28	18
Alien, . .	111	4	100	72	6	101	283	2.55	73	46
Unknown, .	1	-	1	1	-	1	3	3.00	2	-

AGE PERIOD: 60-79.

SEX AND POLITICAL CONDITION.	Number addicted to the Use of Intoxicating Liquors	Excessive Drinkers	Social Drinkers	Home Drinkers	Periodical Drinkers	Occasional Drinkers	Aggregate Number of Drinking Conditions	Average Number of Drinking Conditions	Liquor Habits Unknown	Total Abstainers
Males.	92	1	88	67	8	87	251	2.73	92	47
Citizen born,	13	-	13	8	2	13	36	2.77	13	11
Naturalized, .	24	-	24	18	2	24	68	2.83	24	11
Alien, . .	54	1	50	40	4	49	144	2.67	53	25
Unknown, .	1	-	1	1	-	1	3	3.00	2	-
Females.	7	1	5	3	1	5	15	2.14	10	10
Citizen born,	-	-	-	-	-	-	-	-	2	4
Alien, . .	7	1	5	3	1	5	15	2.14	8	6
BOTH SEXES.	99	2	93	70	9	92	266	2.68	102	57
Citizen born,	13	-	13	8	2	13	36	2.77	15	15
Naturalized, .	24	-	24	18	2	24	68	2.83	24	11
Alien, . .	61	2	55	43	5	54	159	2.61	61	31
Unknown, .	1	-	1	1	-	1	3	3.00	2	-

AGE PERIOD: 80 +.

SEX AND POLITICAL CONDITION.	Number addicted to the Use of Intoxicating Liquors	Excessive Drinkers	Social Drinkers	Home Drinkers	Periodical Drinkers	Occasional Drinkers	Aggregate Number of Drinking Conditions	Average Number of Drinking Conditions	Liquor Habits Unknown	Total Abstainers
Males.	6	-	5	6	2	6	19	3.17	7	5
Citizen born,	2	-	2	2	1	2	7	3.50	1	2
Naturalized, .	3	-	2	3	1	3	9	3.00	5	-
Alien, . .	1	-	1	1	-	1	3	3.00	1	3
Females.	2	1	1	-	-	1	3	1.50	-	1
Citizen born,	1	1	-	-	-	-	1	1.00	-	-
Alien, . .	1	-	1	-	-	1	2	2.00	-	1

Pauperism; Sex, Political Condition, and Liquor Habits of Fathers of Paupers: By Age Periods — Concluded.

AGE PERIOD: 80 + — Concluded.

SEX AND POLITICAL CONDITION.	Number addicted to the Use of Intoxicating Liquors	Excessive Drinkers	Social Drinkers	Home Drinkers	Periodical Drinkers	Occasional Drinkers	Aggregate Number of Drinking Conditions	Average Number of Drinking Conditions	Liquor Habits Unknown	Total Abstainers
BOTH SEXES.	8	1	6	6	2	7	22	2.75	7	6
Citizen born,	3	1	2	2	1	2	8	2.67	1	2
Naturalized, .	3	–	2	3	1	3	9	3.00	5	–
Alien, . .	2	–	2	1	–	2	5	2.50	1	4

RECAPITULATION.

SEX AND POLITICAL CONDITION.	Number addicted to the Use of Intoxicating Liquors	Excessive Drinkers	Social Drinkers	Home Drinkers	Periodical Drinkers	Occasional Drinkers	Aggregate Number of Drinking Conditions	Average Number of Drinking Conditions	Liquor Habits Unknown	Total Abstainers
Males.	1,212	93	1,042	710	117	1,055	3,017	2.49	859	562
Citizen born,	324	50	246	144	55	250	745	2.30	251	186
Naturalized, .	148	2	141	93	11	141	388	2.62	102	70
Alien, . .	736	41	651	469	51	660	1,872	2.68	488	306
Unknown, .	4	–	4	4	–	4	12	3.00	18	–
Females.	274	78	189	133	41	184	625	2.28	170	153
Citizen born,	104	40	58	36	22	58	214	2.06	79	75
Alien, . .	170	38	131	97	19	126	411	2.44	89	78
Unknown, .	–	–	–	–	–	–	–	–	2	–
BOTH SEXES.	1,486	171	1,231	843	158	1,239	3,642	2.45	1,029	715
Citizen born,	428	90	304	180	77	308	959	2.24	330	261
Naturalized, .	148	2	141	93	11	141	388	2.62	102	70
Alien, . .	906	79	782	566	70	786	2,283	2.52	577	384
Unknown, .	4	–	4	4	–	4	12	3.00	20	–

RECAPITULATION: BY AGE PERIODS.

SEX AND AGE PERIODS.	Number addicted to the Use of Intoxicating Liquors	Excessive Drinkers	Social Drinkers	Home Drinkers	Periodical Drinkers	Occasional Drinkers	Aggregate Number of Drinking Conditions	Average Number of Drinking Conditions	Liquor Habits Unknown	Total Abstainers
Males.	1,212	93	1,042	710	117	1,055	3,017	2.49	859	562
Under 1, .	39	14	23	10	11	23	81	2.08	28	11
1-4, .	23	7	13	9	4	13	46	2.00	16	3
5-9, .	14	6	6	6	3	6	27	1.93	19	5

RECAPITULATION: BY AGE PERIODS — Concluded.

SEX AND AGE PERIODS.	Number addicted to the Use of Intoxicating Liquors	Excessive Drinkers	Social Drinkers	Home Drinkers	Periodical Drinkers	Occasional Drinkers	Aggregate Number of Drinking Conditions	Average Number of Drinking Conditions	Liquor Habits Unknown	Total Abstainers
Males — Con.										
10–14, .	16	5	8	4	6	9	32	2.00	25	6
15–19, .	31	4	25	17	4	25	75	2.42	18	11
20–29, .	283	21	249	172	24	249	715	2.53	140	125
30–39, .	319	20	284	177	23	285	789	2.47	219	137
40–49, .	239	11	203	145	19	214	592	2.48	185	129
50–59, .	150	4	138	97	13	138	390	2.60	110	83
60–79, .	92	1	88	67	8	87	251	2.73	92	47
80 +, .	6	–	5	6	2	6	19	3.17	7	5
Females.	274	78	189	133	41	184	625	2.28	170	153
Under 1, .	30	10	18	10	8	18	64	2.10	19	19
1–4, .	12	6	7	2	2	6	23	1.92	10	6
5–9, .	14	8	5	3	3	5	24	1.71	11	2
10–14, .	7	5	3	1	2	2	13	1.67	6	11
15–19, .	24	6	15	12	3	15	51	2.13	23	19
20–29, .	99	21	80	59	15	77	252	2.55	40	45
30–39, .	43	15	29	25	3	29	101	2.35	21	24
40–49, .	24	4	19	13	3	17	56	2.33	17	14
50–59, .	12	1	7	5	1	9	23	1.92	13	2
60–79, .	7	1	5	3	1	5	15	2.14	10	10
80 +, .	2	1	1	–	–	1	3	1.50	–	1
BOTH SEXES.	1,486	171	1,231	843	158	1,239	3,642	2.45	1,029	715
Under 1, .	69	24	41	20	19	41	145	2.10	47	30
1–4, .	35	13	20	11	6	19	69	1.97	26	9
5–9, .	28	14	11	9	6	11	51	1.82	30	7
10–14, .	23	10	11	5	8	11	45	1.96	31	17
15–19, .	55	10	40	29	7	40	126	2.29	41	30
20–29, .	382	42	329	231	39	326	967	2.53	180	170
30–39, .	362	35	313	202	26	314	890	2.46	240	161
40–49, .	263	15	222	158	22	231	648	2.46	202	143
50–59, .	162	5	145	102	14	147	413	2.55	123	85
60–79, .	99	2	93	70	9	92	266	2.68	102	57
80 +, .	8	1	6	6	2	7	22	2.75	7	6

Referring to the recapitulation for both sexes, we note that 1,486 paupers had fathers addicted to the use of intoxicating liquors, there being reported among these fathers 171 excessive drinkers, 1,231 social drinkers, 843 home drinkers,

158 periodical drinkers, and 1,239 occasional drinkers, the total number of drinking conditions represented among the fathers being 3,642, or an average of 2.45 for each person. In 1,029 cases the liquor habits of the fathers were unknown, and in 715 cases the fathers were total abstainers.

The next table shows the liquor habits of the mothers of paupers.

Pauperism; Sex, Political Condition, and Liquor Habits of Mothers of Paupers: By Age Periods.

AGE PERIOD: Under 1.

SEX AND POLITICAL CONDITION.	Number addicted to the Use of Intoxicating Liquors	Excessive Drinkers	Social Drinkers	Home Drinkers	Periodical Drinkers	Occasional Drinkers	Aggregate Number of Drinking Conditions	Average Number of Drinking Conditions	Liquor Habits Unknown	Total Abstainers
Males.	5	-	4	5	-	4	13	2.60	15	58
Citizen born,	5	-	4	5	-	4	13	2.60	15	57
Alien, . .	-	-	-	-	-	-	-	-	-	1
Females.	15	2	10	12	2	12	38	2.53	12	41
Citizen born,	15	2	10	12	2	12	38	2.53	12	40
Alien, . .	-	-	-	-	-	-	-	-	-	1
BOTH SEXES.	20	2	14	17	2	16	51	2.55	27	99
Citizen born,	20	2	14	17	2	16	51	2.55	27	97
Alien, . .	-	-	-	-	-	-	-	-	-	2

AGE PERIOD: 1-4.

SEX AND POLITICAL CONDITION.	Number addicted to the Use of Intoxicating Liquors	Excessive Drinkers	Social Drinkers	Home Drinkers	Periodical Drinkers	Occasional Drinkers	Aggregate Number of Drinking Conditions	Average Number of Drinking Conditions	Liquor Habits Unknown	Total Abstainers
Males.	13	5	8	6	2	7	28	2.15	11	18
Citizen born,	11	4	7	6	2	6	25	2.27	8	18
Alien, . .	2	1	1	-	-	1	3	1.50	2	-
Unknown, .	-	-	-	-	-	-	-	-	1	-
Females.	6	3	3	3	1	3	13	2.17	6	16
Citizen born,	6	3	3	3	1	3	13	2.17	5	15
Alien, . .	-	-	-	-	-	-	-	-	1	1
BOTH SEXES.	19	8	11	9	3	10	41	2.16	17	34
Citizen born,	17	7	10	9	3	9	38	2.24	13	33
Alien, . .	2	1	1	-	-	1	3	1.50	3	1
Unknown, .	-	-	-	-	-	-	-	-	1	-

Pauperism ; Sex, Political Condition, and Liquor Habits of Mothers of Paupers: By Age Periods — Continued.

AGE PERIOD: 5-9.

SEX AND POLITICAL CONDITION.	Number addicted to the Use of Intoxicating Liquors	Excessive Drinkers	Social Drinkers	Home Drinkers	Periodical Drinkers	Occasional Drinkers	Aggregate Number of Drinking Conditions	Average Number of Drinking Conditions	Liquor Habits Unknown	Total Abstainers
Males.	8	6	-	2	-	2	10	1.25	15	15
Citizen born,	6	4	-	2	-	2	8	1.33	11	10
Alien, . .	2	2	-	-	-	-	2	1.00	4	5
Females.	9	6	2	3	-	2	13	1.44	7	11
Citizen born,	8	6	2	2	-	1	11	1.28	5	7
Alien, . .	1	-	-	1	-	1	2	2.00	2	4
BOTH SEXES.	17	12	2	5	-	4	23	1.35	22	26
Citizen born,	14	10	2	4	-	3	19	1.36	16	17
Alien, . .	3	2	-	1	-	1	4	1.33	6	9

AGE PERIOD: 10-14.

SEX AND POLITICAL CONDITION.	Number addicted	Excessive Drinkers	Social Drinkers	Home Drinkers	Periodical Drinkers	Occasional Drinkers	Aggregate Number	Average Number	Liquor Habits Unknown	Total Abstainers
Males.	10	1	5	7	2	6	21	2.10	26	11
Citizen born,	5	1	3	4	-	2	10	2.00	21	9
Alien, . .	5	-	2	3	2	4	11	2.20	5	2
Females.	4	3	1	1	1	1	7	1.75	6	14
Citizen born,	3	2	1	1	1	1	6	2.00	4	12
Alien, . .	1	1	-	-	-	-	1	1.00	2	2
BOTH SEXES.	14	4	6	8	3	7	28	2.00	32	25
Citizen born,	8	3	4	5	1	3	16	2.00	25	21
Alien, . .	6	1	2	3	2	4	12	2.00	7	4

AGE PERIOD: 15-19.

SEX AND POLITICAL CONDITION.	Number addicted	Excessive Drinkers	Social Drinkers	Home Drinkers	Periodical Drinkers	Occasional Drinkers	Aggregate Number	Average Number	Liquor Habits Unknown	Total Abstainers
Males.	13	1	12	10	1	9	33	2.54	16	31
Citizen born,	1	-	1	1	-	1	3	3.00	9	12
Alien, . .	12	1	11	9	1	8	30	2.50	7	19
Females.	9	-	7	8	1	8	24	2.67	18	39
Citizen born,	2	-	1	2	1	2	6	3.00	9	19
Alien, . .	7	-	6	6	-	6	18	2.57	9	20
BOTH SEXES.	22	1	19	18	2	17	57	2.59	34	70
Citizen born,	3	-	2	3	1	3	9	3.00	18	31
Alien, . .	19	1	17	15	1	14	48	2.53	16	39

Pauperism ; Sex, Political Condition, and Liquor Habits of Mothers of Paupers : By Age Periods — Continued.

AGE PERIOD: 20–29.

SEX AND POLITICAL CONDITION.	Number addicted to the Use of Intoxicating Liquors	Excessive Drinkers	Social Drinkers	Home Drinkers	Periodical Drinkers	Occasional Drinkers	Aggregate Number of Drinking Conditions	Average Number of Drinking Conditions	Liquor Habits Unknown	Total Abstainers
Males.	121	3	91	100	6	92	292	2.41	135	292
Citizen born,	13	3	8	10	3	9	33	2.54	40	89
Naturalized, .	5	–	5	5	–	3	13	2.60	4	19
Alien, . .	103	–	78	85	3	80	246	2.39	88	183
Unknown, .	–	–	–	–	–	–	–	–	3	1
Females.	36	1	30	32	4	30	97	2.69	41	107
Citizen born,	5	–	5	5	–	5	15	3.00	13	34
Alien, . .	31	1	25	27	4	25	82	2.65	27	73
Unknown, .	–	–	–	–	–	–	–	–	1	–
BOTH SEXES.	157	4	121	132	10	122	389	2.48	176	399
Citizen born,	18	3	13	15	3	14	48	2.67	53	123
Naturalized, .	5	–	5	5	–	3	13	2.60	4	19
Alien, . .	134	1	103	112	7	105	328	2.45	115	256
Unknown, .	–	–	–	–	–	–	–	–	4	1

AGE PERIOD: 30–39.

SEX AND POLITICAL CONDITION.	Number addicted to the Use of Intoxicating Liquors	Excessive Drinkers	Social Drinkers	Home Drinkers	Periodical Drinkers	Occasional Drinkers	Aggregate Number of Drinking Conditions	Average Number of Drinking Conditions	Liquor Habits Unknown	Total Abstainers
Males.	100	2	95	94	1	82	274	2.74	226	349
Citizen born,	21	1	11	18	1	11	42	2.00	58	104
Naturalized, .	10	–	9	9	–	8	26	2.60	17	35
Alien, .	68	1	74	66	–	62	203	2.99	144	210
Unknown, .	1	–	1	1	–	1	3	3.00	7	–
Females.	11	–	9	11	–	9	29	2.64	27	50
Citizen born,	1	–	–	1	–	–	1	1.00	8	11
Alien, . .	10	–	9	10	–	9	28	2.80	19	39
BOTH SEXES.	111	2	104	105	1	91	303	2.73	253	399
Citizen born,	22	1	11	19	1	11	43	1.95	66	115
Naturalized, .	10	–	9	9	–	8	26	2.60	17	35
Alien, . .	78	1	83	76	–	71	231	2.96	163	249
Unknown, .	1	–	1	1	–	1	3	3.00	7	–

AGE PERIOD: 40–49.

SEX AND POLITICAL CONDITION.	Number addicted to the Use of Intoxicating Liquors	Excessive Drinkers	Social Drinkers	Home Drinkers	Periodical Drinkers	Occasional Drinkers	Aggregate Number of Drinking Conditions	Average Number of Drinking Conditions	Liquor Habits Unknown	Total Abstainers
Males.	87	–	70	81	1	73	225	2.59	189	277
Citizen born,	12	–	8	12	–	9	29	2.42	36	89
Naturalized, .	14	–	12	14	1	8	35	2.50	24	52

Pauperism; Sex, Political Condition, and Liquor Habits of Mothers of Paupers: By Age Periods — Continued.

AGE PERIOD: 40–49 — Concluded.

SEX AND POLITICAL CONDITION.	Number addicted to the Use of Intoxicating Liquors	Excessive Drinkers	Social Drinkers	Home Drinkers	Periodical Drinkers	Occasional Drinkers	Aggregate Number of Drinking Conditions	Average Number of Drinking Conditions	Liquor Habits Unknown	Total Abstainers
Males — Con.										
Alien, . .	61	–	50	55	–	56	161	2.64	127	135
Unknown, .	–	–	–	–	–	–	–	–	2	1
Females.	9	1	8	8	2	7	26	2.89	19	27
Citizen born,	–	–	–	–	–	–	–	–	5	7
Alien, . .	9	1	8	8	2	7	26	2.89	13	20
Unknown, .	–	–	–	–	–	–	–	–	1	–
BOTH SEXES.	96	1	78	89	3	80	251	2.61	208	304
Citizen born,	12	–	8	12	–	9	29	2.42	41	96
Naturalized, .	14	–	12	14	1	8	35	2.50	24	52
Alien, . .	70	1	58	63	2	63	187	2.67	140	155
Unknown, .	–	–	–	–	–	–	–	–	3	1

AGE PERIOD: 50–59.

Males.	75	1	64	73	–	62	200	2.67	102	166
Citizen born,	5	–	4	5	–	4	13	2.60	18	36
Naturalized, .	16	1	14	15	–	12	42	2.63	26	31
Alien, . .	53	–	45	52	–	45	142	2.68	56	99
Unknown, .	1	–	1	1	–	1	3	3.00	2	–
Females.	1	–	–	–	–	1	1	1.00	12	14
Citizen born,	–	–	–	–	–	–	–	–	2	3
Alien, . .	1	–	–	–	–	1	1	1.00	10	11
BOTH SEXES.	76	1	64	73	–	63	201	2.64	114	180
Citizen born,	5	–	4	5	–	4	13	2.60	20	39
Naturalized, .	16	1	14	15	–	12	42	2.63	26	31
Alien, . .	54	–	45	52	–	46	143	2.65	66	110
Unknown, .	1	–	1	1	–	1	3	3.00	2	–

AGE PERIOD: 60–79.

Males.	41	–	35	40	1	31	107	2.61	84	106
Citizen born,	2	–	2	2	–	1	5	2.50	13	22
Naturalized, .	11	–	6	10	–	6	22	2.00	20	28

Pauperism; Sex, Political Condition, and Liquor Habits of Mothers of Paupers: By Age Periods — Concluded.

AGE PERIOD: 60–79 — Concluded.

SEX AND POLITICAL CONDITION.	Number addicted to the Use of Intoxicating Liquors	Excessive Drinkers	Social Drinkers	Home Drinkers	Periodical Drinkers	Occasional Drinkers	Aggregate Number of Drinking Conditions	Average Number of Drinking Conditions	Liquor Habits Unknown	Total Abstainers
Males — Con.										
Alien, . .	27	-	26	27	1	23	77	2.85	50	55
Unknown, .	1	-	1	1	-	1	3	3.00	1	1
Females.	2	-	2	2	-	2	6	3.00	11	14
Citizen born,	-	-	-	-	-	-	-	-	2	4
Alien, . .	2	-	2	2	-	2	6	3.00	9	10
BOTH SEXES.	43	-	37	42	1	33	113	2.63	95	120
Citizen born,	2	-	2	2	-	1	5	2.50	15	26
Naturalized, .	11	-	6	10	-	6	22	2.00	20	28
Alien, . .	29	-	28	29	1	25	83	2.86	59	65
Unknown, .	1	-	1	1	-	1	3	3.00	1	1

AGE PERIOD: 80 +.

Males.	3	-	2	3	-	2	7	2.33	5	10
Citizen born,	1	-	1	1	-	-	2	2.00	-	4
Naturalized, .	2	-	1	2	-	2	5	2.50	4	2
Alien, . .	-	-	-	-	-	-	-	-	1	4
Females.	-	-	-	-	-	-	-	-	-	3
Citizen born,	-	-	-	-	-	-	-	-	-	1
Alien, . .	-	-	-	-	-	-	-	-	-	2
BOTH SEXES.	3	-	2	3	-	2	7	2.33	5	13
Citizen born,	1	-	1	1	-	-	2	2.00	-	5
Naturalized, .	2	-	1	2	-	2	5	2.50	4	2
Alien, . .	-	-	-	-	-	-	-	-	1	6

RECAPITULATION.

SEX AND POLITICAL CONDITION.	Number addicted to the Use of Intoxicating Liquors	Excessive Drinkers	Social Drinkers	Home Drinkers	Periodical Drinkers	Occasional Drinkers	Aggregate Number of Drinking Conditions	Average Number of Drinking Conditions	Liquor Habits Unknown	Total Abstainers
Males.	476	19	386	421	14	370	1,210	2.54	824	1,333
Citizen born,	82	13	49	66	6	49	183	2.23	229	450
Naturalized, .	58	1	47	55	1	39	143	2.47	95	167

RECAPITULATION — Concluded.

Sex and Political Condition.	Number addicted to the Use of Intoxicating Liquors	Excessive Drinkers	Social Drinkers	Home Drinkers	Periodical Drinkers	Occasional Drinkers	Aggregate Number of Drinking Conditions	Average Number of Drinking Conditions	Liquor Habits Unknown	Total Abstainers
Males — Con.										
Alien, . .	333	5	287	297	7	279	875	2.63	484	713
Unknown, .	3	–	3	3	–	3	9	3.00	16	3
Females.	102	16	72	80	11	75	254	2.49	159	336
Citizen born,	40	13	22	26	5	24	90	2.25	65	153
Alien, . .	62	3	50	54	6	51	164	2.65	92	183
Unknown, .	–	–	–	–	–	–	–	–	2	–
BOTH SEXES.	578	35	458	501	25	445	1,464	2.53	983	1,669
Citizen born,	122	26	71	92	11	73	273	2.24	294	603
Naturalized, .	58	1	47	55	1	39	143	2.47	95	167
Alien, . .	395	8	337	351	13	330	1,039	2.63	576	896
Unknown, .	3	–	3	3	–	3	9	3.00	18	3

RECAPITULATION: BY AGE PERIODS.

Sex and Age Periods.	Number addicted to the Use of Intoxicating Liquors	Excessive Drinkers	Social Drinkers	Home Drinkers	Periodical Drinkers	Occasional Drinkers	Aggregate Number of Drinking Conditions	Average Number of Drinking Conditions	Liquor Habits Unknown	Total Abstainers
Males.	476	19	386	421	14	370	1,210	2.54	824	1,333
Under 1, .	5	–	4	5	–	4	13	2.60	15	58
1-4, .	13	5	8	6	2	7	28	2.15	11	18
5-9, .	8	6	–	2	–	2	10	1.25	15	15
10-14, .	10	1	5	7	2	6	21	2.10	26	11
15-19, .	13	1	12	10	1	9	33	2.54	16	31
20-29, .	121	3	91	100	6	92	292	2.41	135	292
30-39, .	100	2	95	94	1	82	274	2.74	226	349
40-49, .	87	–	70	81	1	73	225	2.59	189	277
50-59, .	75	1	64	73	–	62	200	2.67	102	166
60-79, .	41	–	35	40	1	31	107	2.61	84	106
80 +, .	3	–	2	3	–	2	7	2 33	5	10
Females.	102	16	72	80	11	75	254	2.49	159	336
Under 1, .	15	2	10	12	2	12	38	2.53	12	41
1-4, .	6	3	3	3	1	3	13	2 17	6	16
5-9, .	9	6	2	3	–	2	13	1.44	7	11
10-14, .	4	3	1	1	1	1	7	1.75	6	14
15-19, .	9	–	7	8	1	8	24	2.67	18	39

RECAPITULATION: BY AGE PERIODS — Concluded.

SEX AND AGE PERIODS.	Number addicted to the Use of Intoxicating Liquors	Excessive Drinkers	Social Drinkers	Home Drinkers	Periodical Drinkers	Occasional Drinkers	Aggregate Number of Drinking Conditions	Average Number of Drinking Conditions	Liquor Habits Unknown	Total Abstainers
Females-Con.										
20-29, .	36	1	30	32	4	30	97	2.69	41	107
30-39, .	11	-	9	11	-	9	29	2.64	27	50
40-49, .	9	1	8	8	2	7	26	2.89	19	27
50-59, .	1	-	-	-	-	1	1	1.00	12	14
60-79, .	2	-	2	2	-	2	6	3.00	11	14
80 +, .	-	-	-	-	-	-	-	-	-	3
BOTH SEXES.	578	35	458	501	25	445	1,464	2.53	983	1,669
Under 1, .	20	2	14	17	2	16	51	2.55	27	99
1-4, .	19	8	11	9	3	10	41	2.16	17	34
5-9, .	17	12	2	5	-	4	23	1.41	22	26
10-14, .	14	4	6	8	3	7	28	2 00	32	25
15-19, .	22	1	19	18	2	17	57	2.59	34	70
20-29, .	157	4	121	132	10	122	389	2.48	176	399
30-39, .	111	2	104	105	1	91	303	2.73	253	399
40-49, .	96	1	78	89	3	80	251	2 62	208	304
50-59, .	76	1	64	73	-	63	201	2 64	114	180
60-79, .	43	-	37	42	1	33	113	2.63	95	120
80 +, .	3	-	2	3	-	2	7	2.33	5	13

Reproducing the line relating to both sexes in the recapitulation, we find that the number of mothers addicted to the use of intoxicating liquors is 578, among whom there are 35 excessive drinkers, 458 social drinkers, 501 home drinkers, 25 periodical drinkers, and 445 occasional drinkers; the aggregate number of drinking conditions among the mothers being 1,464, or an average of 2.53 per person, this average varying very little from that shown among the fathers. In 1,669 cases the mothers were total abstainers, while the liquor habits of 983 were unknown.

Not only is it true that there are differences of habit with respect to the use of liquor, but it is also a fact that the kind of liquor preferred by those who drink varies. Some select malt liquors only as their beverage, others prefer a more fiery intoxicant, while many use both as opportunity or inclination offers. This difference of taste is of course recognized in the liquor traffic and is met by the supply of different liquors in quantities proportioned to the demand. The next three tables show the kinds of liquor used by the paupers and by their parents. The first table of this series relates to the paupers. In this table the total number of cases reported is 2,949, 2,475 being males and 474 females. The total number of pauper cases considered in the preceding tables was 3,230, but as all under 10 years of age were reported as total abstainers they are omitted from this table, which is presented for the purpose of showing the kinds of liquor used, and is therefore inapplicable to those who are not addicted to the drinking habit.

Pauperism; Sex, Political Condition, and Kinds of Liquor Used by Paupers: By Age Periods.

Age Period: 10-14.

SEX AND POLITICAL CONDITION.	Number addicted to the Use of Intoxicating Liquors	Wines	Lager Beer	Malted Liquor	Distilled Liquor	Aggregate Number of Kinds of Liquor	Average Number of Kinds of Liquor	Particular Kinds of Liquor Unknown	Total Abstainers
Males.	1	–	1	1	–	2	2.00	6	40
Citizen born, .	1	–	1	1	–	2	2.00	6	28
Alien, . .	–	–	–	–	–	–	–	–	12
Females.	1	1	–	–	1	2	2.00	1	22
Citizen born, .	–	–	–	–	–	–	–	–	19
Alien, . .	1	1	–	–	1	2	2 00	1	3
BOTH SEXES.	2	1	1	1	1	4	2 00	7	62
Citizen born, .	1	–	1	1	–	2	2.00	6	47
Alien, . .	1	1	–	–	1	2	2.00	1	15

Age Period: 15-19.

Males.	22	9	21	11	7	48	2.18	6	32
Citizen born, .	7	1	7	4	2	14	2 00	2	13
Alien, . .	15	8	14	7	5	34	2.27	4	19
Females.	7	4	4	3	1	12	1.71	5	54
Citizen born, .	3	1	2	2	1	6	2.00	1	26
Alien, . .	4	3	2	1	–	6	1.50	4	28
BOTH SEXES.	29	13	25	14	8	60	2.07	11	86
Citizen born, .	10	2	9	6	3	20	2.00	3	39
Alien, . .	19	11	16	8	5	40	2.11	8	47

Pauperism; Sex, Political Condition, and Kinds of Liquor Used by Paupers: By Age Periods — Continued.

AGE PERIOD : 20-29

SEX AND POLITICAL CONDITION.	Number addicted to the Use of Intoxicating Liquors	Wines	Lager Beer	Malted Liquor	Distilled Liquor	Aggregate Number of Kinds of Liquor	Average Number of Kinds of Liquor	Particular Kinds of Liquor Unknown	Total Abstainers
Males.	413	123	374	351	281	1,129	2.73	54	81
Citizen born, .	102	32	98	91	73	294	2.88	12	28
Naturalized, .	21	4	17	18	13	52	2.48	2	5
Alien, . .	289	87	238	241	195	781	2.70	37	48
Unknown, .	1	–	1	1	–	2	2 00	3	–
Females.	48	13	42	35	27	117	2.44	11	125
Citizen born, .	11	5	10	10	10	35	3.18	3	38
Alien, . .	37	8	32	25	17	82	2.22	7	87
Unknown, .	–	–	–	–	–	–	–	1	–
BOTH SEXES.	461	136	416	386	308	1,246	2.70	65	206
Citizen born, .	113	37	108	101	83	329	2.91	15	66
Naturalized, .	21	4	17	18	13	52	2.48	2	5
Alien, . .	326	95	290	266	212	863	2.65	44	135
Unknown. .	1	–	1	1	–	2	2.00	4	–

AGE PERIOD : 30-39.

Males.	566	155	497	508	434	1,594	2.82	65	44
Citizen born, .	154	45	140	137	123	445	2.90	19	10
Naturalized, .	55	12	46	47	44	149	2.71	1	6
Alien, . .	356	97	310	323	266	996	2.80	38	28
Unknown, .	1	1	1	1	1	4	4.00	7	–
Females.	35	8	29	28	20	85	2.43	9	44
Citizen born, .	7	1	5	7	5	18	2.57	3	10
Alien, . .	28	7	24	21	15	67	2.39	6	34
BOTH SEXES.	601	163	526	536	454	1,679	2.79	74	88
Citizen born, .	161	46	145	144	128	463	2.88	22	20
Naturalized, .	55	12	46	47	44	149	2.71	1	6
Alien, . .	384	104	334	344	281	1,063	2.77	44	62
Unknown, .	1	1	1	1	1	4	4.00	7	–

AGE PERIOD : 40-49.

Males.	465	123	418	434	386	1,361	2.93	54	34
Citizen born, .	117	37	111	109	92	349	2.98	10	10
Naturalized, .	77	13	72	69	59	213	2.77	6	7

Pauperism; Sex, Political Condition, and Kinds of Liquor Used by Paupers: By Age Periods — Continued.

AGE PERIOD: 40-49 — Concluded.

SEX AND POLITICAL CONDITION.	Number addicted to the Use of Intoxicating Liquors	Wines	Lager Beer	Malted Liquor	Distilled Liquor	Aggregate Number of Kinds of Liquor	Average Number of Kinds of Liquor	Particular Kinds of Liquor Unknown	Total Abstainers
Males — Con.									
Alien, . .	270	73	234	255	234	796	2.95	36	17
Unknown, .	1	-	1	1	1	3	3 00	2	-
Females.	30	6	25	26	21	78	2.60	4	21
Citizen born, .	5	3	5	4	4	16	3.20	-	7
Alien, . .	25	3	20	22	17	62	2.48	3	14
Unknown, .	-	-	-	-	-	-	-	1	-
BOTH SEXES.	495	129	443	460	407	1,439	2.91	58	55
Citizen born, .	122	40	116	113	96	365	2.99	10	17
Naturalized, .	77	13	72	69	59	213	2.77	6	7
Alien, . .	295	76	254	277	251	858	2.91	39	31
Unknown, .	1	-	1	1	1	3	3 00	3	-

AGE PERIOD: 50-59.

Males.	297	58	248	273	237	816	2.75	21	25
Citizen born, .	42	9	36	39	37	121	2.88	7	10
Naturalized, .	65	9	59	62	51	181	2.78	3	5
Alien, . .	189	40	153	171	148	512	2.37	9	10
Unknown, .	1	-	-	1	1	2	2.00	2	-
Females.	10	-	8	8	4	20	2.00	4	13
Citizen born, .	-	-	-	-	-	-	-	1	4
Alien, . .	10	-	8	8	4	20	2.00	3	9
BOTH SEXES.	307	58	256	281	241	836	2.72	25	38
Citizen born, .	42	9	36	39	37	121	2.88	8	14
Naturalized, .	65	9	59	62	51	181	2.78	3	5
Alien, . .	199	40	161	179	152	532	2.67	12	19
Unknown, .	1	-	-	1	1	2	2.00	2	-

AGE PERIOD: 60-79.

Males.	194	32	170	177	151	530	2.73	9	28
Citizen born, .	31	6	27	29	25	87	2.81	1	5
Naturalized, .	47	6	40	41	38	125	2.66	1	11

Pauperism; Sex, Political Condition, and Kinds of Liquor Used by Paupers: By Age Periods — Concluded.

AGE PERIOD: 60-79 — Concluded.

SEX AND POLITICAL CONDITION.	Number addicted to the Use of Intoxicating Liquors	Wines	Lager Beer	Malted Liquor	Distilled Liquor	Aggregate Number of Kinds of Liquor	Average Number of Kinds of Liquor	Particular Kinds of Liquor Unknown	Total Abstainers
Males — Con.									
Alien, . .	113	19	102	106	87	314	2.78	7	12
Unknown, .	3	1	1	1	1	4	1.33	-	-
Females.	10	3	7	7	8	25	2.50	5	12
Citizen born, .	1	-	-	-	1	1	1.00	1	4
Alien, . .	9	3	7	7	7	24	2.67	4	8
BOTH SEXES.	204	35	177	184	159	555	2.72	14	40
Citizen born, .	32	6	27	29	26	88	2.75	2	9
Naturalized, .	47	6	40	41	38	125	2.66	1	11
Alien, . .	122	22	109	113	94	338	2.77	11	20
Unknown, .	3	1	1	1	1	4	1.33	-	-

AGE PERIOD: 80 +.

Males.	9	-	6	8	6	20	2.22	2	7
Citizen born, .	2	-	1	1	1	3	1.50	-	3
Naturalized, .	4	-	3	4	3	10	2.50	2	2
Alien, . .	3	-	2	3	2	7	2.33	-	2
Females.	-	-	-	-	-	-	-	-	3
Citizen born, .	-	-	-	-	-	-	-	-	1
Alien, . .	-	-	-	-	-	-	-	-	2
BOTH SEXES.	9	-	6	8	6	20	2.22	2	10
Citizen born, .	2	-	1	1	1	3	1.50	-	4
Naturalized, .	4	-	3	4	3	10	2.50	2	2
Alien, . .	3	-	2	3	2	7	2.33	-	4

RECAPITULATION.

SEX AND POLITICAL CONDITION.	Number addicted to the Use of Intoxicating Liquors	Wines	Lager Beer	Malted Liquor	Distilled Liquor	Aggregate Number of Kinds of Liquor	Average Number of Kinds of Liquor	Particular Kinds of Liquor Unknown	Total Abstainers
Males.	1,967	500	1,735	1,763	1,502	5,500	2 80	217	291
Citizen born, .	456	130	421	411	353	1,315	2.88	57	107
Naturalized, .	269	44	237	241	208	730	2.71	15	36

RECAPITULATION — Concluded.

Sex and Political Condition.	Number addicted to the Use of Intoxicating Liquors	Wines	Lager Beer	Malted Liquor	Distilled Liquor	Aggregate Number of Kinds of Liquor	Average Number of Kinds of Liquor	Particular Kinds of Liquor Unknown	Total Abstainers
Males — Con.									
Alien,	1,235	324	1,073	1,106	937	3,440	2.79	131	148
Unknown,	7	2	4	5	4	15	2.14	14	-
Females.	141	35	115	107	82	339	2.40	39	294
Citizen born,	27	10	22	23	21	76	2.81	9	109
Alien,	114	25	93	84	61	263	2.31	28	185
Unknown,	-	-	-	-	-	-	-	2	-
Both Sexes.	2,108	535	1,850	1,870	1,584	5,839	2.77	256	585
Citizen born,	483	140	443	434	374	1,391	2.88	66	216
Naturalized,	269	44	237	241	208	730	2.71	15	36
Alien,	1,349	349	1,166	1,190	998	3,703	2.74	159	333
Unknown,	7	2	4	5	4	15	2.14	16	-

RECAPITULATION: BY AGE PERIODS.

Sex and Age Periods.	Number addicted to the Use of Intoxicating Liquors	Wines	Lager Beer	Malted Liquor	Distilled Liquor	Aggregate Number of Kinds of Liquor	Average Number of Kinds of Liquor	Particular Kinds of Liquor Unknown	Total Abstainers
Males.	1,967	500	1,735	1,763	1,502	5,500	2.80	217	291
10-14,	1	-	1	1	-	2	2.00	6	40
15-19,	22	9	21	11	7	48	2.18	6	32
20-29,	413	123	374	351	281	1,129	2.73	54	81
30-39,	566	155	497	508	434	1,594	2.82	65	44
40-49,	465	123	418	434	386	1,361	2.93	54	34
50-59,	297	58	248	273	237	816	2.75	21	25
60-79,	194	32	170	177	151	530	2.73	9	28
80 +,	9	-	6	8	6	20	2.22	2	7
Females.	141	35	115	107	82	339	2.40	39	294
10-14,	1	1	-	-	1	2	2.00	1	22
15-19,	7	4	4	3	1	12	1.71	5	54
20-29,	48	13	42	35	27	117	2.44	11	125
30-39,	35	8	29	28	20	85	2.43	9	44
40-49,	30	6	25	26	21	78	2.60	4	21
50-59,	10	-	8	8	4	20	2.00	4	13
60-79,	10	3	7	7	8	25	2.50	5	12
80 +,	-	-	-	-	-	-	-	-	3

RECAPITULATION: BY AGE PERIODS — Concluded.

SEX AND AGE PERIODS.	Number addicted to the Use of Intoxicating Liquors	Wines	Lager Beer	Malted Liquor	Distilled Liquor	Aggregate Number of Kinds of Liquor	Average Number of Kinds of Liquor	Particular Kinds of Liquor Unknown	Total Abstainers
BOTH SEXES.	2,108	535	1,850	1,870	1,584	5,839	2.77	256	585
10-14, . .	2	1	1	1	1	4	2.00	7	62
15-19, . .	29	13	25	14	8	60	2.07	11	86
20-29, . .	461	136	416	386	308	1,246	2.70	65	206
30-39, . .	601	163	526	536	454	1,679	2.79	74	88
40-49, . .	495	129	443	460	407	1,439	2.91	58	55
50-59, . .	307	58	256	281	241	836	2.72	25	38
60-79, . .	204	35	177	184	159	555	2.72	14	40
80 +, . .	9	-	6	8	6	20	2.22	2	10

In this table the number under each age period is shown in detail, classified by sex and citizen born, naturalized, and alien.

The analysis is confined to the recapitulation. In the final section the facts are shown for both sexes by age periods. The total number of all ages addicted to the use of intoxicating liquors is 2,108. These are classified so as to show the kinds of liquor chiefly used. As in the preceding tables showing the habit as to the use of liquor, here also it is found that in many cases more than one kind of liquor was used, and the same individual is therefore tabulated under more than one head. Thus, among the 2,108 total number of persons there appear 535 instances of wine drinking; 1,850 lager beer; 1,870 malt liquors; and 1,584 distilled liquors; the aggregate number of reports as to kinds of liquor used being 5,839, or an average of 2.77 kinds of liquor to each person. That is of the 2,108 cases, each individual reported himself as addicted to more than two kinds of liquor, the average, however, not quite reaching three kinds. The predominance of the use of lager beer and other malt liquors is shown from the tables, the total number of instances of such use being 3,720, as against 1,584 instances of the use of distilled liquors, and 535 of wine.

The next table shows the kinds of liquor used by the fathers of paupers.

Pauperism; Sex, Political Condition, and Kinds of Liquor Used by Fathers of Paupers: By Age Periods.

AGE PERIOD: UNDER 1.

SEX AND PO-LITICAL CONDITION.	Number addicted to the Use of Intoxicating Liquors	Wines	Lager Beer	Malted Liquor	Distilled Liquor	Aggregate Number of Kinds of Liquor	Average Number of Kinds of Liquor	Particular Kinds of Liquor Unknown	Total Abstainers
Males.	39	16	36	34	32	118	3.03	28	11
Citizen born, .	38	16	35	33	31	115	3.03	27	11
Alien, . .	1	–	1	1	1	3	3.00	1	–
Females.	30	10	25	25	22	82	2.73	19	19
Citizen born, .	29	10	24	24	21	79	2.72	19	19
Alien, . .	1	–	1	1	1	3	3.00	–	–
BOTH SEXES.	69	26	61	59	54	200	2.90	47	30
Citizen born, .	67	26	59	57	52	194	2.90	46	30
Alien, . .	2	–	2	2	2	6	3.00	1	–

AGE PERIOD: 1–4.

Males.	23	10	19	18	13	60	2.61	16	3
Citizen born, .	21	9	18	17	12	56	2.80	13	3
Alien, .	2	1	1	1	1	4	2.00	2	–
Unknown, .	–	–	–	–	–	–	–	1	–
Females.	12	5	13	12	11	41	3.42	10	6
Citizen born, .	12	5	13	12	11	41	3.42	9	5
Alien, . .	–	–	–	–	–	–	–	1	1
BOTH SEXES.	35	15	32	30	24	101	2.89	26	9
Citizen born, .	33	14	31	29	23	97	2.94	22	8
Alien, . .	2	1	1	1	1	4	2.00	3	1
Unknown, .	–	–	–	–	–	–	–	1	–

AGE PERIOD: 5–9.

Males.	14	3	11	13	11	38	2.71	19	5
Citizen born, .	8	2	6	7	7	22	2.75	16	3
Alien, . .	6	1	5	6	4	16	2.67	3	2
Females.	14	3	13	13	12	41	2.93	11	2
Citizen born, .	10	2	10	9	9	30	3.00	9	1
Alien, . .	4	1	3	4	3	11	2.75	2	1

Pauperism ; Sex, Political Condition, and Kinds of Liquor Used by Fathers of Paupers : By Age Periods — Continued.

AGE PERIOD : 5–9 — Concluded.

SEX AND POLITICAL CONDITION.	Number addicted to the Use of Intoxicating Liquors	Wines	Lager Beer	Malted Liquor	Distilled Liquor	Aggregate Number of Kinds of Liquor	Average Number of Kinds of Liquor	Particular Kinds of Liquor Unknown	Total Abstainers
BOTH SEXES.	28	6	24	26	23	79	2.82	30	7
Citizen born, .	18	4	16	16	16	52	2.89	25	4
Alien, . .	10	2	8	10	7	27	2.70	5	3

AGE PERIOD : 10–14.

Males.	16	7	12	12	11	42	2.63	25	6
Citizen born, .	7	1	6	7	6	20	2.86	23	5
Alien, . .	9	6	6	5	5	22	2.44	2	1
Females.	7	3	7	7	6	23	3.29	6	11
Citizen born, .	5	3	5	5	5	18	3.60	3	11
Alien, . .	2	–	2	2	1	5	2.50	3	–
BOTH SEXES.	23	10	19	19	17	65	2.83	31	17
Citizen born, .	12	4	11	12	11	38	3.17	26	16
Alien, . .	11	6	8	7	6	27	2.45	5	1

AGE PERIOD : 15–19.

Males.	31	15	27	19	14	75	2.42	18	11
Citizen born, .	9	3	9	8	6	26	2.89	9	4
Alien, . .	22	12	18	11	8	49	2.23	9	7
Females.	24	5	21	19	18	63	2.63	23	19
Citizen born, .	10	4	9	9	9	31	3.10	10	10
Alien, . .	14	1	12	10	9	32	2.29	13	9
BOTH SEXES.	55	20	48	38	32	138	2.51	41	30
Citizen born, .	19	7	18	17	15	57	3.00	19	14
Alien, . .	36	13	30	21	17	81	2.25	22	16

AGE PERIOD : 20–29.

Males.	283	56	168	206	171	601	2.12	140	125
Citizen born, .	64	7	49	58	43	157	2.45	35	43
Naturalized, .	18	2	13	13	8	36	2.00	4	6
Alien, . .	201	47	106	135	120	408	2.03	97	76
Unknown, .	–	–	–	–	–	–	–	4	–

Pauperism; Sex, Political Condition, and Kinds of Liquor Used by Fathers of Paupers: By Age Periods — Continued.

AGE PERIOD: 20-29 — Concluded.

SEX AND POLITICAL CONDITION.	Number addicted to the Use of Intoxicating Liquors	Wines	Lager Beer	Malted Liquor	Distilled Liquor	Aggregate Number of Kinds of Liquor	Average Number of Kinds of Liquor	Particular Kinds of Liquor Unknown	Total Abstainers
Females.	99	27	62	81	75	245	2.47	40	45
Citizen born, .	22	11	20	19	18	68	3.09	13	17
Alien, . .	77	16	42	62	57	177	2.30	26	28
Unknown, .	-	-	-	-	-	-	-	1	-
BOTH SEXES.	382	83	230	287	246	846	2.22	180	170
Citizen born, .	86	18	69	77	61	225	2.62	48	60
Naturalized, .	18	2	13	13	8	36	2.00	4	6
Alien, . .	278	63	148	197	177	585	2.10	123	104
Unknown, .	-	-	-	-	-	-	-	5	-

AGE PERIOD: 30-39.

Males.	319	50	184	264	216	714	2.24	219	137
Citizen born, .	87	14	61	74	62	211	2.54	56	40
Naturalized, .	28	1	14	23	20	58	2.07	18	16
Alien, . .	203	35	109	166	133	443	2.13	138	81
Unknown, .	1	-	-	1	1	2	2.00	7	-
Females.	43	13	28	36	34	111	2.58	21	24
Citizen born, .	7	3	6	7	7	23	3.29	8	5
Alien, . .	36	10	22	29	27	88	2.44	13	19
BOTH SEXES.	362	63	212	300	250	825	2.28	240	161
Citizen born, .	94	17	67	81	69	234	2.49	64	45
Naturalized, .	28	1	14	23	20	58	2.07	18	16
Alien, . .	239	45	131	195	160	531	2.22	151	100
Unknown, .	1	-	-	1	1	2	2.00	7	-

AGE PERIOD: 40-49.

Males.	239	17	119	200	170	506	2.12	185	129
Citizen born, .	55	3	35	46	39	123	2.24	39	43
Naturalized, .	48	3	16	36	37	92	1.92	23	19
Alien, . .	135	11	68	117	94	290	1.41	121	67
Unknown, .	1	-	-	1	-	1	1.00	2	-
Females.	24	7	11	18	19	55	2.29	17	14
Citizen born, .	5	1	3	3	5	12	2.40	4	3
Alien, . .	19	6	8	15	14	43	2.26	12	11
Unknown, .	-	-	-	-	-	-	-	1	-

Pauperism; Sex, Political Condition, and Kinds of Liquor Used by Fathers of Paupers: By Age Periods — Continued.

AGE PERIOD: 40-49 — Concluded.

SEX AND POLITICAL CONDITION.	Number addicted to the Use of Intoxicating Liquors	Wines	Lager Beer	Malted Liquor	Distilled Liquor	Aggregate Number of Kinds of Liquor	Average Number of Kinds of Liquor	Particular Kinds of Liquor Unknown	Total Abstainers
BOTH SEXES.	263	24	130	218	189	561	2.14	202	143
Citizen born, .	60	4	38	49	44	135	2.25	43	46
Naturalized, .	48	3	16	36	37	92	1.92	23	19
Alien, . .	154	17	76	132	108	333	2.16	133	78
Unknown, .	1	–	–	1	–	1	1.00	3	–

AGE PERIOD: 50-59.

Males.	150	19	60	116	110	305	2.03	110	83
Citizen born, .	20	4	14	16	16	50	2.50	18	21
Naturalized, .	27	4	10	22	20	56	2.07	28	18
Alien, . .	102	11	36	77	73	197	1.93	62	44
Unknown, .	1	–	–	1	1	2	2.00	2	–
Females.	12	1	5	9	8	23	1.92	13	2
Citizen born, .	3	–	1	1	2	4	1.33	2	–
Alien. . .	9	1	4	8	6	19	2.11	11	2
BOTH SEXES.	162	20	65	125	118	328	2.02	123	85
Citizen born, .	23	4	15	17	18	54	2.35	20	21
Naturalized, .	27	4	10	22	20	56	2.07	28	18
Alien, . .	111	12	40	85	79	216	1.95	73	46
Unknown, .	1	–	–	1	1	2	2.00	2	–

AGE PERIOD: 60-79.

Males.	92	6	23	69	72	170	1.85	92	47
Citizen born, .	13	–	4	6	12	22	1.69	13	11
Naturalized, .	24	–	4	19	22	45	1.88	24	11
Alien, . .	54	5	15	44	38	102	1.89	53	25
Unknown, .	1	1	–	–	–	1	1.00	2	–
Females.	7	1	1	4	6	12	1.71	10	10
Citizen born, .	–	–	–	–	–	–	–	2	4
Alien, . .	7	1	1	4	6	12	1.71	8	6
BOTH SEXES.	99	7	24	73	78	182	1.84	102	57
Citizen born, .	13	–	4	6	12	22	1.69	15	15
Naturalized, .	24	–	4	19	22	45	1.88	24	11
Alien, . .	61	6	16	48	44	114	1.87	61	31
Unknown, .	1	1	–	–	–	1	1.00	2	–

Pauperism; Sex, Political Condition, and Kinds of Liquor Used by Fathers of Paupers: By Age Periods — Concluded.

AGE PERIOD: 80 +.

SEX AND POLITICAL CONDITION.	Number addicted to the Use of Intoxicating Liquors	Wines	Lager Beer	Malted Liquor	Distilled Liquor	Aggregate Number of Kinds of Liquor	Average Number of Kinds of Liquor	Particular Kinds of Liquor Unknown	Total Abstainers
Males.	6	-	-	5	5	10	1.67	7	5
Citizen born,	2	-	-	1	2	3	1.50	1	2
Naturalized,	3	-	-	3	2	5	1.67	5	-
Alien,	1	-	-	1	1	2	2.00	1	3
Females.	2	-	-	-	2	2	1.00	-	1
Citizen born,	1	-	-	-	1	1	1.00	-	-
Alien,	1	-	-	-	1	1	1.00	-	1
BOTH SEXES.	8	-	-	5	7	12	1.50	7	6
Citizen born,	3	-	-	1	3	4	1.33	1	2
Naturalized,	3	-	-	3	2	5	1.67	5	-
Alien,	2	-	-	1	2	3	1.50	1	4

RECAPITULATION.

SEX AND POLITICAL CONDITION.	Number addicted to the Use of Intoxicating Liquors	Wines	Lager Beer	Malted Liquor	Distilled Liquor	Aggregate Number of Kinds of Liquor	Average Number of Kinds of Liquor	Particular Kinds of Liquor Unknown	Total Abstainers
Males.	1,212	199	659	956	825	2,639	2.18	859	562
Citizen born,	324	59	237	273	236	805	2.49	251	186
Naturalized,	148	10	57	116	109	292	1.97	102	70
Alien,	736	129	365	564	478	1,536	2.08	488	306
Unknown,	4	1	-	3	2	6	1.50	18	-
Females.	274	75	186	224	213	698	2.55	170	153
Citizen born,	104	39	91	89	88	307	2.95	79	75
Alien,	170	36	95	135	125	391	2.29	89	78
Unknown,	-	-	-	-	-	-	-	2	-
BOTH SEXES.	1,486	274	845	1,180	1,038	3,337	2.25	1,029	715
Citizen born,	428	98	328	362	324	1,112	2.60	330	261
Naturalized,	148	10	57	116	109	292	1.97	102	70
Alien,	906	165	460	699	603	1,927	2.12	577	384
Unknown,	4	1	-	3	2	6	1.50	20	-

RECAPITULATION: BY AGE PERIODS.

SEX AND AGE PERIODS.	Number addicted to the Use of Intoxicating Liquors	Wines	Lager Beer	Malted Liquor	Distilled Liquor	Aggregate Number of Kinds of Liquor	Average Number of Kinds of Liquor	Particular Kinds of Liquor Unknown	Total Abstainers
Males.	1,212	199	659	956	825	2,639	2.18	859	562
Under 1, . .	39	16	36	34	32	118	3.03	28	11
1-4, .	23	10	19	18	13	60	2.61	16	3
5-9, .	14	3	11	13	11	38	2.71	19	5
10-14, .	16	7	12	12	11	42	2.63	25	6
15-19, .	31	15	27	19	14	75	2.42	18	11
20-29, .	283	56	168	206	171	601	2.12	140	125
30-39, .	319	50	184	264	216	714	2.21	219	137
40-49, .	239	17	119	200	170	506	2.12	185	129
50-59, .	150	19	60	116	110	305	2.03	110	83
60-79, .	92	6	23	69	72	170	1.85	92	47
80 +, .	6	-	-	5	5	10	1.67	7	5
Females.	274	75	186	224	213	698	2.55	170	153
Under 1, . .	30	10	25	25	22	82	2.73	19	19
1-4, .	12	5	13	12	11	41	3.42	10	6
5-9, .	14	3	13	13	12	41	2.93	11	2
10-14, .	7	3	7	7	6	23	3.29	6	11
15-19, .	24	5	21	19	18	63	2.63	23	19
20-29, .	99	27	62	81	75	245	2.47	40	45
30-39, .	43	13	28	36	34	111	2.58	21	24
40-49, .	24	7	11	18	19	55	2.29	17	14
50-59, .	12	1	5	9	8	23	1.92	13	2
60-79, .	7	1	1	4	6	12	1.71	10	10
80 +, .	2	-	-	-	2	2	1.00	-	1
BOTH SEXES.	1,486	274	845	1,180	1,038	3,337	2.25	1,029	715
Under 1, . .	69	26	61	59	54	200	2.86	47	30
1-4, .	35	15	32	30	24	101	2.89	26	9
5-9, .	28	6	24	26	23	79	2.82	30	7
10-14, .	23	10	19	19	17	65	2.83	31	17
15-19, .	55	20	48	38	32	138	2.51	41	30
20-29, .	382	83	230	287	246	846	2.21	180	170
30-39, .	362	63	212	300	250	825	2.28	240	161
40-49, .	263	24	130	218	189	561	2.14	202	143
50-59, .	162	20	65	125	118	328	2.02	123	85
60-79, .	99	7	24	73	78	182	1.84	102	57
80 +, .	8	-	-	5	7	12	1.50	7	6

Referring to the recapitulation for both sexes, we find 1,486 cases are reported among the fathers addicted to the use of intoxicating liquors, and of these there are 274 instances of wine drinking; 845 of lager beer drinking; 1,180 of malt liquor; and 1,038 of distilled liquor; the aggregate number of reports as to kinds of liquor used being 3,337, or an average of 2.25 to each person. As in the preceding table, the use of lager beer and other malt liquors far exceeds the use of distilled liquors, the number of cases in the former being 2,025, as against 1,038 instances of distilled liquor drinking, and 274 of wine drinking.

The final table of this series relates to the kinds of liquor used by the mothers of paupers.

Pauperism ; Sex, Political Condition, and Kinds of Liquor Used by Mothers of Paupers : By Age Periods.

AGE PERIOD : Under 1.

SEX AND POLITICAL CONDITION.	Number addicted to the Use of Intoxicating Liquors	Wines	Lager Beer	Malted Liquor	Distilled Liquor	Aggregate Number of Kinds of Liquor	Average Number of Kinds of Liquor	Particular Kinds of Liquor Unknown	Total Abstainers
Males.	5	2	2	3	3	10	2.00	15	58
Citizen born, .	5	2	2	3	3	10	2.00	15	57
Alien, . .	-	-	-	-	-	-	-	-	1
Females.	15	4	13	11	5	33	2.20	12	41
Citizen born, .	15	4	13	11	5	33	2.20	12	40
Alien, . .	-	-	-	-	-	-	-	-	1
BOTH SEXES.	20	6	15	14	8	43	2.15	27	99
Citizen born, .	20	6	15	14	8	43	2.15	27	97
Alien, . .	-	-	-	-	-	-	-	-	2

AGE PERIOD : 1-4.

Males.	13	5	10	8	7	30	2.30	11	18
Citizen born, .	11	4	9	7	6	26	2.36	8	18
Alien, . .	2	1	1	1	1	4	2.00	2	-
Unknown, .	-	-	-	-	-	-	-	1	-
Females.	6	-	5	5	5	15	2.50	6	16
Citizen born, .	6	-	5	5	5	15	2.50	5	15
Alien, . .	-	-	-	-	-	-	-	1	1
BOTH SEXES.	19	5	15	13	12	45	2.37	17	34
Citizen born, .	17	4	14	12	11	41	2 41	13	33
Alien, . .	2	1	1	1	1	4	2.00	2	1
Unknown, .	-	-	-	-	-	-	-	2	-

Pauperism; Sex, Political Condition, and Kinds of Liquor Used by Mothers of Paupers: By Age Periods — Continued.

AGE PERIOD: 5-9.

SEX AND POLITICAL CONDITION.	Number addicted to the Use of Intoxicating Liquors	Wines	Lager Beer	Malted Liquor	Distilled Liquor	Aggregate Number of Kinds of Liquor	Average Number of Kinds of Liquor	Particular Kinds of Liquor Unknown	Total Abstainers
Males.	8	2	5	5	5	17	2.13	15	15
Citizen born, .	6	2	4	4	4	14	2.33	11	10
Alien, . .	2	-	1	1	1	3	1.50	4	5
Females.	9	-	7	7	8	22	2.44	7	11
Citizen born, .	8	-	6	7	7	20	2.50	5	7
Alien, . .	1	-	1	-	1	2	2.00	2	4
BOTH SEXES.	17	2	12	12	13	39	2.29	22	26
Citizen born, .	14	2	10	11	11	34	2.43	16	17
Alien, . .	3	-	2	1	2	5	1.67	6	9

AGE PERIOD: 10-14.

SEX AND POLITICAL CONDITION.	Number addicted to the Use of Intoxicating Liquors	Wines	Lager Beer	Malted Liquor	Distilled Liquor	Aggregate Number of Kinds of Liquor	Average Number of Kinds of Liquor	Particular Kinds of Liquor Unknown	Total Abstainers
Males.	10	4	4	4	5	17	1.70	26	11
Citizen born, .	5	1	2	2	3	8	1.60	21	9
Alien, . .	5	3	2	2	2	9	1.80	5	2
Females.	4	1	4	4	3	12	3.00	6	14
Citizen born, .	3	1	3	3	3	10	3.33	4	12
Alien, . .	1	-	1	1	-	2	2.00	2	2
BOTH SEXES.	14	5	8	8	8	29	2.07	32	25
Citizen born, .	8	2	5	5	6	18	2.25	25	21
Alien, . .	6	3	3	3	2	11	1.83	7	4

AGE PERIOD: 15-19.

SEX AND POLITICAL CONDITION.	Number addicted to the Use of Intoxicating Liquors	Wines	Lager Beer	Malted Liquor	Distilled Liquor	Aggregate Number of Kinds of Liquor	Average Number of Kinds of Liquor	Particular Kinds of Liquor Unknown	Total Abstainers
Males.	13	9	9	5	3	26	2.00	16	31
Citizen born, .	1	-	1	1	-	2	2.00	9	12
Alien, . .	12	9	8	4	3	24	2.00	7	19
Females.	9	3	5	5	6	19	2.11	18	39
Citizen born, .	2	-	2	2	2	6	3.00	9	19
Alien, . .	7	3	3	3	4	13	1.86	9	20
BOTH SEXES.	22	12	14	10	9	45	2.05	34	70
Citizen born, .	3	-	3	3	2	8	2.67	18	31
Alien, . .	19	12	11	7	7	37	1.95	16	39

Pauperism; Sex, Political Condition, and Kinds of Liquor Used by Mothers of Paupers: By Age Periods — Continued.

AGE PERIOD: 20–29.

SEX AND POLITICAL CONDITION.	Number addicted to the Use of Intoxicating Liquors	Wines	Lager Beer	Malted Liquor	Distilled Liquor	Aggregate Number of Kinds of Liquor	Average Number of Kinds of Liquor	Particular Kinds of Liquor Unknown	Total Abstainers
Males.	121	36	48	60	53	197	1.63	135	292
Citizen born, .	13	3	11	13	10	37	2.85	40	89
Naturalized, .	5	2	4	2	1	9	1.80	4	19
Alien, . .	103	31	33	45	42	151	1.47	88	183
Unknown, .	-	-	-	-	-	-	-	3	1
Females.	36	7	16	26	20	69	1.92	41	107
Citizen born, .	5	2	5	5	4	16	3.20	13	34
Alien, . .	31	5	11	21	16	53	1.71	27	73
Unknown, .	-	-	-	-	-	-	-	1	-
BOTH SEXES.	157	43	64	86	73	266	1.69	176	399
Citizen born, .	18	5	16	18	14	53	2.94	53	123
Naturalized, .	5	2	4	2	1	9	1.80	4	19
Alien, . .	134	36	44	66	58	204	1.52	115	256
Unknown, .	-	-	-	-	-	-	-	4	1

AGE PERIOD: 30–39.

Males.	100	22	35	67	47	171	1.71	226	349
Citizen born, .	21	-	10	15	9	34	1.62	58	104
Naturalized, .	10	1	3	9	5	18	1.80	17	35
Alien, . .	68	21	22	42	32	117	1.70	144	210
Unknown, .	1	-	-	1	1	2	2.00	7	-
Females.	11	3	5	6	5	19	1.73	27	50
Citizen born, .	1	-	-	-	1	1	1.00	8	11
Alien, . .	10	3	5	6	4	18	1.80	19	39
BOTH SEXES.	111	25	40	73	52	190	1.71	253	399
Citizen born, .	22	-	10	15	10	35	1.59	66	115
Naturalized, .	10	1	3	9	5	18	1.80	17	35
Alien, . .	78	24	27	48	36	135	1.73	163	249
Unknown, .	1	-	-	1	1	2	2.00	7	-

AGE PERIOD: 40–49.

Males.	87	10	24	64	49	147	1.69	189	277
Citizen born, .	12	1	3	7	9	20	1.67	36	89
Naturalized, .	14	-	3	11	10	24	1.71	24	52

Pauperism; Sex, Political Condition, and Kinds of Liquor Used by Mothers of Paupers: By Age Periods — Continued.

AGE PERIOD: 40-49 — Concluded

SEX AND PO-LITICAL CONDITION.	Number addicted to the Use of Intoxicating Liquors	Wines	Lager Beer	Malted Liquor	Distilled Liquor	Aggregate Number of Kinds of Liquor	Average Number of Kinds of Liquor	Particular Kinds of Liquor Unknown	Total Abstainers
Males — Con.									
Alien, . .	61	9	18	46	30	103	1.69	127	135
Unknown, .	-	-	-	-	-	-	-	2	1
Females.	9	-	2	6	5	13	1.44	19	27
Citizen born, .	-	-	-	-	-	-	-	5	7
Alien, . .	9	-	2	6	5	13	1.44	13	20
Unknown, .	-	-	-	-	-	-	-	1	-
BOTH SEXES.	96	10	26	70	54	160	1.67	208	304
Citizen born, .	12	1	3	7	9	20	1.67	41	96
Naturalized, .	14	-	3	11	10	24	1.71	24	52
Alien, . .	70	9	20	52	35	116	1.65	140	155
Unknown, .	-	-	-	-	-	-	-	3	1

AGE PERIOD: 50-59.

Males.	75	12	21	52	38	123	1.64	102	166
Citizen born, .	5	1	4	3	2	10	2.00	18	36
Naturalized, .	16	4	5	11	9	29	1.81	26	31
Alien, . .	53	7	12	37	26	82	1.55	56	99
Unknown, .	1	-	-	1	1	2	2.00	2	-
Females.	1	-	1	1	1	3	3.00	12	14
Citizen born, .	-	-	-	-	-	-	-	2	3
Alien, . .	1	-	1	1	1	3	3.00	10	11
BOTH SEXES.	76	12	22	53	39	126	1.66	114	180
Citizen born, .	5	1	4	3	2	10	2.00	20	39
Naturalized, .	16	4	5	11	9	29	1.81	26	31
Alien, . .	54	7	13	38	27	85	1.57	66	110
Unknown, .	1	-	-	1	1	2	2.00	2	-

AGE PERIOD: 60-79.

Males.	41	6	6	27	24	63	1.54	84	106
Citizen born, .	2	-	-	-	2	2	1.00	13	22
Naturalized, .	11	-	-	5	9	14	1.27	20	28
Alien, . .	27	5	6	22	13	46	1.70	50	55
Unknown, .	1	1	-	-	-	1	1.00	1	1

Pauperism: Sex, Political Condition, and Kinds of Liquor Used by Mothers of Paupers: By Age Periods — Concluded.

AGE PERIOD: 60-79 — Concluded.

SEX AND PO- LITICAL CONDITION.	Number addicted to the Use of In- toxicat- ing Liquors	Wines	Lager Beer	Malted Liquor	Dis- tilled Liquor	Aggre- gate Number of Kinds of Liquor	Average Number of Kinds of Liquor	Particu- lar Kinds of Liquor Unknown	Total Ab- stainers
Females.	2	1	–	1	1	3	1.50	11	14
Citizen born, .	–	–	–	–	–	–	–	2	4
Alien, . .	2	1	–	1	1	3	1.50	9	10
BOTH SEXES.	43	7	6	28	25	66	1.53	95	120
Citizen born, .	2	–	–	–	2	2	1.00	15	26
Naturalized, .	11	–	–	5	9	14	1.27	20	28
Alien, . .	29	6	6	23	14	49	1.69	59	65
Unknown, .	1	1	–	–	–	1	1.00	1	1

AGE PERIOD: 80 +.

Males.	3	–	–	3	2	5	1.67	5	10
Citizen born, .	1	–	–	1	1	2	2.00	–	4
Naturalized, .	2	–	–	2	1	3	1.50	4	2
Alien, . .	–	–	–	–	–	–	–	1	4
Females.	–	–	–	–	–	–	–	–	3
Citizen born, .	–	–	–	–	–	–	–	–	1
Alien, . .	–	–	–	–	–	–	–	–	2
BOTH SEXES.	3	–	–	3	2	5	1.67	5	13
Citizen born, .	1	–	–	1	1	2	2.00	–	5
Naturalized, .	2	–	–	2	1	3	1.50	4	2
Alien, . .	–	–	–	–	–	–	–	1	6

RECAPITULATION.

SEX AND PO- LITICAL CONDITION.	Number addicted to the Use of In- toxicat- ing Liquors	Wines	Lager Beer	Malted Liquor	Dis- tilled Liquor	Aggre- gate Number of Kinds of Liquor	Average Number of Kinds of Liquor	Particu- lar Kinds of Liquor Unknown	Total Ab- stainers
Males.	476	108	164	298	236	806	1.69	824	1,333
Citizen born, .	82	14	46	56	49	165	2.01	229	450
Naturalized, .	58	7	15	40	35	97	1.67	95	167
Alien, . .	333	86	103	200	150	539	1.62	484	713
Unknown, .	3	1	–	2	2	5	1.67	16	3

RECAPITULATION — Concluded.

SEX AND POLITICAL CONDITION.	Number addicted to the Use of Intoxicating Liquors	Wines	Lager Beer	Malted Liquor	Distilled Liquor	Aggregate Number of Kinds of Liquor	Average Number of Kinds of Liquor	Particular Kinds of Liquor Unknown	Total Abstainers
Females.	102	19	58	72	59	208	2.04	159	336
Citizen born, .	40	7	34	33	27	101	2.53	65	153
Alien, . .	62	12	24	39	32	107	1.73	92	183
Unknown, .	-	-	-	-	-	-	-	2	-
BOTH SEXES.	578	127	222	370	295	1,014	1.75	983	1,669
Citizen born, .	122	21	80	89	76	266	2.18	294	603
Naturalized, .	58	7	15	40	35	97	1.67	95	167
Alien, . .	395	98	127	239	182	646	1.61	576	896
Unknown, .	3	1	-	2	2	5	1.67	18	3

RECAPITULATION: BY AGE PERIODS.

SEX AND AGE PERIODS.	Number addicted to the Use of Intoxicating Liquors	Wines	Lager Beer	Malted Liquor	Distilled Liquor	Aggregate Number of Kinds of Liquor	Average Number of Kinds of Liquor	Particular Kinds of Liquor Unknown	Total Abstainers
Males.	476	108	164	298	236	806	1.69	824	1,333
Under 1, . .	5	2	2	3	3	10	2.00	15	58
1–4, .	13	5	10	8	7	30	2.30	11	18
5–9, .	8	2	5	5	5	17	2.13	15	15
10–14, .	10	4	4	4	5	17	1.70	26	11
15–19, .	13	9	9	5	3	26	2.00	16	31
20–29, .	121	36	48	60	53	197	1.63	135	292
30–39, .	100	22	35	67	47	171	1.71	226	349
40–49, .	87	10	24	64	49	147	1.69	189	277
50–59, .	75	12	21	52	38	123	1.64	102	166
60–79, .	41	6	6	27	24	63	1.54	84	106
80 +, .	3	-	-	3	2	5	1.67	5	10
Females.	102	19	58	72	59	208	2.04	159	336
Under 1, . .	15	4	13	11	5	33	2.20	12	41
1–4, .	6	-	5	5	5	15	2.50	6	16
5–9, .	9	-	7	7	8	22	2.44	7	11
10–14, .	4	1	4	4	3	12	3.00	6	14
15–19, .	9	3	5	5	6	19	2.11	18	39
20–29, .	36	7	16	26	20	69	1.92	41	107
30–39, .	11	3	5	6	5	19	1.73	27	50
40–49, .	9	-	2	6	5	13	1.44	19	27
50–59, .	1	-	1	1	1	3	3.00	12	14
60–79, .	2	1	-	1	1	3	1.50	11	14
80+, .	-	-	-	-	-	-	-	-	3

RECAPITULATION: BY AGE PERIODS — Concluded.

SEX AND AGE PERIODS.	Number addicted to the Use of Intoxicating Liquors	Wines	Lager Beer	Malted Liquor	Distilled Liquor	Aggregate Number of Kinds of Liquor	Average Number of Kinds of Liquor	Particular Kinds of Liquor Unknown	Total Abstainers
BOTH SEXES.	578	127	222	370	295	1,014	1.75	983	1,669
Under 1, . .	20	6	15	14	8	43	1.65	27	99
1-4, .	19	5	15	13	12	45	2.37	17	34
5-9, .	17	2	12	12	13	39	2.29	22	26
10-14, .	14	5	8	8	8	29	2.07	32	25
15-19, .	22	12	14	10	9	45	2.05	34	70
20-29, .	157	43	64	86	73	266	1.69	176	399
30-39, .	111	25	40	73	52	190	1.71	253	399
40-49, .	96	10	26	70	54	160	1.67	208	304
50-59, .	76	12	22	53	39	126	1.66	114	180
60-79, .	43	7	6	28	25	66	1.53	95	120
80+, .	3	–	–	3	2	5	1.67	5	13

The number of mothers of paupers addicted to the use of liquor is 578; of these there are 127 who used wine; 222 lager beer; 370 malt liquor; and 295 distilled liquor; the aggregate number of reports as to kinds of liquor used being 1,014, or an average of 1.75 to each person.

As incidental to the general inquiry, data were collected respecting the use of tobacco and of drugs, including opium, by paupers and their parents. The number of users of drugs was very limited, only three persons among the paupers being thus reported, these being males and citizens born. As to tobacco, the facts are presented in three tables, the first of which, now introduced, relates to the paupers themselves.

Pauperism; Sex, Political Condition, and Use of Tobacco by Paupers: By Age Periods.

AGE PERIOD: 10-14.

SEX AND POLITICAL CONDITION.	Users of Tobacco	Non-users	Number of Paupers
Males.	5	42	47
Citizen born, . . .	4	31	35
Alien, ...	1	11	12
Females.	–	24	24
Citizen born, ...	–	19	19
Alien, ...	–	5	5

Pauperism; Sex, Political Condition, and Use of Tobacco by Paupers: By Age Periods — Continued.

AGE PERIOD: 10-14 — Concluded.

SEX AND POLITICAL CONDITION.	Users of Tobacco	Non-users	Number of Paupers
BOTH SEXES.	5	66	71
Citizen born, ...	4	50	54
Alien, ...	1	16	17

AGE PERIOD: 15-19.

	Users of Tobacco	Non-users	Number of Paupers
Males.	41	19	60
Citizen born, ...	15	7	22
Alien, ...	26	12	38
Females.	–	66	66
Citizen born, ...	–	30	30
Alien, ...	–	36	36
BOTH SEXES.	41	85	126
Citizen born, ...	15	37	52
Alien, ...	26	48	74

AGE PERIOD: 20-29.

	Users of Tobacco	Non-users	Number of Paupers
Males.	410	138	548
Citizen born, ...	111	31	142
Naturalized, ...	20	8	28
Alien, ...	278	96	374
Unknown,.	1	3	4
Females.	9	175	184
Citizen born, ...	2	50	52
Alien, ...	7	124	131
Unknown,.	–	1	1
BOTH SEXES.	419	313	732
Citizen born, ...	113	81	194
Naturalized, ...	20	8	28
Alien, ...	285	220	505
Unknown, ...	1	4	5

AGE PERIOD: 30-39.

	Users of Tobacco	Non-users	Number of Paupers
Males.	568	107	675
Citizen born, ...	149	34	183
Naturalized, ...	56	6	62

Pauperism; Sex, Political Condition, and Use of Tobacco by Paupers: By Age Periods — Continued.

AGE PERIOD: 30–39 — Concluded.

SEX AND POLITICAL CONDITION.	Users of Tobacco	Non-users	Number of Paupers
Males — Con.			
Alien, ...	362	60	422
Unknown, ...	1	7	8
Females.	3	85	88
Citizen born, ...	–	20	20
Alien, ...	3	65	68
BOTH SEXES.	571	192	763
Citizen born, ...	149	54	203
Naturalized, ...	56	6	62
Alien, ...	365	125	490
Unknown, ...	1	7	8

AGE PERIOD: 40–49.

	Users of Tobacco	Non-users	Number of Paupers
Males.	463	90	553
Citizen born, ...	114	23	137
Naturalized, ...	74	16	90
Alien, ...	274	49	323
Unknown, ...	1	2	3
Females.	10	45	55
Citizen born, ...	4	8	12
Alien, ...	6	36	42
Unknown, ...	–	1	1
BOTH SEXES.	473	135	608
Citizen born, ...	118	31	149
Naturalized, ...	74	16	90
Alien, ...	280	85	365
Unknown, ...	1	3	4

AGE PERIOD: 50–59.

	Users of Tobacco	Non-users	Number of Paupers
Males.	285	58	343
Citizen born, ...	46	13	59
Naturalized, ...	61	12	73
Alien, ...	177	31	208
Unknown, ...	1	2	3

Pauperism; Sex, Political Condition, and Use of Tobacco by Paupers: By Age Periods — Continued.

AGE PERIOD: 50-59 — Concluded.

SEX AND POLITICAL CONDITION.	Users of Tobacco	Non-users	Number of Paupers
Females.	8	19	27
Citizen born, ...	–	5	5
Alien, ...	8	14	22
BOTH SEXES.	293	77	370
Citizen born, ...	46	18	64
Naturalized, ...	61	12	73
Alien, ...	185	45	230
Unknown, ...	1	2	3

AGE PERIOD: 60-79.

	Users of Tobacco	Non-users	Number of Paupers
Males.	185	46	231
Citizen born, ...	31	6	37
Naturalized, ...	50	9	59
Alien, ...	104	28	132
Unknown,.	–	3	3
Females.	3	24	27
Citizen born, ...	1	5	6
Alien, ...	2	19	21
BOTH SEXES.	188	70	258
Citizen born, ...	32	11	43
Naturalized, ...	50	9	59
Alien, ...	106	47	153
Unknown, ...	–	3	3

AGE PERIOD: 80 +.

	Users of Tobacco	Non-users	Number of Paupers
Males.	13	5	18
Citizen born, ...	3	2	5
Naturalized, ...	5	3	8
Alien, ...	5	–	5
Females.	2	1	3
Citizen born, ...	1	–	1
Alien, ...	1	1	2

Pauperism; Sex, Political Condition, and Use of Tobacco by Paupers: By Age Periods — Concluded.

AGE PERIOD : 80 + — Concluded.

SEX AND POLITICAL CONDITION.	Users of Tobacco	Non-users	Number of Paupers
BOTH SEXES.	15	6	21
Citizen born, ...	4	2	6
Naturalized, ...	5	3	8
Alien, ...	6	1	7

RECAPITULATION.

SEX AND POLITICAL CONDITION.	Users of Tobacco	Non-users	Number of Paupers
Males.	1,970	505	2,475
Citizen born, ...	473	147	620
Naturalized, ...	266	54	320
Alien, ...	1,227	287	1,514
Unknown,.	4	17	21
Females.	35	439	474
Citizen born, ...	8	137	145
Alien, ...	27	300	327
Unknown, ...	–	2	2
BOTH SEXES.	2,005	944	2,949
Citizen born, ...	481	284	765
Naturalized, ...	266	54	320
Alien, ...	1,254	587	1,841
Unknown,.	4	19	23

RECAPITULATION: BY AGE PERIODS.

SEX AND AGE PERIODS.	Users of Tobacco	Non-users	Number of Paupers
Males.	1,970	505	2,475
10-14, ...	5	42	47
15-19, ...	41	19	60
20-29, ...	410	138	548
30-39, ...	568	107	675
40-49, ...	463	90	553
50-59, ...	285	58	343
60-79, ...	185	46	231
80 +, ...	13	5	18

RECAPITULATION: BY AGE PERIODS — Concluded.

SEX AND AGE PERIODS.	Users of Tobacco	Non-users	Number of Paupers
Females.	35	439	474
10-14, ...	–	24	24
15-19, ...	–	66	66
20-29, ...	9	175	184
30-39, ...	3	85	88
40-49, ...	10	45	55
50-59, ...	8	19	27
60-79, ...	3	24	27
80 +, ...	2	1	3
BOTH SEXES.	2,005	944	2,949
10-14, ...	5	66	71
15-19, ...	41	85	126
20-29, ...	419	313	732
30-39, ...	571	192	763
40-49, ...	473	135	608
50-59, ...	293	77	370
60-79, ...	188	70	258
80 +, ...	15	6	21

In this table the paupers are classified by age periods, and, as compared with the aggregate number of pauper cases canvassed, the table shows a deficit of 281, namely, 158 males and 123 females. This is due to the fact that there were 281 paupers reported under 10 years of age who were non-users of tobacco and who were therefore disregarded in this tabulation. The recapitulation shows 2,005 paupers who were users of tobacco; of these, 1,970 were males and 35 females. Of the males, 473 were citizen born; 266 naturalized; and 1,227 alien; the nativity of four persons being unknown. Of the females who were users of the weed, eight were citizen born and 27 alien. The total number of pauper cases reported above the age of 10 years was 2,949, of whom 2,475 were males and 474 females. It therefore appears that about two-thirds of the total number were addicted to the use of tobacco, about four-fifths of the males having the habit and slightly less than 10 per cent of the females.

The next table presents the facts as to the use of tobacco by fathers of paupers. In this table the classification as to age periods and political condition is maintained.

Pauperism; Sex, Political Condition, and Use of Tobacco by Fathers of Paupers: By Age Periods.

AGE PERIOD : Under 1.

SEX AND POLITICAL CONDITION.	Users of Tobacco	Non-users	Number of Paupers
Males.	47	31	78
Citizen born, ...	46	31	77
Alien, ...	1	–	1
Females.	40	28	68
Citizen born, ...	39	28	67
Alien, ...	1	–	1
BOTH SEXES.	87	59	146
Citizen born, ...	85	59	144
Alien, ...	2	–	2

AGE PERIOD : 1–4.

Males.	24	18	42
Citizen born, ...	23	14	37
Alien, ...	1	3	4
Unknown,.	–	1	1
Females.	15	13	28
Citizen born, ...	15	11	26
Alien, ...	–	2	2
BOTH SEXES.	39	31	70
Citizen born, ...	38	25	63
Alien, ...	1	5	6
Unknown,.	–	1	1

AGE PERIOD : 5–9.

Males.	16	22	38
Citizen born, ...	9	18	27
Alien, ...	7	4	11
Females.	15	12	27
Citizen born, ...	11	9	20
Alien, ...	4	3	7

Pauperism; Sex, Political Condition, and Use of Tobacco by Fathers of Paupers: By Age Periods — Continued.

AGE PERIOD: 5-9 — Concluded.

SEX AND POLITICAL CONDITION.	Users of Tobacco	Non-users	Number of Paupers
BOTH SEXES.	31	34	65
Citizen born, ...	20	27	47
Alien, ...	11	7	18

AGE PERIOD: 10-14.

	Users of Tobacco	Non-users	Number of Paupers
Males.	16	31	47
Citizen born, ...	8	27	35
Alien, ...	8	4	12
Females.	14	10	24
Citizen born, ...	12	7	19
Alien, ...	2	3	5
BOTH SEXES.	30	41	71
Citizen born, ...	20	34	54
Alien, ...	10	7	17

AGE PERIOD: 15-19.

	Users of Tobacco	Non-users	Number of Paupers
Males.	36	24	60
Citizen born, ...	9	13	22
Alien, ...	27	11	38
Females.	33	33	66
Citizen born, ...	16	14	30
Alien, ...	17	19	36
BOTH SEXES.	69	57	126
Citizen born, ...	25	27	52
Alien, ...	44	30	74

AGE PERIOD: 20-29.

	Users of Tobacco	Non-users	Number of Paupers
Males.	319	229	548
Citizen born, ...	79	63	142
Naturalized, ...	22	6	28
Alien, ...	218	156	374
Unknown, ...	–	4	4

Pauperism; Sex, Political Condition, and Use of Tobacco by Fathers of Paupers : By Age Periods— Continued.

AGE PERIOD : 20–29 — Concluded.

SEX AND POLITICAL CONDITION.	Users of Tobacco	Non-users	Number of Paupers
Females.	112	72	184
Citizen born, ...	34	18	52
Alien, ...	78	53	131
Unknown, ...	–	1	1
BOTH SEXES.	431	301	732
Citizen born, ...	113	81	194
Naturalized, ...	22	6	28
Alien, ...	296	209	505
Unknown, ...	–	5	5

AGE PERIOD : 30–39.

	Users of Tobacco	Non-users	Number of Paupers
Males.	345	330	675
Citizen born, ...	88	95	183
Naturalized, ...	35	27	62
Alien, ...	221	201	422
Unknown, ...	1	7	8
Females.	48	40	88
Citizen born, ...	8	12	20
Alien, ...	40	28	68
BOTH SEXES.	393	370	763
Citizen born, ...	96	107	203
Naturalized, ...	35	27	62
Alien, ...	261	229	490
Unknown, ...	1	7	8

AGE PERIOD : 40–49.

	Users of Tobacco	Non-users	Number of Paupers
Males.	275	278	553
Citizen born, ...	70	67	137
Naturalized, ...	52	38	90
Alien, ...	152	171	323
Unknown,.	1	2	3
Females.	29	26	55
Citizen born, ...	8	4	12
Alien, ...	21	21	42
Unknown,.	–	1	1

Pauperism; Sex, Political Condition, and Use of Tobacco by Fathers of Paupers: By Age Periods — Continued.

AGE PERIOD : 40-49 — Concluded.

SEX AND POLITICAL CONDITION.	Users of Tobacco	Non-users	Number of Paupers
BOTH SEXES.	304	304	608
Citizen born, ...	78	71	149
Naturalized, ...	52	38	90
Alien, ...	173	192	365
Unknown,.	1	3	4

AGE PERIOD : 50-59.

	Users of Tobacco	Non-users	Number of Paupers
Males.	160	183	343
Citizen born, ...	25	34	59
Naturalized, ...	30	43	73
Alien, ...	104	104	208
Unknown,.	1	2	3
Females.	12	15	27
Citizen born, ...	3	2	5
Alien, ...	9	13	22
BOTH SEXES.	172	198	370
Citizen born, ...	28	36	64
Naturalized, ...	30	43	73
Alien, ...	113	117	230
Unknown, ...	1	2	3

AGE PERIOD : 60-79.

	Users of Tobacco	Non-users	Number of Paupers
Males.	101	130	231
Citizen born, ...	11	26	37
Naturalized, ...	31	28	59
Alien, ...	59	73	132
Unknown, ...	-	3	3
Females.	12	15	27
Citizen born, ...	2	4	6
Alien, ...	10	11	21
BOTH SEXES.	113	145	258
Citizen born, ...	13	30	43
Naturalized, ...	31	28	59

Pauperism; Sex, Political Condition, and Use of Tobacco by Fathers of Paupers: By Age Periods — Concluded.

AGE PERIOD: 60-79 — Concluded.

SEX AND POLITICAL CONDITION.	Users of Tobacco	Non-users	Number of Paupers
BOTH SEXES — Con.			
Alien, ...	69	84	153
Unknown, ...	–	3	3

AGE PERIOD: 80 +.

	Users of Tobacco	Non-users	Number of Paupers
Males.	4	14	18
Citizen born, ...	2	3	5
Naturalized, ...	1	7	8
Alien, ...	1	4	5
Females.	2	1	3
Citizen born, ...	1	–	1
Alien, ...	1	1	2
BOTH SEXES.	6	15	21
Citizen born, ...	3	3	6
Naturalized, ...	1	7	8
Alien, ...	2	5	7

RECAPITULATION.

SEX AND POLITICAL CONDITION.	Users of Tobacco	Non-users	Number of Paupers
Males.	1,343	1,290	2,633
Citizen born, ...	370	391	761
Naturalized, ...	171	149	320
Alien, ...	799	731	1,530
Unknown, ...	3	19	22
Females.	332	265	597
Citizen born, ...	149	109	258
Alien, ...	183	154	337
Unknown, ...	–	2	2
BOTH SEXES.	1,675	1,555	3,230
Citizen born, ...	519	500	1,019
Naturalized, ...	171	149	320
Alien, ...	982	885	1,867
Unknown, ...	3	21	24

RECAPITULATION: BY AGE PERIODS.

SEX AND AGE PERIODS.	Users of Tobacco	Non-users	Number of Paupers
Males.	1,343	1,290	2,633
Under 1,	47	31	78
1–4,	24	18	42
5–9,	16	22	38
10–14,	16	31	47
15–19,	36	24	60
20–29,	319	229	548
30–39,	345	330	675
40–49,	275	278	553
50–59,	160	183	343
60–79,	101	130	231
80 +,	4	14	18
Females.	332	265	597
Under 1,	40	28	68
1–4,	15	13	28
5–9,	15	12	27
10–14,	14	10	24
15–19,	33	33	66
20–29,	112	72	184
30–39,	48	40	88
40–49,	29	26	55
50–59,	12	15	27
60–79,	12	15	27
80 +,	2	1	3
BOTH SEXES.	1,675	1,555	3,230
Under 1,	87	59	146
1–4,	39	31	70
5–9,	31	34	65
10–14,	30	41	71
15–19,	69	57	126
20–29,	431	301	732
30–39,	393	370	763
40–49,	304	304	608
50–59,	172	198	370
60–79,	113	145	258
80 +,	6	15	21

Referring to the final section of the recapitulation, we note that of the 3,230 cases of pauperism reported, 1,675 had fathers who were users of tobacco, or about 50 per cent of the total number. The details as to nativity and with respect to the different sexes can be readily seen from the table.

The next table presents the same information as to mothers of paupers.

Pauperism; Sex, Political Condition, and Use of Tobacco by Mothers of Paupers: By Age Periods.

AGE PERIOD: Under 1.

SEX AND POLITICAL CONDITION.	Users of Tobacco	Non-users	Number of Paupers
Males.	–	78	78
Citizen born, ...	–	77	77
Alien, ...	–	1	1
Females.	1	67	68
Citizen born, ...	1	66	67
Alien, ...	–	1	1
BOTH SEXES.	1	145	146
Citizen born, ...	1	143	144
Alien, ...	–	2	2

AGE PERIOD: 1–4.

	Users of Tobacco	Non-users	Number of Paupers
Males.	1	41	42
Citizen born, ...	1	36	37
Alien, ...	–	4	4
Unknown, ...	–	1	1
Females.	2	26	28
Citizen born, ...	2	24	26
Alien, ...	–	2	2
BOTH SEXES.	3	67	70
Citizen born, ...	3	60	63
Alien, ...	–	6	6
Unknown, ...	–	1	1

AGE PERIOD: 5–9.

	Users of Tobacco	Non-users	Number of Paupers
Males.	3	35	38
Citizen born, ...	2	25	27
Alien, ...	1	10	11

Pauperism; Sex, Political Condition, and Use of Tobacco by Mothers of Paupers : By Age Periods — Continued

AGE PERIOD: 5-9 — Concluded.

SEX AND POLITICAL CONDITION.	Users of Tobacco	Non-users	Number of Paupers
Females.	-	27	27
Citizen born, ...	-	20	20
Alien, ...	-	7	7
BOTH SEXES.	3	62	65
Citizen born, ...	2	45	47
Alien, ...	1	17	18

AGE PERIOD: 10-14.

	Users of Tobacco	Non-users	Number of Paupers
Males.	2	45	47
Citizen born, ...	-	35	35
Alien, ...	2	10	12
Females.	2	22	24
Citizen born, ...	2	17	19
Alien, ...	-	5	5
BOTH SEXES.	4	67	71
Citizen born, ...	2	52	54
Alien, ...	2	15	17

AGE PERIOD: 15-19.

	Users of Tobacco	Non-users	Number of Paupers
Males.	1	59	60
Citizen born, ...	-	22	22
Alien, ...	1	37	38
Females.	2	64	66
Citizen born, ...	-	30	30
Alien, ...	2	34	36
BOTH SEXES.	3	123	126
Citizen born, ...	-	52	52
Alien, ...	3	71	74

AGE PERIOD: 20-29.

	Users of Tobacco	Non-users	Number of Paupers
Males.	22	526	548
Citizen born, ...	3	139	142
Naturalized, ...	1	27	28

Pauperism; Sex, Political Condition, and Use of Tobacco by Mothers of Paupers: By Age Periods — Continued.

AGE PERIOD: 20-29 — Concluded.

SEX AND POLITICAL CONDITION.	Users of Tobacco	Non-users	Number of Paupers
Males — Con.			
Alien, ...	17	357	374
Unknown,.	1	3	4
Females.	10	174	184
Citizen born, ...	1	51	52
Alien, ...	9	122	131
Unknown,.	-	1	1
BOTH SEXES.	32	700	732
Citizen born, ...	4	190	194
Naturalized, ...	1	27	28
Alien, ...	26	479	505
Unknown,.	1	4	5

AGE PERIOD: 30-39.

	Users of Tobacco	Non-users	Number of Paupers
Males.	16	659	675
Citizen born, ...	5	178	183
Naturalized, ...	1	61	62
Alien, ...	10	412	422
Unknown,.	-	8	8
Females.	5	83	88
Citizen born, ...	-	20	20
Alien, ...	5	63	68
BOTH SEXES.	21	742	763
Citizen born, ...	5	198	203
Naturalized, ...	1	61	62
Alien, ...	15	475	490
Unknown, ...	-	8	8

AGE PERIOD: 40-49.

	Users of Tobacco	Non-users	Number of Paupers
Males.	19	534	553
Citizen born, ...	4	133	137
Naturalized, ...	4	86	90
Alien, ...	11	312	323
Unknown,.	-	3	3

Pauperism ; Sex, Political Condition, and Use of Tobacco by Mothers of Paupers : By Age Periods — Continued.

AGE PERIOD : 40-49 — Concluded.

SEX AND POLITICAL CONDITION.	Users of Tobacco	Non-users	Number of Paupers
Females.	5	50	55
Citizen born, ...	–	12	12
Alien, ...	5	37	42
Unknown,.	–	1	1
BOTH SEXES.	24	584	608
Citizen born, ...	4	145	149
Naturalized, ...	4	86	90
Alien, ...	16	349	365
Unknown,.	–	4	4

AGE PERIOD : 50–59.

	Users of Tobacco	Non-users	Number of Paupers
Males.	7	336	343
Citizen born, ...	–	59	59
Naturalized, ...	2	71	73
Alien, ...	5	203	208
Unknown,.	–	3	3
Females.	4	23	27
Citizen born, ...	–	5	5
Alien, ...	4	18	22
BOTH SEXES.	11	359	370
Citizen born, ...	–	64	64
Naturalized, ...	2	71	73
Alien, ...	9	221	230
Unknown,.	–	3	3

AGE PERIOD : 60–79.

	Users of Tobacco	Non-users	Number of Paupers
Males.	20	211	231
Citizen born, ...	3	34	37
Naturalized, ...	8	51	59
Alien, ...	9	123	132
Unknown,.	–	3	3
Females.	2	25	27
Citizen born, ...	–	6	6
Alien, ...	2	19	21

Pauperism; Sex, Political Condition, and Use of Tobacco by Mothers of Paupers: By Age Periods — Concluded.

AGE PERIOD: 60-79 — Concluded.

SEX AND POLITICAL CONDITION.	Users of Tobacco	Non-users	Number of Paupers
BOTH SEXES.	22	236	258
Citizen born, ...	3	40	43
Naturalized, ...	8	51	59
Alien, ...	11	142	153
Unknown, ...	–	3	3

AGE PERIOD: 80 +.

	Users of Tobacco	Non-users	Number of Paupers
Males.	2	16	18
Citizen born, ...	2	3	5
Naturalized, ...	–	8	8
Alien, ...	–	5	5
Females.	1	2	3
Citizen born, ...	1	–	1
Alien, ...	–	2	2
BOTH SEXES.	3	18	21
Citizen born, ...	3	3	6
Naturalized, ...	–	8	8
Alien, ...	–	7	7

RECAPITULATION.

SEX AND POLITICAL CONDITION.	Users of Tobacco	Non-users	Number of Paupers
Males.	93	2,540	2,633
Citizen born, ...	20	741	761
Naturalized, ...	16	304	320
Alien, ...	56	1,474	1,530
Unknown, ...	1	21	22
Females.	34	563	597
Citizen born, ...	7	251	258
Alien, ...	27	310	337
Unknown, ...	–	2	2
BOTH SEXES.	127	3,103	3,230
Citizen born, ...	27	992	1,019
Naturalized, ...	16	304	320
Alien, ...	83	1,784	1,867
Unknown, ...	1	23	24

RECAPITULATION: BY AGE PERIODS.

Sex and Age Periods.	Users of Tobacco	Non-users	Number of Paupers
Males.	93	2,540	2,633
Under 1,	-(	78	78
1-4,	1,	41	42
5-9,	7	35	38
10-14,		45	47
15-19,		59	60
20-29,	?	526	548
30-39,	3	659	675
40-49,	19	534	553
50-59,	7	336	343
60-79,	20	211	231
80 +,	2	16	18
Females.	34	563	597
Under 1,	1	67	68
1-4,	2	26	28
5-9,	-	27	27
10-14,	2	22	24
15-19,	2	64	66
20-29,	10	174	184
30-39,	5	83	88
40-49,	5	50	55
50-59,	4	23	27
60-79,	2	25	27
80 +,	1	2	3
BOTH SEXES.	127	3,103	3,230
Under 1,	1	145	146
1-4,	3	67	70
5-9,	3	62	65
10-14,	4	67	71
15-19,	3	123	126
20-29,	32	700	732
30-39,	21	742	763
40-49,	24	584	608
50-59,	11	359	370
60-79,	22	236	258
80 +,	3	18	21

Out of the total number of cases of pauperism, namely, 3,230, only 127 had mothers who were users of tobacco.

Among the pauper who reported their mothers as users of
tobacco, 27 were citizen born, 16 naturalized, 83 alien, and
one unknown.

We close the series of tables relating to pauperism with

RECAPITULATION. — *Relation of the Liquor Traffic to Pauperism:
By Sex and Occupations.*

	SEX AND OCCUPATIONS.	Number of Pau-pers.	Is the person's present condition of **Pauperism** due to the use or abuse of **Intoxicating Liquors**			LIQUOR HABITS OF PAUPERS			
			Yes	No	Not Ascertained	Excessive Drinkers	Other Drinkers	Un-known	Total Abstainers
1	MALES.	2,633	1,217	1,041	375	477	1,490	217	449
2	Agents, ...	9	5	4	–	2	6	–	1
3	Artists, ...	2	–	1	1	–	1	1	–
4	Attorneys, ...	1	–	1	–	–	1	–	–
5	Awning makers, . .	1	1	–	–	1	–	–	–
6	Bakers, ...	26	13	11	2	2	21	2	1
7	Barbers, ...	25	14	11	–	2	20	–	3
8	Bar tenders, . . .	1	–	1	–	–	1	–	–
9	Belt makers, . . .	1	–	1	–	–	1	–	–
10	Bill posters, . .	1	1	–	–	–	1	–	–
11	Blacksmiths, . . .	29	19	8	2	6	19	3	1
12	Bleachers, ...	1	1	–	–	–	1	–	–
13	Boat makers, . .	1	1	–	–	–	1	–	–
14	Boiler makers, . . .	4	2	2	–	2	1	–	1
15	Boiler tenders, . .	1	–	1	–	–	1	–	–
16	Bolt makers, . .	1	–	1	–	–	1	–	–
17	Bookkeepers, . .	6	2	3	1	1	3	1	1
18	Boot blacks, . . .	1	–	1	–	–	1	–	–
19	Boot and shoemakers, .	51	26	18	7	14	26	6	5
20	Boxing masters, . .	1	1	–	–	1	–	–	–
21	Brass workers, . .	8	5	3	–	1	7	–	–
22	Brick makers, . . .	1	1	–	–	–	1	–	–
23	Bridge builders, . .	1	–	1	–	–	1	–	–
24	Broom makers, . .	2	2	–	–	–	2	–	–
25	Butchers, ...	5	1	3	1	–	2	1	2
26	Cabinet makers, . .	3	–	3	–	–	2	–	1
27	Carpenters, . . .	40	18	18	4	6	26	4	4
28	Carriage makers, . .	4	3	1	–	1	3	–	–
29	Chair makers, . .	5	4	1	–	1	3	–	1
30	Cigar makers, . .	4	1	1	2	–	2	2	–
31	Civil engineers, . .	1	–	1	–	–	1	–	–
32	Clerks, ...	13	7	5	1	3	6	1	3
33	Coat makers, . . .	2	–	2	–	–	–	1	1

recapitulations in which the leading facts are brought forward and combined with data as to the occupation and place of birth. The first of these recapitulations classifies the facts with relation to occupation.

RECAPITULATION. — *Relation of the Liquor Traffic to Pauperism :*
By Sex and Occupations.

	KINDS OF LIQUOR					TOBACCO		DRUGS		
Wines only	Lager Beer and Malt Liquors only	Distilled Liquors only	Two or All Kinds	Un-known	Inapplicable*	Users	Non-users	Users	Non-users	
15	375	36	1,541	217	449	1,970	663	3	2,630	1
-	3	-	5	-	1	6	3	-	9	2
-	1	-	-	1	-	1	1	-	2	3
-	1	-	-	-	-	1	-	-	1	4
-	-	-	1	-	-	1	-	-	1	5
-	9	-	14	2	1	22	4	-	26	6
-	3	-	19	-	3	21	4	-	25	7
-	1	-	-	-	-	1	-	-	1	8
-	-	-	1	-	-	1	-	-	1	9
-	-	-	1	-	-	1	-	-	1	10
-	-	-	25	3	1	25	4	-	29	11
-	-	-	1	-	-	1	-	-	1	12
-	-	-	1	-	-	1	-	-	1	13
-	-	-	3	-	1	4	-	-	4	14
-	-	-	1	-	-	1	-	-	1	15
-	-	-	1	-	-	1	-	-	1	16
-	1	-	3	1	1	5	1	-	6	17
-	-	-	1	-	-	-	1	-	1	18
-	7	-	33	6	5	41	10	-	51	19
-	-	-	1	-	-	1	-	-	1	20
-	3	-	5	-	-	6	2	-	8	21
-	-	-	1	-	-	1	-	-	1	22
-	1	-	-	-	-	1	-	-	1	23
-	-	-	2	-	-	2	-	-	2	24
-	1	-	1	1	2	2	3	-	5	25
-	1	-	1	-	1	3	-	-	3	26
-	8	1	23	4	4	31	9	-	40	27
-	2	-	2	-	-	2	2	-	4	28
-	1	-	3	-	1	5	-	-	5	29
-	1	-	1	2	-	1	3	-	4	30
-	1	-	-	-	-	1	-	-	1	31
-	-	-	9	1	3	10	3	-	13	32
-	-	-	-	1	1	-	2	-	2	33

* Total Abstainers.

RECAPITULATION. — *Relation of the Liquor Traffic to Pauperism:*
By Sex and Occupations — Continued.

	SEX AND OCCUPATIONS.	Number of Paupers	Is the person's present condition of **Pauperism** due to the use or abuse of **Intoxicating Liquors**			LIQUOR HABITS OF PAUPERS			
			Yes	No	Not Ascertained	Excessive Drinkers	Other Drinkers	Unknown	Total Abstainers
	MALES — Con.								
1	Cooks, ...	42	26	13	3	8	28	3	3
2	Coopers, ...	9	4	4	1	2	4	1	2
3	Cutlers, ...	1	–	1	–	–	1	–	–
4	Cutters (file), . . .	1	–	1	–	–	1	–	–
5	Cutters (meat), . . .	1	–	1	–	–	1	–	–
6	Cutters (paper), . . .	1	–	1	–	–	–	–	1
7	Cutters (shoe), . . .	1	–	1	–	–	1	–	–
8	Cutters (stone), . . .	22	9	13	–	1	19	–	2
9	Domestic servants, . .	5	–	3	2	–	2	2	1
10	Druggists, ...	1	–	1	–	–	–	–	1
11	Dyers, ...	4	2	2	–	–	4	–	–
12	Elevator tenders, . .	2	–	2	–	–	–	–	2
13	Employés (R.R.), . .	15	6	8	1	1	11	2	1
14	Employés (sugar-house), .	1	–	1	–	–	1	–	–
15	Employés (theatre), . .	1	–	1	–	–	–	–	1
16	Engineers, ...	3	2	1	–	1	2	–	–
17	Engravers, ...	1	–	1	–	–	1	–	–
18	Errand boys, . . .	2	–	2	–	–	–	–	2
19	Factory operatives, . .	156	62	79	15	23	99	12	22
20	Farmers, ...	38	13	20	5	3	20	5	10
21	Firemen, ...	47	32	9	6	19	20	7	1
22	Fishermen, ...	10	5	3	2	4	3	2	1
23	Foundrymen, . . .	3	1	2	–	1	2	–	–
24	Furniture makers, . .	8	4	3	1	1	5	2	–
25	Gardeners, ...	11	4	5	2	1	7	2	1
26	Gasfitters, ...	2	2	–	–	–	2	–	–
27	Gilders, ...	2	–	2	–	–	2	–	–
28	Glaziers, ...	2	2	–	–	–	2	–	–
29	Hack drivers, . . .	2	2	–	–	2	–	–	–
30	Harness makers, . .	6	3	2	1	1	2	1	2
31	Hat makers, . . .	3	1	2	–	1	2	–	–
32	Iron workers, . . .	3	1	2	–	–	1	–	2
33	Jewellers, ...	1	–	1	–	–	1	–	–
34	Journalists, . . .	1	–	1	–	–	1	–	–
35	Junk dealers, . . .	6	6	–	–	5	1	–	–
36	Laborers, ...	1,171	633	435	103	253	717	94	107
37	Lathers, ...	2	1	–	1	1	–	1	–
38	Leather workers, . .	25	16	9	–	9	14	1	1
39	Linemen, ...	3	1	1	1	1	1	1	–

RECAPITULATION. — *Relation of the Liquor Traffic to Pauperism: By Sex and Occupations* — Continued.

Wines only	Lager Beer and Malt Liquors only	Distilled Liquors only	Two or All Kinds	Un- known	Inappli- cable*	Users	Non- users	Users	Non- users	
			KINDS OF LIQUOR			TOBACCO		DRUGS		
1	6	–	29	3	3	33	9	1	41	1
–	–	–	6	1	2	7	2	–	9	2
–	–	–	1	–	–	1	–	–	1	3
–	–	–	1	–	–	–	1	–	1	4
–	–	–	1	–	–	1	–	–	1	5
–	–	–	–	–	1	1	–	–	1	6
–	1	–	–	–	–	1	–	–	1	7
–	5	–	15	–	2	21	1	–	22	8
–	2	–	–	2	1	1	4	–	5	9
–	–	–	–	–	1	1	–	–	1	10
–	–	–	4	–	–	4	–	–	4	11
–	–	–	–	–	2	2	–	–	2	12
–	3	–	9	2	1	11	4	–	15	13
–	1	–	–	–	–	–	1	–	1	14
–	–	–	–	–	1	1	–	–	1	15
–	–	–	3	–	–	3	–	–	3	16
–	–	–	1	–	–	1	–	–	1	17
–	–	–	–	–	2	2	–	–	2	18
1	35	–	86	12	22	122	34	–	156	19
–	5	–	18	5	10	28	10	–	38	20
–	5	–	34	7	1	39	8	–	47	21
–	1	–	6	2	1	8	2	–	10	22
–	1	–	2	–	–	3	–	–	3	23
–	–	–	6	2	–	5	3	–	8	24
–	1	–	7	2	1	8	3	–	11	25
–	–	–	2	–	–	2	–	–	2	26
–	–	–	2	–	–	2	–	–	2	27
–	1	–	1	–	–	2	–	–	2	28
–	–	–	2	–	–	2	–	–	2	29
–	1	–	2	1	2	4	2	–	6	30
–	1	–	2	–	–	3	–	–	3	31
–	–	–	1	–	2	3	–	–	3	32
–	1	–	–	–	–	1	–	–	1	33
–	–	–	1	–	–	–	1	–	1	34
–	–	1	5	–	–	6	–	–	6	35
9	153	12	796	94	107	980	191	–	1,171	36
–	–	–	1	1	–	1	1	–	2	37
–	4	–	19	1	1	23	2	–	25	38
–	–	–	2	1	–	2	1	–	3	39

* Total Abstainers.

RECAPITULATION. — *Relation of the Liquor Traffic to Pauperism:
By Sex and Occupations* — Continued.

	SEX AND OCCUPATIONS.	Number of Paupers	Is the person's present condition of **Pauperism** due to the use or abuse of **Intoxicating Liquors**			LIQUOR HABITS OF PAUPERS			
			Yes	No	Not Ascertained	Excessive Drinkers	Other Drinkers	Unknown	Total Abstainers
	MALES — Con.								
1	Locksmiths,	1	–	1	–	–	–	–	1
2	Loom fixers,	4	1	3	–	–	3	–	1
3	Machinists,	38	20	14	4	10	21	3	4
4	Mariners,	74	18	48	8	5	53	8	8
5	Masons,	41	26	13	2	11	24	2	4
6	Mat makers,	1	–	1	–	–	1	–	–
7	Mechanics,	3	2	1	–	1	1	–	1
8	Mercury platers,	1	–	1	–	–	1	–	–
9	Metallic grinders,	2	–	1	1	–	1	1	–
10	Metal workers,	16	5	10	1	3	10	1	2
11	Miners,	1	1	–	–	1	–	–	–
12	Moulders,	11	7	4	–	4	7	–	–
13	Musical instrument makers,	2	–	2	–	–	–	–	2
14	Musicians,	1	1	–	–	1	–	–	–
15	Nurses,	3	2	1	–	–	3	–	–
16	Painters,	53	31	21	1	10	39	1	3
17	Paper box makers,	1	1	–	–	–	1	–	–
18	Paper hangers,	1	1	–	–	–	1	–	–
19	Pattern makers,	1	1	–	–	1	–	–	–
20	Pavers,	2	1	1	–	1	1	–	–
21	Peddlers,	10	2	6	2	–	7	2	1
22	Personal service,	30	12	15	3	6	16	3	5
23	Photographers,	4	4	–	–	–	2	2	–
24	Plasterers,	4	1	3	–	1	3	–	–
25	Plumbers,	4	1	3	–	–	3	1	–
26	Porters,	4	2	2	–	–	3	–	1
27	Printers,	13	5	7	1	2	6	2	3
28	Quarrymen,	12	7	4	1	1	10	–	1
29	Rag pickers,	1	–	1	–	–	1	–	–
30	Reporters,	2	–	2	–	–	1	–	1
31	Riggers,	1	1	–	–	–	1	–	–
32	Roller makers,	1	–	1	–	–	–	1	–
33	Roofers,	1	1	–	–	–	1	–	–
34	Rope makers,	2	2	–	–	1	1	–	–
35	Sail makers,	1	–	1	–	–	1	–	–
36	Salesmen,	7	1	6	–	1	4	–	2
37	Sausage makers,	1	–	1	–	–	1	–	–
38	Saw filers,	1	–	1	–	–	–	–	1
39	Section hands,	1	1	–	–	–	1	–	–

RECAPITULATION. — *Relation of the Liquor Traffic to Pauperism:
By Sex and Occupations* — Continued

Kinds of Liquor						Tobacco		Drugs		
Wines only	Lager Beer and Malt Liquors only	Distilled Liquors only	Two or All Kinds	Un-known	Inappli-cable*	Users	Non-users	Users	Non-users	
-	-	-	-	-	1	-	1	-	1	1
-	1	-	2	-	1	4	-	-	4	2
-	4	-	27	3	4	32	6	-	38	3
1	11	15	31	8	8	47	27	-	74	4
-	5	1	29	2	4	34	7	-	41	5
-	-	-	1	-	-	1	-	-	1	6
-	2	-	-	-	1	2	1	-	3	7
-	1	-	-	-	-	1	-	-	1	8
-	-	-	1	1	-	1	1	-	2	9
-	5	-	8	1	2	15	1	-	16	10
-	-	-	1	-	-	1	-	-	1	11
-	1	-	10	-	-	11	-	-	11	12
-	-	-	-	-	2	-	2	-	2	13
-	-	-	1	-	-	1	-	-	1	14
-	-	-	3	-	-	3	-	-	3	15
-	12	1	36	1	3	44	9	-	53	16
-	-	-	1	-	-	1	-	-	1	17
-	-	-	1	-	-	1	-	-	1	18
-	-	-	1	-	-	1	-	-	1	19
-	-	-	2	-	-	2	-	-	2	20
-	4	-	3	2	1	8	2	-	10	21
-	7	1	14	3	5	21	9	-	30	22
-	-	-	2	2	-	2	2	-	4	23
-	1	-	3	-	-	4	-	-	4	24
-	1	1	1	1	-	3	1	-	4	25
-	2	-	1	-	1	4	-	-	4	26
-	3	-	5	2	3	10	3	-	13	27
-	4	-	7	-	1	11	1	-	12	28
-	-	-	1	-	-	-	1	-	1	29
-	-	-	1	-	1	-	2	-	2	30
-	-	-	1	-	-	1	-	-	1	31
-	-	-	-	1	-	-	1	-	1	32
-	-	-	1	-	-	1	-	-	1	33
-	-	-	2	-	-	2	-	-	2	34
-	1	-	-	-	-	-	1	-	1	35
1	-	-	4	-	2	5	·2	-	7	36
-	1	-	-	-	-	1	-	-	1	37
-	-	-	-	-	1	1	-	1	-	38
-	-	-	1	-	-	1	-	-	1	39

* Total Abstainers.

RECAPITULATION. — *Relation of the Liquor Traffic to Pauperism: By Sex and Occupations* — Continued

	SEX AND OCCUPATIONS.	Number of Paupers	Is the person's present condition of **Pauperism** due to the use or abuse of **Intoxicating Liquors**			LIQUOR HABITS OF PAUPERS			
			Yes	No	Not Ascertained	Excessive Drinkers	Other Drinkers	Unknown	Total Abstainers
	MALES — Con.								
1	Ship carpenters,	1	1	-	-	1	-	-	-
2	Soldiers,	1	-	1	-	-	1	-	-
3	Sorters,	5	4	1	-	1	3	1	-
4	Splint makers,	2	1	-	1	-	-	1	1
5	Stable hands,	56	27	26	3	7	41	4	4
6	Steam drillers,	1	1	-	-	-	1	-	-
7	Steam fitters,	7	5	2	-	1	6	-	-
8	Stone workers,	4	2	2	-	2	-	2	-
9	Sweepers,	1	-	-	1	-	-	-	1
10	Tailors,	30	9	18	3	7	17	3	3
11	Teamsters,	65	33	26	6	15	35	10	5
12	Traders,	1	1	-	-	1	-	-	-
13	Trunk makers,	1	-	1	-	-	1	-	-
14	Upholsterers,	6	3	3	-	1	5	-	-
15	Watchmen,	1	-	1	-	-	1	-	-
16	Whitewashers,	2	2	-	-	-	2	-	-
17	Woodworkers,	2	-	2	-	-	-	1	1
18	None,	214	2	42	170	-	2	9	203
19	Unknown,	9	2	5	2	-	6	1	2
20	FEMALES.	597	57	386	154	28	113	39	417
21	Actresses,	1	-	1	-	-	-	-	1
22	Cigar makers,	1	-	1	-	-	1	-	-
23	Clerks,	1	-	1	-	-	-	-	1
24	Cooks,	17	6	10	1	2	9	1	5
25	Decorators (pottery),	1	-	1	-	-	1	-	-
26	Domestic servants,	267	31	212	24	18	65	20	164
27	Dressmakers,	2	-	1	1	-	-	1	1
28	Factory operatives,	69	10	55	4	4	14	5	46
29	Hairworkers,	1	-	1	-	-	1	-	-
30	Housekeepers,	3	-	2	1	-	-	1	2
31	Housewives,	32	2	26	4	2	7	3	20
32	Laundresses,	10	3	6	1	1	2	1	6
33	Milliners,	1	-	1	-	-	-	-	1
34	Nurses,	2	-	1	1	-	-	1	1
35	Nurse girls,	4	-	4	-	-	-	-	4
36	Peddlers,	3	-	2	1	-	1	1	1
37	Personal service,	8	1	7	-	1	1	-	6

RECAPITULATION. — *Relation of the Liquor Traffic to Pauperism: By Sex and Occupations* — Continued.

| KINDS OF LIQUOR | | | | | | TOBACCO | | DRUGS | | |
Wines only	Lager Beer and Malt Liquors only	Distilled Liquors only	Two or All Kinds	Un-known	Inapplicable*	Users	Non-users	Users	Non-users	
-	-	-	1	-	-	1	-	-	1	1
-	1	-	-	-	-	1	-	-	1	2
-	1	-	3	1	-	4	1	-	5	3
-	-	-	-	1	1	-	2	-	2	4
-	14	-	34	4	4	42	14	-	56	5
-	-	-	1	-	-	1	-	-	1	6
-	2	-	5	-	-	7	-	-	7	7
-	-	-	2	2	-	2	2	-	4	8
-	-	-	-	-	1	-	1	-	1	9
1	5	2	16	3	3	21	9	-	30	10
-	9	1	40	10	5	54	11	-	65	11
-	-	-	1	-	-	1	-	-	1	12
-	-	-	1	-	-	1	-	-	1	13
-	2	-	4	-	-	4	2	-	6	14
-	-	-	1	-	-	1	-	-	1	15
-	-	-	2	-	-	2	-	-	2	16
-	-	-	-	1	1	1	1	-	2	17
-	2	-	-	9	203	10	204	-	214	18
1	1	-	4	1	2	5	4	-	9	19
10	42	2	87	39	417	35	562	-	597	20
-	-	-	-	-	1	-	1	-	1	21
-	-	-	1	-	-	-	1	-	1	22
-	-	-	-	-	1	-	1	-	1	23
-	1	-	10	1	5	2	15	-	17	24
-	1	-	-	-	-	-	1	-	1	25
5	29	1	48	20	164	24	243	-	267	26
-	-	-	-	1	1	-	2	-	2	27
-	6	-	12	5	46	5	64	-	69	28
-	-	-	1	-	-	-	1	-	1	29
-	-	-	-	1	2	-	3	-	3	30
1	3	1	4	3	20	2	30	-	32	31
-	-	-	3	1	6	-	10	-	10	32
-	-	-	-	-	1	-	1	-	1	33
-	-	-	-	1	1	-	2	-	2	34
-	-	-	-	-	4	-	4	-	4	35
1	-	-	-	1	1	-	3	-	3	36
-	1	-	1	-	6	-	8	-	8	37

* Total Abstainers.

RECAPITULATION.—*Relation of the Liquor Traffic to Pauperism: By Sex and Occupations*— Concluded.

SEX AND OCCUPATIONS.	Number of Paupers	Is the person's present condition of **Pauperism** due to the use or abuse of **Intoxicating Liquors**			LIQUOR HABITS OF PAUPERS			
		Yes	No	Not Ascertained	Excessive Drinkers	Other Drinkers	Unknown	Total Abstainers
FEMALES — Con.								
1 Seamstresses, . . .	11	2	8	1	–	3	2	6
2 Store girls, ...	1	–	1	–	–	–	–	1
3 Table girls, ...	8	–	8	–	–	2	–	6
4 Tailoresses, . . .	2	–	2	–	–	1	–	1
5 None, ...	145	2	30	113	–	3	1	141
6 Unknown, ...	7	–	5	2	–	2	2	3

No analysis of this table is required except that necessary to show the manner in which it is to be used, as it is exceedingly graphic and can be readily understood. The first line as to males shows that there were 2,633 instances of male pauperism reported, of whom 1,217 reported that their present condition of pauperism was due to the use or abuse of intoxicating liquor, while 1,041 gave a negative answer upon this point, the information as to 375 not being ascertained. As to liquor habits, 477 were excessive drinkers, while 1,490 were drinkers of other degree; 449 were total abstainers, and for 217 the habits as to the use of liquor was unknown. As to the kinds of liquor used, in 449 instances the question was inapplicable, owing to the fact that the persons were total abstainers; in 217 instances the facts were unknown; 36 reported the use of distilled liquors only; 375 the use of lager beer and malt liquors only; 15 the use of wine only; while in 1,541 instances the use of two kinds of liquor, or of all kinds included in the table, was reported. As to the use of tobacco, among these 2,633 male paupers 1,970 were users and 663 non-users, it being borne in mind, as shown in a preceding table, there were no users of tobacco among those under 10 years of age. As to the intemperate use of drugs, only three cases were reported, 2,630 being non-users of drugs as intoxicants. Under this line in the table are grouped

RECAPITULATION.— *Relation of the Liquor Traffic to Pauperism :*
By Sex and Occupations — Concluded.

	KINDS OF LIQUOR					TOBACCO		DRUGS		
Wines only	Lager Beer and Malt Liquors only	Distilled Liquors only	Two or All Kinds	Un- known	Inappli- cable*	Users	Non- users	Users	Non- users	
-	-	-	3	2	6	2	9	-	11	1
-	-	-	-	-	1	-	1	-	1	2
-	-	-	2	-	6	-	8	-	8	3
1	-	-	-	-	1	-	2	-	2	4
1	-	-	2	1	141	-	145	-	145	5
1	1	-	-	2	3	-	7	-	7	6

* Total Abstainers.

the several occupations of the paupers, their occupation being given as that which was followed before they came into the institution. The most numerous class includes the laborers, that is, those having no distinct trade or profession. This class numbers 1,171; of whom 633, more than 50 per cent, attribute their present condition of pauperism to the use of intoxicating liquors, and 253 of these are excessive drinkers. In this class the users of lager beer and malt liquors only, number 153; while 796 instances are reported of the use of two or all kinds of liquor. The next most numerous class represented among the males are the factory operatives, numbering 156, of whom 62 report their present condition of pauperism as due to the use of intoxicating liquor, 23 being excessive drinkers.

Referring to the section relating to the females in the recapitulation, we find that 597 female paupers are represented, but of these only 57 report their present condition of pauperism as due to the use or abuse of intoxicating liquor, while 386 return a negative answer upon this point. The excessive drinkers among the females number only 28, and drinkers of other degree 113, the total abstainers numbering 417, being largely in the majority. The users of lager beer and malt liquors only, number 42; those addicted to distilled liquors only, 2; those using wines only number 10; while those

using two or all kinds of liquor number 87; the facts as to
39 are unknown, and the questions upon this point are inapplicable in the case of 417 total abstainers. As previously
reported, only 35 females report the use of tobacco, while no
users of drugs as intoxicants are found among them. The
most numerous class as to occupation among the females includes the domestic servants, numbering in the aggregate 267.
In this class are found 31 out of the 57 female paupers who
report their condition of pauperism as due to the use or abuse

RECAPITULATION. — *Relation of the Liquor Traffic to Pauperism: By
Sex and Political Condition.*

SEX AND POLITICAL CONDITION.	Number of Paupers.	Is the person's present condition of **Pauperism** due to the use or abuse of **Intoxicating Liquors**			LIQUOR HABITS OF PAUPERS			
		Yes	No	Not Ascertained	Excessive Drinkers	Other Drinkers	Unknown	Total Abstainers
1	*Males.*	2,633	1,217	1,041	375	477	1,490	217	449
2	Citizen born, . . .	761	288	273	200	103	353	57	248
3	Naturalized or alien, .	1,850	924	765	161	371	1,133	146	200
4	Unknown, ...	22	5	3	14	3	4	14	1
5	*Females.*	597	57	386	154	28	113	39	417
6	Citizen born, . . .	258	14	130	114	6	21	9	222
7	Naturalized or alien, .	337	43	256	38	22	92	28	195
8	Unknown, ...	2	–	–	2	–	–	2	–
9	BOTH SEXES.	3,230	1,274	1,427	529	505	1,603	256	866
10	Citizen born, . . .	1,019	302	403	314	109	374	66	470
11	Naturalized or alien, .	2,187	967	1,021	199	393	1,225	174	395
12	Unknown, ...	24	5	3	16	3	4	16	1

In this table the paupers are classified under the heads
citizen born, naturalized or alien, or birthplace unknown.
From the final lines, including both sexes, we note that of the
3,230 pauper cases reported, 1,019 are citizen born and 2,187
naturalized or alien, the facts being unknown in 24 cases only.
Of the 1,019 who are citizen born, 302 considered their present condition of pauperism due to the use or abuse of intoxicating liquors, this being about one-third of the total number;

of intoxicating liquors, 18 being excessive drinkers, this number being about two-thirds of the total number of excessive drinkers reported among the female paupers. Out of the 35 users of tobacco, 24 are found in the class "domestic servants"; the others comprising two cooks, five factory operatives, two housewives, and two seamstresses.

The final recapitulation classifies the paupers with respect to nativity. This recapitulation is in two sections, the first of which is now presented.

RECAPITULATION.— *Relation of the Liquor Traffic to Pauperism: By Sex and Political Condition.*

KINDS OF LIQUOR						TOBACCO		DRUGS		
Wines only	Lager Beer and Malt Liquors only	Distilled Liquors only	Two or All Kinds	Un-known	Inappli-cable*	Users	Non-users	Users	Non-users	
15	375	36	1,541	217	449	1,970	663	3	2,630	1
-	99	6	351	57	248	473	288	3	758	2
15	276	30	1,183	146	200	1,493	357	-	1,850	3
-	-	-	7	14	1	4	18	-	22	4
10	42	2	87	39	417	35	562	-	597	5
-	3	2	22	9	222	8	250	-	258	6
10	39	-	65	28	195	27	310	-	337	7
-	-	-	-	2	-	-	2	-	2	8
25	417	38	1,628	256	866	2,005	1,225	3	3,227	9
-	102	8	373	66	470	481	538	3	1,016	10
25	315	30	1,248	174	395	1,520	667	-	2,187	11
-	-	-	7	16	1	4	20	-	24	12

* Total Abstainers.

while of the naturalized or alien paupers, 967 are of this class, a somewhat larger proportion. Of the citizen born, 109 are excessive drinkers, and 374 are drinkers of other degree. Of the naturalized or alien, numbering 2,187, 393 are excessive drinkers, and 1,225 are drinkers of other degree. Of the citizen-born paupers 470, or nearly one-half the whole number, are total abstainers; while 395, slightly more than one-seventh, of the naturalized or alien paupers are of this class.

Of the paupers who are citizen born, 373 use two, or all kinds of liquor, while 1,248 of the naturalized or alien paupers make the same report. Of the naturalized or alien paupers, 1,520 are users of tobacco, while 667 are not. On the other

RECAPITULATION. — *Relation of the Liquor Traffic to Pauperism: By Sex, Political Condition, and Place of Birth.*

	SEX, POLITICAL CONDITION, AND PLACE OF BIRTH.	Number of Paupers	Is the person's present condition of **Pauperism** due to the use or abuse of **Intoxicating Liquors**			LIQUOR HABITS OF PAUPERS			
			Yes	No	Not Ascertained	Excessive Drinkers	Other Drinkers	Unknown	Total Abstainers
1	**Males.**	2,633	1,217	1,041	375	477	1,490	217	449
2	*Citizen Born.*	761	288	273	200	103	353	57	248
3	Alabama, ...	1	–	1	–	–	–	–	1
4	Arkansas, ...	1	–	1	–	–	1	–	–
5	California, ...	3	2	1	–	2	1	–	–
6	Connecticut, . . .	27	10	15	2	1	19	1	6
7	District of Columbia, .	2	1	1	–	–	1	–	1
8	Florida, ...	1	1	–	–	–	1	–	–
9	Georgia, ...	2	1	1	–	–	1	1	–
10	Illinois, ...	1	–	1	–	–	–	–	1
11	Indiana, ...	1	1	–	–	–	1	–	–
12	Kansas, ...	1	–	1	–	–	1	–	–
13	Kentucky, ...	2	2	–	–	1	1	–	–
14	Louisiana, ...	2	2	–	–	1	1	–	–
15	Maine, ...	53	18	23	12	10	21	8	14
16	Maryland, . . .	6	2	4	–	–	4	2	–
17	Massachusetts, . . .	400	150	107	143	48	165	19	168
18	Michigan, . . .	5	2	2	1	2	2	1	–
19	Minnesota, ...	4	3	–	1	1	2	1	–
20	Missouri, ...	4	2	1	1	2	–	1	1
21	New Hampshire, . .	39	15	19	5	5	22	2	10
22	New Jersey, . . .	14	5	6	3	3	5	1	5
23	New York, . . .	90	41	32	17	17	48	12	13
24	North Carolina, . .	5	–	4	1	–	1	–	4
25	Ohio, ...	7	2	3	2	1	4	2	–
26	Oregon, ...	2	2	–	–	1	1	–	–
27	Pennsylvania, . .	24	7	15	2	–	17	–	7
28	Rhode Island, . .	23	7	13	3	2	14	2	5
29	South Carolina, . .	3	–	2	1	–	1	1	1
30	Vermont, ...	21	8	7	6	3	9	3	6
31	Virginia, ...	11	2	9	–	2	5	–	4
32	West Virginia, . .	1	1	–	–	1	–	–	–

hand, 481 of the citizen-born paupers are users of tobacco, while 538 are not.

The next section of the recapitulation as to birth shows the place of birth in detail.

RECAPITULATION.—*Relation of the Liquor Traffic to Pauperism: By Sex, Political Condition, and Place of Birth.*

	KINDS OF LIQUOR					TOBACCO		DRUGS		
Wines only	Lager Beer and Malt Liquors only	Distilled Liquors only	Two or All Kinds	Un-known	Inapplicable*	Users	Non-users	Users	Non-users	
15	375	36	1,541	217	449	1,970	663	3	2,630	1
-	99	6	351	57	248	473	288	3	758	2
-	-	-	-	-	1	-	1	-	1	3
-	1	-	-	-	-	1	-	-	1	4
-	1	-	2	-	-	3	-	-	3	5
-	5	-	15	1	6	19	8	-	27	6
-	-	-	1	-	1	1	1	-	2	7
-	1	-	-	-	-	1	-	-	1	8
-	1	-	-	1	-	1	1	-	2	9
-	-	-	-	-	1	-	1	-	1	10
-	-	-	1	-	-	1	-	-	1	11
-	-	-	1	-	-	1	-	-	1	12
-	-	1	1	-	-	2	-	-	2	13
-	-	-	2	-	-	2	-	-	2	14
-	9	-	22	8	14	37	16	2	51	15
-	1	-	3	2	-	3	3	-	6	16
-	40	2	171	19	168	218	182	-	400	17
-	1	-	3	1	-	4	1	-	5	18
-	-	-	3	1	-	2	2	-	4	19
-	-	-	2	1	1	2	2	-	4	20
-	7	1	19	2	10	33	6	-	39	21
-	-	-	8	1	5	10	4	-	14	22
-	11	1	53	12	13	60	30	1	89	23
-	1	-	-	-	4	3	2	-	5	24
-	3	-	2	2	-	5	2	-	7	25
-	-	-	2	-	-	2	-	-	2	26
-	6	-	11	-	7	18	6	-	24	27
-	5	-	11	2	5	17	6	-	23	28
-	-	-	1	1	1	1	2	-	3	29
-	2	-	10	3	6	13	8	-	21	30
-	4	-	3	-	4	7	4	-	11	31
-	-	-	1	-	-	1	-	-	1	32

* Total Abstainers.

RECAPITULATION. — *Relation of the Liquor Traffic to Pauperism : By Sex, Political Condition, and Place of Birth* — Continued.

SEX. POLITICAL CONDITION, AND PLACE OF BIRTH	Number of Paupers	Is the person's present condition of Pauperism due to the use or abuse of Intoxicating Liquors			LIQUOR HABITS OF PAUPERS			
		Yes	No	Not Ascertained	Excessive Drinkers	Other Drinkers	Unknown	Total Abstainers
Males — Con.								
Citizen Born — Con.								
1 Wisconsin, ...	4	1	3	–	–	4	–	–
2 United States (not specified),	1	–	1	–	–	–	–	1
3 *Naturalized or Alien.*	1,850	924	765	161	371	1,133	146	200
4 Africa, ...	14	–	14	–	–	13	–	1
5 Asia, ...	4	–	2	2	–	–	3	1
6 Austria (Bohemia), . .	1	–	1	–	–	1	–	–
7 Austria (not specified), .	12	2	8	2	–	9	1	2
8 Belgium, ...	2	1	1	–	–	2	–	–
9 Born at sea, . . .	1	1	–	–	1	–	–	–
10 British Possessions, Other .	4	3	1	–	1	3	–	–
11 Canada, ...	99	45	38	16	12	58	12	17
12 Cuba, ...	1	–	–	1	–	–	1	–
13 Denmark, ...	7	2	5	–	1	3	–	3
14 England, ...	217	107	90	20	45	123	20	29
15 France, ...	10	7	3	–	2	8	–	–
16 Germany, ...	34	8	23	3	2	23	2	7
17 Greece, ...	6	3	3	–	–	4	–	2
18 Ireland, ...	1,078	630	385	63	262	667	69	80
19 Italy, ...	57	11	42	4	3	47	4	3
20 New Brunswick, . .	48	25	22	1	13	29	1	5
21 Newfoundland, . . .	14	4	9	1	2	7	1	4
22 Norway, ...	4	–	3	1	–	3	–	1
23 Nova Scotia, . . .	46	21	18	7	13	22	5	6
24 Poland, ...	16	–	11	5	–	5	3	8
25 Portugal (Western Islands),	8	–	7	1	–	4	1	3
26 Portugal (not specified), .	4	2	–	2	2	–	1	1
27 Prince Edward Island, .	18	4	9	5	1	11	3	3
28 Russia, ...	41	9	18	14	–	20	8	13
29 Scotland, ...	53	25	21	7	4	41	5	3
30 South America, . . .	1	1	–	–	1	–	–	–
31 Spain, ...	1	1	–	–	1	–	–	–
32 Sweden, ...	26	7	16	3	3	16	3	4
33 Switzerland, . . .	3	2	1	–	1	2	–	–
34 Turkey, ...	6	–	3	3	–	2	3	1
35 Wales, ...	6	2	4	–	–	6	–	–
36 West Indies, . . .	8	1	7	–	1	4	–	3

RECAPITULATION. — *Relation of the Liquor Traffic to Pauperism: By Sex, Political Condition, and Place of Birth* — Continued.

Kinds of Liquor						Tobacco		Drugs		
Wines only	Lager Beer and Malt Liquors only	Distilled Liquors only	Two or All Kinds	Un-known	Inappli-cable*	Users	Non-users	Users	Non-users	
-	1	-	3	-	-	4	-	-	4	1
-	-	-	-	-	1	1	-	-	1	2
15	276	30	1,183	146	200	1,493	357	-	1,850	3
-	-	13	-	-	1	1	13	-	14	4
-	-	-	-	3	1	1	3	-	4	5
-	1	-	-	-	-	1	-	-	1	6
-	4	-	5	1	2	6	6	-	12	7
-	-	-	2	-	-	2	-	-	2	8
-	-	-	1	-	-	1	-	-	1	9
-	-	-	4	-	-	4	-	-	4	10
-	14	1	55	12	17	68	31	-	99	11
-	-	-	-	1	-	-	1	-	1	12
-	4	-	-	-	3	3	4	-	7	13
-	40	1	127	20	29	171	46	-	217	14
1	1	-	8	-	-	9	1	-	10	15
-	13	-	12	2	7	24	10	-	34	16
-	2	-	2	-	2	5	1	-	6	17
-	141	12	776	69	80	943	135	-	1,078	18
7	2	-	41	4	3	36	21	-	57	19
-	7	1	34	1	5	41	7	-	48	20
-	3	-	6	1	4	11	3	-	14	21
-	1	-	2	-	1	1	3	-	4	22
-	6	1	28	5	6	36	10	-	46	23
-	3	-	2	3	8	11	5	-	16	24
2	-	-	2	1	3	6	2	-	8	25
-	-	-	2	1	1	1	3	-	4	26
-	5	-	7	3	3	11	7	-	18	27
3	8	1	8	8	13	22	19	-	41	28
-	12	-	33	5	3	44	9	-	53	29
-	-	-	1	-	-	1	-	-	1	30
-	-	-	1	-	-	1	-	-	1	31
-	7	-	12	3	4	19	7	-	26	32
-	-	-	3	-	-	2	1	-	3	33
1	-	-	1	3	1	-	6	-	6	34
-	2	-	4	-	-	5	1	-	6	35
1	-	-	4	-	3	6	2	-	8	36

* Total Abstainers.

RECAPITULATION.— *Relation of the Liquor Traffic to Pauperism: By Sex, Political Condition, and Place of Birth* — Continued.

SEX, POLITICAL CONDITION, AND PLACE OF BIRTH.	Number of Paupers	Is the person's present condition of **Pauperism** due to the use or abuse of **Intoxicating Liquors**			Liquor Habits of Paupers			
		Yes	No	Not Ascertained	Excessive Drinkers	Other Drinkers	Unknown	Total Abstainers
Males — Con.								
1 *Unknown.*	22	5	3	14	3	4	14	1
2 Ireland,	21	5	3	13	3	4	14	-
3 Not specified,	1	-	-	1	-	-	-	1
4 **Females.**	597	57	386	154	28	113	39	417
5 *Citizen Born.*	258	14	130	114	6	21	9	222
6 California,	1	-	1	-	-	-	1	-
7 Connecticut,	6	-	4	2	-	-	-	6
8 Delaware,	1	-	-	1	-	-	1	-
9 District of Columbia,	1	-	-	1	-	-	1	-
10 Maine,	11	1	7	3	1	2	1	7
11 Massachusetts,	179	8	78	93	2	15	2	160
12 Missouri,	2	-	1	1	-	-	-	2
13 New Hampshire,	9	1	7	1	1	2	-	6
14 New Jersey,	5	-	4	1	-	-	-	5
15 New York,	12	1	7	4	1	-	2	9
16 North Carolina,	1	-	1	-	-	1	-	-
17 Ohio,	4	1	2	1	1	-	-	3
18 Pennsylvania,	3	-	-	3	-	-	1	2
19 Rhode Island,	10	1	6	3	-	1	-	9
20 South Carolina,	2	1	1	-	-	-	-	2
21 Tennessee,	1	-	1	-	-	-	-	1
22 Vermont,	5	-	5	-	-	-	-	5
23 Virginia,	5	-	5	-	-	-	-	5
24 *Naturalized or Alien.*	337	43	256	38	22	92	28	195
25 Asia,	2	-	2	-	-	1	-	1
26 Austria,	4	-	3	1	-	2	1	1
27 Born at sea,	1	-	1	-	-	-	-	1
28 British Possessions, Other.	3	-	3	-	-	2	-	1
29 Canada.	29	1	22	6	-	4	5	20
30 Denmark,	2	-	1	1	-	-	1	1
31 England,	43	3	32	8	1	8	5	29
32 France,	1	-	1	-	-	1	-	-
33 Germany,	10	1	9	-	-	2	-	8
34 Ireland,	144	29	103	12	18	45	8	73
35 Italy,	5	-	4	1	-	-	1	4

RECAPITULATION.— *Relation of the Liquor Traffic to Pauperism: By Sex, Political Condition, and Place of Birth* — Continued.

	KINDS OF LIQUOR						TOBACCO		DRUGS		
Wines only	Lager Beer and Malt Liquors only	Distilled Liquors only	Two or All Kinds	Un-known	Inapplicable*		Users	Non-users	Users	Non-users	
-	-	-	7	14	1		4	18	-	22	1
-	-	-	7	14	-		4	17	-	21	2
-	-	-	-	-	1		-	1	-	1	3
10	42	2	87	39	417		35	562	-	597	4
-	3	2	22	9	222		8	250	-	258	5
-	-	-	-	1	-		-	1	-	1	6
-	-	-	-	-	6		-	6	-	6	7
-	-	-	-	1	-		-	1	-	1	8
-	-	-	-	1	-		-	1	-	1	9
-	-	1	2	1	7		1	10	-	11	10
-	2	1	14	2	160		4	175	-	179	11
-	-	-	-	-	2		-	2	-	2	12
-	-	-	3	-	6		1	8	-	9	13
-	-	-	-	-	5		-	5	-	5	14
-	-	-	1	2	9		-	12	-	12	15
-	1	-	-	-	-		-	1	-	1	16
-	-	-	1	-	3		-	4	-	4	17
-	-	-	-	1	2		-	3	-	3	18
-	-	-	1	-	9		1	9	-	10	19
-	-	-	-	-	2		-	2	-	2	20
-	-	-	-	-	1		-	1	-	1	21
-	-	-	-	-	5		1	4	-	5	22
-	-	-	-	-	5		-	5	-	5	23
10	39	-	65	28	195		27	310	-	337	24
1	-	-	-	-	1		-	2	-	2	25
-	2	-	-	1	1		-	4	-	4	26
-	-	-	-	-	1		-	1	-	1	27
-	1	-	1	-	1		-	3	-	3	28
-	-	-	4	5	20		1	28	-	29	29
-	-	-	-	1	1		-	2	-	2	30
-	3	-	6	5	29		4	39	-	43	31
1	-	-	-	-	-		-	1	-	1	32
-	1	-	1	-	8		-	10	-	10	33
1	22	-	40	8	73		16	128	-	144	34
-	-	-	-	1	4		1	4	-	5	35

* Total Abstainers.

RECAPITULATION. — *Relation of the Liquor Traffic to Pauperism: By Sex, Political Condition, and Place of Birth* — Continued.

SEX, POLITICAL CONDITION, AND PLACE OF BIRTH.	Number of Paupers	Is the person's present condition of **Pauperism** due to the use or abuse of **Intoxicating Liquors**			LIQUOR HABITS OF PAUPERS			
		Yes	No	Not Ascertained	Excessive Drinkers	Other Drinkers	Unknown	Total Abstainers
Females — Con.								
Naturalized or Alien — Con.								
1 New Brunswick, . .	16	5	10	1	2	4	1	9
2 Newfoundland, . . .	3	–	2	1	–	–	1	2
3 Nova Scotia, . . .	16	–	16	–	–	2	–	14
4 Poland, ...	3	–	2	1	–	–	2	1
5 Portugal(Western Islands),	3	–	3	–	–	2	–	1
6 Prince Edward Island, . .	12	2	10	–	–	14	–	8
7 Russia, ...	13	–	10	3	–	9	2	2
8 Scotland, ...	11	2	9	–	1	3	–	7
9 Sweden, ...	14	–	11	3	–	2	1	11
10 Switzerland, . . .	1	–	1	–	–	1	–	–
11 West Indies, . . .	1	–	1	–	–	–	–	1
12 *Unknown.*	2	–	–	2	–	–	2	–
13 Not specified, . . .	2	–	–	2	–	–	2	–
14 **Both Sexes.**	3,230	1,274	1,427	529	505	1,603	256	866
15 *Citizen Born.*	1,019	302	403	314	109	374	66	470
16 Alabama, ...	1	–	1	–	–	–	–	1
17 Arkansas, ...	1	–	1	–	–	1	–	–
18 California, ...	4	2	2	–	2	1	1	–
19 Connecticut, . . .	33	10	19	4	1	19	1	12
20 Delaware, ...	1	–	–	1	–	–	1	–
21 District of Columbia, .	3	1	1	1	–	1	1	1
22 Florida, ...	1	1	–	–	–	1	–	–
23 Georgia, ...	2	1	1	–	–	1	1	–
24 Illinois, ...	1	–	1	–	–	–	–	1
25 Indiana, ...	1	1	–	–	–	1	–	–
26 Kansas, ...	1	–	1	–	–	1	–	–
27 Kentucky, ...	2	2	–	–	1	1	–	–
28 Louisiana, ...	2	2	–	–	1	1	–	–
29 Maine, ...	64	19	30	15	11	23	9	21
30 Maryland, ...	6	2	4	–	–	4	2	–
31 Massachusetts, . . .	579	158	185	236	50	180	21	328
32 Michigan, ...	5	2	2	1	2	2	1	–
33 Minnesota, ...	4	3	–	1	1	2	1	–
34 Missouri, ...	6	2	2	2	2	–	1	3
35 New Hampshire, . .	48	16	26	6	6	24	2	16

RECAPITULATION.— *Relation of the Liquor Traffic to Pauperism: By Sex, Political Condition, and Place of Birth* — Continued.

| | KINDS OF LIQUOR | | | | | TOBACCO | | DRUGS | | |
Wines only	Lager Beer and Malt Liquors only	Distilled Liquors only	Two or All Kinds	Un-known	Inapplicable*	Users	Non-users	Users	Non-users	
-	1	-	5	1	9	-	16	-	16	1
-	-	-	-	1	2	-	3	-	3	2
-	1	-	1	-	14	1	15	-	16	3
-	-	-	-	2	1	-	3	-	3	4
2	-	-	-	-	1	-	3	-	3	5
-	2	-	2	-	8	1	11	-	12	6
5	1	-	3	2	2	1	12	-	13	7
-	2	-	2	-	7	1	10	-	11	8
-	2	-	-	1	11	1	13	-	14	9
-	1	-	-	-	-	-	1	-	1	10
-	-	-	-	-	1	-	1	-	1	11
-	-	-	-	2	-	-	2	-	2	12
-	-	-	-	2	-	-	2	-	2	13
25	417	38	1,628	256	866	2,005	1,225	3	3,227	14
-	102	8	373	66	470	481	538	3	1,016	15
-	-	-	-	-	1	-	1	-	1	16
-	1	-	-	-	-	1	-	-	1	17
-	1	-	2	1	-	3	1	-	4	18
-	5	-	15	1	12	19	14	-	33	19
-	-	-	-	1	-	-	1	-	1	20
-	-	-	1	1	1	1	2	-	3	21
-	-	1	-	-	-	1	-	-	1	22
-	1	-	-	1	-	1	1	-	2	23
-	-	-	-	-	1	-	1	-	1	24
-	-	-	1	-	-	1	-	-	1	25
-	-	-	1	-	-	1	-	-	1	26
-	-	1	1	-	-	2	-	-	2	27
-	-	-	2	-	-	2	-	-	2	28
-	9	1	24	9	21	38	26	2	62	29
-	1	-	3	2	-	3	3	-	6	30
-	42	3	185	21	328	222	357	-	579	31
-	1	-	3	1	-	4	1	-	5	32
-	-	-	3	1	-	2	2	-	4	33
-	-	-	2	1	3	2	4	-	6	34
-	7	1	22	2	16	34	14	-	48	35

* Total Abstainers.

RECAPITULATION. — *Relation of the Liquor Traffic to Pauperism : By Sex, Political Condition, and Place of Birth* — Continued.

	SEX, POLITICAL CONDITION, AND PLACE OF BIRTH.	Number of Paupers	Is the person's present condition of **Pauperism** due to the use or abuse of **Intoxicating Liquors**			LIQUOR HABITS OF PAUPERS			
			Yes	No	Not Ascertained	Excessive Drinkers	Other Drinkers	Unknown	Total Abstainers
	Both Sexes — Con.								
	Citizen Born — Con.								
1	New Jersey, . . .	19	5	10	4	3	5	1	10
2	New York, ...	102	42	39	21	18	48	14	22
3	North Carolina, . . .	6	–	5	1	–	2	–	4
4	Ohio, ...	11	3	5	3	2	4	2	3
5	Oregon, ...	2	2	–	–	1	1	–	–
6	Pennsylvania, . . .	27	7	15	5	–	17	1	9
7	Rhode Island, . . .	33	8	19	6	2	15	2	14
8	South Carolina, . . .	5	1	3	1	–	1	1	3
9	Tennessee, ...	1	–	1	–	–	–	–	1
10	Vermont, ...	26	8	12	6	3	9	3	11
11	Virginia, ...	16	2	14	–	2	5	–	9
12	West Virginia, . . .	1	1	–	–	1	–	–	–
13	Wisconsin, ...	4	1	3	–	–	4	–	–
14	United States (not specified),	1	–	1	–	–	–	–	1
15	*Naturalized or Alien.*	2,187	967	1,021	199	393	1,225	174	395
16	Africa, ...	15	–	14	1	–	13	1	1
17	Asia, ...	5	–	4	1	–	1	2	2
18	Austria (Bohemia), . .	1	–	1	–	–	1	–	–
19	Austria (not specified), .	16	2	11	3	–	11	2	3
20	Belgium, ...	2	1	1	–	–	2	–	–
21	Born at sea, . . .	2	1	1	–	1	–	–	1
22	British Possessions, Other .	7	3	4	–	1	5	–	1
23	Canada, ...	128	46	60	22	12	62	17	37
24	Cuba, ...	1	–	–	1	–	–	1	–
25	Denmark, ...	9	2	6	1	1	3	1	4
26	England, ...	260	110	122	28	46	131	25	58
27	France, ...	11	7	4	–	2	9	–	–
28	Germany, ...	44	9	32	3	2	25	2	15
29	Greece, ...	6	3	3	–	–	4	–	2
30	Ireland, ...	1,222	659	488	75	230	712	77	153
31	Italy, ...	62	11	46	5	3	47	5	7
32	New Brunswick, . .	64	30	32	2	15	33	2	14
33	Newfoundland, . . .	17	4	11	2	2	7	2	6
34	Norway, ...	4	–	3	1	–	3	–	1
35	Nova Scotia, . . .	62	21	34	7	13	24	5	20

RECAPITULATION. — *Relation of the Liquor Traffic to Pauperism : By Sex, Political Condition, and Place of Birth* — Continued.

KINDS OF LIQUOR						TOBACCO		DRUGS		
Wines only	Lager Beer and Malt Liquors only	Distilled Liquors only	Two or All Kinds	Unknown	Inapplicable*	Users	Non-users	Users	Non-users	
-	-	-	8	1	10	10	9	-	19	1
-	11	1	54	14	22	60	42	1	101	2
-	2	-	-	-	4	3	3	-	6	3
-	3	-	3	2	3	5	6	-	11	4
-	-	-	2	-	-	2	-	-	2	5
-	6	-	11	1	9	18	9	-	27	6
-	5	-	12	2	14	18	15	-	33	7
-	-	-	1	1	3	1	4	-	5	8
-	-	-	-	-	1	-	1	-	1	9
-	2	-	10	3	11	14	12	-	26	10
-	4	-	3	-	9	7	9	-	16	11
-	-	-	1	-	-	1	-	-	1	12
-	1	-	3	-	-	4	-	-	4	13
-	-	-	-	-	1	1	-	-	1	14
25	315	30	1,248	174	395	1,520	667	-	2,187	15
-	-	13	-	1	1	1	14	-	15	16
1	-	-	-	2	2	1	4	-	5	17
-	1	-	-	-	-	1	-	-	1	18
-	6	-	5	2	3	6	10	-	16	19
-	-	-	2	-	-	2	-	-	2	20
-	-	-	1	-	1	1	1	-	2	21
-	1	-	5	-	1	4	3	-	7	22
-	14	1	59	17	37	69	59	-	128	23
-	-	-	-	1	-	-	1	-	1	24
-	4	-	-	1	4	3	6	-	9	25
-	43	1	133	25	58	175	85	-	260	26
2	1	-	8	-	-	9	2	-	11	27
-	14	-	13	2	15	24	20	-	44	28
-	2	-	2	-	2	5	1	-	6	29
1	163	12	816	77	153	959	263	-	1,222	30
7	2	-	41	5	7	37	25	-	62	31
-	8	1	39	2	14	41	23	-	64	32
-	3	-	6	2	6	11	6	-	17	33
-	1	-	2	-	1	1	3	-	4	34
-	7	1	29	5	20	37	25	-	62	35

* Total Abstainers.

RECAPITULATION. — *Relation of the Liquor Traffic to Pauperism: By Sex, Political Condition, and Place of Birth* — Concluded.

SEX, POLITICAL CONDITION, AND PLACE OF BIRTH.	Number of Paupers	Is the person's present condition of **Pauperism** due to the use or abuse of **Intoxicating Liquors**			Liquor Habits of Paupers			
		Yes	No	Not Ascertained	Excessive Drinkers	Other Drinkers	Unknown	Total Abstainers
Both Sexes — Con.								
Naturalized or Alien — Con.								
1 Poland, ...	19	–	13	6	–	5	5	9
2 Portugal(Western Islands),	11	–	10	1	–	6	1	4
3 Portugal (not specified), .	4	2	–	2	2	–	1	1
4 Prince Edward Island, .	30	6	19	5	1	15	3	11
5 Russia, ...	54	9	28	17	–	29	10	15
6 Scotland, ...	64	27	30	7	5	44	5	10
7 South America, . . .	1	1	–	–	1	–	–	–
8 Spain, ...	1	1	–	–	1	–	–	–
9 Sweden, ...	40	7	27	6	3	18	4	15
10 Switzerland, . . .	4	2	2	–	1	3	–	–
11 Turkey, ...	6	–	3	3	–	2	3	1
12 Wales, ...	6	2	4	–	–	6	–	–
13 West Indies, . . .	9	1	8	–	1	4	–	4

We summarize the facts as to both sexes only. Of the citizen-born paupers, 1,019 in all, Massachusetts furnishes the largest number, namely, 579; the others being distributed among nearly all the States in the Union, those immediately surrounding Massachusetts having the largest quota. Of the naturalized or alien, the largest number come from Ireland, the next largest from England, and the next largest from Canada. Of the 579 paupers reported as born in Massachusetts, 158 trace their pauperism to the use of intoxicating liquor, while 230 are either excessive drinkers or otherwise addicted to the drink habit, 328 being total abstainers. Of the paupers of Irish nativity, who number 1,222, 659 report their present condition of pauperism as due to the use of intoxicants, while the number addicted to the drink habit includes 280 excessive drinkers and 712 other drinkers, or 992 in all, who are reported as using intoxicants, the total

RECAPITULATION. — *Relation of the Liquor Traffic to Pauperism: By Sex, Political Condition, and Place of Birth* — Concluded.

KINDS OF LIQUOR						TOBACCO		DRUGS		
Wines only	Lager Beer and Malt Liquors only	Distilled Liquors only	Two or All Kinds	Un-known	Inappli-cable*	Users	Non-users	Users	Non-users	
-	3	-	2	5	9	11	8	-	19	1
4	-	-	2	1	4	6	5	-	11	2
-	-	-	2	1	1	1	3	-	4	3
-	7	-	9	3	11	12	18	-	30	4
8	9	1	11	10	15	23	31	-	54	5
-	14	-	35	5	10	45	19	-	64	6
-	-	-	1	-	-	1	-	-	1	7
-	-	-	1	-	-	1	-	-	1	8
-	9	-	12	4	15	20	20	-	40	9
-	1	-	3	-	-	2	2	-	4	10
1	-	-	1	3	1	-	6	-	6	11
-	2	-	4	-	-	5	1	-	6	12
1	-	-	4	-	4	6	3	-	9	13

* Total Abstainers.

abstainers numbering 153. Of the 260 paupers born in England, 110 attribute their pauperism to the use of intoxicants, their being among them 46 excessive drinkers, 131 drinkers of other degree, and 58 total abstainers.

We do not carry the analysis farther, although the same line of facts is presented as to paupers of each nativity shown in the table.

CRIME.

The first table relating to the influence of the use of liquor upon crime shows the total number of criminals convicted of various offences in the courts of the Commonwealth during the twelve months covered by the investigation, classified by age periods, and so as to show the number convicted of drunkenness alone, the number convicted of drunkenness united with other crimes, and the number convicted of crimes other than drunkenness, by sex. This table follows:

Crime ; Sex and Degree of Crime: By Age Periods.

	SEX AND DEGREE OF CRIME.	AGE PERIODS		
		10-14	15-19	20-29
1	Males.	55	1,159	7,994
2	Drunkenness, ...	-	226	4,569
3	Drunkenness and other crimes, . . .	1	23	291
4	Other crimes, ...	54	910	3,134
5	Females.	1	97	1,054
6	Drunkenness, ...	1	15	605
7	Drunkenness and other crimes, . . .	-	-	14
8	Other crimes, ...	-	82	435
9	BOTH SEXES.	56	1,256	9,048
10	Drunkenness, ...	1	241	5,174
11	Drunkenness and other crimes, . . .	1	23	305
12	Other crimes, ...	54	992	3,569

The table shows that the total number of criminal convictions, of all classes, for the year was 26,672, including 23,581 males and 3,091 females. Of the males, 55 were found in the age period 10-14, and of the females one was found in this age period. This one female was convicted of drunkenness; and of the males in this age period, one was convicted of drunkenness and other crimes, while 54 were convicted of crimes other than drunkenness. In the age period 15-19, 1,159 males and 97 females were found. Of the males, 226 were convicted of drunkenness alone, 23 others of drunkenness and other crimes, and 910 of other crimes only. Of the females, 15 were convicted of drunkenness and 82 of other crimes. In the age period 20-29, 7,994 males were found, of whom 4,569 were convicted of drunkenness alone, 291 of drunkenness and other crimes, and 3,134 of other crimes only. In this age period 1,054 females appear, of whom 605 were convicted of drunkenness alone, 14 of drunkenness and other crimes, and 435 of other crimes only. In the age period 30-39, 7,295 males were found, of whom 5,229 were convicted of drunkenness alone, 181 of drunkenness and other crimes, and 1,885 of other crimes only. The females in this

Crime; Sex and Degree of Crime: By Age Periods.

AGE PERIODS						Total	
30-39	40-49	50-59	60-79	80+	Unknown		
7,295	4,390	2,034	644	6	4	23,581	1
5,229	3,402	1,616	492	6	3	15,543	2
181	82	22	8	-	-	608	3
1,885	906	396	144	-	1	7,430	4
1,027	588	227	91	6	-	3,091	5
722	433	184	67	5	-	2,032	6
17	12	6	-	-	-	49	7
288	143	37	24	1	-	1,010	8
8,322	4,978	2,261	735	12	4	26,672	9
5,951	3,835	1,800	559	11	3	17,575	10
198	94	28	8	-	-	657	11
2,173	1,049	433	168	1	1	8,440	12

age period numbered 1,027, of whom 722 were convicted of
drunkenness alone, 17 of drunkenness and other crimes, and
288 of other crimes only. In the age period 40–49, 4,390
males appear, of whom 3,402 were convicted of drunkenness
alone, 82 of drunkenness and other crimes, and 906 of other
crimes only. There were found 588 females in this age
period, of whom 433 were convicted of drunkenness alone,
12 of drunkenness and other crimes, and 143 of other crimes
only. There were 2,034 males in the age period 50–59; of
these, 1,616 were convicted of drunkenness alone, 22 of
drunkenness and other crimes, and 396 of other crimes only.
In the same age period we find 227 females, of whom 184 were
convicted of drunkenness alone, six of drunkenness and other
crimes, and 37 of other crimes only. In the age period 60–79
there are 644 males, of whom 492 were convicted of drunkenness alone, eight of drunkenness and other crimes, and 144
of other crimes only. There are 91 females in this age
period, of whom 67 were convicted of drunkenness alone,
and 24 of other crimes only. There were six male criminals
over 80 years of age, all of whom were convicted of drunkenness. There were also six females over 80 years of age, five

of whom were convicted of drunkenness, and one of other
crimes. Facts as to ages were unknown for four males, three
of whom were convicted of drunkenness, and one of other
crimes. In the aggregate, therefore, it is shown that of the
23,581 male criminals, 15,543 were convicted of drunkenness alone, 608 of drunkenness united with other crimes, and
7,430 of other crimes only. As to the females, who number
3,091, 2,032 were convicted of drunkenness, and 49 of drunkenness united with other crimes, 1,010 being convicted of
other crimes only. Out of the 26,672 cases of criminal conviction, 17,575 were convictions for drunkenness, 657 for
drunkenness united with other crimes, while 8,440 were convictions for other crimes. Upon the face of the returns,

Crime; Sex, Political Condition, and Degree of Crime: By Age Periods.

	SEX, POLITICAL CONDITION, AND DEGREE OF CRIME.	AGE PERIODS		
		10-14	15-19	20-29
	MALES.			
1	*Citizen Born.*	38	890	5,116
2	Drunkenness, ...	–	174	2,882
3	Drunkenness and other crimes, . . .	1	20	171
4	Other crimes, ...	37	696	2,063
5	*Naturalized.*	–	–	632
6	Drunkenness, ...	–	–	382
7	Drunkenness and other crimes, . . .	–	–	29
8	Other crimes, ...	–	–	221
9	*Alien.*	17	269	2,246
10	Drunkenness, ...	–	52	1,305
11	Drunkenness and other crimes, . . .	–	3	91
12	Other crimes, ...	17	214	850
13	**AGGREGATES.**	55	1,159	7,994
14	Drunkenness, ...	–	226	4,569
15	Drunkenness and other crimes, . .	1	23	291
16	Other crimes, ...	54	910	3,134
	FEMALES.			
17	*Citizen Born.*	1	70	590
18	Drunkenness, ...	1	12	335
19	Drunkenness and other crimes, . . .	–	–	7
20	Other crimes, ...	–	58	248

therefore, without taking into account the effect which liquor may have had upon crimes other than drunkenness, a question which we shall consider hereafter in connection with other tables, it appears that out of the grand total, 18,232 convictions, or 68.36 per cent of the whole number, were for drunkenness alone or for drunkenness in connection with other crimes, while 8,440 or 31.64 per cent of the whole number, were for other crimes only. The proportion which drunkenness bears to the total body of crime is thus clearly apparent.

The next table shows the political condition of the criminals, classified by age periods and according to the nature of the crime.

Crime; Sex, Political Condition, and Degree of Crime: By Age Periods.

30-39	40-49	50-59	60-79	80+	Unknown	Total	
4,039	1,970	615	152	4	1	12,825	1
2,866	1,494	481	104	4	1	8,006	2
109	35	9	1	-	-	346	3
1,064	441	125	47	-	-	4,473	4
1,106	1,046	692	248	1	1	3,726	5
819	846	569	199	1	1	· 2,817	6
30	17	3	4	-	-	83	7
257	183	120	45	-	-	826	8
2,150	1,374	727	244	1	2	7,030	9
1,544	1,062	566	189	1	1	4,720	10
42	30	10	3	-	-	179	11
564	282	151	52	-	1	2,131	12
7,295	4,390	2,034	644	6	4	23,581	13
5,229	3,402	1,616	492	6	3	15,543	14
181	82	22	8	-	-	608	15
1,885	906	396	144	-	1	7,430	16
435	169	35	6	-	-	1,306	17
315	114	29	4	-	-	810	18
6	4	1	-	-	-	18	19
114	51	5	2	-	-	478	20

Crime; Sex, Political Condition, and Degree of Crime: By Age Periods
— Concluded.

SEX, POLITICAL CONDITION, AND DEGREE OF CRIME.	AGE PERIODS		
	10-14	15-19	20-29
FEMALES — Con.			
1 *Alien.*	-	27	464
2 Drunkenness, ...	-	3	270
3 Drunkenness and other crimes, . . .	-	-	7
4 Other crimes, ...	-	24	187
5 AGGREGATES.	1	97	1,054
6 Drunkenness, ...	1	15	605
7 Drunkenness and other crimes, . . .	-	-	14
8 Other crimes, ...	-	82	435
BOTH SEXES.			
9 *Citizen Born.*	39	960	5,706
10 Drunkenness, ...	1	186	3,217
11 Drunkenness and other crimes, . . .	1	20	178
12 Other crimes, ...	37	754	2,311
13 *Naturalized.*	-	-	632
14 Drunkenness, ...	-	-	382
15 Drunkenness and other crimes, . . .	-	-	29
16 Other crimes, ...	-	-	221
17 *Alien.*	17	296	2,710
18 Drunkenness, ...	-	55	1,575
19 Drunkenness and other crimes, . .	-	3	98
20 Other crimes, ...	17	238	1,037
21 AGGREGATES.	56	1,256	9,048
22 Drunkenness, ...	1	241	5,174
23 Drunkenness and other crimes, . . .	1	23	305
24 Other crimes, ...	54	992	3,569

Bearing in mind that the total number of convictions was 26,672, we find that of the 23,581 male cases included in this aggregate, 12,825 were citizen born, 3,726 naturalized, and 7,030 alien. Of the citizen-born males, 8,006 were convicted of drunkenness alone, 346 of drunkenness and other crimes, while 4,473 were convicted of other crimes only. Of the naturalized males, 2,817 were convicted of drunkenness alone,

Crime; Sex, Political Condition, and Degree of Crime: By Age Periods
— Concluded.

AGE PERIODS						Total	
30-39	40-49	50-59	60-79	80+	Unknown		
592	419	192	85	6	-	1,785	1
407	319	155	63	5	-	1,222	2
11	8	5	-	-	-	31	3
174	92	32	22	1	-	532	4
1,027	588	227	91	6	-	3,091	5
722	433	184	67	5	-	2,032	6
17	12	6	-	-	-	49	7
288	143	37	24	1	-	1,010	8
4,474	2,139	650	158	4	1	14,131	9
3,181	1,608	510	108	4	1	8,816	10
115	39	10	1	-	-	364	11
1,178	492	130	49	-	-	4,951	12
1,106	1,046	692	248	1	1	3,726	13
819	846	569	199	1	1	2,817	14
30	17	3	4	-	-	83	15
257	183	120	45	-	-	826	16
2,742	1,793	919	329	7	2	8,815	17
1,951	1,381	721	252	6	1	5,942	18
53	38	15	3	-	-	210	19
738	374	183	74	1	1	2,663	20
8,322	4,978	2,261	735	12	4	26,672	21
5,951	3,835	1,800	559	11	3	17,575	22
198	94	28	8	-	-	657	23
2,173	1,049	433	168	1	1	8,440	24

83 of drunkenness and other crimes, while only 826 were convicted of other crimes. Of the alien males, 4,720 were convicted of drunkenness alone, 179 of drunkenness and other crimes, and 2,131 of other crimes only. The females who were citizen born numbered 1,306, while the alien females numbered 1,785, the terms "citizen born" and "alien" as here used being equivalent to native born and foreign born,

respectively.   Of the citizen-born females, 810 were convicted of drunkenness alone, 18 of drunkenness and other
crimes, and 478 of other crimes only.   Of the alien females,
1,222 were convicted of drunkenness alone, 31 of drunkenness
and other crimes, and 532 of other crimes only.   Considering the citizen-born criminals of both sexes, who numbered
14,131, 8,816, or 62.39 per cent of the total number, were convicted of drunkenness alone ; 364, or 2.58 per cent, of drunkenness united with other crimes ; and 4,951, or 35.03 per cent,

*Crime; Degree of Crime and Parent Nativity: By Sex and Political
Condition.*

DEGREE OF CRIME AND PARENT NATIVITY.	MALES			
	Citizen Born	Naturalized	Alien	Total
1 DRUNKENNESS.	8,006	2,817	4,720	15,543
2 Both parents *native*, ...	1,894	7	200	2,101
3 Both parents *foreign*, ...	5,553	2,799	4,499	12,851
4 Both parents *unknown*, . . .	43	2	6	51
5 Father *native*, mother *foreign*, . .	218	6	5	229
6 Father *foreign*, mother *native*, . .	271	1	7	279
7 Father *native*, mother *unknown*, .	9	–	–	9
8 Father *foreign*, mother *unknown*. .	3	2	1	6
9 Father *unknown*, mother *native*, .	8	–	–	8
10 Father *unknown*, mother *foreign*, .	7	–	2	9
11 DRUNKENNESS AND OTHER CRIMES.	346	83	179	608
12 Both parents *native*, ...	64	1	–	65
13 Both parents *foreign*, ...	245	82	179	506
14 Both parents *unknown*, . . .	2	–	–	2
15 Father *native*, mother *foreign*, . .	11	–	–	11
16 Father *foreign*, mother *native*, . .	22	–	–	22
17 Father *native*, mother *unknown*, .	–	–	–	–
18 Father *foreign*, mother *unknown*, .	–	–	–	–
19. Father *unknown*, mother *native*, .	2	–	–	2
20 Father *unknown*, mother *foreign*, .	–	–	–	–
21 OTHER CRIMES.	4,473	826	2,131	7,430
22 Both parents *native*, ...	1,568	7	10	1,585
23 Both parents *foreign*, ...	2,371	817	2,090	5,278
24 Both parents *unknown*, . . .	74	–	5	79
25 Father *native*, mother *foreign*, . .	199	1	11	211
26 Father *foreign*, mother *native*, . .	199	–	8	207
27 Father *native*, mother *unknown*, .	20	–	–	20
28 Father *foreign*, mother *unknown*, .	11	1	5	17

of other crimes only. Of the naturalized criminals, who numbered 3,726, 2,817, or 75.60 per cent, were convicted of drunkenness alone; 83, or 2.23 per cent, of drunkenness united with other crimes; and 826, or 22.17 per cent, of other crimes only. Of the alien criminals, who in the aggregate numbered 8,815, 5,942, or 67.41 per cent, were convicted of drunkenness alone; 210, or 2.38 per cent, of drunkenness united with other crimes; and 2,663, or 30.21 per cent, of other crimes only.

The next table relates to the parent nativity of the criminals.

Crime; Degree of Crime and Parent Nativity: By Sex and Political Condition.

FEMALES			BOTH SEXES				
Citizen Born	Alien	Total	Citizen Born	Naturalized	Alien	Total	
810	1,222	2,032	8,816	2,817	5,942	17,575	1
158	2	160	2,052	7	202	2,261	2
575	1,206	1,781	6,128	2,799	5,705	14,632	3
8	2	10	51	2	8	61	4
28	5	33	246	6	10	262	5
38	6	44	309	1	13	323	6
1	-	1	10	-	-	10	7
-	-	-	3	2	1	6	8
1	-	1	9	-	-	9	9
1	1	2	8	-	3	11	10
18	31	49	364	83	210	657	11
5	-	5	69	1	-	70	12
12	31	43	257	82	210	549	13
-	-	-	2	-	-	2	14
-	-	-	11	-	-	11	15
1	-	1	23	-	-	23	16
-	-	-	-	-	-	-	17
-	-	-	-	-	-	-	18
-	-	-	2	-	-	2	19
-	-	-	-	-	-	-	20
478	532	1,010	4,951	826	2,663	8,440	21
170	3	173	1,738	7	13	1,758	22
230	515	745	2,601	817	2,605	6,023	23
12	2	14	86	-	7	93	24
23	..	23	222	1	11	234	25
28	10	38	227	-	18	245	26
2	-	2	22	-	-	22	27
1	-	1	12	1	5	18	28

Crime; Degree of Crime and Parent Nativity: By Sex and Political Condition — Concluded.

DEGREE OF CRIME AND PARENT NATIVITY.	MALES			
	Citizen Born	Naturalized	Alien	Total
OTHER CRIMES — Con.				
1 Father *unknown*, mother *native*, .	22	–	–	22
2 Father *unknown*, mother *foreign*, .	9	–	2	11
3 AGGREGATES: ALL CRIMES.	12,825	3,726	7,030	23,581
4 Both parents *native*, ...	3,526	15	210	3,751
5 Both parents *foreign*, ...	8,169	3,698	6,768	18,635
6 Both parents *unknown*, . . .	119	2	11	132
7 Father *native*, mother *foreign*, .	428	7	16	451
8 Father *foreign*, mother *native*, .	492	1	15	508
9 Father *native*, mother *unknown*, .	29	–	–	29
10 Father *foreign*, mother *unknown*, .	14	3	6	23
11 Father *unknown*, mother *native*, .	32	–	–	32
12 Father *unknown*, mother *foreign*, .	16	–	4	20

This table shows the full extent of the foreign influence, both with respect to the total body of crime, and also with respect to drunkenness. Both sexes in the aggregate, and each sex separately, are classified so as to show the citizen born, naturalized, and alien independently, the number of each class being as previously cited. Of the 15,543 males who were convicted of drunkenness only, 2,101 had both parents native; on the other hand, 12,851 had both parents foreign, 17 had one parent native and one unknown, and the others, except 51 for whom the facts were not obtainable, had either a foreign mother or a foreign father. Of the females convicted of drunkenness only, who in the aggregate number 2,032, 160 had both parents native, 1,781 had both parents foreign, while two had one parent native and one unknown; and the others, except 10 for whom the facts as to parentage were not ascertained, had either a foreign father or a foreign mother. It follows, therefore, that in the aggregate, out of the 17,575 convictions for drunkenness only, 2,261, or 12.86 per cent, had both parents native, while 14,632, or 83.25 per cent, had both parents foreign; 19 had one parent native and one unknown, and the others, excluding 61 for whom the facts as to parent nativity were un-

Crime; Degree of Crime and Parent Nativity: By Sex and Political Condition — Concluded.

FEMALES			BOTH SEXES				
Citizen Born	Alien	Total	Citizen Born	Naturalized	Alien	Total	
9	-	9	31	-	-	31	1
3	2	5	12	-	4	16	2
1,306	1,785	3,091	14,131	3,726	8,815	26,672	3
333	5	338	3,859	15	215	4,089	4
817	1,752	2,569	8,986	3,698	8,520	21,204	5
20	4	24	139	2	15	156	6
51	5	56	479	7	21	507	7
67	16	83	559	1	31	591	8
3	-	3	32	-	-	32	9
1	-	1	15	3	6	24	10
10	-	10	42	-	-	42	11
4	3	7	20	-	7	27	12

known, aggregating 602, or 3.43 per cent, of the total number, had either father or mother foreign. Of the 608 males convicted of drunkenness in connection with other crimes, 65 had both parents native, while 506 had both parents foreign, two having one parent native and one unknown; the others having either a foreign father or a foreign mother, except two, for whom the facts were unknown. Of the 49 females convicted of drunkenness in connection with other crimes, five had both parents native, and 43 had both parents foreign; in the single remaining case, the father was foreign and the mother native. Summarizing the 657 cases of convictions for drunkenness united with other crimes, we find that 70, or 10.65 per cent, had both parents native, while 549, or 83.56 per cent, had both parents foreign, and 34, or 5.18 per cent, had either father or mother foreign.

It remains to consider the relation of foreign parent nativity to crimes other than those connected with drunkenness. It will suffice to use the summary for both sexes. The number of convictions for these other crimes being 8,440, 1,758, or 20.83 per cent, had both parents native, 6,023, or 71.36 per cent, had both parents foreign, 53 had one parent native and one unknown, while 513, or 6.08 per cent, had either a foreign father or a foreign mother; the facts in 93 cases being unknown.

For the purpose of bringing out the influence of liquor upon crimes other than drunkenness, we now introduce a series of four tables, of which the first contains the tabulated replies to the question " Was the criminal under the influence of liquor at the time the crime was committed."

Was the Criminal under the Influence of Liquor at the Time the Crime was committed.

SEX, DEGREE OF CRIME, AND POLITICAL CONDITION.	Yes	No	Not Ascertained	Total
MALES.	19,509	4,065	7	23,581
Drunkenness, ...	15,541	2	–	15,543
Citizen born, ...	8,005	1	–	8,006
Naturalized, ...	2,817	–	–	2,817
Alien, ...	4,719	1	–	4,720
Drunkenness and *other crimes,* .	601	7	–	608
Citizen born, ...	342	4	–	346
Naturalized, . . .	82	1	–	83
Alien, ...	177	2	–	179
Other crimes, ...	3,367	4,056	7	7,430
Citizen born, ...	2,031	2,439	3	4,473
Naturalized, ...	443	382	1	826
Alien, ...	893	1,235	3	2,131
FEMALES.	2,354	735	2	3,091
Drunkenness, . . .	2,032	–	–	2,032
Citizen born, . . .	810	–	–	810
Alien, ...	1,222	–	–	1,222
Drunkenness and *other crimes,* .	49	–	–	49
Citizen born, . . .	18	–	–	18
Alien, . .	31	–	–	31
Other crimes, . .	273	735	2	1,010
Citizen born, . .	121	356	1	478
Alien, . . .	152	379	1	532
BOTH SEXES.	21,863	4,800	9	26,672
Drunkenness, . .	17,573	2	–	17,575
Citizen born, .	8,815	1	–	8,816
Naturalized, .	2,817	–	–	2,817
Alien, . .	5,941	1	–	5,942

Was the Criminal under the Influence of Liquor at the Time the Crime was committed — Concluded.

SEX, DEGREE OF CRIME, AND POLITICAL CONDITION.	Yes	No	Not Ascertained	Total
BOTH SEXES — Con.				
Drunkenness and *other crimes,* .	650	7	-	657
Citizen born, ...	360	4	-	364
Naturalized, ...	82	1	-	83
Alien, ...	208	2	-	210
Other crimes, ...	3,640	4,791	9	8,440
Citizen born, ...	2,152	2,795	4	4,951
Naturalized, ...	443	382	1	826
Alien, ...	1,045	1,614	4	2,663

Referring to the aggregates, in which both sexes are included, we find that out of the 26,672 cases, the reply to this question was " Yes " in 21,863 instances, this, of course, including 17,573 cases of drunkenness and 650 cases of drunkenness united with other crimes, in which an affirmative reply would naturally be expected on account of the character of the offence. The reply was " No " in 4,800 cases. This includes two cases of drunkenness and seven in which drunkenness was united with other crimes. That is to say, in nine cases in which drunkenness constituted part of the offence for which the criminal was sentenced, the criminal's own reply was that he was not under the influence of liquor at the time the crime was committed. This may be taken to mean that he denied his guilt of the crime for which he was convicted. This number of cases, however, is insignificant compared with the total number of cases. Eliminating the convictions for drunkenness, and for drunkenness and other crimes, we have 8,440 convictions for other crimes. When the conviction is for drunkenness and for drunkenness in connection with other crimes, the effect of the influence of liquor is clear. With respect to these 8,440 other convictions, information was not ascertained in nine cases only. Of the others, in 3,640 cases an affirmative answer was returned to the question, indicating that the criminal was under the influence of liquor at the time the crime was committed. In 4,791 cases the reply was that he was not under the influence of liquor. To put the matter in other words, we find that out of the total number of convictions, 68.73 per cent were directly due to drunkenness and to drunkenness in connection with other crimes, and 81.97 per cent were crimes committed while the criminal was under the influence of liquor, leaving only 18.03 per cent of the total number of convictions to which the influence of liquor cannot be traced. The table enables the reader to observe the relation of political condition and of sex to the special point of inquiry to which the table relates, but this need not be followed out in the analysis.

The next table contains the replies to the question "Was the criminal sober or in liquor when he formed the intent to commit the crime."

Was the Criminal Sober or in Liquor when he formed the Intent to commit the Crime.

SEX, DEGREE OF CRIME, AND POLITICAL CONDITION.	Sober	In Liquor	Not Ascertained	Total
MALES.	4,118	3,899	15,564	23,581
Drunkenness, ...	–	–	15,543	15,543
Citizen born, ...	–	–	8,006	8,006
Naturalized, ...	–	–	2,817	2,817
Alien, ...	–	–	4,720	4,720
Drunkenness and other crimes, .	12	596	–	608
Citizen born, ...	8	338	–	346
Naturalized, ...	–	83	–	83
Alien, ...	4	175	–	179
Other crimes, . . .	4,106	3,303	21	7,430
Citizen born, . . .	2,453	2,013	7	4,473
Naturalized, . .	422	400	4	826
Alien, . . .	1,231	890	10	2,131
FEMALES.	748	307	2,036	3,091
Drunkenness, ...	–	–	2,032	2,032
Citizen born, ...	–	–	810	810
Alien, ...	–	–	1,222	1,222
Drunkenness and other crimes, .	2	45	2	49
Citizen born, .	–	16	2	18
Alien, ...	2	29	–	31
Other crimes, ...	746	262	2	1,010
Citizen born, ...	360	116	2	478
Alien, ...	386	146	–	532

Was the Criminal Sober or in Liquor when he formed the Intent to commit the Crime — Concluded.

SEX, DEGREE OF CRIME, AND POLITICAL CONDITION.	Sober	In Liquor	Not Ascertained	Total
BOTH SEXES.	4,866	4,206	17,600	26,672
Drunkenness, ...	–	–	17,575	17,575
Citizen born, ...	–	–	8,816	8,816
Naturalized, ...	–	–	2,817	2,817
Alien, ...	–	–	5,942	5,942
Drunkenness and *other crimes,* .	14	641	2	657
Citizen born, ...	8	354	2	364
Naturalized, ...	–	83	–	83
Alien, ...	6	204	–	210
Other crimes, ...	4,852	3,565	23	8,440
Citizen born, ...	2,813	2,129	9	4,951
Naturalized, ...	422	400	4	826
Alien, ...	1,617	1,036	10	2,663

Referring to the aggregates, it should first be pointed out that the 17,575 cases of drunkenness are included in the table under the head of cases for which the information under this inquiry was not ascertained, and they may therefore be disregarded in our analysis. As to the 657 convictions for drunkenness combined with other crimes, the replies indicate that in 14 instances the criminal was sober when the intent was formed to commit the crime; in 641 cases the criminal was in liquor when the intent was formed, while in two cases the facts were not ascertained. As to the 8,440 convictions for crimes other than drunkenness, the replies indicate that in 4,852 cases, or 57.49 per cent, the criminal was sober when the intent was formed, while in 3,565 cases the criminal was in liquor, information in 23 cases being unascertained. As in the preceding table, the facts are classified under sex, degree of crime, and political condition.

In the next table, a different phase of the question is presented. In this the replies to the following interrogatory are tabulated: "Did the intemperate habits of the criminal lead to a condition which induced the crime."

Did the Intemperate Habits of the Criminal lead to a Condition which induced the Crime.

SEX, DEGREE OF CRIME, AND POLITICAL CONDITION.	Yes	No	Not Ascertained	Total
MALES.	20,070	3,497	14	23,581
Drunkenness, ...	15,536	5	2	15,543
Citizen born, ...	8,003	3	-	8,006
Naturalized, ...	2,817	-	-	2,817
Alien, ...	4,716	2	2	4,720
Drunkenness and *other crimes*, .	603	5	-	608
Citizen born, ...	343	3	-	346
Naturalized, ...	82	1	-	83
Alien, ...	178	1	-	179
Other crimes, ...	3,931	3,487	12	7,430
Citizen born, ...	2,338	2,131	4	4,473
Naturalized, ...	543	282	1	826
Alien, ...	1,050	1,074	7	2,131
FEMALES.	2,444	645	2	3,091
Drunkenness, ...	2,032	-	-	2,032
Citizen born, . . .	810	-	-	810
Alien, ...	1,222	-	-	1,222
Drunkenness and *other crimes*, .	49	-	-	49
Citizen born, ...	18	-	-	18
Alien, ...	31	-	-	31
Other crimes, . . .	363	645	2	1,010
Citizen born, . . .	165	311	2	478
Alien, . . .	198	334	-	532
BOTH SEXES.	22,514	4,142	16	26,672
Drunkenness, . . .	17,568	5	2	17,575
Citizen born, . .	8,813	3	-	8,816
Naturalized, . . .	2,817	-	-	2,817
Alien, ...	5,938	2	2	5,942
Drunkenness and *other crimes*, .	652	5	-	657
Citizen born, ...	361	3	-	364
Naturalized, ...	82	1	-	83
Alien, ...	209	1	-	210
Other crimes, . . .	4,294	4,132	14	8,440
Citizen born, ...	2,503	2,442	6	4,951
Naturalized, ...	543	282	1	826
Alien, ...	1,248	1,408	7	2,663

We confine our analysis to the aggregates for both sexes. Out of the 26,672 cases, an affirmative reply was made in 22,514, and a negative reply in 4,142, the facts being un-

known in 16 instances. Out of the 22,514 cases in which the
intemperate habits of the criminal led to a condition which
induced the crime, 17,568 were cases of drunkenness alone,
and 652 of drunkenness united with other crimes, while 4,294
were of other crimes only. Hence, disregarding the 18,220
cases in which drunkenness is a factor, and in which an affirmative reply is therefore necessary, there are 4,294 cases of conviction for other crimes, or 50.88 per cent of all the convictions
for crimes other than drunkenness, in which the intemperate
habits of the criminal led to a condition which induced the
crime.

The final table of this series contains the replies to the
question, "Did the intemperate habits of others lead the
criminal to a condition which induced the crime."

Did the Intemperate Habits of Others lead the Criminal to a Condition which
induced the Crime.

SEX, DEGREE OF CRIME, AND POLITICAL CONDITION.	Yes	No	Not Ascertained	Total
MALES.	14,231	9,160	190	23,581
Drunkenness, ...	10,617	4,781	145	15,543
Citizen born, ...	5,671	2,273	62	8,006
Naturalized, ...	1,907	894	16	2,817
Alien, ...	3,039	1,614	67	4,720
Drunkenness and *other crimes,* .	441	161	6	608
Citizen born, ...	256	85	5	346
Naturalized, ...	59	23	1	83
Alien, ...	126	53	–	179
Other crimes, ...	3,173	4,218	39	7,430
Citizen born, ...	1,918	2,538	17	4,473
Naturalized, ...	438	385	3	826
Alien, ...	817	1,295	19	2,131
FEMALES.	1,884	1,180	27	3,091
Drunkenness, ...	1,406	603	23	2,032
Citizen born, ...	613	190	7	810
Alien, ...	793	413	16	1,222
Drunkenness and *other crimes,* .	40	9	–	49
Citizen born, ...	17	1	–	18
Alien, ...	23	8	–	31
Other crimes, ...	438	568	4	1,010
Citizen born, ...	201	275	2	478
Alien, ...	237	293	2	532

Did the Intemperate Habits of Others lead the Criminal to a Condition which induced the Crime — Concluded.

SEX, DEGREE OF CRIME, AND POLITICAL CONDITION.	Yes	No	Not Ascertained	Total
BOTH SEXES.	16,115	10,340	217	26,672
Drunkenness, ...	12,023	5,384	168	17,575
Citizen born, ...	6,284	2,463	69	8,816
Naturalized, ...	1,907	894	16	2,817
Alien, ...	3,832	2,027	83	5,942
Drunkenness and *other crimes,* .	481	170	6	657
Citizen born, ...	273	86	5	364
Naturalized, ...	59	23	1	83
Alien, ...	149	61	–	210
Other crimes, ...	3,611	4,786	43	8,440
Citizen born, ...	2,119	2,813	19	4,951
Naturalized, ...	438	385	3	826
Alien, ...	1,054	1,588	21	2,663

In the replies to this question, the influence of persons other than the criminal is brought out. Out of the 26,672 cases, 16,115 replied that the intemperate habits of others were influential in leading the criminal to a condition which induced the crime. On the other hand, 10,340 returned a negative reply to this question. The information in 217 cases is lacking. Of the cases in which the intemperate habits of others were influential, 12,023 were cases of drunkenness only, and 481 of drunkenness and other crimes; but 3,611, or 42.78 per cent of the total number of convictions for crimes other than drunkenness, are also found in this class.

We next present a table showing in detail the habits of the criminals with respect to the use of liquor. This table is identical in form with that previously presented relating to paupers, and the explanation of the classification employed in the pauper table applies also to this.

Crime; Sex, Degree of Crime, and Liquor Habits of Criminals: By Age Periods.

AGE PERIOD: 10-14.

SEX AND DEGREE OF CRIME.	Number addicted to the Use of Intoxicating Liquors	Excessive Drinkers	Social Drinkers	Home Drinkers	Periodical Drinkers	Occasional Drinkers	Aggregate Number of Drinking Conditions	Average Number of Drinking Conditions	Liquor Habits Un- known	Total Ab- stainers
Males.	3	-	3	1	-	3	7	2.33	-	52
Drunkenness and other crimes, .	1	-	1	-	-	1	2	2.00	-	-
Other crimes, .	2	-	2	1	-	2	5	2.50	-	52
Females.	1	-	1	-	1	1	3	3.00	-	-
Drunkenness, .	1	-	1	-	1	1	3	3.00	-	-
BOTH SEXES.	4	-	4	1	1	4	10	2.50	-	52
Drunkenness, .	1	-	1	-	1	1	3	3.00	-	-
Drunkenness and other crimes, .	1	-	1	-	-	1	2	2.00	-	-
Other crimes, .	2	-	2	1	-	2	5	2.50	-	52

AGE PERIOD: 15-19.

SEX AND DEGREE OF CRIME.	Number addicted	Excessive Drinkers	Social Drinkers	Home Drinkers	Periodical Drinkers	Occasional Drinkers	Aggregate Number	Average Number	Liquor Habits Unknown	Total Abstainers
Males.	625	27	573	208	279	565	1,652	2.64	-	534
Drunkenness, .	226	17	200	92	137	200	646	2.42	-	-
Drunkenness and other crimes, .	23	-	23	11	20	23	77	3.25	-	-
Other crimes, .	376	10	350	105	122	342	929	2.47	-	534
Females.	51	7	38	18	13	42	118	2.31	-	46
Drunkenness, .	15	3	10	6	7	11	37	2.47	-	-
Other crimes, .	36	4	28	12	6	31	81	2.25	-	46
BOTH SEXES.	676	34	611	226	292	607	1,770	2.62	-	580
Drunkenness, .	241	20	210	98	144	211	683	2.83	-	-
Drunkenness and other crimes, .	23	-	23	11	20	23	77	3.25	-	-
Other crimes, .	412	14	378	117	128	373	1,010	2.45	-	580

AGE PERIOD: 20-29.

SEX AND DEGREE OF CRIME.	Number addicted	Excessive Drinkers	Social Drinkers	Home Drinkers	Periodical Drinkers	Occasional Drinkers	Aggregate Number	Average Number	Liquor Habits Unknown	Total Abstainers
Males.	7,565	923	6,061	3,727	4,966	6,108	21,785	2.88	-	429
Drunkenness, .	4,569	709	3,516	2,300	3,311	3,551	13,387	2.93	-	-
Drunkenness and other crimes, .	291	32	236	152	227	239	886	3.05	-	-
Other crimes, .	2,705	182	2,309	1,275	1,428	2,318	7,512	2.78	-	429

Crime; Sex, Degree of Crime, and Liquor Habits of Criminals: By Age
Periods — Continued.

AGE PERIOD: 20–29 — Concluded.

SEX AND DEGREE OF CRIME.	Number addicted to the Use of Intoxicating Liquors	Excessive Drinkers	Social Drinkers	Home Drinkers	Periodical Drinkers	Occasional Drinkers	Aggregate Number of Drinking Conditions	Average Number of Drinking Conditions	Liquor Habits Unknown	Total Abstainers
Females.	917	194	624	469	461	639	2,387	2.60	-	137
Drunkenness, .	605	159	386	285	365	383	1,578	2.59	-	-
Drunkenness and other crimes, .	14	3	10	6	9	11	39	2.79	-	-
Other crimes, .	298	32	228	178	87	245	770	2.58	-	137
BOTH SEXES.	8,482	1,117	6,685	4,196	5,427	6,747	24,172	2.85	-	566
Drunkenness, .	5,174	868	3,902	2,585	3,676	3,934	14,965	2.89	-	-
Drunkenness and other crimes, .	305	35	245	157	235	249	921	3.02	-	-
Other crimes, .	3,003	214	2,538	1,454	1,516	2,564	8,286	2.76	-	566

AGE PERIOD: 30–39

Males.	7,178	1,259	5,292	3,870	4,871	5,312	20,604	2.87	-	117
Drunkenness, .	5,229	1,033	3,732	2,803	3,779	3,766	15,113	2.89	-	-
Drunkenness and other crimes, .	181	31	135	98	138	135	537	2.97	-	-
Other crimes, .	1,768	195	1,425	969	954	1,411	4,954	2.80	-	117
Females.	962	256	604	540	503	600	2,503	2.60	-	65
Drunkenness, .	722	227	426	367	411	417	1,848	2.56	-	-
Drunkenness and other crimes, .	17	3	14	9	12	14	52	3.06	-	-
Other crimes, .	223	26	164	164	80	169	603	2.70	-	65
BOTH SEXES.	8,140	1,515	5,896	4,410	5,374	5,912	23,107	2.84	-	182
Drunkenness, .	5,951	1,260	4,158	3,170	4,190	4,183	16,961	2.85	-	-
Drunkenness and other crimes, .	198	34	148	106	149	148	585	2.97	-	-
Other crimes, .	1,991	221	1,590	1,134	1,035	1,581	5,561	2.79	-	182

AGE PERIOD: 40–49.

Males.	4,329	873	3,016	2,227	2,913	3,060	12,089	2.79	-	61
Drunkenness, .	3,401	741	2,314	1,738	2,415	2,344	9,552	2.81	-	*1
Drunkenness and other crimes, .	82	15	62	46	61	62	246	3.00	-	-
Other crimes, .	846	117	640	443	437	654	2,291	2.71	-	60

* Inebriety caused by the use of narcotics and drugs.

Crime; Sex, Degree of Crime, and Liquor Habits of Criminals: By Age Periods — Continued.

AGE PERIOD: 40-49 — Concluded.

SEX AND DEGREE OF CRIME.	Number addicted to the Use of Intoxicating Liquors	Excessive Drinkers	Social Drinkers	Home Drinkers	Periodical Drinkers	Occasional Drinkers	Aggregate Number of Drinking Conditions	Average Number of Drinking Conditions	Liquor Habits Unknown	Total Abstainers
Females.	555	171	317	296	267	331	1,382	2.49	-	33
Drunkenness, .	433	160	224	207	223	232	1,046	2.42	-	-
Drunkenness and other crimes, .	12	4	7	6	7	6	30	2.50	-	-
Other crimes, .	110	7	86	83	37	93	306	2.73	-	33
BOTH SEXES.	4,884	1,044	3,333	2,523	3,180	3,391	13,471	2.76	-	94
Drunkenness, .	3,834	901	2,538	1,945	2,638	2,576	10,598	2.76	-	*1
Drunkenness and other crimes, .	94	19	69	52	68	68	276	2.94	-	-
Other crimes, .	956	124	726	526	474	747	2,597	2.73	-	93

AGE PERIOD: 50-59.

Males.	2,001	530	1,286	1,048	1,243	1,313	5,420	2.71	-	33
Drunkenness, .	1,616	443	1,021	843	1,070	1,039	4,416	2.73	-	-
Drunkenness and other crimes, .	22	8	11	10	13	12	54	2.45	-	-
Other crimes, .	363	79	254	195	160	262	950	2.62	-	33
Females.	217	59	133	132	117	137	578	2.66	-	10
Drunkenness, .	184	56	110	105	105	111	487	2.65	-	-
Drunkenness and other crimes, .	6	1	5	5	5	5	21	3.50	-	-
Other crimes, .	27	2	18	22	7	21	70	2.59	-	10
BOTH SEXES.	2,218	589	1,419	1,180	1,360	1,450	5,998	2.71	-	43
Drunkenness, .	1,800	499	1,131	948	1,175	1,150	4,903	2.73	-	-
Drunkenness and other crimes, .	28	9	16	15	18	17	75	2.68	-	-
Other crimes, .	390	81	272	217	167	283	1,020	2.62	-	43

AGE PERIOD: 60-79.

Males.	630	174	395	333	368	406	1,676	2.66	-	14
Drunkenness, .	492	149	295	252	301	302	1,299	2.64	-	-
Drunkenness and other crimes, .	8	1	6	7	6	7	27	3.38	-	-
Other crimes, .	130	24	94	74	61	97	350	2.69	-	14

* Inebriety caused by the use of narcotics and drugs.

Crime; Sex, Degree of Crime, and Liquor Habits of Criminals: By Age Periods — Concluded.

AGE PERIOD: 60-79 — Concluded.

SEX AND DEGREE OF CRIME.	Number addicted to the Use of Intoxicating Liquors	Excessive Drinkers	Social Drinkers	Home Drinkers	Periodical Drinkers	Occasional Drinkers	Aggregate Number of Drinking Conditions	Average Number of Drinking Conditions	Liquor Habits Unknown	Total Abstainers
Females.	87	35	42	43	34	46	200	2.30	-	4
Drunkenness, .	67	34	26	28	27	29	144	2.15	-	-
Other crimes, .	20	1	16	15	7	17	56	2.80	-	4
BOTH SEXES.	717	209	437	376	402	452	1,876	2.62	-	18
Drunkenness, .	559	183	321	280	328	331	1,443	2.55	-	-
Drunkenness and other crimes, .	8	1	6	7	6	7	27	3.38	-	-
Other crimes, .	150	25	110	89	68	114	406	2.71	-	18

AGE PERIOD: 80 +.

Males.	6	3	3	3	3	3	15	2.50	-	-
Drunkenness, .	6	3	3	3	3	3	15	2.50	-	-
Females.	6	4	1	1	1	2	9	1.50	-	-
Drunkenness, .	5	3	1	1	1	2	8	1.60	-	-
Other crimes, .	1	1	-	-	-	-	1	1.00	-	-
BOTH SEXES.	12	7	4	4	4	5	24	2.00	-	-
Drunkenness, .	11	6	4	4	4	5	23	2.09	-	-
Other crimes, .	1	1	-	-	-	-	1	1.00	-	-

AGE PERIOD: Unknown.

Males.	4	1	3	2	1	3	10	2.50	-	-
Drunkenness, .	3	1	2	1	1	2	7	2.33	-	-
Other crimes, .	1	-	1	1	-	1	3	3.00	-	-

RECAPITULATION.

SEX AND DEGREE OF CRIME.	Number addicted to the Use of Intoxicating Liquors	Excessive Drinkers	Social Drinkers	Home Drinkers	Periodical Drinkers	Occasional Drinkers	Aggregate Number of Drinking Conditions	Average Number of Drinking Conditions	Liquor Habits Unknown	Total Abstainers
Males.	22,341	3,790	16,632	11,419	14,644	16,773	63,258	2.83	-	1,240
Drunkenness, .	15,542	3,096	11,083	8,032	11,017	11,207	44,435	2.85	-	*1
Drunkenness and other crimes, .	608	87	474	324	465	479	1,829	3.01	-	-
Other crimes, .	6,191	607	5,075	3,063	3,162	5,087	16,994	2.74	-	1,239

* Inebriety caused by the use of narcotics and drugs.

RECAPITULATION — Concluded.

SEX AND DEGREE OF CRIME.	Number addicted to the Use of Intoxicating Liquors	Excessive Drinkers	Social Drinkers	Home Drinkers	Periodical Drinkers	Occasional Drinkers	Aggregate Number of Drinking Conditions	Average Number of Drinking Conditions	Liquor Habits Unknown	Total Abstainers
Females.	2,796	726	1,760	1,499	1,397	1,798	7,180	2.57	-	295
Drunkenness, .	2,032	642	1,184	999	1,140	1,186	5,151	2.53	-	-
Drunkenness and other crimes, .	49	11	36	26	33	36	142	2 90	-	-
Other crimes, .	715	73	540	474	224	576	1,887	2.64	-	295
BOTH SEXES.	25,137	4,516	18,392	12,918	16,041	18,571	70,438	2.80	-	1,535
Drunkenness, .	17,574	3,738	12,267	9,031	12,157	12,393	49,586	2.82	-	*1
Drunkenness and other crimes, .	657	98	510	350	498	515	1,971	3.00	-	-
Other crimes, .	6,906	680	5,615	3,537	3,386	5,663	18,881	2.73	-	1,534

* Inebriety caused by the use of narcotics and drugs.

RECAPITULATION: BY AGE PERIODS.

SEX AND AGE PERIODS.	Number addicted to the Use of Intoxicating Liquors	Excessive Drinkers	Social Drinkers	Home Drinkers	Periodical Drinkers	Occasional Drinkers	Aggregate Number of Drinking Conditions	Average Number of Drinking Conditions	Liquor Habits Unknown	Total Abstainers
Males.	22,341	3,790	16,632	11,419	14,644	16,773	63,258	2.83	-	1,240
10–14, . .	3	-	3	1	-	3	7	2.33	-	52
15–19, . .	625	27	573	208	279	565	1,652	2.64	-	534
20–29, . .	7,565	923	6,061	3,727	4,966	6,108	21,785	2.88	-	429
30–39, . .	7,178	1,259	5,292	3,870	4,871	5,312	20,604	2.87	-	117
40–49, . .	4,329	873	3,016	2,227	2,913	3,060	12,089	2.79	-	61
50–59, . .	2,001	530	1,286	1,048	1,243	1,313	5,420	2.71	-	33
60–79, . .	630	174	395	333	368	406	1,676	2.66	-	14
80 +, . .	6	3	3	3	3	3	15	2.50	-	-
Unknown, .	4	1	3	2	1	3	10	2.50	-	-
Females.	2,796	726	1,760	1,499	1,397	1,798	7,180	2.57	-	295
10–14, . .	1	-	1	-	1	1	3	3.00	-	-
15–19, . .	51	7	38	18	13	42	118	2.31	-	46
20–29, . .	917	194	624	469	461	639	2,387	2.60	-	137
30–39, . .	962	256	604	540	503	600	2,503	2.60	-	65
40–49, . .	555	171	317	296	267	331	1,382	2.49	-	33
50–59, . .	217	59	133	132	117	137	578	2.66	-	10
60–79, . .	87	35	42	43	34	46	200	2.30	-	4
80 +, . .	6	4	1	1	1	2	9	1.50	-	-

RECAPITULATION: BY AGE PERIODS — Concluded.

SEX AND AGE PERIODS.	Number addicted to the Use of Intoxicating Liquors	Excessive Drinkers	Social Drinkers	Home Drinkers	Periodical Drinkers	Occasional Drinkers	Aggregate Number of Drinking Conditions	Average Number of Drinking Conditions	Liquor Habits Unknown	Total Abstainers
BOTH SEXES.	25,137	4,516	18,392	12,918	16,041	18,571	70,438	2.80	-	1,535
10-14, . .	4	-	4	1	1	4	10	2.50	-	52
15-19, . .	676	34	611	226	292	607	1,770	2.62	-	580
20-29, . .	8,482	1,117	6,685	4,196	5,427	6,747	24,172	2.85	-	566
30-39, . .	8,140	1,515	5,896	4,410	5,374	5,912	23,107	2.84	-	182
40-49, . .	4,884	1,044	3,333	2,523	3,180	3,391	13,471	2.76	-	94
50-59, . .	2,218	589	1,419	1,180	1,360	1,450	5,998	2.71	-	43
60-79, . .	717	209	437	376	402	452	1,876	2.62	-	18
80 +, . . .	12	7	4	4	4	5	24	2.00	-	-
Unknown, . .	4	1	3	2	1	3	10	2.50	-	-

The foregoing table includes a classification of the criminals by age periods, and closes with recapitulations to which we now refer. The total number of criminals, without regard to sex, who were addicted to the use of intoxicating liquors, namely, 25,137, is included under the following classification of drinking conditions: excessive drinkers, 4,516; social drinkers, 18,392; home drinkers, 12,918; periodical drinkers, 16,041; and occasional drinkers, 18,571; the total number of drinking conditions under this classification being 70,438, or an average of 2.80, this average being based upon the fact that many of the criminals are classified under more than one of the foregoing heads, as previously explained in the analysis relating to the drinking habits of paupers. The number of total abstainers, disregarded, of course, in this classification of drinking conditions, was 1,535. The tabulation of drinking conditions affecting the criminals who were convicted of crimes other than drunkenness, and who were addicted to the use of intoxicating liquors, discloses 680 excessive drinkers, 5,615 social drinkers, 3,537 home drinkers, 3,386 periodical drinkers, and 5,663 occasional drinkers; the aggregate drinking conditions numbering 18,881, or an average of 2.73 per person.

The recapitulation as to ages, both sexes being considered, shows very few under the age of 15 years, the periods in which the larger number is included being 20-29, 30-39, and 40-49. No excessive drinkers are reported under the age of 15, and there are but 34 so classified in the age period 15–19. In the age period 20–29, however, we find 1,117, and in the age periods 30–39 and 40–49, 1,515 and 1,044 respectively. It is, of course, true that the various combinations noted in analyzing the similar table as to paupers were found in classifying the habits of the criminals.

The next table exhibits the habits of the fathers of criminals.

Crime; Sex, Degree of Crime, and Liquor Habits of Fathers of Criminals: By Age Periods.

AGE PERIOD: 10-14.

SEX AND DEGREE OF CRIME.	Number addicted to the Use of Intoxicating Liquors	Excessive Drinkers	Social Drinkers	Home Drinkers	Periodical Drinkers	Occasional Drinkers	Aggregate Number of Drinking Conditions	Average Number of Drinking Conditions	Liquor Habits Unknown	Total Abstainers
Males.	27	2	18	13	7	22	62	2.30	3	25
Drunkenness and other crimes, .	1	-	1	1	1	1	4	4.00	-	-
Other crimes, .	26	2	17	12	6	21	58	2.20	3	25
Females.	-	-	-	-	..	-	-	-	1	-
Drunkenness, .	-	-	-	-	-	-	-	-	1	-
Both Sexes.	27	2	18	13	7	22	62	2.38	4	25
Drunkenness, .	-	-	-	-	-	-	-	-	1	-
Drunkenness and other crimes, .	1	-	1	1	1	1	4	4.00	-	-
Other crimes, .	26	2	17	12	6	21	58	2.20	3	25

AGE PERIOD: 15-19.

SEX AND DEGREE OF CRIME.	Number addicted to the Use of Intoxicating Liquors	Excessive Drinkers	Social Drinkers	Home Drinkers	Periodical Drinkers	Occasional Drinkers	Aggregate Number of Drinking Conditions	Average Number of Drinking Conditions	Liquor Habits Unknown	Total Abstainers
Males.	630	49	499	399	187	515	1,649	2.62	84	445
Drunkenness, .	131	3	107	94	45	116	365	2.79	14	81
Drunkenness and other crimes, .	16	1	14	10	7	14	46	2.57	-	7
Other crimes, .	483	45	378	295	135	385	1,238	2.56	70	357
Females.	49	10	36	22	4	34	106	2.16	7	41
Drunkenness, .	7	2	4	3	2	4	15	2.14	1	7
Other crimes, .	42	8	32	19	2	30	91	2.17	6	34
Both Sexes.	679	59	535	421	191	549	1,755	2.59	91	486
Drunkenness, .	138	5	111	97	47	120	380	2.75	15	88
Drunkenness and other crimes, .	16	1	14	10	7	14	46	2.87	-	7
Other crimes, .	525	53	410	314	137	415	1,329	2.52	76	391

Crime ; Sex, Degree of Crime, and Liquor Habits of Fathers of Criminals :
By Age Periods — Continued.

AGE PERIOD: 20-29.

SEX AND DEGREE OF CRIME.	Number addicted to the Use of Intoxicating Liquors	Excessive Drinkers	Social Drinkers	Home Drinkers	Periodical Drinkers	Occasional Drinkers	Aggregate Number of Drinking Conditions	Average Number of Drinking Conditions	Liquor Habits Unknown	Total Abstainers
Males.	4,692	164	3,991	3,005	1,332	4,146	12,638	2.69	529	2,773
Drunkenness, .	2,776	89	2,366	1,768	830	2,474	7,527	2.71	276	1,517
Drunkenness and other crimes, .	179	5	145	124	60	154	488	2.74	13	99
Other crimes, .	1,737	70	1,480	1,113	442	1,518	4,623	2.63	240	1,157
Females.	537	43	440	337	129	438	1,387	2.58	106	411
Drunkenness, .	335	27	275	211	84	275	872	2.60	60	210
Drunkenness and other crimes, .	10	1	8	6	2	9	26	2.60	2	2
Other crimes, .	192	15	157	120	43	154	489	2.55	44	199
BOTH SEXES.	5,229	207	4,431	3,342	1,461	4,584	14,025	2.68	635	3,184
Drunkenness, .	3,111	116	2,641	1,979	914	2,749	8,399	2.70	336	1,727
Drunkenness and other crimes, .	189	6	153	130	62	163	514	2.72	15	101
Other crimes, .	1,929	85	1,637	1,233	485	1,672	5,112	2.65	284	1,356

AGE PERIOD: 30-39.

SEX AND DEGREE OF CRIME.	Number addicted to the Use of Intoxicating Liquors	Excessive Drinkers	Social Drinkers	Home Drinkers	Periodical Drinkers	Occasional Drinkers	Aggregate Number of Drinking Conditions	Average Number of Drinking Conditions	Liquor Habits Unknown	Total Abstainers
Males.	4,402	137	3,725	2,895	1,195	3,922	11,874	2.70	649	2,244
Drunkenness, .	3,187	98	2,688	2,064	883	2,855	8,588	2.68	438	1,604
Drunkenness and other crimes, .	95	2	86	65	37	90	280	2.95	22	64
Other crimes, .	1,120	37	951	766	275	977	3,006	2.68	189	576
Females.	516	24	430	328	124	453	1,359	2.63	124	387
Drunkenness, .	367	18	300	223	87	321	949	2.59	74	281
Drunkenness and other crimes, .	7	–	7	6	5	7	25	3.57	4	6
Other crimes, .	142	6	123	99	32	125	385	2.71	46	100
BOTH SEXES.	4,918	161	4,155	3,223	1,319	4,375	13,233	2.69	773	2,631
Drunkenness, .	3,554	116	2,988	2,287	970	3,176	9,537	2.68	512	1,885
Drunkenness and other crimes, .	102	2	93	71	42	97	305	2.99	26	70
Other crimes, .	1,262	43	1,074	865	307	1,102	3,391	2.69	235	676

Crime ; Sex, Degree of Crime, and Liquor Habits of Fathers of Criminals:
By Age Periods — Continued.

AGE PERIOD: 40-49.

SEX AND DEGREE OF CRIME.	Number addicted to the Use of Intoxicating Liquors	Excessive Drinkers	Social Drinkers	Home Drinkers	Periodical Drinkers	Occasional Drinkers	Aggregate Number of Drinking Conditions	Average Number of Drinking Conditions	Liquor Habits Unknown	Total Abstainers
Males.	2,579	77	2,143	1,682	702	2,293	6,897	2.67	508	1,303
Drunkenness, .	1,998	48	1,668	1,320	575	1,789	5,400	2.70	393	1,011
Drunkenness and other crimes, .	52	1	46	32	13	49	141	2.71	9	21
Other crimes, .	529	28	429	330	114	455	1,356	2.56	106	271
Females.	291	8	238	186	49	243	724	2.49	86	211
Drunkenness, .	221	7	183	133	37	195	555	2.51	63	149
Drunkenness and other crimes, .	9	-	7	7	2	7	23	2.56	2	1
Other crimes, .	61	1	48	46	10	41	146	2.39	21	61
BOTH SEXES.	2,870	85	2,381	1,868	751	2,536	7,621	2.66	594	1,514
Drunkenness, .	2,219	55	1,851	1,453	612	1,984	5,955	2.68	456	1,160
Drunkenness and other crimes, .	61	1	53	39	15	56	164	2.69	11	22
Other crimes, .	590	29	477	376	124	496	1,502	2.55	127	332

AGE PERIOD: 50–59.

Males.	1,188	28	986	852	342	1,077	3,285	2.77	319	527
Drunkenness, .	943	24	778	673	278	855	2,608	2.77	261	412
Drunkenness and other crimes, .	13	-	11	8	4	13	36	2.62	4	5
Other crimes, .	232	4	197	171	60	209	641	2.76	54	110
Females.	112	4	97	76	26	101	304	2.71	48	67
Drunkenness, .	89	3	77	61	18	82	241	2.71	40	55
Drunkenness and other crimes, .	4	-	3	3	3	4	13	3.25	1	1
Other crimes, .	19	1	17	12	5	15	50	2.63	7	11
BOTH SEXES.	1,300	32	1,083	928	368	1,178	3,589	2.76	367	594
Drunkenness, .	1,032	27	855	734	296	937	2,849	2.76	301	467
Drunkenness and other crimes, .	17	-	14	11	7	17	49	2.88	5	6
Other crimes, .	251	5	214	183	65	224	691	2.75	61	121

Crime; Sex, Degree of Crime, and Liquor Habits of Fathers of Criminals:
By Age Periods — Concluded.

AGE PERIOD: 60-79.

SEX AND DEGREE OF CRIME.	Number addicted to the Use of Intoxicating Liquors	Excessive Drinkers	Social Drinkers	Home Drinkers	Periodical Drinkers	Occasional Drinkers	Aggregate Number of Drinking Conditions	Average Number of Drinking Conditions	Liquor Habits Unknown	Total Abstainers
Males.	371	8	319	266	107	336	1,036	2.79	115	158
Drunkenness, .	281	5	241	195	86	255	782	2.72	86	125
Drunkenness and other crimes, .	7	–	6	3	–	7	16	2.29	1	–
Other crimes, .	83	3	72	68	21	74	238	2.87	28	33
Females.	40	1	36	30	10	36	113	2.83	27	24
Drunkenness, .	30	1	27	21	8	26	83	2.77	21	16
Other crimes, .	10	–	9	9	2	10	30	3.00	6	8
BOTH SEXES.	411	9	355	296	117	372	1,149	2.77	142	182
Drunkenness, .	311	6	268	216	94	281	865	2.78	107	141
Drunkenness and other crimes, .	7	–	6	3	–	7	16	2.29	1	–
Other crimes, .	93	3	81	77	23	84	268	2.77	34	41

AGE PERIOD: 80 +.

Males.	2	–	1	1	–	2	4	2 00	3	1
Drunkenness, .	2	–	1	1	–	2	4	2.00	3	1
Females.	2	–	1	1	–	2	4	2.00	3	1
Drunkenness, .	1	–	1	1	–	1	3	3.00	3	1
Other crimes, .	1	–	–	–	–	1	1	1.00	–	–
BOTH SEXES.	4	–	2	2	–	4	8	2.00	6	2
Drunkenness, .	3	–	2	2	–	3	7	2.33	6	2
Other crimes, .	1	–	–	–	–	1	1	1.00	–	–

AGE PERIOD: Unknown.

Males.	2	–	2	2	1	2	7	3.50	2	–
Drunkenness, .	1	–	1	1	1	1	4	4.00	2	–
Other crimes, .	1	–	1	1	–	1	3	3 00	–	–

RECAPITULATION.

SEX AND DEGREE OF CRIME.	Number addicted to the Use of Intoxicating Liquors	Excessive Drinkers	Social Drinkers	Home Drinkers	Periodical Drinkers	Occasional Drinkers	Aggregate Number of Drinking Conditions	Average Number of Drinking Conditions	Liquor Habits Unknown	Total Abstainers
Males.	13,893	465	11,684	9,115	3,873	12,315	37,452	2.70	2,212	7,476
Drunkenness, .	9,319	267	7,850	6,116	2,698	8,347	25,278	2.71	1,473	4,751
Drunkenness and other crimes, .	363	9	309	243	122	328	1,011	2.78	49	196
Other crimes, .	4,211	189	3,525	2,756	1,053	3,640	11,163	2.65	690	2,529
Females.	1,547	90	1,278	980	342	1,307	3,997	2.58	402	1,142
Drunkenness, .	1,050	58	867	653	236	904	2,718	2.59	263	719
Drunkenness and other crimes, .	30	1	25	22	12	27	87	2.90	9	10
Other crimes, .	467	31	386	305	94	376	1,192	2.55	130	413
BOTH SEXES.	15,440	555	12,962	10,095	4,215	13,622	41,449	2.68	2,614	8,618
Drunkenness, .	10,369	325	8,717	6,769	2,934	9,251	27,996	2.70	1,736	5,470
Drunkenness and other crimes, .	393	10	334	265	134	355	1,098	2.79	58	206
Other crimes, .	4,678	220	3,911	3,061	1,147	4,016	12,355	2.64	820	2,942

RECAPITULATION: BY AGE PERIODS.

SEX AND AGE PERIODS.	Number addicted to the Use of Intoxicating Liquors	Excessive Drinkers	Social Drinkers	Home Drinkers	Periodical Drinkers	Occasional Drinkers	Aggregate Number of Drinking Conditions	Average Number of Drinking Conditions	Liquor Habits Unknown	Total Abstainers
Males.	13,893	465	11,684	9,115	3,873	12,315	37,452	2.70	2,212	7,476
10-14, . .	27	2	18	13	7	22	62	2.30	3	25
15-19, . .	630	49	499	399	187	515	1,649	2.62	84	445
20-29, . .	4,692	164	3,991	3,005	1,332	4,146	12,638	2.69	529	2,773
30-39, . .	4,402	137	3,725	2,895	1,195	3,922	11,874	2.70	649	2,244
40-49, . .	2,579	77	2,143	1,682	702	2,293	6,897	2.67	508	1,303
50-59, . .	1,188	28	986	852	342	1,077	3,285	2.77	319	527
60-79, . .	371	8	319	266	107	336	1,036	2.79	115	158
80+, . . .	2	-	1	1	-	2	4	2.00	3	1
Unknown, . .	2	-	2	2	1	2	7	3.50	2	-
Females.	1,547	90	1,278	980	342	1,307	3,997	2.58	402	1,142
10-14, . .	-	-	-	-	-	-	-	-	1	-
15-19, . .	49	10	36	22	4	34	106	2.16	7	41
20-29, . .	537	43	440	337	129	438	1,387	2.58	106	411

RECAPITULATION: BY AGE PERIODS — Concluded.

SEX AND AGE PERIODS.	Number addicted to the Use of Intoxicating Liquors	Excessive Drinkers	Social Drinkers	Home Drinkers	Periodical Drinkers	Occasional Drinkers	Aggregate Number of Drinking Conditions	Average Number of Drinking Conditions	Liquor Habits Unknown	Total Abstainers
Females — Con.										
30–39, . .	516	24	430	328	124	453	1,359	2.63	124	387
40–49, . .	291	8	238	186	49	243	724	2.49	96	211
50–59, . .	112	4	97	76	26	101	304	2.71	48	67
60–79, . .	40	1	36	30	10	36	113	2.83	27	24
80 +, . .	2	-	1	1	-	2	4	2.00	3	1
BOTH SEXES.	15,440	555	12,962	10,095	4,215	13,622	41,449	2.68	2,614	8,618
10–14, . .	27	2	18	13	7	22	62	2.30	4	25
15–19, . .	679	59	535	421	191	549	1,755	2.58	91	486
20–29, . .	5,229	207	4,431	3,342	1,461	4,584	14,025	2.68	635	3,184
30–39, . .	4,918	161	4,155	3,223	1,319	4,375	13,233	2.69	773	2,631
40–49, . .	2,870	85	2,381	1,868	751	2,536	7,621	2.66	594	1,514
50–59, . .	1,300	32	1,083	928	368	1,178	3,589	2.76	367	594
60–79, . .	411	9	355	296	117	372	1,149	2.80	142	182
80 +, . .	4	-	2	2	-	4	8	2.00	6	2
Unknown, .	2	-	2	2	1	2	7	3.50	2	-

This table, like the one which precedes it, contains a classification by age periods, with recapitulations. Referring to
the figures for both sexes, we note that 15,440 had fathers
addicted to the use of intoxicating liquors, while 8,618 had
fathers who were total abstainers; these figures representing,
respectively, 57.89 per cent and 32.31 per cent of the total
number of criminals. Of the 15,440 criminals whose fathers
were addicted to the use of liquor, 10,369 were convicted of
drunkenness, 393 of drunkenness united with other crimes,
while 4,678 were convicted of other crimes only. On the
other hand, 5,470 criminals who were convicted of drunkenness had fathers who were total abstainers; and the same is
true of the 206 criminals who were convicted of drunkenness
and other crimes, and the 2,942 who were convicted of other
crimes only. The criminals whose fathers were excessive
drinkers number 555; of these criminals, 220 were convicted
of crimes other than drunkenness. The tabulation of other
forms of the drinking habit to which the fathers of criminals
were addicted results in 12,962 social drinkers, 10,095 home

drinkers, 4,215 periodical drinkers, and 13,622 occasional drinkers, the average to each father being 2.68. The liquor habits of the fathers were unknown in the case of 2,614 criminals; of these, 820 were convicted of crimes other than drunkenness. The table closes with a recapitulation by age periods of the criminals, presented in connection with a classification of the different forms of the drinking habit to which the fathers were addicted.

A similar table as to the mothers of criminals follows:

Crime; Sex, Degree of Crime, and Liquor Habits of Mothers of Criminals: By Age Periods.

AGE PERIOD: 10–14.

SEX AND DEGREE OF CRIME.	Number addicted to the Use of Intoxicating Liquors	Excessive Drinkers	Social Drinkers	Home Drinkers	Periodical Drinkers	Occasional Drinkers	Aggregate Number of Drinking Conditions	Average Number of Drinking Conditions	Liquor Habits Unknown	Total Abstainers
Males.	11	–	4	11	1	6	22	2.00	3	41
Drunkenness and other crimes, .	–	–	–	–	–	–	–	–	–	1
Other crimes, .	11	–	4	11	1	6	22	2.00	3	40
Females.	–	–	–	–	–	–	–	–	–	1
Drunkenness, .	–	–	–	–	–	–	–	–	–	1
BOTH SEXES.	11	–	4	11	1	6	22	2.00	3	42
Drunkenness, .	–	–	–	–	–	–	–	–	–	1
Drunkenness and other crimes, .	–	–	–	–	–	–	–	–	–	1
Other crimes, .	11	–	4	11	1	6	22	2.00	3	40

AGE PERIOD: 15–19.

Males.	216	8	162	190	32	131	523	2.42	52	891
Drunkenness, .	42	–	33	39	4	24	100	2.38	7	177
Drunkenness and other crimes, .	6	–	6	6	2	3	17	2.83	2	15
Other crimes, .	168	8	123	145	26	104	406	2.42	43	699
Females.	23	7	12	13	2	12	46	2.00	8	66
Drunkenness, .	5	2	1	3	1	2	9	1.80	–	10
Other crimes, .	18	5	11	10	1	10	37	2.06	8	56

Crime ; Sex, Degree of Crime, and Liquor Habits of Mothers of Criminals:
By Age Periods — Continued.

AGE PERIOD: 15–19 — Concluded.

SEX AND DEGREE OF CRIME.	Number addicted to the Use of Intoxicating Liquors	Excessive Drinkers	Social Drinkers	Home Drinkers	Periodical Drinkers	Occasional Drinkers	Aggregate Number of Drinking Conditions	Average Number of Drinking Conditions	Liquor Habits Unknown	Total Abstainers
BOTH SEXES.	239	15	174	203	34	143	569	2.34	60	957
Drunkenness, .	47	2	34	42	5	26	109	2.32	7	187
Drunkenness and other crimes, .	6	–	6	6	2	3	17	2.83	2	15
Other crimes, .	186	13	134	155	27	114	443	2.39	51	755

AGE PERIOD: 20–29.

Males.	1,459	24	1,115	1,310	142	915	3,506	2.40	392	6,143
Drunkenness, .	846	15	630	765	98	516	2,024	2.39	212	3,511
Drunkenness and other crimes, .	55	2	39	45	4	33	123	2.25	7	229
Other crimes, .	558	7	446	500	40	366	1,359	2.43	173	2,403
Females.	245	8	190	210	30	154	592	2.42	67	742
Drunkenness, .	168	4	129	145	24	100	402	2.39	36	401
Drunkenness and other crimes, .	4	1	3	3	–	2	9	2.25	1	9
Other crimes, .	73	3	58	62	6	52	181	2.48	30	332
BOTH SEXES.	1,704	32	1,305	1,520	172	1,069	4,098	2.40	459	6,885
Drunkenness, .	1,014	19	759	910	122	616	2,426	2.39	248	3,912
Drunkenness and other crimes, .	59	3	42	48	4	35	132	2.24	8	238
Other crimes, .	631	10	504	562	46	418	1,540	2.44	203	2,735

AGE PERIOD: 30–39.

Males.	1,442	10	1,129	1,321	163	952	3,575	2.48	440	5,413
Drunkenness, .	985	8	761	912	116	629	2,426	2.47	312	3,932
Drunkenness and other crimes, .	33	–	21	27	6	23	77	2.22	18	130
Other crimes, .	424	2	347	382	41	300	1,072	2.53	110	1,351
Females.	247	6	185	212	33	168	604	2.45	85	695
Drunkenness, .	175	5	126	149	25	118	423	2.39	52	495
Drunkenness and other crimes, .	2	–	2	2	–	1	5	2.50	2	13
Other crimes, .	70	1	57	61	8	49	176	2.51	31	187

Crime ; Sex, Degree of Crime, and Liquor Habits of Mothers of Criminals :
By Age Periods — Continued.

AGE PERIOD: 30–39 — Concluded.

SEX AND DEGREE OF CRIME.	Number addicted to the Use of Intoxicating Liquors	Excessive Drinkers	Social Drinkers	Home Drinkers	Periodical Drinkers	Occasional Drinkers	Aggregate Number of Drinking Conditions	Average Number of Drinking Conditions	Liquor Habits Unknown	Total Abstainers
BOTH SEXES	1,689	16	1,314	1,533	196	1,120	4,179	2.48	525	6,108
Drunkenness, .	1,160	13	887	1,061	141	747	2,849	2.46	364	4,427
Drunkenness and other crimes, .	35	–	23	29	6	24	82	2.34	20	143
Other crimes, .	494	3	404	443	49	349	1,248	2.53	141	1,538

AGE PERIOD: 40–49.

Males.	892	10	697	810	106	571	2,194	2.45	365	3,133
Drunkenness, .	688	8	529	627	93	426	1,683	2.44	282	2,432
Drunkenness and other crimes, .	18	1	14	16	2	11	44	2.44	7	57
Other crimes, .	186	1	154	167	11	134	467	2.51	76	644
Females.	142	2	112	128	17	86	345	2.43	63	383
Drunkenness, .	106	2	83	95	14	63	257	2.42	47	280
Drunkenness and other crimes, .	5	–	5	5	1	1	12	2.40	–	7
Other crimes, .	31	–	24	28	2	22	76	2.45	16	96
BOTH SEXES.	1,034	12	809	938	123	657	2,539	2.46	428	3,516
Drunkenness, .	794	10	612	722	107	489	1,940	2.70	329	2,712
Drunkenness and other crimes, .	23	1	19	21	3	12	56	2.43	7	64
Other crimes, .	217	1	178	195	13	156	543	2.50	92	740

AGE PERIOD: 50–59.

Males.	524	2	417	473	54	350	1,296	2.51	243	1,267
Drunkenness, .	413	2	332	377	47	277	1,035	2.51	199	1,004
Drunkenness and other crimes, .	4	–	2	3	–	3	8	2.00	2	16
Other crimes, .	107	–	83	93	7	70	253	2.40	42	247
Females.	71	–	59	65	6	48	178	2.51	40	116
Drunkenness, .	58	–	49	55	4	38	146	2.52	32	94
Drunkenness and other crimes, .	4	–	3	3	1	3	10	2.50	1	1
Other crimes, .	9	–	7	7	1	7	22	2.44	7	21

*Crime ; Sex, Degree of Crime, and Liquor Habits of Mothers of Criminals:
By Age Periods —* Concluded.

AGE PERIOD : 50–59 — Concluded.

SEX AND DEGREE OF CRIME.	Number addicted to the Use of Intoxicating Liquors	Excessive Drinkers	Social Drinkers	Home Drinkers	Periodical Drinkers	Occasional Drinkers	Aggregate Number of Drinking Conditions	Average Number of Drinking Conditions	Liquor Habits Unknown	Total Abstainers
BOTH SEXES.	595	2	476	538	60	398	1,474	2.48	283	1,383
Drunkenness, .	471	2	381	432	51	315	1,181	2.51	231	1,098
Drunkenness and other crimes, .	8	-	5	6	1	6	18	2.25	3	17
Other crimes, .	116	-	90	100	8	77	275	2.37	49	268

AGE PERIOD : 60–79.

Males.	164	-	132	143	21	105	401	2.45	97	383
Drunkenness, .	115	-	89	100	15	67	271	2.36	78	299
Drunkenness and other crimes, .	4	-	3	3	-	3	9	2.25	-	4
Other crimes, .	45	-	40	40	6	35	121	2.69	19	80
Females.	24	-	18	20	5	14	57	2.37	25	42
Drunkenness, .	18	-	14	15	4	9	42	2.33	21	28
Other crimes, .	6	-	4	5	1	5	15	2.60	4	14
BOTH SEXES.	188	-	150	163	26	119	458	2 26	122	425
Drunkenness, .	133	-	103	115	19	76	313	2.36	99	327
Drunkenness and other crimes, .	4	-	3	3	-	3	9	2.25	-	4
Other crimes, .	51	-	44	45	7	40	136	2.67	23	94

AGE PERIOD : 80 +.

Males.	1	-	1	1	-	1	3	3.00	3	2
Drunkenness. .	1	-	1	1	-	1	3	3.00	3	2
Females.	2	-	1	1	-	2	4	2.00	2	2
Drunkenness, .	1	-	1	1	-	1	3	3.00	2	2
Other crimes, .	1	-	-	-	-	1	1	1.00	-	-
BOTH SEXES.	3	-	2	2	-	3	7	2.33	5	4
Drunkenness, .	2	-	2	2	-	2	6	3.00	5	4
Other crimes, .	1	-	-	-	-	1	1	1.00	-	-

AGE PERIOD : Unknown.

Males.	1	-	-	-	-	1	1	1.00	3	-
Drunkenness, .	-	-	-	-	-	-	-	-	3	-
Other crimes, .	1	-	-	-	-	1	1	1.00	-	-

RECAPITULATION.

Sex and Degree of Crime.	Number addicted to the Use of Intoxicating Liquors	Excessive Drinkers	Social Drinkers	Home Drinkers	Periodical Drinkers	Occasional Drinkers	Aggregate Number of Drinking Conditions	Average Number of Drinking Conditions	Liquor Habits Unknown	Total Abstainers
Males.	4,710	54	3,657	4,259	519	3,032	11,521	2.45	1,598	17,273
Drunkenness, .	3,090	33	2,375	2,821	373	1,940	7,542	2.44	1,096	11,357
Drunkenness and other crimes, .	120	3	85	100	14	76	278	2.32	36	452
Other crimes, .	1,500	18	1,197	1,338	132	1,016	3,701	2.47	466	5,464
Females.	754	23	577	649	93	484	1,826	2.42	290	2,047
Drunkenness, .	531	13	403	463	72	331	1,282	2.41	190	1,311
Drunkenness and other crimes, .	15	1	13	13	2	7	36	2.40	4	30
Other crimes, .	208	9	161	173	19	146	508	2.44	96	706
BOTH SEXES	5,464	77	4,234	4,908	612	3,516	13,347	2.44	1,888	19,320
Drunkenness, .	3,621	46	2,778	3,284	445	2,271	8,824	2.44	1,286	12,668
Drunkenness and other crimes, .	135	4	98	113	16	83	314	2.33	40	482
Other crimes, .	1,708	27	1,358	1,511	151	1,162	4,209	2.47	562	6,170

RECAPITULATION: BY AGE PERIODS.

Sex and Age Periods.	Number addicted to the Use of Intoxicating Liquors	Excessive Drinkers	Social Drinkers	Home Drinkers	Periodical Drinkers	Occasional Drinkers	Aggregate Number of Drinking Conditions	Average Number of Drinking Conditions	Liquor Habits Unknown	Total Abstainers
Males.	4,710	54	3,657	4,259	519	3,032	11,521	2.45	1,598	17,273
10-14, . .	11	–	4	11	1	6	22	2.00	3	41
15-19, . .	216	8	162	190	32	131	523	2.42	52	891
20-29, . .	1,459	24	1,115	1,310	142	915	3,506	2.40	392	6,143
30-39, . .	1,442	10	1,129	1,321	163	952	3,575	2.48	440	5,413
40-49, . .	892	10	697	810	106	571	2,194	2.45	365	3,133
50-59, . .	524	2	417	473	54	350	1,296	2.51	243	1,267
60-79, . .	164	–	132	143	21	105	401	2.45	97	383
80 +, . .	1	–	1	1	–	1	3	3.00	3	2
Unknown, .	1	–	–	–	–	1	1	1.00	3	–
Females.	754	23	577	649	93	484	1,826	2.42	290	2,047
10-14, . .	–	–	–	–	–	–	–	–	–	1
15-19, . .	23	7	12	13	2	12	46	2.00	8	66
20-29, . .	245	8	190	210	30	154	592	2.42	67	742
30-39, . .	247	6	185	212	33	168	604	2.45	85	695
40-49, . .	142	2	112	128	17	86	345	2.43	63	383
50-59, . .	71		59	65	6	48	178	2.51	40	116

RECAPITULATION: BY AGE PERIODS — Concluded.

SEX AND AGE PERIODS.	Number addicted to the Use of Intoxicating Liquors	Excessive Drinkers	Social Drinkers	Home Drinkers	Periodical Drinkers	Occasional Drinkers	Aggregate Number of Drinking Conditions	Average Number of Drinking Conditions	Liquor Habits Unknown	Total Abstainers
Females — Con.										
60-79, . .	24	-	18	20	5	14	57	2.37	25	42
80 +, . .	2	-	1	1	-	2	4	2.00	2	2
BOTH SEXES.	5,464	77	4,234	4,908	612	3,516	13,347	2.44	1,888	19,320
10-14, . .	11	-	4	11	1	6	22	2.00	3	42
15-19, . .	239	15	174	203	34	143	569	2.38	60	957
20-29, . .	1,704	32	1,305	1,520	172	1,069	4,098	2.40	459	6,885
30-39, . .	1,689	16	1,314	1,533	196	1,120	4,179	2.48	525	6,108
40-49, . .	1,034	12	809	938	123	657	2,539	2.46	428	3,516
50-59, . .	595	2	476	538	60	398	1,474	2.48	283	1,383
60-79, . .	188	-	150	163	26	119	458	2.46	122	425
80 +, . .	3	-	2	2	-	3	7	2.33	5	4
Unknown, .	1	-	-	-	-	1	1	1.00	3	-

Referring to the recapitulation in which both sexes are
included, we find that in the case of 5,464 criminals the
mothers were addicted to the use of intoxicating liquors; but,
on the other hand, in the case of 19,320 criminals, the mothers
were total abstainers. This, of course, shows a very much
larger proportion of total abstainers among the mothers than
was found to be the case among the fathers. Of the criminals
who were convicted of drunkenness only, 3,621 had mothers
who were addicted to the use of intoxicating liquors, while in
12,668 cases the mothers were total abstainers. Of the criminals convicted of drunkenness with other crimes, 135 had
mothers who were addicted to the use of liquor, while 482 had
mothers who were total abstainers. Of the criminals convicted of crimes other than drunkenness, 1,708 had mothers
addicted to the use of liquor, while 6,170 had mothers who
were total abstainers. The tabulation as to the drinking
habits of the mothers in detail shows a comparatively small
number of excessive drinkers, only 77 falling under this head.
The social drinkers among the mothers numbered 4,234; the
home drinkers, 4,908; the periodical drinkers, 612; and the
occasional drinkers, 3,516; each mother being tabulated
under an average of 2.44 heads. In 1,888 cases the liquor

habits of the mothers were unknown. As in the preceding table, a recapitulation by age periods concludes the table.

The next presentation indicates the kinds of liquor used by the criminals, with classifications by sex, degree of crime, and age periods.

Crime; Sex, Degree of Crime, and Kinds of Liquor Used by Criminals: By Age Periods.

AGE PERIOD: 10-14.

SEX AND DEGREE OF CRIME.	Number addicted to the Use of Intoxicating Liquors	Wines	Lager Beer	Malted Liquor	Distilled Liquor	Aggregate Number of Kinds of Liquor	Average Number of Kinds of Liquor	Particular Kinds of Liquor Unknown	Total Abstainers
Males.	3	–	2	1	2	5	1.67	–	52
Drunkenness and other crimes, .	1	–	–	–	1	1	1.00	–	–
Other crimes, .	2	–	2	1	1	4	2.00	–	52
Females.	1	–	1	1	1	3	3.00	–	–
Drunkenness, .	1	–	1	1	1	3	3.00	–	–
BOTH SEXES.	4	–	3	2	3	8	2.00	–	52
Drunkenness, .	1	–	1	1	1	3	3.00	–	–
Drunkenness and other crimes, .	1	–	–	–	1	1	1.00	–	–
Other crimes, .	2	–	2	1	1	4	2.00	–	52

AGE PERIOD: 15-19.

Males.	625	167	553	415	355	1,490	2.38	–	534
Drunkenness, .	226	62	205	172	134	573	2.54	–	–
Drunkenness and other crimes, .	23	9	21	15	13	58	2.52	–	–
Other crimes, .	376	96	327	228	208	859	2.28	–	534
Females.	51	8	50	33	25	116	2.27	–	46
Drunkenness, .	15	3	15	13	10	41	2.73	–	–
Other crimes, .	36	5	35	20	15	75	2 08	–	46
BOTH SEXES.	676	175	603	448	380	1,606	2.38	–	580
Drunkenness, .	241	65	220	185	144	614	2.55	–	–
Drunkenness and other crimes, .	23	9	21	15	13	58	2.52	–	–
Other crimes, .	412	101	362	248	223	934	2.27	–	580

Crime; Sex, Degree of Crime, and Kinds of Liquor Used by Criminals: By Age Periods — Continued.

AGE PERIOD: 20-29.

SEX AND DEGREE OF CRIME.	Number addicted to the Use of Intoxicating Liquors	Wines	Lager Beer	Malted Liquor	Distilled Liquor	Aggregate Number of Kinds of Liquor	Average Number of Kinds of Liquor	Particular Kinds of Liquor Unknown	Total Abstainers
Males.	7,565	2,633	7,014	6,589	5,797	22,033	2.91	-	429
Drunkenness, .	4,569	*1,657	4,248	4,167	3,657	13,729	3.00	-	-
Drunkenness and other crimes, .	291	69	280	263	235	847	2.91	-	-
Other crimes, .	2,705	907	2,486	2,159	1,905	7,457	2.76	-	429
Females.	917	247	862	716	599	2,424	2.64	-	137
Drunkenness, .	605	167	567	501	429	1,664	2.75	-	-
Drunkenness and other crimes, .	14	5	14	13	10	42	3.00	-	-
Other crimes, .	298	75	281	202	160	718	2.41	-	137
BOTH SEXES.	8,482	2,880	7,876	7,305	6,396	24,457	2.88	-	566
Drunkenness, .	5,174	*1,824	4,815	4,668	4,086	15,393	2.98	-	-
Drunkenness and other crimes, .	305	74	294	276	245	889	2.91	-	-
Other crimes, .	3,003	982	2,767	2,361	2,065	8,175	2.72	-	566

AGE PERIOD: 30-39.

SEX AND DEGREE OF CRIME.	Number addicted	Wines	Lager Beer	Malted Liquor	Distilled Liquor	Aggregate Number	Average Number	Particular Unknown	Total Abstainers
Males.	7,178	2,684	6,746	6,559	6,075	22,064	3.07	-	117
Drunkenness, .	5,229	*1,948	4,950	4,892	4,550	16,340	3.12	-	-
Drunkenness and other crimes, .	181	61	167	155	145	528	2.36	-	-
Other crimes, .	1,768	675	1,629	1,512	1,380	5,196	2.94	-	117
Females.	962	313	873	808	700	2,694	2.80	-	65
Drunkenness, .	722	232	655	628	545	2,060	2.85	-	-
Drunkenness and other crimes, .	17	6	15	14	12	47	2.76	-	-
Other crimes, .	223	75	203	166	143	587	2.63	-	65
BOTH SEXES.	8,140	2,997	7,619	7,367	6,775	24,758	3.04	-	182
Drunkenness, .	5,951	*2,180	5,605	5,520	5,095	18,400	3.09	-	-
Drunkenness and other crimes, .	198	67	182	169	157	575	2.90	-	-
Other crimes, .	1,991	750	1,832	1,678	1,523	5,783	2.91	-	182

* Includes one cider.

Crime; Sex, Degree of Crime, and Kinds of Liquor Used by Criminals: By Age Periods — Continued.

AGE PERIOD: 40-49.

SEX AND DEGREE OF CRIME.	Number addicted to the Use of Intoxicating Liquors	Wines	Lager Beer	Malted Liquor	Distilled Liquor	Aggregate Number of Kinds of Liquor	Average Number of Kinds of Liquor	Particular Kinds of Liquor Unknown	Total Abstainers
Males.	4,329	1,603	4,055	3,985	3,752	13,395	3.09	–	61
Drunkenness, .	3,401	1,242	3,207	3,194	3,023	10,666	3.14	–	†1
Drunkenness and other crimes, .	82	27	77	75	64	243	2.96	–	–
Other crimes, .	846	*334	771	716	665	2,486	2.94	–	60
Females.	555	182	507	473	406	1,568	2:83	–	33
Drunkenness, .	433	142	402	381	327	1,252	2.89	–	–
Drunkenness and other crimes, .	12	3	12	11	9	35	2.92	–	–
Other crimes, .	110	37	93	81	70	281	2.55	–	33
BOTH SEXES.	4,884	1,785	4,562	4,458	4,158	14,963	3.06	–	94
Drunkenness, .	3,834	1,384	3,609	3,575	3,350	11,918	3.11	–	†1
Drunkenness and other crimes, .	94	30	89	86	73	278	2.96	–	–
Other crimes, .	956	*371	864	797	735	2,767	2.89	–	93

AGE PERIOD: 50-59.

SEX AND DEGREE OF CRIME.	Number addicted to the Use of Intoxicating Liquors	Wines	Lager Beer	Malted Liquor	Distilled Liquor	Aggregate Number of Kinds of Liquor	Average Number of Kinds of Liquor	Particular Kinds of Liquor Unknown	Total Abstainers
Males.	2,001	758	1,844	1,823	1,735	6,160	3 08	–	33
Drunkenness, .	1,616	598	1,491	1,487	1,413	4,989	3.09	–	–
Drunkenness and other crimes, .	22	10	19	19	21	69	3.14	–	–
Other crimes, .	363	150	334	317	301	1,102	3.04	–	33
Females.	217	52	190	189	166	597	2.75	–	10
Drunkenness, .	184	43	164	166	143	516	2.80	–	–
Drunkenness and other crimes, .	6	–	5	3	5	13	2.17	–	–
Other crimes, .	27	9	21	20	18	68	2.52	–	10
BOTH SEXES.	2,218	810	2,034	2,012	1,901	6,757	3.04	–	43
Drunkenness, .	1,800	641	1,655	1,653	1,556	5,505	3.06	–	–
Drunkenness and other crimes, .	28	10	24	22	26	82	2.93	–	–
Other crimes, .	390	159	355	337	319	1,170	3 00	–	43

* Includes one cider.   † Inebriety caused by the use of narcotics and drugs.

*Crime; Sex, Degree of Crime, and Kinds of Liquor Used by Criminals: By
Age Periods* — Concluded.

AGE PERIOD: 60-79.

SEX AND DEGREE OF CRIME.	Number addicted to the Use of Intoxicating Liquors	Wines	Lager Beer	Malted Liquor	Distilled Liquor	Aggregate Number of Kinds of Liquor	Average Number of Kinds of Liquor	Particular Kinds of Liquor Unknown	Total Abstainers
Males.	630	209	565	551	550	1,875	2.98	–	14
Drunkenness, .	492	*168	452	435	437	1,492	3.03	–	–
Drunkenness and other crimes, .	8	1	7	8	7	23	2.89	–	–
Other crimes, .	130	40	106	108	106	360	2.77	–	14
Females.	87	28	81	76	74	259	2.98	–	4
Drunkenness, .	67	23	64	63	61	211	3.15	–	–
Other crimes, .	20	5	17	13	13·	48	2.40	–	4
BOTH SEXES.	717	237	646	627	624	2,134	2.98	–	18
Drunkenness, .	559	*191	516	498	498	1,703	3.05	–	–
Drunkenness and other crimes, .	8	1	7	8	7	23	2.89	–	–
Other crimes, .	150	45	123	121	119	408	2.72	–	18

AGE PERIOD: 80 +.

Males.	6	2	6	6	6	20	3.33	–	–
Drunkenness, .	6	2	6	6	6	20	3.33	–	–
Females.	6	3	4	6	4	17	2.83	–	–
Drunkenness, .	5	2	3	5	3	13	2.60	–	–
Other crimes, .	1	1	1	1	1	4	4.00	–	–
BOTH SEXES.	12	5	10	12	10	37	3.08	–	–
Drunkenness, .	11	4	9	11	9	33	3.00	–	–
Other crimes, .	1	1	1	1	1	4	4.00	–	–

AGE PERIOD: Unknown.

Males.	4	2	2	2	4	10	2.50	–	–
Drunkenness, .	3	2	2	2	3	9	3.00	–	–
Other crimes, .	1	–	–	–	1	1	1.00	–	–

* Includes one cider.

RECAPITULATION.

SEX AND DEGREE OF CRIME.	Number addicted to the Use of Intoxicating Liquors	Wines	Lager Beer	Malted Liquor	Distilled Liquor	Aggregate Number of Kinds of Liquor	Average Number of Kinds of Liquor	Particular Kinds of Liquor Unknown	Total Abstainers
Males.	22,341	8,058	20,787	19,931	18,276	67,052	3.00	-	1,240
Drunkenness, .	15,542	5,679	14,561	14,355	13,223	47,818	3.08	-	†1
Drunkenness and other crimes, .	608	177	571	535	486	1,769	2.91	-	-
Other crimes, .	6,191	2,202	5,655	5,041	4,567	17,465	2.82	-	1,239
Females.	2,796	833	2,568	2,302	1,975	7,678	2.75	-	295
Drunkenness, .	2,032	612	1,871	1,758	1,519	5,760	2.83	-	-
Drunkenness and other crimes, .	49	14	46	41	36	137	2.80	-	-
Other crimes, .	715	207	651	503	420	1,781	2.49	-	295
BOTH SEXES.	25,137	8,891	23,355	22,233	20,251	74,730	2.97	-	1,535
Drunkenness, .	17,574	6,291	16,432	16,113	14,742	53,578	3.05	-	†1
Drunkenness and other crimes, .	657	191	617	576	522	1,906	2.92	-	-
Other crimes, .	6,906	2,409	6,306	5,544	4,987	19,246	2.79	-	1,534

† Inebriety caused by the use of narcotics and drugs.

RECAPITULATION: BY AGE PERIODS.

SEX AND AGE PERIODS.	Number addicted to the Use of Intoxicating Liquors	Wines	Lager Beer	Malted Liquor	Distilled Liquor	Aggregate Number of Kinds of Liquor	Average Number of Kinds of Liquor	Particular Kinds of Liquor Unknown	Total Abstainers
Males.	22,341	8,058	20,787	19,931	18,276	67,052	3.00	-	1,240
10–14, . . .	3	-	2	1	2	5	1.67	-	52
15–19, . . .	625	167	553	415	355	1,490	2.38	-	534
20–29, . . .	7,565	2,633	7,014	6,589	5,797	22,033	2.91	-	429
30–39, . . .	7,178	2,684	6,746	6,559	6,075	22,064	3.07	-	117
40–49, . . .	4,329	1,603	4,055	3,985	3,752	13,395	3.09	-	61
50–59, . . .	2,001	758	1,844	1,823	1,735	6,160	3.08	-	33
60–79, . . .	630	209	565	551	550	1,875	2.98	-	14
80 +, . . .	6	2	6	6	6	20	3.33	-	-
Unknown, . .	4	2	2	2	4	10	2.50	-	-
Females.	2,796	833	2,568	2,302	1,975	7,678	2.75	-	295
10–14, . . .	1	-	1	1	1	3	3.00	-	-
15–19, . . .	51	8	50	33	25	116	2.27	-	46

RECAPITULATION: BY AGE PERIODS — Concluded.

SEX AND AGE PERIODS.	Number addicted to the Use of Intoxicating Liquors	Wines	Lager Beer	Malted Liquor	Distilled Liquor	Aggregate Number of Kinds of Liquor	Average Number of Kinds of Liquor	Particular Kinds of Liquor Unknown	Total Abstainers
Females — Con.									
20-29, . . .	917	247	862	716	599	2,424	2.64	-	137
30-39, . . .	962	313	873	808	700	2,694	2.80	-	65
40-49, . . .	555	182	507	473	406	1,568	2.83	-	33
50-59, . . .	217	52	190	189	166	597	2.75	-	10
60-79, . . .	87	28	81	76	74	259	2.98	-	4
80 +, . . .	6	3	4	6	4	17	2.83	-	-
BOTH SEXES.	25,137	8,891	23,355	22,233	20,251	74,730	2.97	-	1,535
10-14, . . .	4	-	3	2	3	8	2.00	-	52
15-19, . . .	676	175	603	448	380	1,606	2.38	-	580
20-29, . . .	8,482	2,830	7,876	7,305	6,396	24,457	2.88	-	566
30-39, . . .	8,140	2,997	7,619	7,367	6,775	24,758	3.04	-	182
40-49, . . .	4,884	1,785	4,562	4,458	4,158	14,963	3.06	-	94
50-59, . . .	2,218	810	2,034	2,012	1,901	6,757	3.05	-	43
60-79, . . .	717	237	646	627	624	2,134	2.98	-	18
80 +, . . .	12	5	10	12	10	37	3.08	-	-
Unknown, . .	4	2	2	2	4	10	2.50	-	-

Referring to the recapitulation for both sexes, we find among the 25,137 criminals addicted to the use of liquor, 8,891 instances in which wine was used, 23,355 lager beer, 22,233 malted liquors, and 20,251 distilled liquors, the classification resulting in an aggregate number of kinds of liquor amounting to 74,730, or an average of 2.97 kinds per person. The 17,575 persons convicted of drunkenness only, included 6,291 who stated that they used wine, 16,432 who used lager beer, 16,113 who used malted liquors other than lager beer, 14,742 who used distilled liquors, and one who used narcotics and drugs. The 657 criminals who were convicted of drunkenness and other crimes included 191 wine drinkers, 617 lager beer drinkers, 576 users of malted liquors, and 522 who used distilled liquors. These figures do not indicate the exclusive use of any particular form of liquor among the criminals, for although nearly the entire number used lager beer, a very large proportion also used distilled liquors. The same fact is brought out in connection with the 6,906 criminals who were convicted of crimes other than drunkenness. Among these, there were 2,409 who used wine, 6,306 who used lager beer, 5,544 who used malted liquors, while 4,987 used distilled liquors.

The next table shows the kinds of liquor used by the fathers of criminals, the classification contained in the table being the same as in the preceding presentations.

Crime; Sex, Degree of Crime, and Kinds of Liquor Used by Fathers of Criminals: By Age Periods.

AGE PERIOD: 10-14.

SEX AND DEGREE OF CRIME.	Number addicted to the Use of Intoxicating Liquors	Wines	Lager Beer	Malted Liquor	Distilled Liquor	Aggregate Number of Kinds of Liquor	Average Number of Kinds of Liquor	Particular Kinds of Liquor Unknown	Total Abstainers
Males.	27	1	21	9	15	46	1.70	3	25
Drunkenness and other crimes, .	1	-	1	1	1	3	3.00	-	-
Other crimes, .	26	1	20	8	14	43	1.65	3	25
Females.	-	-	-	-	-	-	-	1	-
Drunkenness, .	-	-	-	-	-	-	-	1	-
BOTH SEXES.	27	1	21	9	15	46	1.70	4	25
Drunkenness, .	-	-	-	-	-	-	-	1	
Drunkenness and other crimes, .	1	-	1	1	1	3	3.00	-	-
Other crimes, .	26	1	20	8	14	43	1.65	3	25

AGE PERIOD: 15-19.

Males.	630	146	434	404	440	1,424	2.26	84	445
Drunkenness, .	131	30	96	105	96	327	2.50	14	81
Drunkenness and other crimes, .	16	4	14	16	11	45	2.81	-	7
Other crimes, .	483	112	324	283	333	1,052	2.18	70	357
Females.	49	3	41	39	36	119	2.43	7	41
Drunkenness, .	7	-	5	6	7	18	2.57	1	7
Other crimes, .	42	3	36	33	29	101	2.40	6	34
BOTH SEXES.	679	149	475	443	476	1,543	2.27	91	486
Drunkenness, .	138	30	101	111	103	345	2.50	15	88
Drunkenness and other crimes, .	16	4	14	16	11	45	2.81	-	7
Other crimes, .	525	115	360	316	362	1,153	2.20	76	391

Crime: Sex, Degree of Crime, and Kinds of Liquor Used by Fathers of Criminals: By Age Periods — Continued.

AGE PERIOD: 20-29.

SEX AND DEGREE OF CRIME.	Number addicted to the Use of Intoxicating Liquors	Wines	Lager Beer	Malted Liquor	Distilled Liquor	Aggregate Number of Kinds of Liquor	Average Number of Kinds of Liquor	Particular Kinds of Liquor Unknown	Total Abstainers
Males.	4,692	1,044	3,327	3,766	3,523	11,660	2.48	529	2,773
Drunkenness, .	2,776	551	1,992	2,321	2,110	6,974	2.69	276	1,517
Drunkenness and other crimes, .	179	22	127	142	134	425	2.37	13	99
Other crimes, .	1,737	471	1,208	1,303	1,279	4,261	2.45	240	1,157
Females.	537	80	375	441	398	1,294	2.40	106	411
Drunkenness, .	335	39	227	274	252	792	2.36	60	210
Drunkenness and other crimes, ..	10	3	7	10	7	27	2.70	2	2
Other crimes, .	192	38	141	157	139	475	2.48	44	199
BOTH SEXES.	5,229	1,124	3,702	4,207	3,921	12,954	2.48	635	3,184
Drunkenness, .	3,111	590	2,219	2,595	2,362	7,766	2.56	336	1,727
Drunkenness and other crimes, .	189	25	134	152	141	452	2.39	15	101
Other crimes, .	1,929	509	1,349	1,460	1,418	4,736	2.45	284	1,356

AGE PERIOD: 30-39.

Males.	4,402	883	2,795	3,496	3,483	10,657	2.42	658	2,244
Drunkenness, .	3,187	587	2,027	2,595	2,558	7,767	2.44	444	1,604
Drunkenness and other crimes, .	95	19	63	73	73	228	2.40	22	64
Other crimes, .	1,120	277	705	828	852	2,662	2.38	192	576
Females.	516	63	323	419	398	1,203	2.30	124	387
Drunkenness, .	367	42	230	307	286	865	2.36	74	281
Drunkenness and other crimes, .	7	–	6	6	7	19	2.71	4	6
Other crimes, .	142	21	87	106	105	319	2.25	46	100
BOTH SEXES.	4,918	946	3,118	3,915	3,881	11,860	2.41	782	2,631
Drunkenness, .	3,554	629	2,257	2,902	2,844	8,632	2.43	518	1,885
Drunkenness and other crimes, .	102	19	69	79	80	247	2.42	26	70
Other crimes, .	1,262	298	792	934	957	2,981	2.36	238	676

Crime; Sex, Degree of Crime, and Kinds of Liquor Used by Fathers of Criminals: By Age Periods — Continued.

AGE PERIOD : 40-49.

SEX AND DEGREE OF CRIME.	Number addicted to the Use of Intoxicating Liquors	Wines	Lager Beer	Malted Liquor	Distilled Liquor	Aggregate Number of Kinds of Liquor	Average Number of Kinds of Liquor	Particular Kinds of Liquor Unknown	Total Abstainers
Males.	2,579	516	1,508	2,022	2,097	6,143	2.38	512	1,303
Drunkenness, .	1,998	360	1,178	1,622	1,648	4,808	2.41	397	1,011
Drunkenness and other crimes, .	52	9	32	44	41	126	2.42	9	21
Other crimes, .	529	147	298	356	408	1,209	2.29	106	271
Females.	291	37	128	226	236	627	2.15	88	211
Drunkenness, .	221	24	99	171	177	471	2.13	65	149
Drunkenness and other crimes, .	9	1	3	8	9	21	2.33	2	1
Other crimes, .	61	12	26	47	50	135	2.21	21	61
BOTH SEXES.	2,870	553	1,636	2,248	2,333	6,770	2.35	600	1,514
Drunkenness, .	2,219	384	1,277	1,793	1,825	5,279	2.38	462	1,160
Drunkenness and other crimes, .	61	10	35	52	50	147	2.41	11	22
Other crimes, .	590	159	324	403	458	1,344	2.27	127	332

AGE PERIOD : 50-59.

Males.	1,188	229	581	899	1,018	2,727	2.30	320	527
Drunkenness, .	943	174	458	723	816	2,171	2.31	262	412
Drunkenness and other crimes, .	13	2	9	9	10	30	2.31	4	5
Other crimes, .	232	53	114	167	192	526	2.27	54	110
Females.	112	14	36	85	99	234	2.10	48	67
Drunkenness, .	89	11	29	70	80	190	2.13	40	55
Drunkenness and other crimes, .	4	–	1	2	4	7	1.75	1	1
Other crimes, .	19	3	6	13	15	37	1.95	7	11
BOTH SEXES.	1,300	243	617	984	1,117	2,961	2.21	368	594
Drunkenness, .	1,032	185	487	793	896	2,361	2.29	302	467
Drunkenness and other crimes, .	17	2	10	11	14	37	2.18	5	6
Other crimes, .	251	56	120	180	207	563	2.24	61	121

Crime; Sex, Degree of Crime, and Kinds of Liquor Used by Fathers of Criminals: By Age Periods — Concluded.

AGE PERIOD : 60-79.

SEX AND DEGREE OF CRIME.	Number addicted to the Use of Intoxicating Liquors	Wines	Lager Beer	Malted Liquor	Distilled Liquor	Aggregate Number of Kinds of Liquor	Average Number of Kinds of Liquor	Particular Kinds of Liquor Unknown	Total Abstainers
Males.	371	76	165	267	327	835	2.25	115	158
Drunkenness, .	281	48	125	209	254	636	2.26	86	125
Drunkenness and other crimes, .	7	–	1	3	6	10	1.43	1	–
Other crimes, .	83	28	39	55	67	189	2.28	28	33
Females. .	40	3	9	29	32	73	1.83	27	24
Drunkenness, .	30	1	8	22	23	54	1.80	21	16
Other crimes, .	10	2	1	7	9	19	1.90	6	8
BOTH SEXES.	411	79	174	296	359	908	2.21	142	182
Drunkenness, .	311	49	133	231	277	690	2.22	107	141
Drunkenness and other crimes, .	7	–	1	3	6	10	1.43	1	–
Other crimes, .	93	30	40	62	76	208	2.24	34	41

AGE PERIOD : 80 +.

Males.	2	1	1	1	1	4	2.00	3	1
Drunkenness, .	2	1	1	1	1	4	2.00	3	1
Females.	2	–	1	1	1	3	1.50	3	1
Drunkenness, .	1	–	–	1	1	2	2.00	3	1
Other crimes, .	1	–	1	–	–	1	1.00	–	–
BOTH SEXES.	4	1	2	2	2	7	1.50	6	2
Drunkenness, .	3	1	1	2	2	6	2.00	6	2
Other crimes, .	1	–	1	–	–	1	1.00	–	–

AGE PERIOD : Unknown.

Males.	2	–	–	–	2	2	1.00	2	–
Drunkenness, .	1	–	–	–	1	1	1.00	2	–
Other crimes, .	1	–	–	–	1	1	1.00	–	–

RECAPITULATION.

Sex and Degree of Crime.	Number addicted to the Use of Intoxicating Liquors	Wines	Lager Beer	Malted Liquor	Distilled Liquor	Aggregate Number of Kinds of Liquor	Average Number of Kinds of Liquor	Particular Kinds of Liquor Unknown	Total Abstainers
Males.	13,893	2,896	8,832	10,864	10,906	33,498	2.41	2,226	7,476
Drunkenness,	9,319	1,751	5,877	7,576	7,484	22,688	2.43	1,484	4,751
Drunkenness and other crimes,	363	56	247	288	276	867	2.38	49	196
Other crimes,	4,211	1,089	2,708	3,000	3,146	9,943	2.36	693	2,529
Females.	1,547	200	913	1,240	1,200	3,553	2.30	404	1,142
Drunkenness,	1,050	117	598	851	826	2,392	2.28	265	719
Drunkenness and other crimes,	30	4	17	26	27	74	2.47	9	10
Other crimes,	467	79	298	363	347	1,087	2.33	130	413
BOTH SEXES.	15,440	3,096	9,745	12,104	12,106	37,051	2.40	2,630	8,618
Drunkenness,	10,369	1,868	6,475	8,427	8,310	25,080	2.42	1,749	5,470
Drunkenness and other crimes,	393	60	264	314	303	941	2.39	58	206
Other crimes,	4,678	1,168	3,006	3,363	3,493	11,030	2.36	823	2,942

RECAPITULATION: BY AGE PERIODS.

Sex and Age Periods.	Number addicted to the Use of Intoxicating Liquors	Wines	Lager Beer	Malted Liquor	Distilled Liquor	Aggregate Number of Kinds of Liquor	Average Number of Kinds of Liquor	Particular Kinds of Liquor Unknown	Total Abstainers
Males.	13,893	2,896	8,832	10,864	10,906	33,498	2.41	2,226	7,476
10–14,	27	1	21	9	15	46	1.70	3	25
15–19,	630	146	434	404	440	1,424	2.26	84	445
20–29,	4,692	1,044	3,327	3,766	3,523	11,660	2.48	529	2,773
30–39,	4,402	883	2,795	3,496	3,483	10,657	2.42	658	2,244
40–49,	2,579	516	1,508	2,022	2,097	6,143	2.38	512	1,303
50–59,	1,188	229	581	899	1,018	2,727	2.30	320	527
60–79,	371	76	165	267	327	835	2.25	115	158
80 +,	2	1	1	1	1	4	2.00	3	1
Unknown,	2	–	–	–	2	2	1.00	2	–
Females.	1,547	200	913	1,240	1,200	3,553	2.30	404	1,142
10–14,	–	–	–	–	–	–	–	1	–
15–19,	49	3	41	39	36	119	2.43	7	41

RECAPITULATION: BY AGE PERIODS — Concluded.

SEX AND AGE PERIODS.	Number addicted to the Use of Intoxicating Liquors	Wines	Lager Beer	Malted Liquor	Distilled Liquor	Aggregate Number of Kinds of Liquor	Average Number of Kinds of Liquor	Particular Kinds of Liquor Unknown	Total Abstainers
Females — Con.									
20-29, . . .	537	80	375	441	398	1,294	2.40	106	411
30-39, . . .	516	63	323	419	398	1,203	2.30	124	387
40-49, . . .	291	37	128	226	236	627	2.15	88	211
50-59, . . .	112	14	36	85	99	234	2.10	48	67
60-79, . . .	40	3	9	29	32	73	1.83	27	24
80 +, . . .	2	–	1	1	1	3	1.50	3	1
BOTH SEXES.	15,440	3,096	9,745	12,104	12,106	37,051	2.40	2,630	8,618
10-14, . . .	27	1	21	9	15	46	1.70	4	25
15-19, . . .	679	149	475	443	476	1,543	2.77	91	486
20-29, . . .	5,229	1,124	3,702	4,207	3,921	12,954	2.47	635	3,184
30-39, . . .	4,918	946	3,118	3,915	3,881	11,860	2.42	782	2,631
40-49, . . .	2,870	553	1,636	2,248	2,333	6,770	2.36	600	1,514
50-59, . . .	1,300	243	617	984	1,117	2,961	2.28	368	594
60-79, . . .	411	79	174	296	359	908	2.16	142	182
80 +, . . .	4	1	2	2	2	7	1.75	6	2
Unknown, . .	2	–	–	–	2	2	1.00	2	–

As before, we confine our analysis to the recapitulation for both sexes. Disregarding the 8,618 cases in which the fathers were total abstainers, and the 2,630 in which the particular kinds of liquor used by the fathers was unknown, we find among the 15,440 cases in which the fathers were addicted to the use of intoxicating liquors, 3,096 who reported the use of wine, 9,745 lager beer, 12,104 malted liquors, and 12,106 distilled liquors. These figures indicate that the use of distilled liquors exceeds the use of lager beer, and is fully equal to the use of malted liquors other than lager beer. Among the fathers of criminals convicted of crimes other than drunkenness, who were addicted to the use of intoxicating liquors, the aggregate number being 4,678, we find 1,168 wine drinkers, 3,006 lager beer drinkers, 3,316 who used malted liquors, and 3,493 who used distilled liquors.

A similar table, showing the kinds of liquor used by the mothers of criminals, follows.

Crime; Sex, Degree of Crime, and Kinds of Liquor Used by Mothers of Criminals: By Age Periods.

AGE PERIOD: 10–14.

SEX AND DEGREE OF CRIME.	Number addicted to the Use of Intoxicating Liquors	Wines	Lager Beer	Malted Liquor	Distilled Liquor	Aggregate Number of Kinds of Liquor	Average Number of Kinds of Liquor	Particular Kinds of Liquor Unknown	Total Abstainers
Males.	11	1	8	3	2	14	1.27	3	41
Drunkenness and other crimes, .	–	–	–	–	–	–	–	–	1
Other crimes, .	11	1	8	3	2	14	1.27	3	40
Females.	–	–	–	–	–	–	–	–	1
Drunkenness, .	–	–	–	–	–	–	–	–	1
BOTH SEXES.	11	1	8	3	2	14	1.27	3	42
Drunkenness, .	–	–	–	–	–	–	–	–	1
Drunkenness and other crimes, .	–	–	–	–	–	–	–	–	1
Other crimes, .	11	1	8	3	2	14	1.27	3	40

AGE PERIOD: 15–19.

SEX AND DEGREE OF CRIME.	Number addicted	Wines	Lager Beer	Malted Liquor	Distilled Liquor	Aggregate	Average	Particular Unknown	Total Abstainers
Males.	216	65	150	114	91	420	1.94	52	891
Drunkenness, .	42	11	30	27	17	85	2.02	7	177
Drunkenness and other crimes, .	6	2	4	5	3	14	2.33	2	15
Other crimes, .	168	52	116	82	71	321	1.91	43	699
Females.	23	2	20	19	13	54	2.35	8	66
Drunkenness, .	5	1	4	5	3	13	2.60	–	10
Other crimes, .	18	1	16	14	10	41	2.28	8	56
BOTH SEXES.	239	67	170	133	104	474	1.98	60	957
Drunkenness, .	47	12	34	32	20	98	2.09	7	187
Drunkenness and other crimes, .	6	2	4	5	3	14	2.33	2	15
Other crimes, .	186	53	132	96	81	362	1.95	51	755

AGE PERIOD: 20–29.

SEX AND DEGREE OF CRIME.	Number addicted	Wines	Lager Beer	Malted Liquor	Distilled Liquor	Aggregate	Average	Particular Unknown	Total Abstainers
Males.	1,459	343	937	1,021	601	2,902	1.99	393	6,143
Drunkenness, .	846	161	548	628	381	1,718	2.03	212	3,511
Drunkenness and other crimes, .	55	7	41	46	24	118	2.15	7	229
Other crimes, .	558	175	348	347	196	1,066	1.91	174	2,403

Crime; Sex, Degree of Crime, and Kinds of Liquor Used by Mothers of Criminals: By Age Periods — Continued.

AGE PERIOD: 20-29 — Concluded.

SEX AND DEGREE OF CRIME.	Number addicted to the Use of Intoxicating Liquors	Wines	Lager Beer	Malted Liquor	Distilled Liquor	Aggregate Number of Kinds of Liquor	Average Number of Kinds of Liquor	Particular Kinds of Liquor Unknown	Total Abstainers
Females.	245	40	159	189	109	497	2.03	68	742
Drunkenness, .	168	21	108	133	75	337	2.01	36	401
Drunkenness and other crimes, .	4	1	2	3	2	8	2.00	1	9
Other crimes, .	73	18	49	53	32	152	2.08	31	332
BOTH SEXES.	1,704	383	1,096	1,210	710	3,399	1.99	461	6,885
Drunkenness, .	1,014	182	656	761	456	2,055	2.03	248	3,912
Drunkenness and other crimes, .	59	8	43	49	26	126	2.14	8	238
Other crimes, .	631	193	397	400	228	1,218	1.93	205	2,735

AGE PERIOD: 30-39.

Males.	1,442	288	825	1,041	656	2,810	1.95	444	5,413
Drunkenness, .	985	163	567	752	459	1,941	1.97	315	3,932
Drunkenness and other crimes, .	33	3	14	24	13	54	1.64	18	130
Other crimes, .	424	122	244	265	184	815	1.92	111	1,351
Females.	247	33	151	176	121	481	1.95	85	695
Drunkenness, .	175	20	106	130	85	341	1.95	52	495
Drunkenness and other crimes, .	2	–	2	2	1	5	2.50	2	13
Other crimes, .	70	13	43	44	35	135	1.93	31	187
BOTH SEXES.	1,689	321	976	1,217	777	3,291	1.95	529	6,108
Drunkenness, .	1,160	183	673	882	544	2,282	1.97	367	4,427
Drunkenness and other crimes, .	35	3	16	26	14	59	1.69	20	143
Other crimes, .	494	135	287	309	219	950	1.92	142	1,538

AGE PERIOD: 40-49.

Males.	892	166	434	660	459	1,719	1.93	366	3,133
Drunkenness, .	688	107	341	540	368	1,356	1.97	283	2,432
Drunkenness and other crimes, .	18	–	9	14	8	31	1.72	7	57
Other crimes, .	186	59	84	106	83	332	1.78	76	644

Crime: Sex, Degree of Crime, and Kinds of Liquor Used by Mothers of Criminals: By Age Periods — Continued.

AGE PERIOD: 40-49 — Concluded.

SEX AND DEGREE OF CRIME.	Number addicted to the Use of Intoxicating Liquors	Wines	Lager Beer	Malted Liquor	Distilled Liquor	Aggregate Number of Kinds of Liquor	Average Number of Kinds of Liquor	Particular Kinds of Liquor Unknown	Total Abstainers
Females.	142	18	60	101	77	256	1.80	63	383
Drunkenness,	106	12	51	76	54	193	1.81	47	280
Drunkenness and other crimes,	5	–	–	4	3	7	1.40	–	7
Other crimes,	31	6	9	21	20	56	1.81	16	96
BOTH SEXES.	1,034	184	494	761	536	1,975	1.91	429	3,516
Drunkenness,	794	119	392	616	422	1,549	1.95	330	2,712
Drunkenness and other crimes,	23	–	9	18	11	38	1.65	7	64
Other crimes,	217	65	93	127	103	388	1.79	92	740

AGE PERIOD: 50-59.

Males.	524	94	198	379	305	976	1.86	245	1,267
Drunkenness,	413	64	153	315	256	788	1.91	201	1,004
Drunkenness and other crimes,	4	1	2	1	2	6	1.50	2	16
Other crimes,	107	29	43	63	47	182	1.70	42	247
Females.	71	7	20	56	50	133	1.87	40	116
Drunkenness,	58	5	16	46	40	107	1.84	32	94
Drunkenness and other crimes,	4	–	1	2	4	7	1.75	1	1
Other crimes,	9	2	3	8	6	19	2.11	7	21
BOTH SEXES.	595	101	218	435	355	1,109	1.86	285	1,383
Drunkenness,	471	69	169	361	296	895	1.90	233	1,098
Drunkenness and other crimes,	8	1	3	3	6	13	1.63	3	17
Other crimes,	116	31	46	71	53	201	1.73	49	268

AGE PERIOD: 60-79.

Males.	164	30	55	112	111	308	1.88	97	383
Drunkenness,	115	12	35	82	84	213	1.85	78	299
Drunkenness and other crimes,	4	–	1	2	3	6	1.50	–	4
Other crimes,	45	18	19	28	24	89	1.98	19	80

Crime; Sex, Degree of Crime, and Kinds of Liquor Used by Mothers of
Criminals: By Age Periods — Concluded.

AGE PERIOD: 60-79 — Concluded.

SEX AND DEGREE OF CRIME.	Number addicted to the Use of Intoxicating Liquors	Wines	Lager Beer	Malted Liquor	Distilled Liquor	Aggregate Number of Kinds of Liquor	Average Number of Kinds of Liquor	Particular Kinds of Liquor Unknown	Total Abstainers
Females.	24	2	5	16	19	42	1.75	25	42
Drunkenness, .	18	–	5	12	15	32	1.78	21	28
Other crimes, .	6	2	–	4	4	10	1.67	4	14
BOTH SEXES.	188	32	60	128	130	350	1.86	122	425
Drunkenness, .	133	12	40	94	99	245	1.84	99	327
Drunkenness and other crimes, .	4	–	1	2	3	6	1.50	–	4
Other crimes, .	51	20	19	32	28	99	1.94	23	94

AGE PERIOD: 80 +.

Males.	1	1	1	–	–	2	2.00	3	2
Drunkenness, .	1	1	1	–	–	2	2.00	3	2
Females.	2	–	1	1	1	3	1.50	2	2
Drunkenness, .	1	–	–	1	1	2	2.00	2	2
Other crimes, .	1	–	1	–	–	1	1.00	–	–
BOTH SEXES.	3	1	2	1	1	5	1.67	5	4
Drunkenness, .	2	1	1	1	1	4	2.00	5	4
Other crimes, .	1	–	1	–	–	1	1.00	–	–

AGE PERIOD: Unknown.

Males.	1	–	–	–	1	1	1.00	3	–
Drunkenness, .	–	–	–	–	–	–	–	3	–
Other crimes, .	1	–	–	–	1	1	1.00	–	–

RECAPITULATION.

SEX AND DEGREE OF CRIME.	Number addicted to the Use of Intoxicating Liquors	Wines	Lager Beer	Malted Liquor	Distilled Liquor	Aggregate Number of Kinds of Liquor	Average Number of Kinds of Liquor	Particular Kinds of Liquor Unknown	Total Abstainers
Males.	4,710	988	2,608	3,330	2,226	9,152	1.94	1,606	17,273
Drunkenness, .	3,090	519	1,675	2,344	1,565	6,103	1.97	1,102	11,357
Drunkenness and other crimes, .	120	13	71	92	53	229	1.91	36	452
Other crimes, .	1,500	456	862	894	608	2,820	1.88	468	5,464
Females.	754	102	416	558	390	1,466	1.94	291	2,047
Drunkenness, .	531	59	290	403	273	1,025	1.93	190	1,311
Drunkenness and other crimes, .	15	1	5	11	10	27	1.80	4	30
Other crimes, .	208	42	121	144	107	414	1.99	97	706
BOTH SEXES.	5,464	1,090	3,024	3,888	2,616	10,618	1.94	1,897	19,320
Drunkenness, .	3,621	578	1,965	2,747	1,838	7,128	1.97	1,292	12,668
Drunkenness and other crimes, .	135	14	76	103	63	256	1.90	40	482
Other crimes, .	1,708	498	983	1,038	715	3,234	1.89	565	6,170

RECAPITULATION : BY AGE PERIODS.

SEX AND AGE PERIODS.	Number addicted to the Use of Intoxicating Liquors	Wines	Lager Beer	Malted Liquor	Distilled Liquor	Aggregate Number of Kinds of Liquor	Average Number of Kinds of Liquor	Particular Kinds of Liquor Unknown	Total Abstainers
Males.	4,710	988	2,608	3,330	2,226	9,152	1.94	1,606	17,273
10-14, . . .	11	1	8	3	2	14	1.27	3	41
15-19, . . .	216	65	150	114	91	420	1.94	52	891
20-29, . . .	1,459	343	937	1,021	601	2,902	1.99	393	6,143
30-39, . . .	1,442	288	825	1,041	656	2,810	1.95	444	5,413
40-49, . . .	892	166	434	660	459	1,719	1.93	366	3,133
50-59, . . .	524	94	198	379	305	976	1.86	245	1,267
60-79, . . .	164	30	55	112	111	308	1.88	97	383
80 +, . . .	1	1	1	–	–	2	2.00	3	2
Unknown, . .	1	–	–	–	1	1	1.00	3	–
Females.	754	102	416	558	390	1,466	1.94	291	2,047
10-14, . . .	–	–	–	–	–	–	–	–	1
15-19, . . .	23	2	20	19	13	54	2.35	8	66
20-29, . . .	245	40	159	189	109	497	2.03	68	742

RECAPITULATION: BY AGE PERIODS — Concluded

SEX AND AGE PERIODS.	Number addicted to the Use of Intoxicating Liquors	Wines	Lager Beer	Malted Liquor	Distilled Liquor	Aggregate Number of Kinds of Liquor	Average Number of Kinds of Liquor	Particular Kinds of Liquor Un-known	Total Abstainers
Females — Con.									
30-39, . . .	247	33	151	176	121	481	1.95	85	695
40-49, . . .	142	18	60	101	77	256	1.80	63	383
50-59, . . .	71	7	20	56	50	133	1.87	40	116
60-79, . . .	24	2	5	16	19	42	1.75	25	42
80 +, . . .	2	–	1	1	1	3	1.50	2	2
BOTH SEXES.	6,464	1,090	3,024	3,888	2,616	10,618	1.94	1,897	19,320
10-14, . . .	11	1	8	3	2	14	1.27	3	42
15-19, . . .	239	67	170	133	104	474	1.98	60	957
20-29, . . .	1,704	383	1,096	1,210	710	3,399	1.99	461	6,885
30-39, . . .	1,689	321	976	1,217	777	3,291	1.95	529	6,108
40-49, . . .	1,034	184	494	761	536	1,975	1.91	429	3,516
50-59, . . .	595	101	218	435	355	1,109	1.86	285	1,383
60-79, . . .	188	32	60	128	130	350	1.86	122	425
80 +, . . .	3	1	2	1	1	5	1.67	6	4
Unknown, . .	1	–	–	–	1	1	1.00	3	–

Disregarding the 19,320 cases in which the mothers were total abstainers, and the 1,897 cases in which the particular kinds of liquor used by the mothers was unknown, we find among the 5,464 cases in which the mothers of criminals were addicted to the use of intoxicating liquors, 1,090 instances of wine drinking, 3,024 lager beer, 3,888 malted liquors, and 2,616 distilled liquors. Among the 1,708 criminals who were convicted of crimes other than drunkenness, and whose mothers were addicted to the use of liquor, we find for the mothers, 498 instances of wine drinking, 983 lager beer, 1,038 malted liquors, and 715 distilled liquors, these, of course, being included in the total of each class which we have just cited, the difference between these figures and the total, representing the mothers in each class of criminals who were convicted of drunkenness or of drunkenness in connection with other crimes.

The series of three tables, which follows, presents the facts as to the use of tobacco by criminals, and by the fathers and mothers of criminals. The first table relates to the criminals themselves.

Crime; Sex, Degree of Crime, and Use of Tobacco by Criminals: By Age Periods.

AGE PERIOD: 10-14.

SEX AND DEGREE OF CRIME.	Users of Tobacco	Non-users	Number of Criminals
Males.	27	28	55
Drunkenness and other crimes, .	–	1	1
Other crimes, ...	27	27	54
Females.	–.	1	1
Drunkenness, ...	–	1	1
BOTH SEXES.	27	29	56
Drunkenness, ...	–	1	1
Drunkenness and other crimes, . .	–	1	1
Other crimes, ...	27	27	54

AGE PERIOD: 15-19.

	Users of Tobacco	Non-users	Number of Criminals
Males.	861	298	1,159
Drunkenness, ...	194	32	226
Drunkenness and other crimes, . .	21	2	23
Other crimes, ...	646	264	910
Females.	6	91	97
Drunkenness, ...	1	14	15
Other crimes, ...	5	77	82
BOTH SEXES.	867	389	1,256
Drunkenness, ...	195	46	241
Drunkenness and other crimes, . .	21	2	23
Other crimes, ...	651	341	992

AGE PERIOD: 20-29.

	Users of Tobacco	Non-users	Number of Criminals
Males.	7,506	488	7,994
Drunkenness, ...	4,395	174	4,569
Drunkenness and other crimes, . .	280	11	291
Other crimes, ...	2,831	303	3,134
Females.	163	891	1,054
Drunkenness, ...	115	490	605
Drunkenness and other crimes, . .	1	13	14
Other crimes, ...	47	388	435

Crime; Sex, Degree of Crime, and Use of Tobacco by Criminals: By Age Periods — Continued.

AGE PERIOD: 20-29 — Concluded.

SEX AND DEGREE OF CRIME.	Users of Tobacco	Non-users	Number of Criminals
BOTH SEXES.	7,669	1,379	9,048
Drunkenness, ...	4,510	664	5,174
Drunkenness and other crimes, . .	281	24	305
Other crimes, ...	2,878	691	3,569

AGE PERIOD: 30-39.

	Users of Tobacco	Non-users	Number of Criminals
Males.	6,970	325	7,295
Drunkenness, ...	5,050	179	5,229
Drunkenness and other crimes, . .	175	6	181
Other crimes, ...	1,745	140	1,885
Females.	204	823	1,027
Drunkenness, ...	171	551	722
Drunkenness and other crimes, .	4	13	17
Other crimes, ...	29	259	288
BOTH SEXES.	7,174	1,148	8,322
Drunkenness, ...	5,221	730	5,951
Drunkenness and other crimes, . .	179	19	198
Other crimes, ...	1,774	399	2,173

AGE PERIOD: 40-49.

	Users of Tobacco	Non-users	Number of Criminals
Males.	4,200	190	4,390
Drunkenness, ...	3,291	111	3,402
Drunkenness and other crimes, .	80	2	82
Other crimes, ...	829	77	906
Females.	142	446	588
Drunkenness, ...	115	318	433
Drunkenness and other crimes, . .	2	10	12
Other crimes, ...	25	118	143
BOTH SEXES.	4,342	636	4,978
Drunkenness, ...	3,406	429	3,835
Drunkenness and other crimes, . .	82	12	94
Other crimes, ...	854	195	1,049

Crime; Sex, Degree of Crime, and Use of Tobacco by Criminals: By Age Periods — Continued.

AGE PERIOD: 50–59.

SEX AND DEGREE OF CRIME.	Users of Tobacco	Non-users	Number of Criminals
Males.	1,938	96	2,034
Drunkenness, ...	1,550	66	1,616
Drunkenness and other crimes, . .	21	1	22
Other crimes, ...	367	29	396
Females.	72	155	227
Drunkenness, ...	69	115	184
Drunkenness and other crimes, . .	–	6	6
Other crimes, ...	3	34	37
BOTH SEXES.	2,010	251	2,261
Drunkenness, ...	1,619	181	1,800
Drunkenness and other crimes, . .	21	7	28
Other crimes, ...	370	63	433

AGE PERIOD: 60–79.

	Users of Tobacco	Non-users	Number of Criminals
Males.	602	42	644
Drunkenness, ...	473	19	492
Drunkenness and other crimes, . .	8	–	8
Other crimes, ...	121	23	144
Females.	37	54	91
Drunkenness, ...	30	37	67
Other crimes, ...	7	17	24
BOTH SEXES.	639	96	735
Drunkenness, ...	503	56	559
Drunkenness and other crimes, . .	8	–	8
Other crimes, ...	128	40	168

AGE PERIOD: 80 +.

	Users of Tobacco	Non-users	Number of Criminals
Males.	6	–	6
Drunkenness, . .	6	–	6
Females.	2	4	6
Drunkenness, ...	2	3	5 *
Other crimes, ...	–	1	1

Crime; Sex, Degree of Crime, and Use of Tobacco by Criminals: By Age Periods — Concluded.

AGE PERIOD : 80 + — Concluded.

SEX AND DEGREE OF CRIME.	Users of Tobacco	Non-users	Number of Criminals
BOTH SEXES.	8	4	12
Drunkenness, ...	8	3	11
Other crimes, ...	-	1	1

AGE PERIOD : Unknown.

	Users of Tobacco	Non-users	Number of Criminals
Males.	2	2	4
Drunkenness, ...	2	1	3
Other crimes, ...	-	1	1

RECAPITULATION.

SEX AND DEGREE OF CRIME.	Users of Tobacco	Non-users	Number of Criminals
Males.	22,112	1,469	23,581
Drunkenness, ...	14,961	582	15,543
Drunkenness and other crimes, . .	585	23	608
Other crimes, ...	6,566	864	7,430
Females.	626	2,465	3,091
Drunkenness, ...	503	1,529	2,032
Drunkenness and other crimes, .	7	42	49
Other crimes, ...	116	894	1,010
BOTH SEXES.	22,738	3,934	26,672
Drunkenness, ...	15,464	2,111	17,575
Drunkenness and other crimes, . .	592	65	657
Other crimes, ...	6,682	1,758	8,440

RECAPITULATION : BY AGE PERIODS.

SEX AND AGE PERIODS.	Users of Tobacco	Non-users	Number of Criminals
Males.	22,112	1,469	23,581
10-14, ...	27	28	55
15-19, ...	861	298	1,159
20-29, ...	7,506	488	7,994
30-39, ...	6,970	325	7,295

RECAPITULATION: BY AGE PERIODS — Concluded.

SEX AND AGE PERIODS.	Users of Tobacco	Non-users	Number of Criminals
Males — Con.			
40–49, ...	4,200	190	4,390
50–59, ...	1,938	96	2,034
60–79, ...	602	42	644
80 +, ...	6	-	6
Unknown, ...	2	2	4
Females.	626	2,465	3,091
10–14, ...	-	1	1
15–19, ...	6	91	97
20–29, ...	163	891	1,054
30–39, ...	204	823	1,027
40–49, ...	142	446	588
50–59, ...	72	155	227
60–79, ...	37	54	91
80 +, ...	2	4	6
BOTH SEXES.	22,738	3,934	26,672
10–14, ...	27	29	56
15–19, ...	867	389	1,256
20–29, ...	7,669	1,379	9,048
30–39, ...	7,174	1,148	8,322
40–49, ...	4,342	636	4,978
50–59, ...	2,010	251	2,261
60–79, ...	639	96	735
80 +, ...	8	4	12
Unknown, ...	2	2	4

As in the preceding tables, the classification by ages and by the degree of crime is preserved. We confine our analysis, however, to the recapitulation for both sexes, from which it appears that among the 26,672 criminals, there were 22,738 who used tobacco, the non-users numbering 3,934. Of the 22,738 who used tobacco, 15,464 were convicted of drunkenness, 592 of drunkenness and other crimes, while 6,682 were convicted of other crimes only. Those not using it who were convicted of drunkenness, and of drunkenness in connection with other crimes, number 2,176, while the non-users who were convicted of crimes other than drunkenness, number 1,758. Among the 3,091 female criminals there were 626

users of tobacco, of whom 510 were convicted of drunkenness
and of drunkenness in connection with other crimes; the remaining 116 were convicted of other crimes only.
The next table of the series relates to the fathers of criminals.

Crime; Sex, Degree of Crime, and Use of Tobacco by Fathers of Criminals:
By Age Periods.

AGE PERIOD: 10–14.

SEX AND DEGREE OF CRIME.	Users of Tobacco	Non-users	Number of Criminals
Males.	37	18	55
Drunkenness and other crimes, . .	1	–	1
Other crimes, ...	36	18	54
Females.	–	1	1
Drunkenness, . .	–	1	1
BOTH SEXES.	37	19	56
Drunkenness, ...	–	1	1
Drunkenness and other crimes, . .	1	–	1
Other crimes, ...	36	18	54

AGE PERIOD: 15-19.

	Users of Tobacco	Non-users	Number of Criminals
Males.	865	294	1,159
Drunkenness, ...	176	50	226
Drunkenness and other crimes, . .	21	2	23
Other crimes, ...	668	242	910
Females.	65	32	97
Drunkenness, . . .	11	4	15
Other crimes, . . .	54	28	82
BOTH SEXES.	930	326	1,256
Drunkenness, ...	187	54	241
Drunkenness and other crimes, . .	21	2	23
Other crimes, ...	722	270	992

AGE PERIOD: 20-29.

	Users of Tobacco	Non-users	Number of Criminals
Males.	6,139	1,855	7,994
Drunkenness, ...	3,586	983	4,569
Drunkenness and other crimes, . .	220	71	291
Other crimes, ...	2,333	801	3,134

Crime; Sex, Degree of Crime, and Use of Tobacco by Fathers of Criminals:
By Age Periods — Continued.

AGE PERIOD: 20-29 — Concluded.

SEX AND DEGREE OF CRIME.	Users of Tobacco	Non-users	Number of Criminals
Females.	730	324	1,054
Drunkenness, ...	447	158	605
Drunkenness and other crimes, . .	10	4	14
Other crimes, ...	273	162	435
BOTH SEXES.	6,869	2,179	9,048
Drunkenness, ...	4,033	1,141	5,174
Drunkenness and other crimes, . .	230	75	305
Other crimes, ...	2,606	963	3,569

AGE PERIOD: 30-39.

	Users of Tobacco	Non-users	Number of Criminals
Males.	5,551	1,744	7,295
Drunkenness, ...	4,011	1,218	5,229
Drunkenness and other crimes, . .	127	54	181
Other crimes, ...	1,413	472	1,885
Females.	711	316	1,027
Drunkenness, ...	519	204	722
Drunkenness and other crimes, . .	9	8	17
Other crimes, ...	184	104	288
BOTH SEXES.	6,262	2,060	8,322
Drunkenness, ...	4,529	1,422	5,951
Drunkenness and other crimes, . .	136	62	198
Other crimes, ...	1,597	576	2,173

AGE PERIOD: 40–49.

	Users of Tobacco	Non-users	Number of Criminals
Males.	3,201	1,189	4,390
Drunkenness, ...	2,503	899	3,402
Drunkenness and other crimes, .	62	20	82
Other crimes, ...	636	270	906
Females.	396	192	588
Drunkenness, ...	295	138	433
Drunkenness and other crimes, . .	10	2	12
Other crimes, ...	91	52	143

Crime ; Sex, Degree of Crime, and Use of Tobacco by Fathers of Criminals :
By Age Periods — Continued.

AGE PERIOD : 40–49 — Concluded.

SEX AND DEGREE OF CRIME.	Users of Tobacco	Non-users	Number of Criminals
BOTH SEXES.	3,597	1,381	4,978
Drunkenness, ...	2,798	1,037	3,835
Drunkenness and other crimes, . .	72	22	94
Other crimes, ...	727	322	1,049

AGE PERIOD : 50–59.

	Users of Tobacco	Non-users	Number of Criminals
Males.	1,422	612	2,034
Drunkenness, ...	1,133	483	1,616
Drunkenness and other crimes, . .	16	6	22
Other crimes, ...	273	123	396
Females.	151	76	227
Drunkenness, ...	124	60	184
Drunkenness and other crimes, . .	5	1	6
Other crimes, ...	22	15	37
BOTH SEXES.	1,573	688	2,261
Drunkenness, ...	1,257	543	1,800
Drunkenness and other crimes, . .	21	7	28
Other crimes, ...	295	138	433

AGE PERIOD : 60–79.

	Users of Tobacco	Non-users	Number of Criminals
Males.	437	207	644
Drunkenness, ...	340	152	492
Drunkenness and other crimes, . .	7	1	8
Other crimes, ...	90	54	144
Females.	48	43	91
Drunkenness, ...	36	31	67
Other crimes, ...	12	12	24
BOTH SEXES.	485	250	735
Drunkenness, ...	376	183	559
Drunkenness and other crimes, . .	7	1	8
Other crimes, ...	102	66	168

Crime; Sex, Degree of Crime, and Use of Tobacco by Fathers of Criminals:
By Age Periods — Concluded.

AGE PERIOD : 80 +.

SEX AND DEGREE OF CRIME.	Users of Tobacco	Non-users	Number of Criminals
Males.	3	3	6
Drunkenness, ...	3	3	6
Females.	2	4	6
Drunkenness, ...	1	4	5
Other crimes, ...	1	-	1
BOTH SEXES.	5	7	12
Drunkenness, ...	4	7	11
Other crimes, ...	1	-	1

AGE PERIOD : Unknown.

	Users of Tobacco	Non-users	Number of Criminals
Males.	1	3	4
Drunkenness, ...	1	2	3
Other crimes, ...	-	1	1

RECAPITULATION.

SEX AND DEGREE OF CRIME.	Users of Tobacco	Non-users	Number of Criminals
Males.	17,656	5,925	23,581
Drunkenness, ...	11,753	3,790	15,543
Drunkenness and other crimes, . .	454	154	608
Other crimes, ...	5,449	1,981	7,430
Females.	2,103	988	3,091
Drunkenness, ...	1,432	600	2,032
Drunkenness and other crimes, . .	34	15	49
Other crimes, ...	637	373	1,010
BOTH SEXES.	19,759	6,913	26,672
Drunkenness, ...	13,185	4,390	17,575
Drunkenness and other crimes, . .	488	169	657
Other crimes, ...	6,086	2,354	8,440

RECAPITULATION: BY AGE PERIODS.

Sex and Age Periods.	Users of Tobacco	Non-users	Number of Criminals
Males.	17,656	5,925	23,581
10-14,	37	18	55
15-19,	865	294	1,159
20-29,	6,139	1,855	7,994
30-39,	5,551	1,744	7,295
40-49,	3,201	1,189	4,390
50-59,	1,422	612	2,034
60-79,	437	207	644
80 +,	3	3	6
Unknown,	1	3	4
Females.	2,103	988	3,091
10-14,	-	1	1
15-19,	65	32	97
20-29,	730	324	1,054
30-39,	711	316	1,027
40-49,	396	192	588
50-59,	151	76	227
60-79,	48	43	91
80 +,	2	4	6
Both Sexes.	19,759	6,913	26,672
10-14,	37	19	56
15-19,	930	326	1,256
20-29,	6,869	2,179	9,048
30-39,	6,262	2,060	8,322
40-49,	3,597	1,381	4,978
50-59,	1,573	688	2,261
60-79,	485	250	735
80 +,	5	7	12
Unknown,	1	3	4

This table is identical in form with the one which precedes it. Out of the 26,672 criminals, there were 19,759 whose fathers used tobacco; of these criminals, 6,086 were convicted of crimes other than drunkenness, the remainder being convicted of drunkenness and of drunkenness in connection with other crimes. The criminals whose fathers were non-users of tobacco number 6,913; of these, 2,354 were convicted of crimes other than drunkenness, and the remainder of drunkenness and of drunkenness in connection with other crimes.

The next table relates to the mothers of criminals.

*Crime ; Sex, Degree of Crime, and Use of Tobacco by Mothers of Criminals:
By Age Periods.*

AGE PERIOD : 10–14.

SEX AND DEGREE OF CRIME.	Users of Tobacco	Non-users	Number of Criminals
Males.	-	55	55
Drunkenness and other crimes,	-	1	1
Other crimes, ...	-	54	54
Females.	-	1	1
Drunkenness, ...	-	1	1
BOTH SEXES.	-	56	56
Drunkenness, ...	-	1	1
Drunkenness and other crimes, . .	-	1	1
Other crimes, ...	-	54	54

AGE PERIOD : 15–19.

Males.	30	1,129	1,159
Drunkenness, ...	6	220	226
Drunkenness and other crimes, .	-	23	23
Other crimes, ...	24	886	910
Females.	1	96	97
Drunkenness, ...	-	15	15
Other crimes, ...	1	81	82
BOTH SEXES.	31	1,225	1,256
Drunkenness, ...	6	235	241
Drunkenness and other crimes, . .	-	23	23
Other crimes, ...	25	967	992

AGE PERIOD : 20–29.

Males.	225	7,769	7,994
Drunkenness, ...	129	4,440	4,569
Drunkenness and other crimes, . .	6	285	291
Other crimes, ...	90	3,044	3,134
Females.	35	1,019	1,054
Drunkenness, ...	24	581	605
Drunkenness and other crimes, . .	-	14	14
Other crimes, ...	11	424	435

Crime: Sex, Degree of Crime, and Use of Tobacco by Mothers of Criminals:
By Age Periods — Continued.

AGE PERIOD: 20-29 — Concluded.

SEX AND DEGREE OF CRIME.	Users of Tobacco	Non-users	Number of Criminals
BOTH SEXES.	260	8,788	9,048
Drunkenness, ...	153	5,021	5,174
Drunkenness and other crimes, . .	6	299	305
Other crimes, ...	101	3,468	3,569

AGE PERIOD: 30-39.

	Users of Tobacco	Non-users	Number of Criminals
Males.	278	7,017	7,295
Drunkenness, ...	202	5,027	5,229
Drunkenness and other crimes, .	8	173	181
Other crimes, ...	68	1,817	1,885
Females.	59	968	1,027
Drunkenness, ...	45	677	722
Drunkenness and other crimes, . .	1	16	17
Other crimes, ...	13	275	288
BOTH SEXES.	337	7,985	8,322
Drunkenness, ...	247	5,704	5,951
Drunkenness and other crimes, . .	9	189	198
Other crimes, ...	81	2,092	2,173

AGE PERIOD: 40-49.

	Users of Tobacco	Non-users	Number of Criminals
Males.	234	4,156	4,390
Drunkenness, ...	175	3,227	3,402
Drunkenness and other crimes, .	3	79	82
Other crimes, ...	56	850	906
Females.	32	556	588
Drunkenness, ...	25	408	433
Drunkenness and other crimes, .	-	12	12
Other crimes, ...	7	136	143
BOTH SEXES.	266	4,712	4,978
Drunkenness, ...	200	3,635	3,835
Drunkenness and other crimes, . .	3	91	94
Other crimes, ...	63	986	1,049

Crime; Sex, Degree of Crime, and Use of Tobacco by Mothers of Criminals:
By Age Periods — Continued.

AGE PERIOD : 50–59.

SEX AND DEGREE OF CRIME.	Users of Tobacco	Non-users	Number of Criminals
Males.	129	1,905	2,034
Drunkenness, ...	99	1,517	1,616
Drunkenness and other crimes, . .	1	21	22
Other crimes, ...	29	367	396
Females.	13	214	227
Drunkenness, ...	11	173	184
Drunkenness and other crimes, . .	1	5	6
Other crimes, ...	1	36	37
BOTH SEXES.	142	2,119	2,261
Drunkenness, ...	110	1,690	1,800
Drunkenness and other crimes, . .	2	26	28
Other crimes, ...	30	403	433

AGE PERIOD : 60–79.

	Users of Tobacco	Non-users	Number of Criminals
Males.	51	593	644
Drunkenness, ...	39	453	492
Drunkenness and other crimes, . .	2	6	8
Other crimes, ...	10	134	144
Females.	3	88	91
Drunkenness, ...	2	65	67
Other crimes, ...	1	23	24
BOTH SEXES.	54	681	735
Drunkenness, ...	41	518	559
Drunkenness and other crimes, . .	2	6	8
Other crimes, ...	11	157	168

AGE PERIOD : 80 +.

	Users of Tobacco	Non-users	Number of Criminals
Males.	–	6	6
Drunkenness, ...	–	6	6
Females.	–	6	6
Drunkenness, ...	–	5	5
Other crimes, ...	–	1	1

Crime ; Sex, Degree of Crime, and Use of Tobacco by Mothers of Criminals :
By Age Periods — Concluded.

AGE PERIOD : 80 + — Concluded.

SEX AND DEGREE OF CRIME.	Users of Tobacco	Non-users	Number of Criminals
BOTH SEXES.	–	12	12
Drunkenness, ...	–	11	11
Other crimes, ...	–	1	1

AGE PERIOD : Unknown.

	Users of Tobacco	Non-users	Number of Criminals
Males.	–	4	4
Drunkenness, ...	–	3	3
Other crimes, ...	–	1	1

RECAPITULATION.

SEX AND DEGREE OF CRIME.	Users of Tobacco	Non-users	Number of Criminals
Males.	947	22,634	23,581
Drunkenness, ...	650	14,893	15,543
Drunkenness and other crimes, .	20	588	608
Other crimes, ...	277	7,153	7,430
Females.	143	2,948	3,091
Drunkenness, ...	107	1,925	2,032
Drunkenness and other crimes, .	2	47	49
Other crimes, ...	34	976	1,010
BOTH SEXES.	1,090	25,582	26,672
Drunkenness, ...	757	16,818	17,575
Drunkenness and other crimes, . .	22	635	657
Other crimes, ...	311	8,129	8,440

RECAPITULATION : BY AGE PERIODS.

SEX AND AGE PERIODS.	Users of Tobacco	Non-users	Number of Criminals
Males.	947	22,634	23,581
10-14, ...	–	55	55
15-19, ...	30	1,129	1,159

RECAPITULATION: BY AGE PERIODS — Concluded.

SEX AND AGE PERIODS.	Users of Tobacco	Non-users	Number of Criminals
Males — Con.			
20-29, ...	225	7,769	7,994
30-39, ...	278	7,017	7,295
40-49, ...	234	4,156	4,390
50-59, ...	129	1,905	2,034
60-79, ...	51	593	644
80 +, ...	-	6	6
Unknown, ...	-	4	4
Females.	143	2,948	3,091
10-14, ...	-	1	1
15-19, ...	1	96	97
20-29, ...	35	1,019	1,054
30-39, ...	59	968	1,027
40-49, ...	32	556	588
50-59, ...	13	214	227
60-79, ...	3	88	91
80 +, ...	-	6	6
BOTH SEXES.	1,090	25,582	26,672
10-14, ...	-	56	56
15-19, ...	31	1,225	1,256
20-29, ...	260	8,788	9,048
30-39, ...	337	7,985	8,322
40-49, ...	266	4,712	4,978
50-59, ...	142	2,119	2,261
60-79, ...	54	681	735
80 +, ...	-	12	12
Unknown, ...	-	4	4

In the case of 1,090 criminals out of 26,672, the aggregate number, the mothers were users of tobacco. The criminals who had these mothers included 311 who were convicted of crimes other than drunkenness, and 779 who were convicted of drunkenness or of drunkenness in connection with other crimes.

Besides the use of tobacco, it was found that 96 male criminals and 27 female criminals were addicted to intoxication produced by drugs, of which opium was chief. The number of fathers of criminals who used drugs to excess was 26, and the number of mothers of criminals thus using drugs was 25. These facts indicate that among the criminal classes the use of drugs as an intoxicant does not largely prevail.

RECAPITULATION. — *Relation of the Liquor Traffic to Crime : By Sex and Occupations.*

	SEX AND OCCUPATIONS.	Number of Criminals	Was the Criminal under the **Influence of Liquor** at the Time the **Crime** was committed		
			Yes	No	Not Ascertained
1	*Males.*	23,581	19,509	4,065	7
2	Agents, canvassers, collectors, travelling salesmen, etc., ...	97	67	29	1
3	Blacksmiths and wheelwrights, ...	317	282	35	–
4	Bookbinders, ...	22	18	4	–
5	Bookkeepers, clerks and salesmen, ...	349	228	121	–
6	Boot and shoemakers, ...	1,578	1,367	211	–
7	Bottlers, ...	14	10	4	–
8	Brickmakers, ...	11	10	1	–
9	Broom and brush makers, ...	9	6	3	–
10	Building trades, ...	2,535	2,198	336	1
11	Button makers, ...	9	6	3	
12	Candy makers, ...	20	14	6	–
13	Carriage and bicycle makers, ...	14	10	4	–
14	Cigar makers, ...	83	61	22	–
15	Coachmen and stable employés, ...	646	543	102	1
16	Dealers, traders, peddlers (all kinds), . . .	865	592	273	–
17	Electricians and electric work employés, . .	43	29	14	–
18	Farmers and farm laborers, ...	672	546	125	1
19	Furniture makers and finishers, ...	136	115	21	–
20	Glass workers, ...	36	25	11	–
21	Hat makers and finishers, ...	43	34	9	–
22	Hotel, boarding-house, and restaurant proprietors, and employés, ...	60	33	27	–
23	Housewives and domestic service, ...	195	146	49	–
24	Laborers, ...	7,566	6,501	1,062	3
25	Leather makers and workers, ...	458	429	29	–
26	Machinists, ...	497	404	93	–
27	Mariners and fishermen, ...	507	436	71	–
28	Messengers and porters, ...	85	36	49	–
29	Metal workers, ...	689	606	83	–
30	Musical instrument makers, ...	19	17	2	–
31	Paper makers, ...	69	63	6	–
32	Personal service, ...	1,172	872	300	–

In the next table, the leading facts as to the use of liquor are recapitulated, in connection with the occupations of the criminal.

RECAPITULATION.— *Relation of the Liquor Traffic to Crime: By Sex and Occupations.*

LIQUOR HABITS OF CRIMINALS			KINDS OF LIQUOR					TOBACCO		
Excessive Drinkers	Other Drinkers	Total Abstainers	Wines only	Lager Beer and Malt Liquors only	Distilled Liquors only	Two or All Kinds	Inapplicable*	Users	Non-users	
3,790	18,551	1,240	101	3,613	626	18,001	1,240	22,112	1,460	1
9	80	8	-	26	8	55	8	85	12	2
52	253	12	-	38	11	256	12	305	12	3
3	18	1	-	5	-	16	1	20	2	4
44	261	44	2	56	13	234	44	309	40	5
268	1,239	71	4	173	51	1,279	71	1,479	99	6
-	14	-	-	5	1	8	-	13	1	7
1	9	1	-	1	-	9	1	10	1	8
1	7	1	-	-	-	8	1	7	2	9
446	2,014	75	3	369	79	2,009	75	2,412	123	10
1	5	3	-	-	-	6	3	8	1	11
2	17	1	-	6	-	13	1	18	2	12
-	12	2	-	5	-	7	2	13	1	13
7	72	4	-	19	2	58	4	75	8	14
92	527	27	-	114	21	484	27	608	38	15
135	640	90	24	120	27	604	90	768	97	16
6	33	4	-	8	-	31	4	42	1	17
106	513	53	5	111	31	472	53	604	68	18
26	102	8	1	31	-	96	8	133	3	19
3	28	5	-	8	2	21	5	34	2	20
7	36	-	-	11	1	31	-	41	2	21
5	45	10	1	10	1	38	10	52	8	22
27	155	13	2	25	8	147	13	176	19	23
1,371	5,974	221	28	1,046	144	6,127	221	7,210	356	24
71	381	6	1	48	15	388	6	435	23	25
67	401	29	2	83	*11	372	29	468	29	26
73	422	12	1	86	16	392	12	487	20	27
5	50	30	-	25	3	27	30	63	22	28
115	560	14	2	111	16	546	14	661	28	29
3	16	-	-	5	1	13	-	18	1	30
10	57	2	-	10	2	55	2	66	3	31
187	889	96	8	192	41	835	96	1,083	89	32

* Total Abstainers.

RECAPITULATION. — *Relation of the Liquor Traffic to Crime: By Sex and Occupations* — Concluded.

	SEX AND OCCUPATIONS.	Number of Criminals	Was the Criminal under the **Influence of Liquor** at the Time the **Crime** was committed		
			Yes	No	Not Ascertained
	Males — Con.				
1	Printers (compositors and pressmen), . .	250	198	52	–
2	Professional service, ...	135	77	58	–
3	Rubber factory operatives, ...	37	34	3	–
4	Stone cutters and polishers, ...	221	192	29	–
5	Tailors and seamstresses (all kinds), . .	204	156	48	–
6	Textile factory operatives, ...	1,622	1,393	229	–
7	Transportation, teamsters, expressmen, etc., .	1,508	1,256	252	–
8	Watch and clock repairers, . . .	8	6	2	–
9	Woodworkers and finishers, ...	216	182	34	–
10	Other occupations, ...	60	49	11	–
11	Not stated (including "Unknown"), . .	504	262	242	–
12	*Females.*	3,091	2,354	735	2
13	Bookkeepers, clerks, and saleswomen, . . .	15	7	8	–
14	Boot and shoemakers, ...	15	12	3	–
15	Button makers, ...	1	1	–	–
16	Candy makers, ...	4	2	2	–
17	Cigar makers, ...	2	2	–	–
18	Dealers, traders, peddlers (all kinds), . . .	14	5	9	–
19	Hotel, boarding-house, and restaurant proprietors, and employés, ...	61	34	27	–
20	Housewives and domestic service, ...	2,220	1,728	491	1
21	Personal service, ...	105	65	40	–
22	Professional service, ...	19	9	9	1
23	Rubber factory operatives, ...	5	–	5	–
24	Tailors and seamstresses, ...	89	57	32	–
25	Textile factory operatives, ...	448	380	68	–
26	Woodworkers and finishers, ...	5	3	2	–
27	Not stated (including "Unknown"), . . .	88	49	39	–

This table is similar in arrangement with one previously introduced, relating to the occupations of paupers. The first line shows that of the 23,581 male criminals, 19,509 replied "Yes" and 4,065, "No" to the question, "Was the criminal under the influence of liquor at the time the crime was committed," the information not being ascertained in seven instances only. These male criminals include 3,790 excessive

RECAPITULATION. — *Relation of the Liquor Traffic to Crime: By Sex and Occupations* — Concluded.

LIQUOR HABITS OF CRIMINALS			KINDS OF LIQUOR					TOBACCO		
Excessive Drinkers	Other Drinkers	Total Abstainers	Wines only	Lager Beer and Malt Liquors only	Distilled Liquors only	Two or All Kinds	Inapplicable*	Users	Non-users	
34	198	18	1	45	7	179	18	227	23	1
20	91	24	6	27	5	73	24	117	18	2
5	32	-	-	13	1	23	-	36	1	3
34	182	5	-	39	6	171	5	208	13	4
45	147	12	4	26	6	156	12	187	17	5
181	1,377	64	-	365	24	1,169	64	1,547	75	6
227	1,206	75	3	235	49	1,146	75	1,432	76	7
1	7	-	-	-	2	6	-	7	1	8
40	165	11	-	31	4	170	11	206	10	9
10	43	7	-	9	2	42	7	52	8	10
50	273	181	3	76	15	229	181	390	114	11
726	2,070	295	25	680	102	1,989	295	626	2,465	12
2	8	5	-	4	-	6	5	2	13	13
4	9	2	1	2	1	9	2	5	10	14
-	1	-	-	-	-	1	-	-	1	15
1	2	1	-	-	-	3	1	1	3	16
-	2	-	-	-	1	1	-	1	1	17
4	6	4	-	4	1	5	4	2	12	18
8	41	12	3	14	2	30	12	14	47	19
546	1,488	186	13	483	73	1,465	186	466	1,754	20
26	64	15	1	20	2	67	15	19	86	21
4	9	6	2	3	-	8	6	1	18	22
-	4	1	-	2	1	1	1	-	5	23
18	52	19	-	19	2	49	19	11	78	24
89	335	24	4	116	18	286	24	87	361	25
-	3	2	-	-	-	3	2	2	3	26
24	46	18	1	13	1	55	18	15	73	27

* Total Abstainers.

drinkers, while drinkers of other degree number 18,551; the total abstainers numbering 1,240. With regard to the kinds of liquor used, 101 used wines only, 3,613 used lager beer and malt liquors only, 626 distilled liquors only, while 18,001 used two or all kinds of liquor; information upon this point being inapplicable in 1,240 instances in which the criminals were total abstainers. The users of tobacco number 22,112, and the non-users 1,469. With respect to occupations, the most numerous class includes the laborers, who number 7,566, of whom only 1,062 were not under the influence of liquor at the time the crime was committed. The laborers include 1,371 excessive drinkers and 221 total abstainers, the others being drinkers of other degree than excessive. Respecting the kinds of liquor used by the laborers, 6,127 used two or all kinds; 1,046 lager beer and malt liquors only, 144 distilled liquors only, and 28 wines only. The non-users of tobacco in this class number 356. The next most numerous class includes persons employed in the building trades, who number 2,535, only 336 being free from the influence of liquor at the time the crime was committed, of whom 446 are classed as excessive drinkers, 2,014 as drinkers not excessive, while 75 were total abstainers. The users of lager beer and malt liquors among these criminals number 369, 79 used distilled liquors only, and three wines only, while 2,009 used two or all kinds of liquor. The next most numerous classes, respectively, are the textile factory operatives, numbering 1,622; boot and shoe-makers, numbering 1,578; employés in transportation, teamsters, expressmen, etc., numbering 1,508; and the persons engaged in personal service, numbering 1,172. The facts as to the use of liquor by each of these classes may be plainly seen in the table, and need not be repeated here.

RECAPITULATION. — *Relation of the Liquor Traffic to Crime : By Sex and Nature of Crime.*

SEX AND NATURE OF CRIME.	Number of Criminals	Was the Criminal under the **Influence of Liquor** at the Time the **Crime** was committed		
		Yes	No	Not Ascertained
1 *Males.*	23,581	19,509	4,065	7
2 Abortion, ...	3	–	3	–
3 Abuse of female child, ...	6	1	5	–
4 Adultery, ...	50	17	33	–
5 Appropriating horse or horse and team, . .	20	14	6	–
6 Assault or assault and battery, ...	1,566	960	605	1
7 Assault, felonious, ...	12	3	9	–
8 Assault on officer, ...	67	34	33	–

The female criminals, who number in the aggregate 3,091, include 2,354 who replied " Yes " and 735 who replied " No " to the question, " Was the criminal under the influence of liquor at the time the crime was committed." They also include 726 excessive drinkers, and 2,070 drinkers of other degree, together with 295 total abstainers. Among the females there were 102 who used distilled liquors only, 680 who used lager beer and malt liquors only, 25 who used wines only, and 1,989 who used two or all kinds of liquor ; while 626 were users of tobacco. The most numerous class, as to occupations among the females, includes housewives and persons in domestic service, who number in the aggregate 2,220 ; of these, only 491 were not under the influence of liquor at the time the crime was committed. The excessive drinkers in this class number 546 ; the total abstainers only 186 ; the others being classed as drinkers not excessive. The users of lager beer and malt liquors only, number 483 ; distilled liquors only, 73 ; wines only, 13 ; while 1,465 used two or all kinds of liquor, and 466 used tobacco. The most numerous classes, next to the housewives and persons in domestic service, include the textile factory operatives, who number 448, and persons in personal service, who number 105.

In the next table the facts as to the use of liquor are presented in connection with the nature of the crime, under a classification by sexes.

RECAPITULATION.— *Relation of the Liquor Traffic to Crime: By Sex and Nature of Crime.*

LIQUOR HABITS OF CRIMINALS			KINDS OF LIQUOR					TOBACCO		
Excessive Drinkers	Other Drinkers	Total Abstainers	Wines only	Lager Beer and Malt Liquors only	Distilled Liquors only	Two or All Kinds	Inapplicable*	Users	Non-users	
3,790	18,551	1,240	101	3,613	626	18,001	1,240	22,112	1,469	1
-	1	2	1	-	-	-	2	2	1	2
-	5	1	1	1	-	3	1	4	2	3
3	41	6	1	8	1	34	6	45	5	4
2	14	4	-	3	-	13	4	19	1	5
127	1,291	148	10	363	30	1,015	148	1,426	140	6
1	8	3	1	1	-	7	3	9	3	7
5	60	2	-	12	2	51	2	60	7	8

* Total Abstainers.

RECAPITULATION. — *Relation of the Liquor Traffic to Crime: By Sex and Nature of Crime* — Continued.

SEX AND NATURE OF CRIME.	Number of Criminals	Was the Criminal under the **Influence of Liquor** at the Time the **Crime** was committed		
		Yes	No	Not Ascertained
Males — Con.				
1 . Assault with intent to commit rape, . . .	4	2	2	–
2 Assault with weapon, ...	58	30	28	–
3 Breaking and entering, ...	391	168	223	–
4 Breaking glass, ...	72	55	17	–
5 Burglars' tools, having, ...	2	1	1	–
6 Burning buildings, ...	7	1	6	–
7 ' Cheating, ...	10	2	8	–
8 Common nuisance, ...	13	3	10	–
9 ' Contempt, ...	19	4	15	–
10 ' Counterfeiting or uttering counterfeits, . . .	- 9	–	9	–
11 Cruelty, ...	44	20	24	–
12 Disorderly house, keeping, ...	31	12	19	–
13 Disturbing a meeting, ...	12	5	7	–
14 ¦ Disturbing the peace, ...	750	600	150	–
15 ¦ Drunkard, common, ...	56	56	–	–
16 ' Drunkenness, ...	15,487	15,486	1	–
17 Embezzlement, ...	79	22	57	–
18 Escape, ...	21	2	19	–
19 Evading carfare, ...	45	30	15	–
20 False pretences (defrauding), ...	90	33	57	–
21 Forgery, ...	26	9	17	–
22 Fornication, ...	168	18	150	–
23 Fraud, ...	11	1	10	–
24 Gaming laws, violating, ...	54	3	51	–
25 House of ill-fame, ...	6	–	6	–
26 Incest, ...	3	–	3	–
27 Indecent assault, ...	23	9	14	–
28 Indecent exposure, ...	34	21	13	–
29 Indecent language, ...	10	8	2	–
30 Larceny, ...	1,960	1,093	867	–
31 Lewdness, ...	21	16	5	–
32 Liquor carrying, ...	4	–	4	–
33 Liquor keeping, ...	78	15	63	–
34 Liquor nuisance, ...	53	2	51	–
35 Liquor selling, ...	169	29	140	–
36 Malicious mischief, ...	72	52	20	–
37 Malicious trespass, ...	55	11	44	–
38 Manslaughter, ...	17	11	6	–

RECAPITULATION. — *Relation of the Liquor Traffic to Crime: By Sex and Nature of Crime* — Continued.

LIQUOR HABITS OF CRIMINALS			KINDS OF LIQUOR					TOBACCO		
Excessive Drinkers	Other Drinkers	Total Abstainers	Wines only	Lager Beer and Malt Liquors only	Distilled Liquors only	Two or All Kinds	Inapplicable*	Users	Non-users	
-	3	1	-	-	-	3	1	4	-	1
4	46	8	4	10	3	33	8	51	7	2
18	253	120	3	66	28	174	120	307	84	3
12	55	5	-	13	-	54	5	64	8	4
-	2	-	-	-	-	2	-	1	1	5
-	5	2	-	2	-	3	2	3	4	6
-	6	4	-	1	-	5	4	7	3	7
-	12	1	1	4	-	7	1	11	2	8
1	14	4	-	4	-	11	4	17	2	9
-	7	2	1	2	-	4	2	7	2	10
2	37	5	-	9	3	27	5	42	2	11
5	24	2	-	4	2	23	2	29	2	12
-	8	4	-	2	-	6	4	9	3	13
49	648	53	1	150	24	522	53	693	57	14
49	7	-	-	5	2	49	-	52	4	15
3,043	12,443	1	29	2,130	358	12,969	1	14,928	559	16
4	54	21	1	13	2	42	21	62	17	17
6	14	1	-	1	-	19	1	19	2	18
5	36	4	-	7	1	33	4	43	2	19
4	65	21	2	15	3	49	21	83	7	20
4	14	8	-	1	5	12	8	18	8	21
3	132	33	1	39	3	92	33	149	19	22
-	9	2	1	3	-	5	2	9	2	23
-	36	18	-	3	12	21	18	36	18	24
-	4	2	-	-	-	4	2	5	1	25
-	1	2	-	-	-	1	2	2	1	26
-	19	4	-	5	1	13	4	21	2	27
1	29	4	-	7	-	23	4	32	2	28
2	6	2	-	2	-	6	2	8	2	29
173	1,416	371	11	302	87	1,189	371	1,739	221	30
4	14	3	-	2	1	15	3	18	3	31
-	4	-	-	-	-	4	-	4	-	32
3	72	3	-	10	6	59	3	72	6	33
3	49	1	-	11	3	38	1	51	2	34
8	151	10	4	25	7	123	10	147	22	35
7	56	9	-	15	1	47	9	69	3	36
1	35	19	-	14	1	21	19	42	13	37
1	14	2	-	5	1	9	2	12	5	38

* Total Abstainers.

RECAPITULATION. — *Relation of the Liquor Traffic to Crime: By Sex and Nature of Crime* — Continued.

	SEX AND NATURE OF CRIME.	Number of Criminals	Was the Criminal under the **Influence of Liquor** at the Time the **Crime** was committed		
			Yes	No	Not Ascertained
	Males — Con.				
1	Murder, ...	4	1	3	-
2	Neglect of family, ...	152	72	80	-
3	Nightwalker, common, ...	1	-	1	-
4	Nuisance, maintaining, ...	3	1	2	-
5	Peddling, ...	39	-	39	-
6	Perjury, ...	2	2	-	-
7	Polygamy, ...	11	3	8	-
8	Profanity, ...	16	7	9	-
9	Rape, ...	5	-	5	-
10	Receiving stolen goods (or money), . . .	53	12	41	-
11	Rescue, ...	5	1	4	-
12	Riot or riotous assault, ...	5	-	5	-
13	Robbery, ...	46	38	8	-
14	Stubborn children, ...	40	3	37	-
15	Sunday law, violating, ...	11	2	9	-
16	Threats, ...	37	19	18	-
17	Truancy, ...	1	-	1	-
18	Vagabonds and idle persons (tramps), . .	905	359	542	4
19	Violation of probation, ...	1	-	1	-
20	Violation of school law, ...	3	-	3	-
21	Violating town or city by-laws (or ordinances), .	238	78	159	1
22	Walking on railroad tracks, ...	252	37	215	-
23	Other offences, ...	63	15	47	1
24	*Females.*	3,091	2,354	735	2
25	Adultery, ...	36	10	26	-
26	Assault or assault and battery, ...	86	25	61	-
27	Assault on officer, ...	2	2	-	-
28	Assault with weapon, ...	3	1	2	-
29	Breaking and entering, ...	2	1	1	-
30	Breaking glass, ...	10	4	6	-
31	Burning buildings, ...	1	1	-	-
32	Cheating, ...	1		1	-
33	Common nuisance, ...	2	-	2	-
34	Contempt, ...	2	-	2	-
35	Cruelty, ...	1	1	-	-
36	Disorderly house, keeping, ...	25	9	16	-
37	Disturbing the peace, ...	210	119	91	-

RECAPITULATION. — *Relation of the Liquor Traffic to Crime: By Sex and Nature of Crime* — Continued.

Liquor Habits of Criminals			Kinds of Liquor					Tobacco		
Excessive Drinkers	Other Drinkers	Total Abstainers	Wines only	Lager Beer and Malt Liquors only	Distilled Liquors only	Two or All Kinds	Inapplicable*	Users	Non-users	
-	3	1	-	-	-	3	1	4	-	1
6	130	16	-	43	5	88	16	143	9	2
-	-	1	-	-	-	-	1	-	1	3
-	2	1	-	-	-	2	1	2	1	4
-	21	18	10	7	-	4	18	21	18	5
1	1	-	-	-	2	-	∴	1	1	6
-	5	6	-	2	1	2	6	9	2	7
-	15	1	-	6	1	8	1	16	-	8
-	5	-	-	2	-	3	-	5	-	9
-	40	13	2	10	3	25	13	44	9	10
1	3	1	-	1	-	3	1	4	1	11
-	3	2	-	-	2	1	2	3	2	12
2	44	-	-	9	2	35	-	43	3	13
1	11	28	-	4	2	6	28	26	14	14
-	8	3	-	2	-	6	3	11	-	15
2	34	1	1	13	-	22	1	36	1	16
-	-	1	-	-	-	-	1	-	1	17
197	614	94	1	111	14	685	94	846	59	18
-	1	-	-	-	-	1	-	1	-	19
-	3	-	-	1	-	2	-	1	2	20
16	151	71	13	60	2	92	71	170	68	21
12	195	45	-	57	2	148	45	241	11	22
2	42	19	1	15	3	25	19	54	9	23
726	2,070	295	25	680	102	1,989	295	626	2,465	24
2	24	10	1	12	2	11	10	4	32	25
2	62	22	-	30	1	33	22	13	73	26
2	-	-	-	-	-	2	-	-	2	27
-	3	-	-	2	-	1	-	-	3	28
1	1	-	-	1	-	1	-	-	2	29
1	7	2	-	3	-	5	2	1	9	30
1	-	-	-	1	-	-	-	-	1	31
-	-	1	-	-	-	-	1	-	1	32
-	1	1	-	1	-	-	1	-	2	33
-	-	2	-	-	-	-	2	1	1	34
-	-	1	-	-	-	-	1	-	1	35
-	21	4	1	4	1	15	4	1	24	36
19	162	29	-	59	11	111	29	29	181	37

* Total Abstainers.

RECAPITULATION. — *Relation of the Liquor Traffic to Crime: By Sex and Nature of Crime* — Continued.

	SEX AND NATURE OF CRIME.	Number of Criminals	Was the Criminal under the **Influence of Liquor** at the Time the **Crime** was committed		
			Yes	No	Not Ascertained
	Females — Con.				
1	Drunkard, common, ...	19	19	–	–
2	Drunkenness, ...	2,013	2,013	–	–
3	Escape, ...	1	–	1	–
4	False pretences (defrauding), ...	11	1	10	–
5	Forgery, ...	1	–	1	–
6	Fornication, ...	211	31	180	–
7	Fraud, ...	3	–	3	–
8	House of ill-fame, ...	6	–	6	–
9	Larceny, ...	147	44	103	–
10	Lewdness, ...	28	12	16	–
11	Liquor keeping, ...	20	1	18	1
12	Liquor nuisance, ...	13	–	13	–
13	Liquor selling, ...	51	2	48	1
14	Malicious mischief, ...	6	2	4	–
15	Malicious trespass, ...	2	–	2	–
16	Neglect of family, ...	2	–	2	–
17	Nightwalker, common, ...	96	22	74	–
18	Peddling, ...	3	–	3	–
19	Perjury, ...	1	–	1	–
20	Polygamy, ...	4	1	3	–
21	Profanity, ...	2	1	1	–
22	Receiving stolen goods (or money), . . .	4	1	3	–
23	Stubborn children , ...	6	–	6	–
24	Vagabonds and idle persons (tramps), . .	52	26	26	–
25	Violating town or city by-laws (ordinances), .	3	3	–	–
26	Walking on railroad tracks, ...	2	1	1	–
27	Other offences, ...	3	1	2	–
28	BOTH SEXES.	26,672	21,863	4,800	9
29	Abortion, ...	3	–	3	–
30	Abuse of female child, ...	6	1	5	–
31	Adultery, ...	86	27	59	–
32	Appropriating horse or horse and team, . .	20	14	6	–
33	Assault or assault and battery, . . .	1,652	985	666	1
34	Assault, felonious, ...	12	3	9	–
35	Assault on officer, ...	69	36	33	–
36	Assault with intent to commit rape, . .	4	2	2	–
37	Assault with weapon, ...	61	31	30	–

RECAPITULATION. — *Relation of the Liquor Traffic to Crime: By Sex and Nature of Crime — Continued.*

LIQUOR HABITS OF CRIMINALS			KINDS OF LIQUOR					TOBACCO		
Excessive Drinkers	Other Drinkers	Total Abstainers	Wines only	Lager Beer and Malt Liquors only	Distilled Liquors only	Two or All Kinds	Inapplicable*	Users	Non-users	
17	2	–	–	2	–	17	–	4	15	1
630	1,383	–	11	439	74	1,489	–	499	1,514	2
–	1	–	–	1	–	–	–	–	1	3
–	4	7	1	–	–	3	7	1	10	4
–	–	1	–	–	–	–	1	–	1	5
10	130	71	5	40	4	91	71	28	183	6
1	–	2	1	–	–	–	2	–	3	7
–	4	2	–	2	–	2	2	–	6	8
6	66	75	2	18	3	49	75	11	136	9
4	17	7	1	6	1	13	7	2	26	10
–	16	4	–	1	–	15	4	1	19	11
–	11	2	–	3	–	8	2	2	11	12
–	41	10	1	19	1	20	10	4	47	13
–	4	2	–	2	–	2	2	–	6	14
–	–	2	–	–	–	–	2	–	2	15
–	1	1	–	1	–	–	1	–	2	16
16	65	15	–	22	2	57	15	14	82	17
–	1	2	1	–	–	–	2	–	3	18
–	–	1	–	–	–	–	1	–	1	19
–	2	2	–	–	–	2	2	–	4	20
1	1	–	–	1	–	1	–	–	2	21
–	3	1	–	–	–	3	1	–	4	22
1	2	3	–	–	–	3	3	–	6	23
10	31	11	–	8	2	31	11	10	42	24
2	1	–	–	–	–	3	–	1	2	25
–	1	1	–	–	–	1	1	–	2	26
–	2	1	–	2	–	–	1	–	3	27
4,516	20,621	1,535	126	4,293	728	19,990	1,535	22,738	3,934	28
–	1	2	1	–	–	–	2	2	1	29
–	5	1	1	1	–	3	1	4	2	30
5	65	16	2	20	3	45	16	49	37	31
2	14	4	–	3	–	13	4	19	1	32
129	1,353	170	10	393	31	1,048	170	1,439	213	33
1	3	3	1	1	–	7	3	9	3	34
7	60	2	–	12	2	53	2	60	9	35
–	3	1	–	–	–	3	1	4	–	36
4	49	8	4	12	3	34	8	51	10	37

* Total Abstainers.

RECAPITULATION. — *Relation of the Liquor Traffic to Crime.· By Sex and Nature of Crime* — Continued.

	SEX AND NATURE OF CRIME.	Number of Criminals	Was the Criminal under the **Influence of Liquor** at the Time the **Crime** was committed		
			Yes	No·	Not Ascertained
	BOTH SEXES — Con.				
1	Breaking and entering, ...	393	169	224	–
2	Breaking glass, ...	82	59	23	–
3	Burglars' tools, having, ...	2	1	1	–
4	Burning buildings, ...	8	2	6	–
5	Cheating, ...	11	2	9	–
6	Common nuisance, ...	15	3	12	–
7	Contempt, ...	21	4	17	–
8	Counterfeiting or uttering counterfeits, . . .	9	–	9	–
9	Cruelty, ...	45	21	24	–
10	Disorderly house, keeping, ...	56	21	35	–
11	Disturbing a meeting, ...	12	5	7	–
12	Disturbing the peace, ...	960	719	241	–
13	Drunkard, common, ...	75	75	–	–
14	Drunkenness, ...	17,500	17,499	1	–
15	Embezzlement, ...	79	22	57	–
16	Escape, ...	22	2	20	–
17	Evading car-fare, ...	45	30	15	–
18	False pretences (defrauding), ...	101	34	67	–
19	Forgery, ...	27	9	18	–
20	Fornication, ...	379	49	330	–
21	Fraud, ...	14	1	13	–
22	Gaming laws, violating, ...	54	3	51	–
23	House of ill-fame, ...	12	–	12	–
24	Incest, . ·	3	–	3	–
25	Indecent assault, ...	23	9	14	–
26	Indecent exposure, ...	34	21	13	–
27	Indecent language, ...	10	8	2	–
28	Larceny, ...	2,107	1,137	970	–
29	Lewdness, ...	49	28	21	–
30	Liquor carrying, ...	4	–	4	–
31	Liquor keeping, ...	98	16	81	1
32	Liquor nuisance, ...	66	2	64	–
33	Liquor selling, ...	220	31	188	1
34	Malicious mischief, ...	78	54	24	–
35	Malicious trespass, ...	57	11	46	–
36	Manslaughter, ...	17	11	6	–
37	Murder, ...	4	1	3	–
38	Neglect of family, ...	154	72	82	–

RECAPITULATION.— *Relation of the Liquor Traffic to Crime: By Sex and Nature of Crime* — Continued.

| Liquor Habits of Criminals | | | Kinds of Liquor | | | | | Tobacco | | |
Excessive Drinkers	Other Drinkers	Total Abstainers	Wines only	Lager Beer and Malt Liquors only	Distilled Liquors only	Two or All Kinds	Inapplicable *	Users	Non-users	
19	254	120	3	67	28	175	120	307	86	1
13	62	7	-	16	-	59	7	65	17	2
-	2	-	-	-	-	2	-	1	1	3
1	5	2	-	3	-	3	2	3	5	4
-	6	5	-	1	-	5	5	7	4	5
-	13	2	1	5	-	7	2	11	4	6
1	14	6	-	4	-	11	6	18	3	7
..	7	2	1	2	-	4	2	7	2	8
2	37	6	-	9	3	27	6	42	3	9
5	45	6	1	8	3	38	6	30	26	10
-	8	4	-	2	-	6	4	9	3	11
68	810	82	1	209	35	633	82	722	238	12
66	9	-	-	7	2	66	-	56	19	13
3,673	13,826	1	40	2,569	432	14,458	1	15,427	2,073	14
4	54	21	1	13	2	42	21	62	17	15
6	15	1	-	2	-	19	1	19	3	16
5	36	4	-	7	1	33	4	43	2	17
4	69	28	3	15	3	52	28	84	17	18
4	14	9	-	1	5	12	9	18	9	19
13	262	104	6	79	7	183	104	177	202	20
1	9	4	2	3	-	5	4	9	5	21
-	36	18	-	3	12	21	18	36	18	22
-	8	4	-	2	-	6	4	5	7	23
-	1	2	-	-	-	1	2	2	1	24
-	19	4	-	5	1	13	4	21	2	25
1	29	4	-	7	-	23	4	32	2	26
2	6	2	-	2	-	6	2	8	2	27
179	1,482	446	13	320	90	1,238	446	1,750	357	28
8	31	10	1	8	2	28	10	20	29	29
-	4	-	-	-	-	4	-	4	-	30
3	88	7	-	11	6	74	7	73	25	31
3	60	3	-	14	3	46	3	53	13	32
8	192	20	5	44	8	143	20	151	69	33
7	60	11	-	17	1	49	11	69	9	34
1	35	21	-	14	1	21	21	42	15	35
1	14	2	-	5	1	9	2	12	5	36
-	3	1	-	-	-	3	1	4	-	37
6	131	17	-	44	5	88	17	143	11	38

* Total Abstainers.

RECAPITULATION. — *Relation of the Liquor Traffic to Crime: By Sex and Nature of Crime* — Concluded.

SEX AND NATURE OF CRIME.	Number of Criminals	Was the Criminal under the **Influence of Liquor** at the Time the **Crime** was committed		
		Yes	No	Not Ascertained
BOTH SEXES — Con.				
1 Nightwalker, common,	97	22	75	–
2 Nuisance, maintaining,	3	1	2	–
3 Peddling,	42	–	42	–
4 Perjury,	3	2	1	–
5 Polygamy,	15	4	11	–
6 Profanity,	18	8	10	–
7 Rape,	5	–	5	–
8 Receiving stolen goods (or money),	57	13	44	–
9 Rescue,	5	1	4	–
10 Riot or riotous assault,	5	–	5	–
11 Robbery,	46	38	8	–
12 Stubborn children,	46	3	43	–
13 Sunday law, violating,	11	2	9	–
14 Threats,	37	19	18	–
15 Truancy,	1	–	1	–
16 Vagabonds, and idle persons (tramps),	957	385	568	4
17 Violation of probation,	1	–	1	–
18 Violation of school law,	3	–	3	–
19 Violating town or city by-laws (ordinances),	241	81	159	1
20 Walking on railroad track,	254	38	216	–
21 Other offences,	66	16	49	1

Disregarding in the analysis the classification by sex, we simply point out that, as previously stated, the persons committed for drunkenness, including common drunkards, are very largely in the majority; and the classification of the leading points of the investigation embodied in the head lines of the table, enables the reader to see at a glance a summary of all the facts relating to these criminals.

Next to drunkenness, the largest number of criminals grouped under any single head comprises those sentenced for larceny, who number 2,107, of whom 1,137 were under the influence of liquor at the time the crime was committed, including 179 excessive drinkers; 1,652 sentenced for assault

RECAPITULATION. — *Relation of the Liquor Traffic to Crime: By Sex and Nature of Crime* — Concluded.

LIQUOR HABITS OF CRIMINALS			KINDS OF LIQUOR					TOBACCO		
Excessive Drinkers	Other Drinkers	Total Abstainers	Wines only	Lager Beer and Malt Liquors only	Distilled Liquors only	Two or All Kinds	Inapplicable *	Users	Non-users	
16	65	16	–	22	2	57	16	14	83	1
–	2	1	–	–	–	2	1	2	1	2
–	22	20	11	7	–	4	20	21	21	3
1	1	1	–	–	2	–	1	1	2	4
–	7	8	–	2	1	4	8	9	6	5
1	16	1	–	7	1	9	1	16	2	6
–	5	–	–	2	–	3	–	5	–	7
–	43	14	2	10	3	28	14	44	13	8
1	3	1	–	1	–	3	1	4	1	9
–	3	2	–	–	2	1	2	3	2	10
2	44	–	–	9	2	35	–	43	3	11
2	13	31	–	4	2	9	31	26	20	12
–	8	3	–	2	–	6	3	11	–	13
2	34	1	1	13	–	22	1	36	1	14
–	–	1	–	–	–	–	1	–	1	15
207	645	105	1	119	16	716	105	856	101	16
–	1	–	–	–	–	1	–	1	–	17
–	3	–	–	1	–	2	–	1	2	18
18	152	71	13	60	2	95	71	171	70	19
12	196	46	–	57	2	149	46	241	13	20
2	44	20	1	17	3	25	20	54	12	21

* Total Abstainers.

and battery, of whom 985 were under the influence of liquor at the time the crime was committed, and who include 129 excessive drinkers; 960 persons sentenced for disturbing the peace, of whom 719 were in liquor at the time, and who include 68 excessive drinkers; 957 vagabonds and idle persons (tramps), of whom 385 were in liquor when the crime was committed, and who include 207 excessive drinkers.

The tables which follow recapitulate the leading facts in connection with sex, political condition, and place of birth of the criminals. The first table relates to sex and political condition, the other showing the place of birth in detail.

RECAPITULATION. — *Relation of the Liquor Traffic to Crime: By Sex and Political Condition.*

	SEX AND POLITICAL CONDITION.	Number of Criminals	Was the Criminal under the **Influence of Liquor** at the Time the **Crime** was committed		
			Yes	No	Not Ascertained
1	*Males.*	23,581	19,509	4,065	7
2	Citizen born, . .	12,825	10,378	2,444	3
3	Naturalized or alien, .	10,756	9,131	1,621	4
4	*Females.*	3,091	2,354	735	2
5	Citizen born, ...	1,306	949	356	1
6	Naturalized or alien, ...	1,785	1,405	379	1
7	BOTH SEXES.	26,672	21,863	4,800	9
8	Citizen born, ...	14,131	11,327	2,800	4
9	Naturalized or alien, ...	12,541	10,536	2,000	5

RECAPITULATION. — *Relation of the Liquor Traffic to Crime: By Sex, Political Condition, and Place of Birth.*

	SEX, POLITICAL CONDITION, AND PLACE OF BIRTH.	Number of Criminals	Was the Criminal under the **Influence of Liquor** at the Time the **Crime** was committed		
			Yes	No	Not Ascertained
1	MALES.	23,581	19,509	4,065	7
2	*Citizen Born.*	12,825	10,378	2,444	3
3	Alabama, ...	3	2	1	-
4	California, ...	35	20	15	-
5	Colorado, ...	4	3	1	-
6	Connecticut, ...	362	275	87	-
7	Dakota (not specified), ...	1	-	1	-
8	Delaware, ... , . .	2	1	1	-
9	District of Columbia, ...	19	12	7	-
10	Florida, ...	10	4	6	-
11	Georgia, ...	15	9	6	-
12	Illinois, ...	70	40	29	1
13	Indiana, ...	14	9	5	-
14	Iowa, ...	8	6	2	-

RECAPITULATION. — *Relation of the Liquor Traffic to Crime: By Sex and Political Condition.*

Liquor Habits of Criminals			Kinds of Liquor					Tobacco		
Excessive Drinkers	Other Drinkers	Total Abstainers	Wines only	Lager Beer and Malt Liquors only	Distilled Liquors only	Two or All Kinds	Inapplicable*	Users	Nonusers	
3,790	18,551	1,240	101	3,613	626	18,001	1,240	22,112	1,469	1
2,031	9,938	856	34	1,967	409	9,559	856	12,026	799	2
1,759	8,613	384	67	1,646	217	8,442	384	10,086	670	3
726	2,070	295	25	680	102	1,989	295	626	2,465	4
290	856	160	13	272	50	811	160	252	1,054	5
436	1,214	135	12	408	52	1,178	135	374	1,411	6
4,516	20,621	1,535	126	4,293	728	19,990	1,535	22,738	3,934	7
2,321	10,794	1,016	47	2,239	459	10,370	1,016	12,278	1,853	8
2,195	9,827	519	79	2,054	269	9,620	519	10,460	2,081	9

RECAPITULATION. — *Relation of the Liquor Traffic to Crime: By Sex, Political Condition, and Place of Birth.*

Liquor Habits of Criminals			Kinds of Liquor					Tobacco		
Excessive Drinkers	Other Drinkers	Total Abstainers	Wines only	Lager Beer and Malt Liquors only	Distilled Liquors only	Two or All Kinds	Inapplicable*	Users	Nonusers	
3,790	18,551	1,240	101	3,613	626	18,001	1,240	22,112	1,469	1
2,031	9,938	856	34	1,967	409	9,559	856	12,026	799	2
-	3	-	-	-	-	3	-	3	-	3
4	27	4	1	9	1	20	4	33	2	4
1	3	-	-	1	-	3	-	4	-	5
46	294	22	2	50	15	273	22	339	23	6
-	-	1	-	-	-	-	1	-	1	7
-	2	-	-	-	-	2	-	2	-	8
2	13	4	-	4	1	10	4	15	4	9
-	8	2	-	1	-	7	2	9	1	10
2	10	3	-	2	-	10	3	12	3	11
6	60	4	1	14	2	49	4	66	4	12
1	10	3	-	2	-	9	3	12	2	13
2	5	1	-	-	-	7	1	7	1	14

* Total Abstainers.

RECAPITULATION. — *Relation of the Liquor Traffic to Crime: By Sex,*
Political Condition, and Place of Birth — Continued.

SEX, POLITICAL CONDITION, AND PLACE OF BIRTH.	Number of Criminals	Was the Criminal under the **Influence of Liquor** at the Time the **Crime** was committed		
		Yes	No	Not Ascertained
MALES — Con.				
Citizen Born — Con.				
1 Kansas, ...	5	2	3	-
2 Kentucky, ...	20	13	7	-
3 Louisiana, ...	10	8	2	-
4 Maine, ...	606	490	116	-
5 Maryland, ...	46	29	17	-
6 Massachusetts, ...	9,067	7,493	1,572	2
7 Michigan, ...	31	19	12	-
8 Minnesota, ...	7	2	5	-
9 Mississippi, ...	3	1	2	-
10 Missouri, ...	25	11	14	-
11 Montana, ...	4	4	-	-
12 Nebraska, ...	2	1	1	-
13 Nevada, ...	2	2	-	-
14 New Hampshire, ...	412	347	65	-
15 New Jersey, ...	94	77	17	-
16 New York, ...	890	709	181	-
17 North Carolina, ...	29	17	12	-
18 Ohio, ...	48	33	15	-
19 Oregon, ...	3	2	1	-
20 Pennsylvania, ...	182	136	46	-
21 Rhode Island, ...	382	308	74	-
22 South Carolina, ...	14	6	8	-
23 South Dakota, ...	1	-	1	-
24 Tennessee, ...	7	5	2	-
25 Texas, ...	8	4	4	-
26 Utah, ...	2	-	2	-
27 Vermont, ...	241	193	48	-
28 Virginia, ...	104	58	46	-
29 Washington, ...	1	1	-	-
30 West Virginia, ...	10	5	5	-
31 Wisconsin, ...	23	20	3	-
32 Wyoming, ...	1	-	1	-
33 Unknown, ...	2	1	1	-
34 *Naturalized or Alien.*	10,756	9,131	1,621	4
35 Africa, ...	4	2	2	-
36 Asia, ...	12	2	10	-

RECAPITULATION.— *Relation of the Liquor Traffic to Crime: By Sex, Political Condition, and Place of Birth* — Continued.

LIQUOR HABITS OF CRIMINALS			KINDS OF LIQUOR					TOBACCO		
Excessive Drinkers	Other Drinkers	Total Abstainers	Wines only	Lager Beer and Malt Liquors only	Distilled Liquors only	Two or All Kinds	Inapplicable *	Users	Non-users	
1	1	3	-	-	-	2	3	5	-	1
2	17	1	-	5	3	11	1	16	4	2
4	6	-	-	2	-	8	-	10	-	3
87	475	44	-	103	21	438	44	561	45	4
9	32	5	-	6	-	35	5	44	2	5
1,534	6,959	574	23	1,349	280	6,841	574	8,524	543	6
2	25	4	-	6	-	21	4	29	2	7
1	3	3	-	1	-	3	3	6	1	8
-	1	2	-	-	-	1	2	1	2	9
2	20	3	-	5	-	17	3	23	2	10
-	4	-	-	-	1	3	-	4	-	11
1	-	1	-	-	1	-	1	2	-	12
1	1	-	-	-	-	2	-	1	1	13
63	325	24	1	64	17	306	24	380	32	14
19	72	3	-	6	4	81	3	89	5	15
118	709	63	2	157	23	645	63	836	54	16
1	25	3	-	7	2	17	3	26	3	17
8	37	3	-	6	2	37	3	46	2	18
1	2	-	-	-	-	3	-	3	-	19
17	147	18	1	31	4	128	18	174	8	20
46	314	22	-	69	16	275	22	356	26	21
2	10	2	1	1	1	9	2	14	-	22
-	1	-	-	-	-	1	-	1	-	23
-	6	1	-	2	-	4	1	5	2	24
2	6	-	-	3	-	5	-	8	-	25
-	2	-	-	-	-	2	-	2	-	26
36	194	11	-	38	12	180	11	230	11	27
5	80	19	2	13	2	68	19	94	10	28
-	1	-	-	1	-	-	-	1	-	29
2	5	3	-	1	-	6	3	9	1	30
3	20	-	-	7	1	15	-	22	1	31
-	1	-	-	-	-	1	-	1	-	32
-	2	-	-	1	-	1	-	1	1	33
1,759	8,613	384	67	1,646	217	8,442	384	10,086	670	34
-	4	-	-	1	2	1	-	3	1	35
-	7	5	4	-	-	3	5	7	5	36

* Total Abstainers.

RECAPITULATION. — *Relation of the Liquor Traffic to Crime: By Sex, Political Condition, and Place of Birth* — Continued.

SEX, POLITICAL CONDITION, AND PLACE OF BIRTH.	Number of Criminals	Was the Criminal under the **Influence of Liquor** at the Time the **Crime** was committed		
		Yes	No	Not Ascertained
MALES — Con.				
Naturalized or Alien — Con.				
1 Austria (Hungary), ...	5	3	1	1
2 Austria (not specified), ...	12	8	4	-
3 Belgium, ...	13	6	7	-
4 Born at sea, ...	7	5	2	-
5 British Possessions, Other	15	15	-	-
6 Canada, ...	873	668	205	-
7 Central America, ...	3	3	-	-
8 China, ...	26	-	26	-
9 Cuba, ...	1	-	1	-
10 Denmark, ...	21	16	5	-
11 England, ...	1,239	1,046	193	-
12 France, ...	38	32	6	-
13 Germany (Prussia), ...	2	-	2	-
14 Germany (not specified), ...	160	105	55	-
15 Greece, ...	23	-	23	-
16 Holland, ...	2	1	1	-
17 Ireland, ...	6,101	5,555	544	2
18 Italy, ...	196	68	127	1
19 Mexico, ...	1	-	1	-
20 New Brunswick, ...	339	287	52	-
21 Newfoundland, ...	126	114	12	-
22 Norway, ...	48	43	5	-
23 Nova Scotia, ...	470	382	88	-
24 Poland, ...	60	26	34	-
25 Portugal (Western Islands), ...	23	8	15	-
26 Portugal (not specified), ...	7	5	2	-
27 Prince Edward Island, ...	133	106	27	-
28 Russia, ...	143	87	56	-
29 Scotland, ...	351	313	38	-
30 South America, ...	5	3	2	-
31 Spain, ...	2	1	1	-
32 Sweden, ...	238	186	52	-
33 Switzerland, ...	8	6	2	-
34 Turkey, ...	6	1	5	-
35 Wales, ...	26	24	2	-
36 West Indies, ...	17	4	13	-

RECAPITULATION. — *Relation of the Liquor Traffic to Crime: By Sex,. Political Condition, and Place of Birth* — Continued.

Liquor Habits of Criminals			Kinds of Liquor					Tobacco		
Excessive Drinkers	Other Drinkers	Total Abstainers	Wines only	Lager Beer and Malt Liquors only	Distilled Liquors only	Two or All Kinds	Inapplicable*	Users	Non-users	
-	4	1	-	-	2	2	1	4	1	1
2	9	1	-	1	-	10	1	12	-	2
2	9	2	-	1	-	10	2	9	4	3
3	4	-	-	2	-	5	-	7	-	4
3	12	-	-	2	-	13	-	14	1	5
80	732	52	2	144	33	642	52	798	75	6
-	3	-	-	-	-	3	-	3	-	7
-	13	13	-	-	13	-	13	7	19	8
-	-	1	-	-	-	-	1	1	-	9
2	17	2	-	5	-	14	2	20	1	10
169	1,020	50	1	279	18	891	50	1,161	78	11
3	34	1	-	4	1	32	1	36	2	12
-	1	1	-	-	-	1	1	1	1	13
16	135	9	-	45	-	106	9	148	12	14
-	14	9	10	2	-	2	9	11	12	15
-	1	1	-	1	-	-	1	2	-	16
1,209	4,809	83	14	806	109	5,089	83	5,851	250	17
9	163	24	20	24	1	127	24	165	31	18
-	-	1	-	-	-	-	1	1	-	19
53	272	14	-	43	5	277	14	317	22	20
24	97	5	-	18	-	103	5	123	3	21
3	44	1	-	10	-	37	1	48	-	22
55	383	32	-	59	12	367	32	429	41	23
3	50	7	4	18	3	28	7	45	15	24
-	19	4	-	5	1	13	4	22	1	25
2	5	-	1	1	-	5	-	4	3	26
13	112	8	-	23	3	99	8	120	13	27
15	106	22	9	29	7	76	22	114	29	28
59	286	6	-	62	2	281	6	334	17	29
-	4	1	-	1	-	3	1	5	-	30
1	1	-	-	-	1	1	-	2	-	31
17	203	18	2	53	4	161	18	211	27	32
3	5	-	-	-	-	8	-	6	2	33
-	2	4	-	1	-	1	4	6	-	34
3	23	-	-	2	-	24	-	25	1	35
1	10	6	-	4	-	7	6	14	3	36

* Total Abstainers.

RECAPITULATION.— *Relation of the Liquor Traffic to Crime: By Sex, Political Condition, and Place of Birth* — Continued.

SEX, POLITICAL CONDITION, AND PLACE OF BIRTH.	Number of Criminals	Was the Criminal under the **Influence of Liquor** at the Time the **Crime** was committed		
		Yes	No	Not Ascertained
1 FEMALES.	3,091	2,354	735	2
2 *Citizen Born.*	1,306	949	356	1
3 California, ...	3	2	1	-
4 Connecticut, ...	22	15	7	-
5 District of Columbia, ...	7	5	2	-
6 Georgia, ...	2	-	2	-
7 Illinois, ...	5	3	2	-
8 Kansas, ...	1	-	1	-
9 Kentucky, ...	1	-	1	-
10 Louisiana, ...	2	1	1	-
11 Maine, ...	85	55	30	-
12 Maryland, ...	6	3	3	-
13 Massachusetts, ...	915	694	220	1
14 Michigan, ...	3	3	-	-
15 Minnesota, ...	1	1	-	-
16 New Hampshire, ...	50	34	16	-
17 New Jersey, ...	3	1	2	-
18 New York, ...	76	59	17	-
19 North Carolina, ...	10	6	4	-
20 Ohio, ...	7	3	4	-
21 Pennsylvania, ...	15	11	4	-
22 Rhode Island, ...	40	34	6	-
23 Vermont, ...	28	11	17	-
24 Virginia, ...	20	5	15	-
25 Wisconsin, ...	2	2	-	-
26 United States (not specified), ...	2	1	1	-
27 *Naturalized or Alien.*	1,785	1,405	379	1
28 Asia, ...	1	-	1	-
29 Austria (Bohemia), ...	1	-	1	-
30 Austria (Hungary), ...	1	-	1	-
31 Belgium, ...	1	1	-	-
32 Born at sea, ...	2	1	1	-
33 British Possessions, Other	2	2	-	-
34 Canada, ...	109	69	40	-
35 England, ...	238	191	47	-
36 France, ...	6	4	2	-
37 Germany, ...	7	3	4	-

RECAPITULATION. — *Relation of the Liquor Traffic to Crime: By Sex, Political Condition, and Place of Birth* — Continued.

| Liquor Habits of Criminals | | | Kinds of Liquor | | | | | Tobacco | | |
Excessive Drinkers	Other Drinkers	Total Abstainers	Wines only	Lager Beer and Malt Liquors only	Distilled Liquors only	Two or All Kinds	Inapplicable *	Users	Non-users	
726	2,070	295	25	680	102	1,989	295	626	2,465	1
290	856	160	13	272	50	811	160	252	1,054	2
-	2	1	-	1	-	1	1	-	3	3
2	15	5	-	5	4	8	5	6	16	4
-	6	1	-	1	-	5	1	1	6	5
1	1	-	-	1	-	1	-	1	1	6
-	4	1	-	-	-	4	1	1	1	7
-	-	1	-	-	-	-	1	-	1	8
-	1	-	-	1	-	-	-	-	1	9
-	2	-	-	-	1	1	-	1	1	10
20	52	13	4	14	4	50	13	14	71	11
-	4	2	-	1	-	3	2	1	5	12
223	595	97	6	192	29	591	97	185	730	13
-	3	-	-	1	-	2	-	1	2	14
-	1	-	-	-	-	1	-	1	-	15
9	35	6	2	15	3	24	6	3	47	16
-	3	-	-	-	-	3	-	-	3	17
16	55	5	-	17	2	52	5	11	65	18
2	6	2	1	1	-	6	2	2	8	19
1	2	4	-	-	-	3	4	-	7	20
1	12	2	-	4	-	9	2	3	12	21
8	31	1	-	9	4	26	1	10	30	22
5	13	10	-	4	1	13	10	8	20	23
2	10	8	-	5	1	6	8	2	18	24
-	2	-	-	-	-	2	-	-	2	25
-	1	1	-	-	1	-	1	1	1	26
436	1,214	135	12	408	52	1,178	135	374	1,411	27
-	-	1	-	-	-	-	1	-	1	28
-	-	1	-	-	-	-	1	1	-	29
-	-	1	-	-	-	-	1	-	1	30
1	-	-	-	-	-	1	-	-	1	31
1	-	1	-	-	-	1	1	-	2	32
1	1	-	-	-	-	2	-	-	2	33
17	70	22	1	18	6	62	22	22	87	34
48	172	18	1	60	5	154	18	43	195	35
2	4	-	1	1	1	3	-	1	5	36
1	6	-	-	2	-	5	-	-	7	37

* Total Abstainers.

RECAPITULATION. — *Relation of the Liquor Traffic to Crime: By Sex, Political Condition, and Place of Birth* — Continued.

SEX, POLITICAL CONDITION, AND PLACE OF BIRTH.	Number of Criminals	Was the Criminal under the **Influence of Liquor** at the Time the **Crime** was committed		
		Yes	No	Not Ascertained
FEMALES — Con.				
Naturalized or Alien — Con.				
1 Ireland,	1,086	904	181	1
2 Italy,	8	-	8	-
3 New Brunswick,	61	47	14	-
4 Newfoundland,	10	10	-	-
5 Nova Scotia,	115	76	39	-
6 Poland,	3	-	3	-
7 Portugal (Western Islands),	4	1	3	-
8 Portugal (not specified),	2	-	2	-
9 Prince Edward Island,	30	19	11	-
10 Russia,	3	-	3	-
11 Scotland,	77	67	10	-
12 Spain,	1	1	-	-
13 Sweden,	8	2	6	-
14 Switzerland,	1	1	-	-
15 Turkey,	1	-	1	-
16 Wales,	7	6	1	-
17 **BOTH SEXES.**	26,672	21,863	4,800	9
18 *Citizen Born.*	14,131	11,327	2,800	4
19 Alabama,	3	2	1	-
20 California,	38	22	16	-
21 Colorado,	4	3	1	-
22 Connecticut,	384	290	94	-
23 Dakota (not specified),	1	-	1	-
24 Delaware,	2	1	1	-
25 District of Columbia,	26	17	9	-
26 Florida,	10	4	6	-
27 Georgia,	17	9	8	-
28 Illinois,	75	43	31	1
29 Indiana,	14	9	5	-
30 Iowa,	8	6	2	-
31 Kansas,	6	2	4	-
32 Kentucky,	21	13	8	-
33 Louisiana,	12	9	3	-
34 Maine,	691	545	146	-
35 Maryland,	52	32	20	-

RECAPITULATION.— *Relation of the Liquor Traffic to Crime: By Sex, Political Condition, and Place of Birth* — Continued.

| Liquor Habits of Criminals | | | Kinds of Liquor | | | | | Tobacco | | |
Excessive Drinkers	Other Drinkers	Total Abstainers	Wines only	Lager Beer and Malt Liquors only	Distilled Liquors only	Two or All Kinds	Inapplicable *	Users	Non-users	
297	746	43	2	262	29	750	43	257	829	1
-	6	2	-	1	-	5	2	1	7	2
21	36	4	-	8	2	47	4	13	48	3
2	8	-	-	1	-	9	-	2	8	4
18	73	24	2	24	6	59	24	13	102	5
-	1	2	-	-	-	1	2	-	3	6
-	4	-	-	-	-	4	-	-	4	7
-	1	1	-	1	-	-	1	1	1	8
5	21	4	-	8	1	17	4	1	29	9
-	2	1	2	-	-	-	1	-	3	10
15	57	5	3	20	2	47	5	15	62	11
1	-	-	-	-	-	1	-	1	-	12
1	3	4	-	1	-	3	4	-	8	13
1	-	-	-	-	-	1	-	1	-	14
-	-	1	-	-	-	-	1	-	1	15
4	3	-	-	1	-	6	-	2	5	16
4,516	20,621	1,535	126	4,293	728	19,990	1,535	22,738	3,934	17
2,321	10,794	1,016	47	2,239	459	10,370	1,016	12,278	1,853	18
-	3	-	-	-	-	3	-	3	-	19
4	29	5	1	10	1	21	5	33	5	20
1	3	-	-	1	-	3	-	4	-	21
48	309	27	2	55	19	281	27	345	39	22
-	-	1	-	-	-	-	1	-	1	23
-	2	-	-	-	-	2	-	2	-	24
2	19	5	-	5	1	15	5	16	10	25
-	8	2	-	1	-	7	2	9	1	26
3	11	3	-	3	-	11	3	13	4	27
6	64	5	1	14	2	53	5	67	8	28
1	10	3	-	2	-	9	3	12	2	29
2	5	1	-	-	-	7	1	7	1	30
1	1	4	-	-	-	2	4	5	1	31
2	18	1	-	6	3	11	1	16	5	32
4	8	-	-	2	1	9	-	11	1	33
107	527	57	4	117	25	488	57	575	116	34
9	36	7	-	7	-	38	7	45	7	35

* Total Abstainers.

RECAPITULATION.— *Relation of the Liquor Traffic to Crime: By Sex, Political Condition, and Place of Birth* — Continued.

	SEX, POLITICAL CONDITION, AND PLACE OF BIRTH.	Number of Criminals	Was the Criminal under the Influence of Liquor at the Time the Crime was committed		
			Yes	No	Not Ascertained
	BOTH SEXES — Con.				
	Citizen Born — Con.				
1	Massachusetts,	9,982	8,187	1,792	3
2	Michigan,	34	22	12	--
3	Minnesota,	8	3	5	--
4	Mississippi,	3	1	2	--
5	Missouri,	25	11	14	--
6	Montana,	4	4	--	--
7	Nebraska,	2	1	1	--
8	Nevada,	2	2	--	--
9	New Hampshire,	462	381	81	--
10	New Jersey,	97	78	19	--
11	New York,	966	768	198	--
12	North Carolina,	39	23	16	--
13	Ohio,	55	36	19	--
14	Oregon,	3	2	1	--
15	Pennsylvania,	197	147	50	--
16	Rhode Island,	422	342	80	--
17	South Carolina,	14	6	8	--
18	South Dakota,	1	--	1	--
19	Tennessee,	7	5	2	--
20	Texas,	8	4	4	--
21	Utah,	2	--	2	--
22	Vermont,	269	204	65	--
23	Virginia,	124	63	61	--
24	Washington,	1	1	--	--
25	West Virginia,	10	5	5	--
26	Wisconsin,	25	22	3	--
27	Wyoming,	1	--	1	--
28	United States (not specified),	2	1	1	--
29	Unknown,	2	1	1	--
30	*Naturalized or Alien.*	12,541	10,536	2,000	5
31	Africa,	4	2	2	--
32	Asia,	13	2	11	--
33	Austria (Bohemia),	1	--	1	--
34	Austria (Hungary),	6	3	2	1
35	Austria (not specified),	12	8	4	--
36	Belgium,	14	7	7	--

RECAPITULATION. — *Relation of the Liquor Traffic to Crime: By Sex, Political Condition, and Place of Birth* — Continued.

Liquor Habits of Criminals			Kinds of Liquor					Tobacco		
Excessive Drinkers	Other Drinkers	Total Abstainers	Wines only	Lager Beer and Malt Liquors only	Distilled Liquors only	Two or All Kinds	Inapplicable *	Users	Non-users	
1,757	7,554	671	29	1,541	309	7,432	671	8,709	1,273	1
2	28	4	-	7	-	23	4	30	4	2
1	4	3	-	1	-	4	3	7	1	3
-	1	2	-	-	-	1	2	1	2	4
2	20	3	-	5	-	17	3	23	2	5
-	4	-	-	-	1	3	-	4	-	6
1	-	1	-	-	1	-	1	2	-	7
1	1	-	-	-	-	2	-	1	1	8
72	360	30	3	79	20	330	30	383	79	9
19	75	3	-	6	4	84	3	89	8	10
134	764	68	2	174	25	697	68	847	119	11
3	31	5	1	8	2	23	5	28	11	12
9	39	7	-	6	2	40	7	46	9	13
1	2	-	-	-	-	3	-	3	-	14
18	159	20	1	35	4	137	20	177	20	15
54	345	23	-	78	20	301	23	366	56	16
2	10	2	1	1	1	9	2	14	-	17
-	1	-	-	-	-	1	-	1	-	18
-	6	1	-	2	-	4	1	5	2	19
2	6	-	-	3	-	5	-	8	-	20
-	2	-	-	-	-	2	-	2	-	21
41	207	21	-	42	13	193	21	238	31	22
7	90	27	2	18	3	74	27	96	28	23
-	1	-	-	1	-	-	-	1	-	24
2	5	3	-	1	-	6	3	9	1	25
3	22	-	-	7	1	17	-	22	3	26
-	1	-	-	-	-	1	-	1	-	27
-	1	1	-	-	1	-	1	1	1	28
-	2	-	-	1	-	1	-	1	1	29
2,195	9,827	519	79	2,054	269	9,620	519	10,460	2,081	30
-	4	-	-	1	2	1	-	3	1	31
-	7	6	4	-	-	3	6	7	6	32
-	-	1	-	-	-	-	1	1	-	33
-	4	2	-	-	2	2	2	4	2	34
2	9	1	-	1	-	10	1	12	-	35
3	9	2	-	1	-	11	2	9	5	36

* Total Abstainers.

RECAPITULATION. — *Relation of the Liquor Traffic to Crime: By Sex, Political Condition, and Place of Birth* — Concluded.

SEX, POLITICAL CONDITION, AND PLACE OF BIRTH.	Number of Criminals	Was the Criminal under the Influence of Liquor at the Time the Crime was committed		
		Yes	No	Not Ascertained
BOTH SEXES — Con.				
Naturalized or Alien — Con.				
1　Born at sea,	9	6	3	–
2　British Possessions, Other	17	17	–	–
3　Canada,	982	737	245	–
4　Central America,	3	3	–	–
5　China,	26	–	26	–
6　Cuba,	1	–	1	–
7　Denmark,	21	16	5	–
8　England,	1,477	1,237	240	–
9　France,	44	36	8	–
10　Germany (Prussia),	2	–	2	–
11　Germany (not specified),	167	108	59	–
12　Greece,	23	–	23	–
13　Holland,	2	1	1	–
14　Ireland,	7,187	6,459	725	3
15　Italy,	204	68	135	1
16　Mexico,	1	–	1	–
17　New Brunswick,	400	334	66	–
18　Newfoundland,	136	124	12	–
19　Norway,	48	43	5	–
20　Nova Scotia,	585	458	127	–
21　Poland,	63	26	37	–
22　Portugal (Western Islands),	27	9	18	–
23　Portugal (not specified),	9	5	4	–
24　Prince Edward Island,	163	125	38	–
25　Russia,	146	87	59	–
26　Scotland,	428	380	48	–
27　South America,	5	3	2	–
28　Spain,	3	2	1	–
29　Sweden,	246	188	58	–
30　Switzerland,	9	7	2	–
31　Turkey,	7	1	6	–
32　Wales,	33	30	3	–
33　West Indies,	17	4	13	–

The first table indicates that, disregarding the classification by sex, of the 26,672 criminals, including 14,131 citizen born

RECAPITULATION. — *Relation of the Liquor Traffic to Crime: By Sex, Political Condition, and Place of Birth* — Concluded.

LIQUOR HABITS OF CRIMINALS			KINDS OF LIQUOR					TOBACCO		
Excessive Drinkers	Other Drinkers	Total Abstainers	Wines only	Lager Beer and Malt Liquors only	Distilled Liquors only	Two or All Kinds	Inapplicable *	Users	Non-users	
4	4	1	-	2	-	6	1	7	2	1
4	13	-	-	2	-	15	-	14	3	2
106	802	74	3	162	39	704	74	820	162	3
-	3	-	-	-	-	3	-	3	-	4
-	13	13	-	-	13	-	13	7	19	5
-	-	1	-	-	-	-	1	1	-	6
2	17	2	-	5	-	14	2	20	1	7
217	1,192	68	2	339	23	1,045	68	1,204	273	8
5	38	1	1	5	2	35	1	37	7	9
-	1	1	-	-	-	1	1	1	1	10
17	141	9	-	47	-	111	9	148	19	11
-	14	9	10	2	-	2	9	11	12	12
-	1	1	-	1	-	-	1	2	-	13
1,506	5,555	126	16	1,068	138	5,839	126	6,108	1,079	14
9	169	26	20	25	1	132	26	166	38	15
-	-	1	-	-	-	-	1	1	-	16
74	308	18	-	51	7	324	18	330	70	17
26	105	5	-	19	-	112	5	125	11	18
3	44	1	-	10	-	37	1	48	-	19
73	456	56	2	83	18	426	56	442	143	20
3	51	9	4	18	3	29	9	45	18	21
-	23	4	-	5	1	17	4	22	5	22
2	6	1	1	2	-	5	1	5	4	23
18	133	12	-	31	4	116	12	121	42	24
15	108	23	11	29	7	76	23	114	32	25
74	343	11	3	82	4	328	11	349	79	26
-	4	1	-	1	-	3	1	5	-	27
2	1	-	-	-	1	2	-	3	-	28
18	206	22	2	54	4	164	22	211	35	29
4	5	-	-	-	-	9	-	7	2	30
-	2	5	-	1	-	1	5	6	1	31
7	26	-	-	3	-	30	-	27	6	32
1	10	6	-	4	-	7	6	14	3	33

* Total Abstainers.

and 12,541 naturalized or alien, there were 21,863 who replied " Yes " to the question, " Was the criminal under the influence

of liquor at the time the crime was committed," including
11,327 citizen born and 10,536 naturalized or alien; the
aggregate number who replied "No" to this question being
4,800, of whom 2,800 were citizen born and 2,000 naturalized
or alien. The aggregate number of excessive drinkers, namely,
4,516, include 2,321 citizen born and 2,195 naturalized or alien.
Drinkers of other degree, who number in the aggregate 20,621,
include 10,794 citizen born and 9,827 naturalized or alien.
The total abstainers among the criminals number in the aggregate 1,535, of whom 1,016 were citizen born and 519 naturalized or alien. Users of wines only, among the citizen born,
number 47; among the naturalized or alien, 79. Those who
used lager beer and malt liquors only include 2,239 citizen
born and 2,054 naturalized or alien. Distilled liquors only
were used by 459 who were citizen born and 269 who were
naturalized or alien. Of the citizen-born criminals, 10,370
used two or all kinds of liquor, while 9,620 who were naturalized or alien fall within the same class.

RECAPITULATION. — *Crime : Sentences : By Political Condition and
Degree of Crime.*

	POLITICAL CONDITION AND DEGREE OF CRIME.	FINES ONLY			IMPRISONMENT ONLY		
		Number	Aggregate Fines	Average Fine	Number	Aggregate Time (Days)	Average Time (Days)
1	*Citizen Born.*	6,479	$60,221.85	$9.29	7,323	3,157,592	431
2	Drunkenness, . .	4,528	27,470.36	6.07	4,158	535,375	129
3	Drunkenness and other						
	crimes, . . .	132	2,289.48	17.34	168	55,729	332
4	Other crimes, . .	1,819	30,462.01	16.20	2,997	2,566,488	856
5	*Naturalized or Alien.*	6,426	64,208.87	9.99	5,841	1,120,120	192
6	Drunkenness, . .	4,739	28,597.01	6.03	3,939	501,387	127
7	Drunkenness and other						
	crimes, . . .	133	1,974 00	14.83	109	23,439	215
8	Other crimes, . .	1,554	33,637.86	21.65	1,793	595,294	332
9	AGGREGATES.	12,905	124,430.72	9.64	13,164	4,277,712	325
10	Drunkenness, . .	9,267	56,067.37	6.05	8,097	1,036,762	128
11	Drunkenness and other						
	crimes, . . .	265	4,263.48	16.09	277	79,168	236
12	Other crimes, . .	3,373	64,099.87	19.00	4,790	3,161,782	660

Turning to the second table which shows the place of birth in detail, we find that among the males who were citizen born, 12,825 in all, those born in Massachusetts number 9,067. Of the females, 1,306 in all, those born in Massachusetts number 915. Of the naturalized or alien males, 10,756 in all, 6,101 were born in Ireland, 1,239 in England, 873 in Canada, 470 in Nova Scotia, and 339 in New Brunswick; the others being distributed among the various other foreign countries. Of the females of foreign birth, who number 1,785, there are 1,086 who were born in Ireland, 238 in England, 109 in Canada, 115 in Nova Scotia, 77 in Scotland, and 61 in New Brunswick; the others being distributed among the other foreign countries; and the table shows in detail the facts as to the use of liquor by the criminals of each of the nativities represented.

We now introduce a table which shows the nature of sentences imposed upon criminals for offences in which the use of liquor is a factor, or for other offences.

RECAPITULATION. — *Crime ; Sentences : By Political Condition and Degree of Crime.*

	FINES AND IMPRISONMENT				BONDS, BONDS AND FINES					
		AGGREGATE		AVERAGE		Num-ber of Bonds	Num-ber of Bonds and Fines	Total Surety	Total Fines	Average Surety	Average Fine
Num-ber	Fines	Time (Days)	Fine	Time (Days)							
137	$6,411.00	13,815	$46.79	101	16	23	$5,510.00	$313.96	$141.29	$13.65	1
9	101.00	840	11.22	93	6	4	650.00	19.00	65.00	4.75	2
51	582.00	4,530	11.41	89	3	5	900.00	32.68	112.50	6.53	3
77	5,728.00	8,445	74.39	110	7	14	3,960.00	262.28	188.57	18.73	4
181	7,217.00	12,901	39.87	71	27	27	8,308.00	194.60	153.85	7.20	5
59	383.00	1,475	6.50	25	1	4	400.00	18.00	80.00	4.50	6
44	733.00	3,350	16.66	76	-	4	403.00	46.00	100.75	11.50	7
78	6,101.00	8,076	78.47	104	26	19	7,505.00	130.60	166.77	6.87	8
318	13,628.00	26,716	42.84	84	43	50	13,818.00	508.56	148.58	10.17	9
68	484.00	2,315	7.12	34	7	8	1,050.00	37.00	70.00	4.63	10
95	1,315.00	7,880	13.84	83	3	9	1,303.00	78.68	108.58	8.74	11
155	11,829.00	16,521	76.32	107	33	33	11,465.00	392.88	173.71	11.91	12

We summarize the facts in the aggregate. It appears that during the year there were 12,905 criminals who were sentenced to fine only, and 13,164 to imprisonment only, while 318 were sentenced to fine and imprisonment. The persons convicted of drunkenness include 9,267 who were sentenced to fine only, the aggregate amount of fines being $56,067.37, or an average fine of $6.05. For drunkenness and other crimes, 265 persons were sentenced to fine only, the fines in the aggregate amounting to $4,263.48, or an average of $16.09. Persons sentenced to fine only for crimes other than drunkenness number 3,373, the aggregate amount of fines in these cases being $64,099.87, or an average of $19. In 8,097 cases of drunkenness, the criminals were sentenced to imprisonment only, the aggregate number of days of imprisonment being 1,036,762, or an average of 128 days for each person. There were 277 persons sentenced to imprisonment only, for drunkenness together with other crimes, the aggregate time of imprisonment being 79,168 days, or an average of 286 days for each person. For crimes other than drunkenness, 4,790 persons were sentenced to imprisonment only, the time aggregating 3,161,782 days, or an average of 660 days each. The sentence of fine and imprisonment was imposed in 68 cases of drunkenness, the aggregate amount of fines being $484, and the aggregate time of imprisonment 2,315 days; or an average of $7.12 fine and 34 days' imprisonment to each person. For drunkenness in connection with other crimes, 95 persons were sentenced to fine and imprisonment, the aggregate amount of fines in these cases being $1,315, and the aggregate time of imprisonment 7,880 days; or an average of $13.84 fine and 83 days' imprisonment in each case. For crimes other than drunkenness, 155 criminals were sentenced to fine and imprisonment, the aggregate fines amounting to $11,829, and the aggregate imprisonment to 16,521 days; or an average of $76.32 fine and 107 days' imprisonment. The relations of the fines and imprisonment imposed for drunkenness only, and for drunkenness united with other crimes, to the fines and imprisonment imposed for crimes other than drunkenness may be clearly seen from these figures, which represent the return to the public, either in money or in days of imprisonment, for the violations of law during the 12 months covered by the investigation. The aggregate number of bonds in the criminal cases which we have covered was 43, while there were 50 cases of bonds and fines; the average surety being $148.58 and the average fine in connection with bonds $10.17. Of the cases in which bonds were given, 10 related to drunkenness and to drunkenness with other crimes, while 33 related to other crimes only. Of the bond and fine cases, 17 related to drunkenness and to drunkenness in connection with other crimes, and 33 to other crimes only.

In 192 cases, alternative sentences, namely, either fines or imprisonment, were imposed. The nature of these cases, classified by political condition, place of birth, and degree of crime is shown in the following table:

Crime; Alternative Sentences: By Political Condition, Place of Birth, and Degree of Crime.

POLITICAL CONDITION, PLACE OF BIRTH, AND DEGREE OF CRIME.	FINES OR IMPRISONMENT				
	Number	Total Fines	Total Time (Days)	Average Fine	Average Time (Days)
Citizen Born.	153	$1,882.00	5,373	$12.30	35
Connecticut, ...	1	5.00	3	5.00	3
Drunkenness, ...	1	5.00	3	5.00	3
Maine, ...	10	107.00	420	10.70	42
Drunkenness, ...	6	40.00	180	6.67	30
Other crimes, ...	4	67.00	210	16.75	60
Massachusetts, ...	109	1,400.00	3,870	12.84	36
Drunkenness, ...	78	480.00	1,910	6.15	24
Drunkenness and other crimes, .	3	52.00	110	17.33	37
Other crimes, ...	28	868.00	1,850	31.00	66
New Hampshire, ...	8	55.00	240	6.88	30
Drunkenness, ...	7	40.00	180	5.71	26
Other crimes, ...	1	15.00	60	15.00	60
New Jersey, ...	3	25.00	75	8.33	25
Drunkenness, ...	3	25.00	75	8.33	25
New York, ...	4	45.00	165	11.25	41
Drunkenness, ...	3	15.00	45	5.00	15
Drunkenness and other crimes, .	1	30.00	120	30.00	120
Ohio, ...	1	5.00	15	5.00	15
Drunkenness, ...	1	5.00	15	5.00	15
Pennsylvania, ...	2	25.00	45	12.50	23
Drunkenness, ...	1	5.00	15	5.00	15
Other crimes, ...	1	20.00	30	20.00	30

Crime; Alternative Sentences: By Political Condition, Place of Birth, and Degree of Crime — Concluded.

POLITICAL CONDITION, PLACE OF BIRTH, AND DEGREE OF CRIME.	FINES OR IMPRISONMENT				
	Number	Total Fines	Total Time (Days)	Average Fine	Average Time (Days)
Citizen Born — Con.					
Rhode Island, ...	10	170.00	405	17.00	41
Drunkenness, ...	7	35.00	105	5.00	15
Other crimes, ...	3	135.00	300	45.00	100
Vermont, ...	5	45.00	135	9.00	27
Drunkenness, ...	4	25.00	120	6.25	30
Drunkenness and other crimes, .	1	20.00	15	20.00	15
Naturalized or Alien.	39	789.00	2,095	20.23	54
Canada, ...	8	180.00	535	22.50	67
Drunkenness, ...	5	110.00	270	22.00	54
Drunkenness and other crimes, .	1	25.00	55	25.00	55
Other crimes, ...	2	45.00	210	22.50	105
England, ...	2	20.00	90	10.00	45
Other crimes, ...	2	20.00	90	10.00	45
France, ...	1	5.00	15	5.00	15
Drunkenness, ...	1	5.00	15	5.00	15
Ireland, ...	14	420.00	1,020	30.00	73
Drunkenness and other crimes, .	1	15.00	60	15.00	60
Other crimes, ...	13	405.00	960	31.15	74
Nova Scotia, ...	10	74.00	300	7.40	30
Drunkenness, ...	8	40.00	120	5.00	15
Drunkenness and other crimes, .	1	14.00	60	14.00	60
Other crimes, ...	1	20.00	120	20.00	120
Portugal (Western Islands), . .	1	75.00	90	75.00	90
Other crimes, ...	1	75.00	90	75.00	90
Scotland, ...	1	5.00	15	5.00	15
Drunkenness, ...	1	5.00	15	5.00	15
Sweden, ...	2	10.00	30	5.00	15
Drunkenness, ...	2	10.00	30	5.00	15
AGGREGATES.	192	2,671.00	7,468	13.91	39
Citizen born, ...	153	1,882.00	5,373	12.30	35
Naturalized or alien, ...	39	789.00	2,095	20.23	54

In the aggregate, 192 cases appear, including 153 criminals who were citizen born and 39 who were naturalized or alien. The average fine imposed in these cases was $13.91, and the average imprisonment, 39 days. The cases include 128 persons sentenced for drunkenness only; eight, sentenced for drunkenness and other crimes ; and 56, for other crimes only. These cases are classified under the place of birth of the criminals who were convicted of the specified crimes.

We have already shown the influence of the foreign strain in respect to crime. The following table shows the number of criminals who could not speak the English language :

Crime ; Number of Criminals who could not Speak the English Language : By Nature of Crime.

NATURE OF CRIME.	Number of Criminals	Number *Not* Speaking English
BOTH SEXES.	26,672	134
Drunkenness, ...	17,575	41
Liquor offences,.	388	4
Other crimes, ...	8,709	89

As shown by the table, of the whole number of criminals, 134 could not speak the English language. Of these, 41 were committed for drunkenness, 4 for other liquor offences, and 89 for other crimes. That is, putting the facts in terms of percentage, 0.50 per cent of the total number of criminals could not speak English ; of those committed for drunkenness, 0.23 per cent could not speak English ; of those committed for other liquor offences, 1.03 per cent could not speak English ; and of those committed for other crimes, 1.02 per cent could not speak English. The criminals who could not speak English include the following : Italian, 40 ; French, 29 ; Finnish, 17 ; Chinese, 13 ; Greek, nine ; German, six ; Polish, five ; Swedish, five ; Russian, four ; Portuguese, three ; Hungarian, two ; Danish, one. Of these, the Chinese, Hungarian, and Danish were convicted of crimes other than drunkenness ; those who were convicted of drunkenness or of other liquor offences comprise 18 who spoke French ; 11, Finnish ; six, Italian ; three, Polish ; two, German ; two, Swedish ; and one each Portuguese, Russian, and Greek.

For purposes of comparison, we next present, for the State as a whole, the number of sentences for drunkenness, liquor offences, and for all other offences, separately, for a series of years, beginning with 1860 and closing with the 12 months covered by the present investigation.

CLASSIFICATION.	1860	1865	1870	1875	1879	1894-95
Drunkenness, ...	6,334	8,060	18,880	23,553	16,211	17,575
Liquor offences,*	583	599	6,930	1,751	460	388
All other offences, . . .	9,600	8,620	13,895	15,107	11,482	8,709
AGGREGATES (ALL OFFENCES),	16,517	17,279	39,705	40,411	28,153	26,672

In 1860, the total number of sentences for all offences was
16,517; in 1865, the number was 17,279; while in the next
five years a very great increase appears, the number in 1870
being 39,705. In 1875 the number was 40,411; but in 1879
there were only 28,153 sentences; and in the 12 months covered by the present investigation, only 26,672. The greatest
variation appears in the sentences for drunkenness and liquor
offences. The sentences for drunkenness in 1860 numbered
6,334; and in 1865, 8,060. In 1870 they rose to 18,880; in
1875, to 23,553; declining in 1879 to 16,211; and numbering
for the 12 months covered by the present investigation, 17,575.
Thus, if a comparison is made between 1860 and the 12 months
now under consideration, we find an increase in sentences for
all offences amounting to 61.93 per cent, while the increase in
sentences for drunkenness only, amounts to 36.04 per cent.
The sentences for liquor offences * other than drunkenness,
which in 1860 numbered 583, and in 1865, 599, aggregated in
1870, 6,930; declining in 1875 to 1,751; in 1879 to only 460;
and in the 12 months covered by the present investigation to
only 388. The sentences for all offences other than drunkenness and liquor offences numbered 9,600 in 1860, and in the
12 months at present under consideration, 8,709; a decline of
9.28 per cent, although, of course, the population has very
largely increased.

This table is interesting because it shows very clearly that
the increase in crime, which is apparent if we base our comparisons on the whole number of sentences, is due to the
increase of sentences for drunkenness; while the wide varia-
tions in the number of yearly sentences for drunkenness, and,
to a certain extent, for other liquor offences, between periods

---

* Including liquor selling, liquor keeping, liquor carrying, and all violations of
the license laws.

closely connected, can only be explained by the statutory changes which have affected the status of the crimes themselves, and by the changes in public policy with respect to the liquor traffic, which have more or less influenced the administration of the law relating to them. There is apparently nothing else which accounts for the enormous increase in sentences shown in 1870 and in 1875 as compared with 1865, followed by a remarkable decline between 1875 and 1879. These changes are also, to a limited degree, reflected in the sentences for crimes other than drunkenness and liquor offences. For example, the sentences for other offences, which show a decline between 1860 and 1865 from 9,600 to 8,620, rose to 13,895 in 1870, and to 15,107 in 1875 ;* since which time they have shown a decline. The increases noted are, however, very much less than the increases shown for the same years in sentences for drunkenness. It is, of course, true that some of the sentences for offences other than drunkenness and purely liquor offences are for crimes upon which the use of liquor has an influence. This has been sufficiently brought out in preceding tables. The figures plainly indicate that while there is shown a considerable increase in the number of sentences during the 12 months covered by the present investigation as compared with the year 1860, this increase is wholly due to sentences for drunkenness, for, if these sentences are excluded from the comparison, a decline is apparent. In other words, although one who notes the increase in the aggregate number of sentences shown in this table might be justified in stating that crime has increased in Massachusetts since 1860, it should be clearly pointed out that this increase is not due to sentences for offences such as are universally recognized as criminal, but rather to sentences for drunkenness, which is made a crime by statute law, varying in different States, and from time to time in our own State.

The effect of legislation upon the crime of drunkenness must be taken into account in any such comparison, or entirely erroneous deductions will be drawn. In 1860, for ex-

---

* The highest point, although not shown in the table, was actually reached in 1873, when the number of sentences for all offences was 46,132, those for drunkenness numbering 23,842. See Report of this Bureau for 1880, Part III, "Statistics of Crime."

ample, no person could be fined for single acts of drunkenness; the offender must have been a common drunkard. Persons found drunk could be detained only until sober. This law, as pointed out in a previous report of this Bureau,* caused a decrease in sentences for drunkenness during the years 1860, 1861, and 1862, although it was repealed by Chapter 136 of the Acts of 1861. Subsequently, down to the present time, the offence has been subjected to various legal modifications.† Since 1860 there have been other changes in legislation which must be borne in mind. The prohibitory law of 1855 was in force until 1868 when a license law was passed. A re-enactment of the prohibitory law went into effect July 1, 1869. In 1870 the legislature permitted the free sale of "ale, porter, strong beer, and lager beer," everywhere, unless prohibited by vote of each city or town. The "beer law," so called, remained substantially the same until 1873, when it was repealed. In 1875 the prohibitory law was again repealed and the present local option license system adopted.

The figures shown in the preceding table, are in the following presentation, compared with the population for each of the years named, so as to show the number of sentences to each 1,000 of the population, for each of the specified offences.

YEARS.	Population	PROPORTION TO EACH 1,000 OF POPULATION			
		Drunken-ness	Liquor Offences	All Other Offences	All Offences
1860, ...	1,231,066	5.15	0.47	7.80	13.42
1865, ...	1,267,030	6.36	0.47	6.80	13.63
1870, ...	1,457,351	12.96	4.75	9.53	27.24
1875, ...	1,651,912	14.26	1.06	9.15	24.47
1879, ...	‡1,783,085	9.09	0.26	6.44	15.79
1894-95, ...	§2,500,183	7.03	0.16	3.48	10.67

This table illustrates the point already made that the apparent increase of crime since 1860 is due to sentences for drunk-

* Report for 1880; Part III. "Statistics of Crime."
† See Chap. 221, Acts of 1880; Chap. 247, Acts of 1880; Chap. 276, Acts of 1881; Chap. 365, Acts of 1885; Chap. 375, Acts of 1885; Chap. 377, Acts of 1888; and Chap. 427, Acts of 1891.
‡ Population for 1880.　　　§ Population for 1895.

enness, and that if drunkenness and other liquor offences be excluded from the comparison, crime has declined. The sentences for all offences other than drunkenness in 1860 numbered 7.80 to each 1,000 of the population; in 1865, 6.80; and in 1870, 9.53. They declined to 9.15 in 1875; to 6.44 in 1879; and were found to be but 3.48 per 1,000 in the 12 months covered by the present investigation. The sentences for liquor offences other than drunkenness, when apportioned to each 1,000 of the population, are comparatively few. In the year 1870, for reasons peculiar to that period, due to the statutes then in force, such sentences numbered 4.75 to each 1,000 of the population; but in the other years compared in the table they are so few in number that they need not be particularly considered. The sentences for drunkenness in 1860 numbered 5.15 to each 1,000 of the population; the highest point was reached in 1875, when such sentences numbered 14.26 to each 1,000; in the 12 months at present under consideration they numbered 7.03. Sentences for all offences, including drunkenness, numbered 13.42 to each 1,000 of the population in 1860; they numbered only 10.67 to each 1,000 of the population in the 12 months now under consideration; a relative decline, although, as we have shown, the sentences for all offences in the aggregate exhibit a numerical increase, and the sentences for drunkenness have increased both numerically and relatively to the population.

In connection with the relation of the use of liquor to crime, we have collected data relative to the number of arrests for drunkenness and for all offences other than drunkenness, in the different cities and towns. The following table exhibits the number of such arrests during the 12 months covered by the investigation for each of the cities, and for the towns independently of the cities, by counties, in comparison with the population.

Number of Arrests, classified by Nature of Crime, and Proportion to Each 1,000 of Population.

COUNTIES, CITIES, AND TOWNS.	Population	Number of Arrests for Drunkenness	Number of Arrests for All Offences Other than Drunkenness	Total Number of Arrests for All Offences including Drunkenness	PROPORTION TO EACH 1,000 OF POPULATION		
					Number of Arrests for Drunkenness	Number of Arrests for All Offences Other than Drunkenness	Total Number of Arrests for All Offences including Drunkenness
BARNSTABLE.	27,654	16	118	134	0.58	4.27	4.85
Towns, .	27,654	16	118	134	0.58	4.27	4.85
BERKSHIRE.	86,292	1,591	1,534	3,125	18.44	17.77	36.21
North Adams,	19,135	582	417	999	30.42	21.79	52.21
Pittsfield, .	20,461	667	472	1,139	32.60	23.07	55.67
Towns, . .	46,696	342	645	987	7.32	13.81	21.13
BRISTOL.	219,019	3,930	3,386	7,316	17.94	15.46	33.40
Fall River, .	89,203	1,822	1,833	3,655	20.43	20.54	40.97
New Bedford,	55,251	1,149	806	1,955	20.80	14.58	35.38
Taunton, . .	27,115	835	309	1,144	30.79	11.40	42.19
Towns, . .	47,450	124	438	562	2.61	9.23	11.84
DUKES.	4,238	3	26	29	0.71	6.13	6.84
Towns, .	4,238	3	26	29	0.71	6.13	6.84
ESSEX.	330,393	8,014	4,414	12,428	24.26	13.36	37.62
Beverly, . .	11,806	133	83	216	11.27	7.03	18.30
Gloucester, .	28,211	576	293	869	20.41	10.39	30.80
Haverhill, .	30,209	759	644	1,403	25.12	21.32	46.44
Lawrence, .	52,164	2,031	889	2,920	38.94	17.04	55.98
Lynn, . .	62,354	2,201	1,054	3,255	35.30	16.90	52.20
Newburyport,	14,552	690	193	883	47.41	13.26	60.67
Salem, . .	34,473	799	400	1,199	23.18	11.60	34.78
Towns, . .	96,624	825	858	1,683	8.54	8.88	17.42
FRANKLIN.	40,145	165	251	416	4.11	6.25	10.36
Towns, . .	40,145	165	251	416	4.11	6.25	10.36
HAMPDEN.	152,938	2,675	2,040	4,715	17.49	13.34	30.83
Chicopee,. .	16,420	268	263	531	16.32	16.02	32.34
Holyoke, . .	40,322	795	651	1,446	19.72	16.14	35.86
Springfield, .	51,522	1,346	900	2,246	26.12	17.47	43.59
Towns, . .	44,674	266	226	492	5.95	5.06	11.01
HAMPSHIRE.	54,710	491	237	728	8.97	4.33	13.30
Northampton,.	16,746	346	98	444	20.66	5.85	26.51
Towns, . .	37,964	145	139	284	3.82	3.66	7.48

Number of Arrests, classified by Nature of Crime, and Proportion to Each 1,000 of Population — Concluded.

COUNTIES, CITIES, AND TOWNS.	Population	Number of Arrests for Drunkenness	Number of Arrests for All Offences Other than Drunkenness	Total Number of Arrests for All Offences including Drunkenness	PROPORTION TO EACH 1,000 OF POPULATION		
					Number of Arrests for Drunkenness	Number of Arrests for All Offences Other than Drunkenness	Total Number of Arrests for All Offences including Drunkenness
MIDDLESEX.	499,217	10,801	6,720	17,521	21.64	13.46	35.10
CAMBRIDGE, .	81,643	1,922	1,428	3,350	23.54	17.49	41.03
EVERETT, . .	18,573	397	203	600	21.37	10.93	32.30
LOWELL, . .	84,367	3,773	1,645	5,418	44.72	19.50	64.22
MALDEN, . .	29,708	258	430	688	8.68	14.47	23.15
MARLBOROUGH,	14,977	352	152	504	23.50	10.15	33.65
MEDFORD, . .	14,474	214	173	387	14.79	·11.95	26.74
NEWTON, . .	27,590	398	394	792	14.43	14.28	28.71
SOMERVILLE, .	52,200	977	603	1,580	18.72	11.55	30.27
WALTHAM, .	20,876	744	350	1,094	35.64	16.76	52.40
WOBURN, . .	14,178	559	212	771	39.43	14.95	54.38
Towns, . .	140,631	1,207	1,130	2,337	8.58	8.04	16.62
NANTUCKET.	3,016	36	6	42	11.94	1.99	13.93
Towns, . .	3,016	36	6	42	11.94	1.99	13.93
NORFOLK.	134,819	1,242	1,433	2,675	9.21	10.63	19.84
QUINCY, . .	20,712	271	208	479	13.08	10.04	23.12
Towns, . .	114,107	971	1,225	2,196	8.51	10.74	19.25
PLYMOUTH.	101,498	912	994	1,906	8.99	9.79	18.78
BROCKTON, .	33,165	624	504	1,128	18.81	15.20	34.01
Towns, . .	68,333	288	490	778	4.21	7.17	11.38
SUFFOLK.	539,799	26,807	17,717	44,524	49.66	32.82	82.48
BOSTON, . .	496,920	26,036	16,736	42,772	52.39	33.68	86.07
CHELSEA, . .	31,264	636	778	1,414	20.34	24.88	45.22
Towns, . .	11,615	135	203	338	11.62	17.48	29.10
WORCESTER.	306,445	4,792	3,183	7,975	15.64	10.38	26.02
FITCHBURG, .	26,409	420	390	810	15.90	14.77	30.67
WORCESTER, .	98,767	2,592	1,307	3,899	26.24	13.23	39.47
Towns, . .	181,269	1,780	1,486	3,266	9.82	8.20	18.02
THE STATE.	2,500,183	61,475	42,059	103,534	24.59	16.82	41.41
Cities, . .	1,635,767	55,172	34,818	89,990	33.73	21.28	55.01
Towns, . .	864,416	6,303	7,241	13,544	7.29	8.38	15.67

For the State as a whole, the population of the cities according to the census of 1895, being 1,635,767, we find that during the 12 months covered by the investigation, there were, in the cities alone, 89,990 arrests for all offences, including drunkenness, or 55.01 arrests to each 1,000 of the population. In the towns alone during the same time, there were 13,544 arrests, or 15.67 arrests to each 1,000 of the population, the aggregate population of the towns being 864,416. In the State as a whole, without considering the cities and towns independently, the arrests for all offences numbered 41.41 to each 1,000 of the population. These figures show a very great preponderance of arrests in cities over those in towns to each 1,000 of the population. The arrests for drunkenness only, in the cities, numbered 33.73 to each 1,000 of the population, while similar arrests in towns numbered only 7.29. The arrests in the cities for all offences other than drunkenness numbered 21.28 to each 1,000 of the population, while in the towns they numbered 8.38. It is undoubtedly true that the law with respect to drunkenness and minor crimes and misdemeanors is more vigorously enforced in the cities than in the towns generally, and in the larger towns than in the smaller. A person under the influence of liquor is much more in evidence in a city than in the country, and more likely to be arrested. In the State as a whole, without considering the cities and towns separately, the arrests for drunkenness alone numbered 24.59 to each 1,000 of the population. Expressing these figures in percentages, we note that, of all the arrests, 59.38 per cent in the State, 61.31 per cent in the cities, and 46.54 per cent in the towns, were for drunkenness alone. In the towns the arrests for crimes other than drunkenness to each 1,000 of the population exceeded the arrests for drunkenness; but, on the other hand, in the cities the arrests for drunkenness to each 1,000 of the population were considerably in excess of the arrests for other crimes; and this statement of course holds true for the State as a whole. The largest number of arrests for drunkenness to each 1,000 of the population in the cities was found in Boston, namely 52.39; and the smallest number in Malden, namely 8.68. The cities in which the number of arrests for drunkenness to each 1,000 of the population exceeded the average number found in the cities of the Commonwealth, are

as follows, the number being annexed in each case : Boston,
52.39 ; Lawrence, 38.94 ; Lowell, 44.72 ; Lynn, 35.30 ; New-
buryport, 47.41 ; Waltham, 35.64 ; Woburn, 39.43.

The status of the liquor traffic under the law is fixed anew
every 12 months by the suffrages of the people upon the question of license. During the 12 months covered by the investigation, many towns were entirely under the license system, while
in many others no license prevailed ; in others still, the policy
upon this question was changed during the year. The following table gives the facts upon this point and shows the number
of arrests in each group of cities and towns, with the proportion to each 1,000 of the population.

	Number of Cities and Towns	Population	Number of Arrests for Drunkenness	Number of Arrests for All Offences Other than Drunkenness	Total Number of Arrests for All Offences including Drunkenness	PROPORTION TO EACH 1,000 OF POPULATION		
						Number of Arrests for Drunkenness	Number of Arrests for All Offences Other than Drunkenness	Total Number of Arrests for All Offences including Drunkenness
THE STATE.	353	2,500,183	61,475	42,059	103,534	24.59	16.82	41.41
License cities and towns, .	53	1,275,163	46,211	28,482	74,693	36.24	22.34	58.58
No license cities and towns, .	260	924,046	9,181	9,483	18,664	9.94	10.26	20.20
License and no license cities and towns, .	40	300,974	6,083	4,094	10,177	20.21	13.60	33.81

According to this table, out of the 353 cities and towns in
the Commonwealth, 53 were entirely under the policy of
license during the 12 months. These 53 cities and towns included an aggregate population of 1,275,163, or about 50 per
cent of the population of the State. The number of arrests for
drunkenness in these places was 46,211, or 36.24 to each 1,000
of the population. The number of arrests for all offences other
than drunkenness was 28,482, or 22.34 to each 1,000 of the
population. In the aggregate, there were 74,693 arrests for
all offences, or 58.58 to each 1,000 of the population.

The no-license cities and towns numbered 260, including an
aggregate population of 924,046. In these cities and towns
the number of arrests for drunkenness was 9,181, or 9.94 to
each 1,000 of the population. The number of arrests for all

offences other than drunkenness was 9,483, or 10.26 to each 1,000 of the population; and, in the aggregate, the number of arrests for all offences was 18,664, or 20.20 to each 1,000 of the population. There were 40 cities and towns which changed their policy upon the license question during the 12 months. These cities and towns included an aggregate population of 300,974. The number of arrests for drunkenness in these places was 6,083, or 20.21 to each 1,000 of the population; the number of arrests for all offences other than drunkenness was 4,094, or 13.60 to each 1,000 of the population; and the total number of arrests for all offences was 10,177, or 33.81 to each 1,000 of the population. In comparing the number of arrests to each 1,000 of the population in no-license cities and towns with the number in license cities and towns, it should, of course, be borne in mind that the city of Boston, with a population of nearly half a million, forms a considerable

Number of Arrests, under License and No License, classified by Nature of Crime, with Averages per Month.

	COUNTIES, CITIES, AND TOWNS.	NUMBER OF MONTHS		NUMBER OF ARRESTS FOR DRUNKENNESS		NUMBER OF ARRESTS FOR ALL OFFENCES OTHER THAN DRUNKENNESS	
		License	No License	License	No License	License	No License
1	BARNSTABLE.	–	12.00	–	16	–	118
2	Barnstable, . . .	–	12.00	–	3	–	35
3	Bourne, . . .	–	12.00	–	–	–	8
4	Brewster, . . .	–	12.00	–	–	–	–
5	Chatham, . . .	–	12.00	–	1	–	–
6	Dennis, . . .	–	12.00	–	–	–	5
7	Eastham, . . .	–	12.00	–	–	–	–
8	Falmouth, . . .	–	12.00	–	–	–	13
9	Harwich, . . .	–	12.00	–	2	–	–
10	Mashpee, . . .	–	12.00	–	–	–	4
11	Orleans, . . .	–	12.00	–	1	–	8
12	Provincetown, . .	–	12.00	–	6	–	25
13	Sandwich, . . .	–	12.00	–	3	–	11
14	Truro, ...	–	12.00	–	–	–	–
15	Wellfleet, . . .	–	12.00	–	–	–	–
16	Yarmouth, . . .	–	12.00	–	–	–	9
17	BERKSHIRE.	4.31	7.69	1,194	397	1,074	460
18	Adams, . . .	8.00	4.00	39	28	106	55
19	Alford,. . . .	7.00	5.00	–	–	2	1

part of the license territory, and that there are conditions affecting arrests in large cities other than the policy of the city upon the question of license. These conditions operate to cause a larger number of arrests in such municipalities than are found in smaller places. This, of course, tends to increase the number of arrests to each 1,000 of the population in the group of license cities and towns as against the number shown in the no-license cities and towns. When, however, the policy of a given city or town is changed within 12 months, a comparison of arrests under each system may be made without the misleading element to which we have just alluded.

The following table shows the number of arrests, and also the number of months under license and no license during the year covered by the investigation, in each of the cities and towns, the arrests being classified so as to show the total number under each policy, and the average number per month.

Number of Arrests, under License and No License, classified by Nature of Crime, with Averages per Month.

TOTAL NUMBER OF ARRESTS FOR ALL OFFENCES INCLUDING DRUNKENNESS		AVERAGE NUMBER OF ARRESTS PER MONTH FOR DRUNKENNESS		AVERAGE NUMBER OF ARRESTS PER MONTH FOR ALL OFFENCES OTHER THAN DRUNKENNESS		AVERAGE NUMBER OF ARRESTS PER MONTH FOR ALL OFFENCES INCLUDING DRUNKENNESS		
License	No License	License	No License	License	No License	License	No License	
-	134	-	1.34	-	9.83	-	11.17	1
-	38	-	0.25	-	2.92	-	3.17	2
-	8	-	-	-	0.67	-	0.67	3
-	-	-	-	-	-	-	-	4
-	1	-	0.08	-	-	-	0.08	5
-	5	-	-	-	0.42	-	0.42	6
-	-	-	-	-	-	-	-	7
-	13	-	-	-	1.08	-	1.08	8
-	2	-	0.17	-	-	-	0.17	9
-	4	-	-	-	0.33	-	0.33	10
-	9	-	0.08	-	0.67	-	0.75	11
-	31	-	0.50	-	2.08	-	2.58	12
-	14	-	0.25	-	0.92	-	1.17	13
-	-	-	-	-	-	-	-	14
-	-	-	-	-	-	-	-	15
-	9	-	-	-	0.75	-	0.75	16
2,268	857	277.03	51.62	249.19	59.82	526.22	111.44	17
145	83	4.88	7.00	13.25	13.75	18.13	20.75	18
2	1	-	-	0.29	0.20	0.29	0.20	19

Number of Arrests, under License and No License, classified by Nature of Crime, with Averages per Month — Continued.

	COUNTIES, CITIES, AND TOWNS.	NUMBER OF MONTHS		NUMBER OF ARRESTS FOR DRUNKENNESS		NUMBER OF ARRESTS FOR ALL OFFENCES OTHER THAN DRUNKENNESS	
		License	No License	License	No License	License	No License
	BERKSHIRE—Con.						
1	Becket, . . .	–	12.00	–	–	–	3
2	Cheshire, . . .	3.00	9.00	–	7	–	–
3	Clarksburg, . . .	–	12.00	–	7	–	4
4	Dalton, . . .	–	12.00	–	4	–	22
5	Egremont, . . .	–	12.00	–	1	–	14
6	Florida, . . .	–	12.00	–	–	–	1
7	Great Barrington, .	12.00	–	122	–	173	–
8	Hancock, . . .	–	12.00	–	–	–	–
9	Hinsdale, . . .	8.00	4.00	10	13	3	9
10	Lanesborough, . .	–	12.00	–	–	–	2
11	Lee, ...	12.00	–	44	–	75	–
12	Lenox, ...	12.00	–	3	–	39	–
13	Monterey, . . .	–	12.00	–	5	–	8
14	Mount Washington, .	–	12.00	–	–	–	–
15	New Ashford, . .	–	12.00	–	–	–	–
16	New Marlborough, .	–	12.00	–	11	–	8
17	NORTH ADAMS, .	12.00	–	582	–	417	–
18	Otis, ...	12.00	–	–	–	6	–
19	Peru, ...	–	12.00	–	2	–	3
20	PITTSFIELD, . .	4.00	8.00	373	294	198	274
21	Richmond, . . .	–	12.00	–	–	–	–
22	Sandisfield, . . .	12.00	–	2	–	6	–
23	Savoy, ...	8.00	4.00	–	1	–	2
24	Sheffield, . . .	–	12.00	–	3	–	24
25	Stockbridge, . .	4.00	8.00	1	2	8	10
26	Tyringham, . . .	–	12.00	–	–	–	2
27	Washington, . .	8.00	4.00	–	–	1	1
28	West Stockbridge, .	12.00	–	2	–	18	–
29	Williamstown, . .	4.00	8.00	16	19	22	17
30	Windsor, . . .	–	12.00	–	–	–	–
31	BRISTOL.	2.00	10.00	3,829	101	3,015	371
32	Acushnet, . . .	–	12.00	–	–	–	3
33	Attleborough, . .	–	12.00	–	17	–	134
34	Berkley, . . .	–	12.00	–	1	–	3
35	Dartmouth, . . .	–	12.00	–	7	–	24
36	Dighton, . . .	–	12.00	–	–	–	2
37	Easton, . . .	–	12.00	–	48	–	57
38	Fairhaven, . . .	–	12.00	–	3	–	5
39	FALL RIVER, . .	12.00	–	1,822	–	1,833	–

Number of Arrests, under License and No License, classified by Nature of Crime, with Averages per Month. — Continued.

TOTAL NUMBER OF ARRESTS FOR ALL OFFENCES INCLUDING DRUNKENNESS		AVERAGE NUMBER OF ARRESTS PER MONTH FOR DRUNKENNESS		AVERAGE NUMBER OF ARRESTS PER MONTH FOR ALL OFFENCES OTHER THAN DRUNKENNESS		AVERAGE NUMBER OF ARRESTS PER MONTH FOR ALL OFFENCES INCLUDING DRUNKENNESS		
License	No License	License	No License	License	No License	License	No License	
–	3	–	–	–	0.25	–	0.25	1
–	7	–	0.78	–	–	–	0.78	2
–	11	–	0.58	–	0.33	–	0.91	3
–	26	–	0.33	–	1.83	–	2.16	4
–	15	–	0.08	–	1.17	–	1.25	5
–	1	–	–	–	0.08	–	0.08	6
295	–	10.17	–	14.42	–	24.59	–	7
–	–	–	–	–	–	⌣	–	8
13	22	1.25	3.25	0.38	2.25	1.63	5.50	9
–	2	–	–	–	0.17	–	0.17	10
119	–	3.67	–	6.25	–	9.92	–	11
42	–	0.25	–	3.25	–	3.50	–	12
–	13	–	0.42	–	0.67	–	1.09	13
–	–	–	–	–	–	–	–	14
–	–	–	–	–	–	–	–	15
–	19	–	0.92	–	0.67	–	1.59	16
999	–	48.50	–	34.75	–	83.25	–	17
6	–	–	–	–	0.50	–	0.50	18
–	5	–	0.17	–	0.25	–	0.42	19
571	568	93.25	36.75	49.50	34.25	142.75	71.00	20
–	–	–	–	–	–	–	–	21
8	–	0.17	–	0.50	–	0.67	–	22
–	3	–	0.25	–	0.50	–	0.75	23
–	27	–	0.25	–	2.00	–	2.25	24
9	12	0.25	0.25	2.00	1.25	2.25	1.50	25
–	2	–	–	–	0.17	–	0.17	26
1	1	–	–	0.13	0.25	0.13	0.25	27
20	–	0.17	–	1.50	–	1.67	–	28
38	36	4.00	2.37	5.50	2.13	9.50	4.50	29
–	–	–	–	–	–	–	–	30
6,844	472	1,914.50	10.10	1,507.50	37.10	3,422.00	47.20	31
–	3	–	–	–	0.25	–	0.25	32
–	151	–	1.42	–	11.17	–	12.59	33
–	4	–	0.08	–	0.25	–	0.33	34
–	31	–	0.58	–	2.00	–	2.58	35
–	2	–	–	–	0.16	–	0.16	36
–	105	–	4.00	–	4.75	–	8.75	37
–	8	–	0.25	–	0.42	–	0.67	38
3,655	–	151.83	–	152.75	–	304.58	–	39

Number of Arrests, under License and No License, classified by Nature of Crime, with Averages per Month— Continued.

COUNTIES, CITIES, AND TOWNS.	NUMBER OF MONTHS		NUMBER OF ARRESTS FOR DRUNKENNESS		NUMBER OF ARRESTS FOR ALL OFFENCES OTHER THAN DRUNKENNESS	
	License	No License	License	No License	License	No License
BRISTOL — Con.						
1 Freetown,	–	12.00	–	1	–	5
2 Mansfield,	–	12.00	–	1	–	24
3 NEW BEDFORD,	12.00	–	1,149	–	806	–
4 North Attleborough,	4.00	8.00	23	6	67	47
5 Norton,	–	12.00	–	–	–	3
6 Raynham,	–	12.00	–	8	–	29
7 Rehoboth,	–	12.00	–	–	–	5
8 Seekonk,	–	12.00	–	–	–	4
9 Somerset,	–	12.00	–	–	–	16
10 Swansea,	–	12.00	–	–	–	2
11 TAUNTON,	12.00	–	835	–	309	–
12 Westport,	–	12.00	–	9	–	8
13 **DUKES.**	–	12.00	–	3	–	26
14 Chilmark,	–	12.00	–	–	–	–
15 Cottage City,	–	12.00	–	2	–	14
16 Edgartown,	–	12.00	–	–	–	8
17 Gay Head,	–	12.00	–	–	–	–
18 Gosnold,	–	12.00	–	–	–	–
19 Tisbury,	–	12.00	–	1	–	3
20 West Tisbury,	–	12.00	–	–	–	1
21 **ESSEX.**	2.17	9.83	5,987	2,027	2,646	1,768
22 Amesbury,	–	12.00	–	100	–	136
23 Andover,	–	12.00	–	14	–	26
24 BEVERLY,	–	12.00	–	133	–	83
25 Boxford,	–	12.00	–	–	–	1
26 Bradford,	–	12.00	–	4	–	2
27 Danvers,	–	12.00	–	61	–	101
28 Essex,	–	12.00	–	2	–	4
29 Georgetown,	4.00	8.00	13	16	5	7
30 GLOUCESTER,	12.00	–	576	–	293	–
31 Groveland,	–	12.00	–	4	–	3
32 Hamilton,	–	12.00	–	2	–	2
33 HAVERHILL,	8.00	4.00	653	106	485	159
34 Ipswich,	4.00	8.00	28	23	19	24
35 LAWRENCE,	12.00	–	2,031	–	889	–
36 LYNN,	4.00	8.00	1,260	941	426	628
37 Lynnfield,	–	12.00	–	1	–	–
38 Manchester,	–	12.00	–	12	–	4

Number of Arrests, under License and No License, classified by Nature of Crime, with Averages per Month — Continued.

TOTAL NUMBER OF ARRESTS FOR ALL OFFENCES INCLUDING DRUNKENNESS		AVERAGE NUMBER OF ARRESTS PER MONTH FOR DRUNKENNESS		AVERAGE NUMBER OF ARRESTS PER MONTH FOR ALL OFFENCES OTHER THAN DRUNKENNESS		AVERAGE NUMBER OF ARRESTS PER MONTH FOR ALL OFFENCES INCLUDING DRUNKENNESS		
License	No License	License	No License	License	No License	License	No License	
–	6	–	0.08	–	0.42	–	0.50	1
–	25	–	0.08	–	2.00	–	2.08	2
1,955	–	95.75	–	67.17	–	162.92	–	3
90	53	5.75	0.75	16.75	5.88	22.50	6.63	4
–	3	–	–	–	0.25	–	0.25	5
–	37	–	0.67	–	2.42	–	3.09	6
–	5	–	–	–	0.42	–	0.42	7
–	4	–	–	–	0.33	–	0.33	8
–	16	–	–	–	1.33	–	1.33	9
–	2	–	–	–	0.17	–	0.17	10
1,144	–	69.58	–	25.75	–	95.33	–	11
–	17	–	0.75	–	0.67	–	1.42	12
–	29	–	0.25	–	2.17	–	2.42	13
–	–	–	–	–	–	–	–	14
–	16	–	0.17	–	1.17	–	1.34	15
–	8	–	–	–	0.67	–	0.67	16
–	–	–	–	–	–	–	–	17
–	–	–	–	–	–	–	–	18
–	4	–	0.08	–	0.25	–	0.33	19
–	1	–	–	–	0.08	–	0.08	20
8,633	3,795	2,758.99	206.21	1,219.35	179.86	3,978.34	386.07	21
–	236	–	8.33	–	11.33	–	19.66	22
–	40	–	1.17	–	2.17	–	3.34	23
–	216	–	11.08	–	6.92	–	18.00	24
–	1	–	–	–	0.08	–	0.08	25
–	6	–	0.33	–	0.17	–	0.50	26
–	162	–	5.08	–	8.42	–	13.50	27
–	6	–	0.17	–	0.33	–	0.50	28
18	23	3.25	2.00	1.25	0.88	4.50	2.88	29
869	–	48.00	–	24.42	–	72.42	–	30
–	7	–	0.33	–	0.25	–	0.58	31
–	4	–	0.17	–	0.17	–	0.34	32
1,138	265	81.63	26.50	60.63	39.75	142.26	66.25	33
47	47	7.00	2.88	4.75	3.00	11.75	5.88	34
2,920	–	169.25	–	74.08	–	243.33	–	35
1,686	1,569	315.00	117.63	106.50	78.50	421.50	196.13	36
–	1	–	0.08	–	–	–	0.08	37
–	16	–	1.00	–	0.33	–	1.33	38

Number of Arrests, under License and No License, classified by Nature of Crime, with Averages per Month — Continued.

	COUNTIES, CITIES, AND TOWNS.	NUMBER OF MONTHS		NUMBER OF ARRESTS FOR DRUNKENNESS		NUMBER OF ARRESTS FOR ALL OFFENCES OTHER THAN DRUNKENNESS	
		License	No License	License	No License	License	No License
	ESSEX — Con.						
1	Marblehead, . .	–	12.00	–	133	–	43
2	Merrimac, . . .	–	12.00	–	6	–	13
3	Methuen, . . .	–	12.00	–	32	–	52
4	Middleton, . . .	–	12.00	–	–	–	3
5	Nahant, . . .	12.00	–	24	–	41	–
6	Newbury, . . .	–	12.00	–	–	–	–
7	NEWBURYPORT, . .	12.00	–	690	–	193	–
8	North Andover, . .	–	12.00	–	6	–	19
9	Peabody, . . .	4.00	8.00	150	95	83	90
10	Rockport, . . .	–	12.00	–	63	–	35
11	Rowley, . . .	–	12.00	–	2	–	5
12	SALEM,. . . .	4.00	8.00	562	237	212	188
13	Salisbury, . . .	–	12.00	–	15	–	62
14	Saugus, . . .	–	12.00	–	8	–	39
15	Swampscott, . .	–	12.00	–	6	–	29
16	Topsfield, . . .	–	12.00	–	1	–	1
17	Wenham, . . .	–	12.00	–	2	–	4
18	West Newbury, . .	–	12.00	–	2	–	5
19	FRANKLIN.	2.54	9.46	77	88	118	133
20	Ashfield, . . .	–	12.00	–	–	–	–
21	Bernardston, . .	–	12.00	–	–	–	–
22	Buckland, . . .	12.00	–	2	–	–	–
23	Charlemont, . .	–	12.00	–	–	–	9
24	Colrain, . . .	–	12.00	–	–	–	3
25	Conway, . . .	–	12.00	–	–	–	–
26	Deerfield, . . .	6.00	6.00	–	–	–	–
27	Erving, . . .	12.00	–	2	–	4	–
28	Gill, ...	–	12.00	–	–	–	5
29	Greenfield, . . .	4.00	8.00	42	46	22	21
30	Hawley, . . .	–	12.00	–	–	–	–
31	Heath, ...	–	12.00	–	–	–	–
32	Leverett, . . .	–	12.00	–	–	–	3
33	Leyden, . . .	–	12.00	–	–	–	1
34	Monroe, . . .	–	12.00	–	–	–	5
35	Montague, . . .	8.00	4.00	29	12	83	49
36	New Salem, . .	–	12.00	–	–	–	–
37	Northfield, . . .	–	12.00	–	–	–	1
38	Orange, . . .	–	12.00	–	29	–	32
39	Rowe, ...	–	12.00	–	–	–	4

Number of Arrests, under License and No License, classified by Nature of Crime, with Averages per Month — Continued.

TOTAL NUMBER OF ARRESTS FOR ALL OFFENCES INCLUDING DRUNKENNESS		AVERAGE NUMBER OF ARRESTS PER MONTH FOR DRUNKENNESS		AVERAGE NUMBER OF ARRESTS PER MONTH FOR ALL OFFENCES OTHER THAN DRUNKENNESS		AVERAGE NUMBER OF ARRESTS PER MONTH FOR ALL OFFENCES INCLUDING DRUNKENNESS		
License	No License	License	No License	License	No License	License	No License	
–	176	–	11.08	–	3.58	–	14.66	1
–	19	–	0.50	–	1.08	–	1.58	2
–	84	–	2.67	–	4.33	–	7.00	3
–	3	–	–	–	0.25	–	0.25	4
65	–	2.00	–	3.42	–	5.42	–	5
–	–	–	–	–	–	–	–	6
883	–	57.50	–	16.08	–	73.58	–	7
–	25	–	0.50	–	1.58	–`	2.08	8
233	185	37.50	11.88	20.75	11.25	58.25	23.13	9
–	98	–	5.25	–	2.92	–	8.17	10
–	7	–	0.17	–	0.42	–	0.59	11
774	425	140.50	29.63	53.00	23.50	193.50	53.13	12
–	77	–	1.25	–	5.17	–	6.42	13
–	47	–	0.67	–	3.25	–	3.92	14
–	35	–	0.50	–	2.42	–	2.92	15
–	2	–	0.08	–	0.08	–	0.16	16
–	6	–	0.17	–	0.33	–	0.50	17
–	7	–	0.17	–	0.42	–	0.59	18
195	221	30.31	9.30	46.46	14.06	76.77	23.36	19
–	–	–	–	–	–	–	–	20
–	–	–	–	–	–	–	–	21
2	–	0.17	–	–	–	0.17	–	22
–	9	–	–	–	0.75	–	0.75	23
–	3	–	–	–	0.25	–	0.25	24
–	–	–	–	–	–	–	–	25
–	–	–	–	–	–	–	–	26
6	–	0.17	–	0.33	–	0.50	–	27
–	5	–	–	–	0.42	–	0.42	28
64	67	10.50	5.75	5.50	2.63	16.00	8.38	29
–	–	–	–	–	–	–	–	30
–	–	–	–	–	–	–	–	31
–	3	–	–	–	0.25	–	0.25	32
–	1	–	–	–	0.08	–	0.08	33
–	5	–	–	–	0.42	–	0.42	34
112	61	3.63	3.00	10.37	12.25	14.00	15.25	35
–	–	–	–	–	–	–	–	36
–	1	–	–	–	0.08	–	0.08	37
–	61	–	2.42	–	2.67	–	5.09	38
–	4	–	–	–	0.33	–	0.33	39

7	HAMPDEN.	4.33	7.67	2,649	26	1,987	83
8	Agawam.	-	12.00	-	2	-	3
9	Blandford.	-	12.00	-	1	-	-
10	Brimfield.	-	12.00	-	1	-	-
11	Chester.	12.00	-	6	-	14	-
12	Chicopee.	12.00	-	368	-	368	-
13	East Longmeadow.	-	12.00	-	1	-	1
14	Granville.	-	12.00	-	-	-	1
15	Hampden.	-	12.00	-	1	-	4
16	Holland.	-	12.00		-	-	-
17	HOLYOKE.	12.00	-	793	-	631	-
18	Longmeadow.	-	12.00	-	-	-	-
19	Ludlow.	-	-	-	-	-	-
20	Monson.	-	12.00		17	-	36
21	Montgomery.	-	12.00	-	-	-	1
22	Palmer.	12.00	-	115	-	101	-
23	Russell.	12.00	-	-	-	1	-
24	Southwick.	7.00	5.00	-	1	-	-
25	SPRINGFIELD.*	12.00	-	1,816	-	900	-
26	Tolland.	-	12.00	-	-	-	4
27	Wales.	-	12.00	-	1	-	2
28	Westfield.	12.00	-	119	-	57	-
29	West Springfield.	-	-	-	-	-	
30	Wilbraham.		12.00	-	1	-	2
31	HAMPSHIRE.	1.74	10.26	868	123	117	128
32	Amherst.		12.00	-	27	-	12

Number of Arrests, under License and No License, classified by Nature of Crime, with Averages per Month — Continued.

TOTAL NUMBER OF ARRESTS FOR ALL OFFENCES INCLUDING DRUNKENNESS		AVERAGE NUMBER OF ARRESTS PER MONTH FOR DRUNKENNESS		AVERAGE NUMBER OF ARRESTS PER MONTH FOR ALL OFFENCES OTHER THAN DRUNKENNESS		AVERAGE NUMBER OF ARRESTS PER MONTH FOR ALL OFFENCES INCLUDING DRUNKENNESS		
License	No License	License	No License	License	No License	License	No License	
-	1	-	0.08	-	-	-	0.08	1
-	-	-	-	-	-	-	-	2
-	-	-	-	-	-	-	-	3
-	-	-	-	-	-	-	-	4
6	-	0.17	-	0.33	-	0.50	-	5
5	-	-	-	0.42	-	0.42	-	6
4,636	79	611.78	3.39	458.89	6.91	1,070.67	10.30	7
-	5	-	0.17	-	0.25	-	0.42	8
-	1	-	0.08	-	-	-	0.08	9
-	1	-	0.08	-	-	-	0.08	10
20	-	0.50	-	1.17	-	1.67	-	11
531	-	22.33	-	21.92	-	44.25	-	12
-	2	-	0.08	-	0.08	-	0.16	13
-	1	-	-	-	0.08	-	0.08	14
-	5	-	0.08	-	0.33	-	0.41	15
-	-	-	-	-	-	-	-	16
1,446	-	66.25	-	54.25	-	120.50	-	17
-	-	-	-	-	-	-	-	18
-	-	-	-	-	-	-	-	19
-	* 53	-	1.42	-	3.00	-	4.42	20
-	1	-	-	-	0.08	-	0.08	21
216	-	9.58	-	8.42	-	18.00	-	22
1	-	-	-	0.08	-	0.08	-	23
-	1	-	0.20	-	-	-	0.20	24
2,246	-	112.17	-	75.00	-	187.17	-	25
-	4	-	-	-	0.33	-	0.33	26
-	2	-	0.08	-	0.08	-	0.16	27
176	-	9.92	-	4.75	-	14.67	-	28
-	-	-	-	-	-	-	-	29
-	3	-	0.08	-	0.17	-	0.25	30
485	243	211.50	11.99	67.24	11.70	278.74	23.69	31
-	39	-	2.25	-	1.00	-	3.25	32
3	7	0.50	0.25	0.25	0.63	0.75	0.88	33
-	-	-	-	-	-	-	-	34
-	-	-	-	-	-	-	-	35
10	14	0.63	2.50	0.63	1.00	1.26	3.50	36
-	12	-	0.42	-	0.58	-	1.00	37
-	-	-	-	-	-	-	-	38

Number of Arrests, under License and No License, classified by Nature of Crime, with Averages per Month — Continued.

COUNTIES, CITIES, AND TOWNS.	NUMBER OF MONTHS		NUMBER OF ARRESTS FOR DRUNKENNESS		NUMBER OF ARRESTS FOR ALL OFFENCES OTHER THAN DRUNKENNESS	
	License	No License	License	No License	License	No License
HAMPSHIRE — Con.						
1 Granby, . . .	–	12.00	–	–	–	–
2 Greenwich, . . .	–	12.00	–	–	–	1
3 Hadley, . . .	12.00	–	1	–	–	–
4 Hatfield, . . .	–	12.00	–	–	–	–
5 Huntington, . .	–	12.00	–	1	–	2
6 Middlefield, . . .	–	12.00	–	–	–	–
7 NORTHAMPTON, . .	12.00	–	346	–	98	–
8 Pelham, . . .	–	12.00	–	–	–	2
9 Plainfield, . . .	–	12.00	–	–	–	–
10 Prescott, . . .	–	12.00	–	–	–	–
11 Southampton, . .	–	12.00	–	–	–	3
12 South Hadley, . .	4.00	8.00	14	13	13	13
13 Ware, ...	–	12.00	–	63	–	65
14 Westhampton, . .	–	12.00	–	–	–	–
15 Williamsburg, . .	–	12.00	–	2	–	6
16 Worthington, . .	–	12.00	–	–	–	–
17 **MIDDLESEX.**	2.19	9.81	6,030	4,771	2,740	3,980
18 Acton, ...	–	12.00	–	–	–	8
19 Arlington, . . .	–	12.00	–	46	–	89
20 Ashby, ...	–	12.00	–	–	2	23
21 Ashland, . . .	–	12.00	–	1	–	14
22 Ayer, ...	12.00	–	23	–	28	–
23 Bedford, . . .	–	12.00	–	1	–	1
24 Belmont, . . .	–	12.00	–	9	–	16
25 Billerica, . . .	–	12.00	–	13	–	13
26 Boxborough, . .	–	12.00	–	–	–	–
27 Burlington, . . .	–	12.00	–	1	–	–
28 CAMBRIDGE, . .	–	12.00	–	1,922	–	1,428
29 Carlisle, . . .	–	12.00	–	–	–	1
30 Chelmsford, . . .	–	12.00	–	3	–	–
31 Concord, . . .	–	12.00	–	32	–	48
32 Dracut, . . .	–	–	–	–	–	–
33 Dunstable, . . .	–	12.00	–	–	–	–
34 EVERETT, . . .	–	12.00	–	397	–	203
35 Framingham, . .	4.00	8.00	78	35	47	61
36 Groton, . . .	–	12.00	–	–	–	–
37 Holliston, . . .	–	12.00	–	24	–	7
38 Hopkinton, . . .	4.00	8.00	1	6	2	5
39 Hudson, . . .	12.00	–	83	–	74	–

Number of Arrests, under License and No License, classified by Nature of Crime, with Averages per Month — Continued.

TOTAL NUMBER OF ARRESTS FOR ALL OFFENCES INCLUDING DRUNKENNESS		AVERAGE NUMBER OF ARRESTS PER MONTH FOR DRUNKENNESS		AVERAGE NUMBER OF ARRESTS PER MONTH FOR ALL OFFENCES OTHER THAN DRUNKENNESS		AVERAGE NUMBER OF ARRESTS PER MONTH FOR ALL OFFENCES INCLUDING DRUNKENNESS		
License	No License	License	No License	License	No License	License	No License	
–	–	–	–	–	–	–	–	1
–	1	–	–	–	0.08	–	0.08	2
1	–	0.08	–	–	–	0.08	–	3
–	–	–	–	–	–	–	–	4
–	3	–	0.08	–	0.17	–	0.25	5
–	–	–	–	–	–	–	–	6
444	–	28.83	–	8.17	–	37.00	–	7
–	2	–	–	–	0.17	–	0.17	8
–	–	–	–	–	–	–	–	9
–	–	–	–	–	–	–	–	10
–	3	–	–	–	0.25	–	0.25	11
27	26	3.50	1.63	3.25	1.63	6.75	3.26	12
–	128	–	5.25	–	5.42	–	10.67	13
–	–	–	–	–	–	–	–	14
–	8	–	0.17	–	0.50	–	0.67	15
–	–	–	–	–	–	–	–	16
8,770	8,751	2,753.43	486.34	1,251.14	405.71	4,004.57	892.05	17
–	8	–	–	–	0.67	–	0.67	18
–	135	–	3.83	–	7.42	–	11.25	19
–	23	–	–	–	1.92	–	1.92	20
–	15	–	0.08	–	1.17	–	1.25	21
51	–	1.92	–	2.33	–	4.25	–	22
–	2	–	0.08	–	0.08	–	0.16	23
–	25	–	0.75	–	1.33	–	2.08	24
–	26	–	1.08	–	1.08	–	2.16	25
–	–	–	–	–	–	–	–	26
–	1	–	0.08	–	–	–	0.08	27
–	3,350	–	16,016.67	–	11,900.00	–	27,916.67	28
–	1	–	–	–	0.08	–	0.08	29
–	3	–	0.25	–	–	–	0.25	30
–	80	–	2.67	–	4.00	–	6.67	31
–	–	–	–	–	–	–	–	32
–	–	–	–	–	–	–	–	33
–	600	–	33.08	–	16.92	–	50.00	34
125	96	19.50	4.37	11.75	7.63	31.25	.12.00	35
–	–	–	–	–	–	–	–	36
–	31	–	2.00	–	0.58	–	2.58	37
3	11	0.25	0.75	0.50	0.63	0.75	1.38	38
157	–	6.91	–	6.17	–	13.08	–	39

Number of Arrests, under License and No License, classified by Nature of Crime, with Averages per Month — Continued.

COUNTIES, CITIES, AND TOWNS.	NUMBER OF MONTHS		NUMBER OF ARRESTS FOR DRUNKENNESS		NUMBER OF ARRESTS FOR ALL OFFENCES OTHER THAN DRUNKENNESS	
	License	No License	License	No License	License	No License
MIDDLESEX — Con.						
1 Lexington, ...	-	12.00	-	35	-	48
2 Lincoln, . . .	-	12.00	-	-	-	4
3 Littleton. . . .	-	12.00	-	-	-	8
4 Lowell,* . . .	12.00	-	3.773	-	1,645	-
5 Malden. . . .	-	12.00	-	258	-	430
6 Marlborough, . .	12.00	-	352	-	152	-
7 Maynard. . . .	4.00	8.00	6	4	4	12
8 Medford, . . .	8.00	4.00	161	58	119	54
9 Melrose. . . .	-	12.00	-	95	-	85
10 Natick, . . .	4.00	8.00	201	88	54	61
11 Newton. . . .	-	12.00	-	398	-	394
12 North Reading, .	-	12.00	-	1	-	11
13 Pepperell, . . .	12.00	-	28	-	48	-
14 Reading. . . .	-	12.00	-	15	-	27
15 Sherborn. . . .	-	12.00	-	2	-	3
16 Shirley. . . .	8.00	4.00	21	6	5	4
17 Somerville, . .	-	12.00	-	977	-	603
18 Stoneham, . .	-	12.00	-	102	-	53
19 Stow. . . .	-	12.00	-	3	-	3
20 Sudbury, . . .	-	12.00	-	2	-	4
21 Tewksbury, . .	-	12.00	-	3	-	30
22 Townsend, . .	-	12.00	-	1	-	1
23 Tyngsborough, .	-	12.00	-	-	-	1
24 Wakefield, . .	-	12.00	-	46	-	51
25 Waltham, . . .	12.00	-	744	-	350	-
26 Watertown, . .	-	12.00	-	68	-	78
27 Wayland, .	-	12.00	-	2	-	12
28 Westford. .	-	12.00	-	-	-	3
29 Weston. .	-	12.00	-	1	-	9
30 Wilmington, .	-	12.00	-	-	-	-
31 Winchester, .	-	12.00	-	121	-	74
32 Woburn. .	12.00	-	559	-	212	-
33 NANTUCKET.	12.00	-	36	-	6	-
34 Nantucket, . .	12.00	-	36	-	6	-
35 NORFOLK.	1.04	10.96	159	1,088	145	1,288
36 Avon, ...	-	12.00	-	5	-	9
37 Bellingham, .	-	12.00	-	2	-	5
38 Braintree. . .	-	12.00	-	68	-	72

* Includes Dracut.

Number of Arrests, under License and No License, classified by Nature of Crime, with Averages per Month — Continued

Total Number of Arrests for All Offences Including Drunkenness		Average Number of Arrests per Month for Drunkenness		Average Number of Arrests per Month for All Offences Other than Drunkenness		Average Number of Arrests per Month for All Offences Including Drunkenness		
License	No License	License	No License	License	No License	License	No License	
-	83	-	2.92	-	4.00	-	6.92	1
-	4	-	-	-	0.33	-	0.33	2
-	8	-	-	-	0.67	-	0.67	3
5,418	-	314.42	-	137.08	-	451.50	-	4
-	688	-	21.50	-	35.83	-	57.33	5
504	-	29.33	-	12.67	-	42.00	-	6
10	16	1.50	0.50	1.00	1.50	2.50	2.00	7
280	107	20.12	13.25	14.88	13.50	35.00	26.75	8
-	180	-	7.92	-	7.08	-	15.00	9
255	149	50.25	11.00	13.50	7.63	63.75	18.63	10
-	792	-	33.17	-	32.83	-	66.00	11
-	12	-	0.08	-	0.92	-	1.00	12
76	-	2.33	-	4.00	-	6.33	-	13
-	42	-	1.25	-	2.25	-	3.50	14
-	5	-	0.17	-	0.25	-	0.42	15
26	10	2.62	1.50	0.63	1.00	3.25	2.50	16
-	1,580	-	81.42	-	50.25	-	131.67	17
-	155	-	8.50	-	4.42	-	12.92	18
-	6	-	0.25	-	0.25	-	0.50	19
-	6	-	0.17	-	0.33	-	0.50	20
-	33	-	0.25	-	2.50	-	2.75	21
-	2	-	0.08	-	0.08	-	0.16	22
-	1	-	-	-	0.08	-	0.08	23
-	97	-	3.83	-	4.25	-	8.08	24
1,094	-	62.00	-	29.17	-	91.17	-	25
-	146	-	5.67	-	6.50	-	12.17	26
-	14	-	0.17	-	1.00	-	1.17	27
-	3	-	-	-	0.25	-	0.25	28
-	10	-	0.08	-	0.75	-	0.83	29
-	-	-	-	-	-	-	-	30
-	195	-	10.08	-	6.17	-	16.25	31
771	-	46.58	-	17.67	-	64.25	-	32
42	-	3.00	-	0.50	-	3.50	-	33
42	-	3.00	-	0.50	-	3.50	-	34
304	2,371	152.89	98.81	139.42	117.52	292.31	216.33	35
-	14	-	0.42	-	0.75	-	1.17	36
-	7	-	0.17	-	0.42	-	0.59	37
-	140	-	5.67	-	6.00	-	11.67	38

Number of Arrests, under License and No License, classified by Nature of Crime, with Averages per Month — Continued.

COUNTIES, CITIES, AND TOWNS.	NUMBER OF MONTHS		NUMBER OF ARRESTS FOR DRUNKENNESS		NUMBER OF ARRESTS FOR ALL OFFENCES OTHER THAN DRUNKENNESS	
	License	No License	License	No License	License	No License
NORFOLK — Con.						
1 Brookline, . . .	–	12.00	–	207	–	295
2 Canton, . . .	–	12.00	–	45	–	42
3 Cohasset, . . .	12.00	–	12	–	23	–
4 Dedham, . . .	4.00	8.00	126	29	36	30
5 Dover, ...	–	12.00	–	–	–	3
6 Foxborough, . .	–	12.00	–	6	–	16
7 Franklin, . . .	–	12.00	–	16	–	16
8 Holbrook, . . .	–	12.00	–	11	–	21
9 Hyde Park, . . .	–	12.00	–	103	–	128
10 Medfield, . . .	–	12.00	–	7	–	19
11 Medway, . . .	12.00	–	21	–	86	–
12 Millis, ...	–	12.00	–	9	–	6
13 Milton, ...	–	12.00	–	26	–	34
14 Needham, . . .	–	12.00	–	21	–	26
15 Norfolk, . . .	–	12.00	–	1	–	2
16 Norwood, . . .	–	12.00	–	24	–	38
17 Quincy, . . .	–	12.00	–	271	–	208
18 Randolph, . . .	–	12.00	–	40	–	73
19 Sharon, . . .	–	12.00	–	41	–	49
20 Stoughton, . . .	–	12.00	–	57	–	49
21 Walpole, . . .	–	12.00	–	4	–	8
22 Wellesley, . . .	–	12.00	–	5	–	43
23 Weymouth, . . .	–	12.00	–	80	–	88
24 Wrentham, . . .	–	12.00	–	5	–	8
25 **PLYMOUTH.**	0.89	11.11	61	851	79	915
26 Abington, . . .	–	12.00	–	42	–	59
27 Bridgewater, . .	–	12.00	–	13	–	30
28 Brockton, . . .	–	12.00	–	624	–	504
29 Carver, . . .	–	12.00	–	4	–	4
30 Duxbury, . . .	4.00	8.00	–	–	–	–
31 East Bridgewater, .	–	12.00	–	9	–	10
32 Halifax, . . .	–	12.00	–	–	–	–
33 Hanover, . . .	–	12.00	–	–	–	5
34 Hanson, . . .	–	12.00	–	1	–	7
35 Hingham, . . .	–	12.00	–	14	–	8
36 Hull, ...	12.00	–	59	–	68	–
37 Kingston, . . .	–	12.00	–	–	–	1
38 Lakeville, . . .	–	12.00	–	1	–	1
39 Marion, . . .	–	12.00	–	–	–	10

Number of Arrests, under License and No License, classified by Nature of Crime, with Averages per Month — Continued.

TOTAL NUMBER OF ARRESTS FOR ALL OFFENCES INCLUDING DRUNKENNESS		AVERAGE NUMBER OF ARRESTS PER MONTH FOR DRUNKENNESS		AVERAGE NUMBER OF ARRESTS PER MONTH FOR ALL OFFENCES OTHER THAN DRUNKENNESS		AVERAGE NUMBER OF ARRESTS PER MONTH FOR ALL OFFENCES INCLUDING DRUNKENNESS		
License	No License	License	No License	License	No License	License	No License	
-	502	-	17.25	-	24.58	-	41.83	1
-	87	-	3.75	-	3.50	-	7.25	2
35	-	1.00	-	1.92	-	2.92	-	3
162	59	31.50	3.63	9.00	3.75	40.50	7.38	4
-	3	-	-	-	0.25	-	0.25	5
-	22	-	0.50	-	1.33	-	1.83	6
-	32	-	1.33	-	1.33	-	2.66	7
-	32	-	0.92	-	1.75	-	2.67	8
-	231	-	8.58	-	10.67	-	19.25	9
-	26	-	0.58	-	1.58	-	2.16	10
107	-	1.75	-	7.17	-	8.92	-	11
-	15	-	0.75	-	0.50	-	1.25	12
-	60	-	2.17	-	2.83	-	5.00	13
-	47	-	1.75	-	2.17	-	3.92	14
-	3	-	0.08	-	0.17	-	0.25	15
-	62	-	2.00	-	3.17	-	5.17	16
-	479	-	22.58	-	17.33	-	39.91	17
-	113	-	3.33	-	6.08	-	9.41	18
-	90	-	3.41	-	4.09	-	7.50	19
-	106	-	4.75	-	4.09	-	8.84	20
-	12	-	0.33	-	0.67	-	1.00	21
-	48	-	0.42	-	3.58	-	4.00	22
-	168	-	6.67	-	7.33	-	14.00	23
-	13	-	0.41	-	0.67	-	1.08	24
140	1,766	68.54	76.60	88.76	82.36	157.30	158.96	25
-	101	-	3.50	-	4.92	-	8.42	26
-	43	-	1.08	-	2.50	-	3.58	27
-	1,128	-	52.00	-	42.00	-	94.00	28
-	8	-	0.33	-	0.33	-	0.66	29
-	-	-	-	-	-	-	-	30
-	19	-	0.75	-	0.83	-	1.58	31
-	-	-	-	-	-	-	-	32
-	5	-	-	-	0.42	-	0.42	33
-	8	-	0.08	-	0.58	-	0.66	34
-	22	-	1.17	-	0.67	-	1.84	35
127	-	4.92	-	5.67	-	10.59	-	36
-	1	-	-	-	0.08	-	0.08	37
-	2	-	0.08	-	0.08	-	0.16	38
-	10	-	-	-	0.83	-	0.83	39

Number of Arrests, under License and No License, classified by Nature of Crime, with Averages per Month — Continued.

	COUNTIES, CITIES, AND TOWNS.	NUMBER OF MONTHS		NUMBER OF ARRESTS FOR DRUNKENNESS		NUMBER OF ARRESTS FOR ALL OFFENCES OTHER THAN DRUNKENNESS	
		License	No License	License	No License	License	No License
	PLYMOUTH — Con.						
1	Marshfield, ...	–	12.00	–	3	–	3
2	Mattapoisett, . .	–	12.00	–	–	–	6
3	Middleborough, . .	–	12.00	–	36	–	36
4	Norwell, . . .	–	12.00	–	–	–	3
5	Pembroke, . . .	–	12.00	–	–	–	–
6	Plymouth, . . .	–	12.00	–	19	–	94
7	Plympton, . . .	–	12.00	–	–	–	–
8	Rochester, . . .	–	12.00	–	–	–	5
9	Rockland, . . .	–	12.00	–	44	–	12
10	Scituate, . . .	8.00	4.00	2	3	11	19
11	Wareham, . . .	–	12.00	–	16	–	28
12	West Bridgewater, .	–	12.00	–	4	–	6
13	Whitman, . . .	–	12.00	–	18	–	64
14	SUFFOLK.	3.00	9.00	26,036	771	16,736	981
15	BOSTON, .	12.00	–	26,036	–	16,736	–
16	CHELSEA, . .	–	12.00	–	636	–	778
17	Revere, . .	–	12.00	–	117	–	188
18	Winthrop, . .	–	12.00	–	18	–	15
19	WORCESTER.	3.05	8.95	3,718	1,074	1,974	1,209
20	Ashburnham, . .	–	12.00	–	8	–	7
21	Athol, . . .	12.00	–	107	–	45	–
22	Auburn, . . .	–	12.00	–	3	–	1
23	Barre, ...	–	12.00	–	5	–	12
24	Berlin, . . .	–	12.00	–	–	–	3
25	Blackstone, . .	12.00	–	62	–	72	–
26	Bolton, ...	–	12.00	–	–	–	5
27	Boylston, . . .	–	12.00	–	2	–	4
28	Brookfield, . .	12.00	–	134	–	67	–
29	Charlton, . . .	–	12.00	–	8	–	11
30	Clinton, . . .	12.00	–	205	–	73	–
31	Dana, . . .	–	12.00	–	–	–	–
32	Douglas, . . .	8.00	4.00	1	4	12	9
33	Dudley, . . .	–	12.00	–	16	–	8
34	FITCHBURG, . .	–	12.00	–	420	–	390
35	Gardner, . . .	8.00	4.00	81	35	45	18
36	Grafton, . . .	12.00	–	27	–	13	–
37	Hardwick, . . .	–	12.00	–	19	–	24
38	Harvard, . . .	–	12.00	–	8	–	1

Number of Arrests, under License and No License, classified by Nature of Crime, with Averages per Month — Continued.

Total Number of Arrests for All Offences Including Drunkenness		Average Number of Arrests per Month for Drunkenness		Average Number of Arrests per Month for All Offences Other than Drunkenness		Average Number of Arrests per Month Including Drunkenness		
License	No License	License	No License	License	No License	License	No License	
–	6	–	0.25	–	0.25	–	0.50	1
–	6	–	–	–	0.50	–	0.50	2
–	72	–	3.00	–	3.00	–	6.00	3
–	3	–	–	–	0.25	–	0.25	4
–	–	–	–	–	–	–	–	5
–	113	–	1.58	–	7.83	–	9.41	6
–	–	–	–	–	–	–	–	7
–	5	–	–	–	0.42	– `	0.42	8
–	56	–	3.67	–	1.00	–	4.67	9
13	22	0.25	0.75	1.38	4.75	1.63	5.50	10
–	44	–	1.33	–	2.33	–	3.66	11
–	10	–	0.33	–	0.50	–	0.83	12
–	82	–	1.50	–	5.33	–	6.83	13
42,772	1,752	8,678.67	85.67	5,578.67	109.00	14,257.34	194.67	14
42,772	–	2,169.67	–	1,394.67	–	3,564.34	–	15
–	1,414	–	53.00	–	64.83	–	117.83	16
–	305	–	9.75	–	15.67	–	25.42	17
–	33	–	1.50	–	1.25	–	2.75	18
5,692	2,283	1,219.02	120.00	647.21	135.08	1,866,23	255.08	19
–	15	–	0.67	–	0.58	–	1.25	20
152	–	8.92	–	3.75	–	–	12.67	21
–	4	–	0.25	–	0.08	–	0.33	22
–	17	–	0.42	–	1.00	–	1.42	23
–	3	–	–	–	0.25	–	0.25	24
134	–	5.17	–	6.00	–	11.17	–	25
–	5	–	–	–	0.42	–	0.42	26
–	6	–	0.17	–	0.33	–	0.50	27
201	–	11.17	–	5.58	–	16.75	–	28
–	19	–	0.67	–	0.92	–	1.59	29
278	–	17.08	–	6.08	–	23.16	–	30
–	–	–	–	–	–	–	–	31
13	13	0.13	1.00	1.50	2.25	1.63	3.25	32
–	24	–	1.33	–	0.67	–	2.00	33
–	810	–	35.00	–	32.50	–	67.50	34
126	53	10.12	8.75	5.63	4.50	15.75	13.25	35
40	–	2.25	–	1.08	–	3.33	–	36
–	43	–	1.58	–	2.00	–	3.58	37
–	9	–	0.67	–	0.08	–	0.75	38

Number of Arrests, under License and No License, classified by Nature of
Crime, with Averages per Month — Concluded.

COUNTIES, CITIES, AND TOWNS.	NUMBER OF MONTHS		NUMBER OF ARRESTS FOR DRUNKENNESS		NUMBER OF ARRESTS FOR ALL OFFENCES OTHER THAN DRUNKENNESS	
	License	No License	License	No License	License	No License
WORCESTER — Con.						
1 Holden,	–	12.00	–	2	–	7
2 Hopedale,	–	12.00	–	5	–	1
3 Hubbardston,	–	12.00	–	2	–	6
4 Lancaster,	–	12.00	–	5	–	2
5 Leicester,	4.00	8.00	–	–	–	4
6 Leominster,	–	12.00	–	95	–	105
7 Lunenburg,	–	12.00	–	10	–	24
8 Mendon,	–	12.00	–	5	–	2
9 Milford,	12.00	–	316	–	77	–
10 Millbury,	8.00	4.00	17	3	16	7
11 New Braintree,	–	12 00	–	–	–	–
12 Northborough,	–	12.00	–	–	–	1
13 Northbridge,	–	12.00	–	22	–	36
14 North Brookfield,	–	12.00	–	36	–	39
15 Oakham,	4.00	8.00	3	–	3	–
16 Oxford,	4.00	8.00	–	4	14	19
17 Paxton,	–	12.00	–	1	–	–
18 Petersham,	12.00	–	–	–	2	–
19 Phillipston,	–	12.00	–	–	–	5
20 Princeton,	–	12.00	–	–	–	1
21 Royalston,	–	12.00	–	–	–	–
22 Rutland,	–	12.00	–	–	–	6
23 Shrewsbury,	–	12.00	–	1	–	3
24 Southborough,	–	12.00	–	120	–	18
25 Southbridge,	12.00	–	50	–	81	–
26 Spencer,	–	12.00	–	106	–	222
27 Sterling,	–	12.00	–	1	–	3
28 Sturbridge,	–	12.00	–	15	–	17
29 Sutton,	12.00	–	14	–	17	–
30 Templeton,	–	12.00	–	6	–	16
31 Upton,	–	12.00	–	4	–	1
32 Uxbridge,	8.00	4.00	3	–	20	13
33 Warren,	–	12.00	–	40	–	30
34 Webster,	12.00	–	94	–	104	–
35 Westborough,	4.00	8.00	12	8	6	19
36 West Boylston,	–	12.00	–	18	–	36
37 West Brookfield,	–	12.00	–	19	–	22
38 Westminster,	–	12.00	–	–	–	2
39 Winchendon,	–	12.00	–	18	–	49
40 WORCESTER,	12.00	–	2,592	–	1,307	–

Number of Arrests, under License and No License, classified by Nature of Crime, with Averages per Month — Concluded.

TOTAL NUMBER OF ARRESTS FOR ALL OFFENCES INCLUDING DRUNKENNESS		AVERAGE NUMBER OF ARRESTS PER MONTH FOR DRUNKENNESS		AVERAGE NUMBER OF ARRESTS PER MONTH FOR ALL OFFENCES OTHER THAN DRUNKENNESS		AVERAGE NUMBER OF ARRESTS PER MONTH FOR ALL OFFENCES INCLUDING DRUNKENNESS		
License	No License	License	No License	License	No License	License	No License	
-	9	-	0.17	-	0.58	-	0.75	1
-	6	-	0.42	-	0.08	-	0.50	2
-	8	-	0.17	-	0.50	-	0.67	3
-	7	-	0.42	-	0.17	-	0.59	4
-	4	-	-	-	0.50	-	0.50	5
-	200	-	7.92	-	8.75	-	16.67	6
-	34	-	0.83	-	2.00	-	2.83	7
-	7	-	0.42	-	0.17	-	0.59	8
393	-	26.33	-	6.42	-	32.75	-	9
33	10	2.13	0.75	2.00	1.75	4.13	2.50	10
-	-	-	-	-	-	-	-	11
-	1	-	-	-	0.08	-	0.08	12
-	58	-	1.83	-	3.00	-	4.83	13
-	75	-	3.00	-	3.25	-	6.25	14
6	-	0.75	-	0.75	-	1.50	-	15
14	23	-	0.50	3.50	2.38	3.50	2.88	16
-	1	-	0.08	-	-	-	0.08	17
2	-	-	-	0.17	-	0.17	-	18
-	5	-	-	-	0.42	-	0.42	19
-	1	-	-	-	0.08	-	0.08	20
-	-	-	-	-	-	-	-	21
-	6	-	-	-	0.50	-	0.50	22
-	4	-	0.08	-	0.25	-	0.33	23
-	138	-	10.00	-	1.50	-	11.50	24
131	-	4.17	-	6.75	-	10.92	-	25
-	328	-	8.83	-	18.50	-	27.33	26
-	4	-	0.08	-	0.25	-	0.33	27
-	32	-	1.25	-	1.42	-	2.67	28
31	-	1.17	-	1.42	-	2.59	-	29
-	22	-	0.50	-	1.33	-	1.83	30
-	5	-	0.33	-	0.08	-	0.41	31
23	13	0.38	-	2.50	3.25	2.88	3.25	32
-	70	-	3.33	-	2.50	-	5.83	33
198	-	7.83	-	8.67	-	16.50	-	34
18	27	3.00	1.00	1.50	2.38	4.50	3.38	35
-	54	-	1.50	-	3.00	-	4.50	36
-	41	-	1.58	-	1.83	-	3.41	37
-	2	-	-	-	0.17	-	0.17	38
-	67	-	1.50	-	4.08	-	5.58	39
3,899	-	216.00	-	108.92	-	324.92	-	40

254　　　　STATISTICS OF LABOR.　　　[Pub. Doc.

The towns which changed their policy with respect to license during the year are as follows: in Berkshire County: Adams, Alford, Cheshire, Hinsdale, Savoy, Stockbridge, Washington, and Williamstown; in Bristol County: North Attleborough; in Essex County: Georgetown, Ipswich, and Peabody; in Franklin County: Deerfield, Greenfield, and Montague; in Hampden County: Southwick; in Hampshire County: Belchertown, Easthampton, and South Hadley;

	CITIES.	NUMBER OF MONTHS		NUMBER OF ARRESTS FOR DRUNKENNESS		NUMBER OF ARRESTS FOR ALL OFFENCES OTHER THAN DRUNKENNESS	
		License	No License	License	No License	License	No License
1	Beverly,	–	12.00	–	133	–	83
2	Boston,	12.00	–	26,036	–	16,736	–
3	Brockton,	–	12.00	–	624	–	504
4	Cambridge,	–	12.00	–	1,922	–	1,428
5	Chelsea,	–	12.00	–	636	–	778
6	Chicopee,	12.00	–	268	–	263	–
7	Everett,	–	12.00	–	397	–	203
8	Fall River,	12.00	–	1,822	–	1,833	–
9	Fitchburg,	–	12.00	–	420	–	390
10	Gloucester,	12.00	–	576	–	293	–
11	Haverhill,	8.00	4.00	653	106	485	159
12	Holyoke,	12.00	–	795	–	651	–
13	Lawrence,	12.00	–	2,031	–	889	–
14	Lowell,*	12.00	–	3,773	–	1,645	–
15	Lynn,	4.00	8.00	1,260	941	426	628
16	Malden,	–	12.00	–	258	–	430
17	Marlborough,	12.00	–	352	–	152	–
18	Medford,	8.00	4.00	161	53	119	54
19	New Bedford,	12.00	–	1,149	–	806	–
20	Newburyport,	12.00	–	690	–	193	–
21	Newton,	–	12.00	–	398	–	394
22	North Adams,	12.00	–	582	–	417	–
23	Northampton,	12.00	–	346	–	98	–
24	Pittsfield,	4.00	8.00	373	294	198	274
25	Quincy,	–	12.00	–	271	–	208
26	Salem,	4.00	8.00	562	237	212	188
27	Somerville,	–	12.00	–	977	–	603
28	Springfield,†	12.00	–	1,346	–	900	–
29	Taunton,	12.00	–	835	–	309	–
30	Waltham,	12.00	–	744	–	350	–
31	Woburn,	12.00	–	559	–	212	–
32	Worcester,	12.00	–	2,592	–	1,307	–

* Includes Dracut.　　　　† Includes Ludlow and West Springfield.

in Middlesex County: Framingham, Hopkinton, Maynard, Natick, and Shirley; in Norfolk County: Dedham; in Plymouth County: Duxbury and Scituate; in Worcester County: Douglas, Gardner, Leicester, Millbury, Oakham, Oxford, Uxbridge, and Westborough. The towns of Adams, Cheshire, Hinsdale, Savoy, Washington, Montague, Southwick, Belchertown, Easthampton, Hopkinton, Scituate, Douglas, Leicester, and Uxbridge show a larger average number of arrests per

TOTAL NUMBER OF ARRESTS FOR ALL OFFENCES INCLUDING DRUNKENNESS		AVERAGE NUMBER OF ARRESTS PER MONTH FOR DRUNKENNESS		AVERAGE NUMBER OF ARRESTS PER MONTH FOR ALL OFFENCES OTHER THAN DRUNKENNESS		AVERAGE NUMBER OF ARRESTS PER MONTH FOR ALL OFFENCES INCLUDING DRUNKENNESS		
License	No License	License	No License	License	No License	License	No License	
–	216	–	11.08	–	6.92	–	18.00	1
42,772	–	2,169.67	–	1,394.67	–	3,564.34	–	2
–	1,128	–	52.00	–	42.00	–	94.00	3
–	3,350	–	16,016.67	–	11,900.00	–	27,916.67	4
–	1,414	–	53.00	–	64.83	–	117.83	5
531	–	22.33	–	21.92	–	44.25	–	6
–	600	–	33.08	–	16.92	–	50.00	7
3,655	–	151.83	–	152.75	–	304.58	–	8
–	810	–	35.00	–	32.50	–	67.50	9
869	–	48.00	–	24.42	–	72.42	–	10
1,138	265	81.63	26.50	60.63	39.75	142.26	66.25	11
1,446	–	66.25	–	54.25	–	120.50	–	12
2,920	–	169.25	–	74.08	–	243.33	–	13
5,418	–	314.42	–	137.08	–	451.50	–	14
1,686	1,569	315.00	117.63	106.50	78.50	421.50	196.13	15
–	688	–	21.50	–	35.83	–	57.33	16
504	–	29.33	–	12.67	–	42.00	–	17
280	107	20.12	13.25	14.88	13.50	35.00	26.75	18
1,955	–	95.75	–	67.17	–	162.92	–	19
883	–	57.50	–	16.08	–	73.58	–	20
–	792	–	33.17	–	32.83	–	66.00	21
999	–	48.50	–	34.75	–	83.25	–	22
444	–	28.83	–	8.17	–	37.00	–	23
571	568	93.25	36.75	49.50	34.25	142.75	71.00	24
–	479	–	22.58	–	17.33	–	39.91	25
774	425	140.50	29.63	53.00	23.50	193.50	53.13	26
–	1,580	–	81.42	–	50.25	–	131.67	27
2,246	–	112.17	–	75.00	–	187.17	–	28
1,144	–	69.58	–	25.75	–	95.33	–	29
1,094	–	62.00	–	29.17	–	91.17	–	30
771	–	46.58	–	17.67	–	64.25	–	31
3,899	–	216.00	–	108 92	–	324.92	–	32

month under no license than under license; but the number
in either case is quite small in these towns. In the following towns the average number of arrests per month for
drunkenness, is larger, and usually, as will be seen from the
table, considerably larger, under license than under no license :
Williamstown, North Attleborough, Georgetown, Ipswich,
Peabody, Greenfield, Montague, Belchertown, South Hadley,
Framingham, Maynard, Natick, Shirley, Dedham, Gardner,
Millbury, Oakham, Uxbridge, and Westborough. No arrests
for drunkenness under either system are reported in Alford,
Washington, Deerfield, Duxbury, or Leicester. In the town
of Stockbridge there was one arrest for drunkenness during
four months of license, and two arrests during eight months
of no license.

The facts as to the cities are presented in the table on pages
254 and 255, so as to be easily compared.

Of the cities, Boston, Chicopee, Fall River, Gloucester,
Holyoke, Lawrence, Lowell, Marlborough, New Bedford, New-
buryport, North Adams, Northampton, Springfield, Taunton,
Waltham, Woburn, and Worcester were under license during
the entire 12 months. Beverly, Brockton, Cambridge, Chel-
sea, Everett, Fitchburg, Malden, Newton, Quincy, and Som-
erville were under no license. Haverhill, Lynn, Medford,
Pittsfield, and Salem changed their policy during the year.
In Haverhill, there were eight months of license and four
months of no license; the average number of arrests per
month for drunkenness in the license period was 81.63, and
under no license, 26.50. In Lynn, there were four months
of license and eight months of no license; the average number
of arrests per month for drunkenness under license was 315.00,
and under no license, 117.63. In Medford, there were eight
months of license and four months of no license; the average
number of arrests per month for drunkenness under license
was 20.12, and under no license, 13.25. In Pittsfield, there
were four months of license and eight months of no license;
the average number of arrests per month for drunkenness under
license was 93.25, and under no license, 36.75. In Salem
there were also four months of license and eight months of no
license; the average number of arrests per month for drunken-

ness under license was 140.50, and under no license, 29.63.
It is not necessary to point out the changes in the average
number of arrests per month for all offences, as they closely
follow the fluctuations in the arrests for drunkenness, inas-
much as arrests for drunkenness are included in the aggregate
figure. The average number of arrests per month for all
offences other than drunkenness in the cities which changed
their policy with respect to license during the year are as
follows: Haverhill, under license, 60.63; under no license,
39.75; Lynn, under license, 106.50; under no license, 78.50;
Medford, under license, 14.88; under no license, 13.50; Pittsfield, under license, 49.50; under no license, 34.25; Salem,
under license, 53.00; under no license, 23.50. It may be well
to point out again that these offences other than drunkenness
include many crimes upon which, as shown by preceding tables,
the use of liquor has an influence.

The next table bears upon the legal residence of the persons
convicted during the 12 months, and is introduced for the purpose of showing whether the town or city in which the crime
was committed was also the town or city in which the criminal
had a legal residence. It is sometimes alleged that, in the
case of towns adjacent to each other, but under contrary poli-
cies with respect to the liquor traffic, the number of arrests in
the towns where license prevails may be increased by crimes
committed by persons who have come in from the no-license
towns for the purpose of obtaining liquor, and that the number
of arrests for drunkenness or other crimes induced by liquor
in the license towns is thus increased by the presence of
offenders who should be credited, on the score of residence, to
no-license towns. This table shows the number of convictions
for drunkenness, liquor offences, and other offences, in each
city and town during the year, and whether or not the legal
residence of the criminal was in the town or city in which the
offence occurred.

Towns and Cities in which Crimes were committed, classified by Nature of Crime, with Legal Residence.

TOWNS AND CITIES IN WHICH CRIMES WERE COMMITTED AND LEGAL RESIDENCE.	NATURE OF CRIME				
	Drunken-ness	Liquor Offences	Total Drunk-enness and Liquor Offences	Other Crimes	All Crimes
Abington.	8	–	8	14	22
In town specified, . . .	6	–	6	–	6
Not in town specified, . .	2	–	2	14	16
Acushnet.	–	–	–	2	2
In town specified, . . .	–	–	–	–	–
Not in town specified, . .	–	–	–	2	2
Adams.	4	–	4	24	28
In town specified, . . .	1	–	1	12	13
Not in town specified, . .	3	–	3	12	15
Alford.	–	–	–	2	2
In town specified, . . .	–	–	–	2	2
Not in town specified, . .	–	–	–	–	–
Amesbury.	10	–	10	14	24
In town specified, . .	9	–	9	11	20
Not in town specified, .	1	–	1	3	4
Amherst.	9	–	9	8	17
In town specified, . . .	6	–	6	5	11
Not in town specified, . .	3	–	3	3	6
Andover.	–	–	–	5	5
In town specified, . . .	–	–	–	4	4
Not in town specified, . .	–	–	–	1	1
Arlington.	9	1	10	9	19
In town specified, . . .	7	1	8	7	15
Not in town specified, . .	2	–	2	2	4
Ashburnham.	1	3	4	1	5
In town specified, . . .	–	3	3	1	4
Not in town specified, . .	1	–	1	–	1
Ashland.	1	1	2	4	6
In town specified, . . .	–	1	1	3	4
Not in town specified, . .	1	–	1	1	2

*Towns and Cities in which Crimes were committed, classified by Nature of
Crime, with Legal Residence* — Continued.

TOWNS AND CITIES IN WHICH CRIMES WERE COMMITTED AND LEGAL RESIDENCE.	NATURE OF CRIME				
	Drunkenness	Liquor Offences	Total Drunkenness and Liquor Offences	Other Crimes	All Crimes
Athol.	34	–	34	18	52
In town specified, . . .	12	–	12	13	25
Not in town specified, . .	22	–	22	5	27
At Sea.	–	–	–	1	1
In town specified, . . .	–	–	–	–	–
Not in town specified, . .	–	–	–	1	1
Attleborough.	4	3	7	26	33
In town specified, . . .	4	3	7	18	25
Not in town specified, . .	–	–	–	8	8
Auburn.	–	1	1	1	2
In town specified, . . .	–	1	1	1	2
Not in town specified, . .	–	–	–	–	–
Avon.	1	1	2	4	6
In town specified, . . .	–	1	1	1	2
Not in town specified, . .	1	–	1	3	4
Ayer.	9	–	9	7	16
In town specified, . . .	1	–	1	2	3
Not in town specified, . .	8	–	8	5	13
Barnstable.	–	–	–	8	8
In town specified, . . .	–	–	–	4	4
Not in town specified, . .	–	–	–	4	4
Barre.	1	–	1	2	3
In town specified, . . .	1	–	1	2	3
Not in town specified, . .	–	–	–	–	–
Bedford.	–	–	–	2	2
In town specified, . . .	–	–	–	2	2
Not in town specified, . .	–	–	–	–	–
Belchertown.	–	–	–	1	1
In town specified, . . .	–	–	–	–	–
Not in town specified, . .	–	–	–	1	1

Towns and Cities in which Crimes were committed, classified by Nature of Crime, with Legal Residence — Continued.

TOWNS AND CITIES IN WHICH CRIMES WERE COMMITTED AND LEGAL RESIDENCE.	NATURE OF CRIME				
	Drunkenness	Liquor Offences	Total Drunkenness and Liquor Offences	Other Crimes	All Crimes
Bellingham.	1	-	1	2	3
In town specified, .	1	-	1	2	3
Not in town specified,	-	-	-	-	-
Belmont.	5	-	5	1	6
In town specified, . .	2	-	2	1	3
Not in town specified, .	3	-	3	-	3
BEVERLY.	38	1	39	21	60
In city specified, . .	26	-	26	11	37
Not in city specified, . .	12	1	13	10	23
Billerica.	1	-	1	1	2
In town specified, . . .	-	-	-	1	1
Not in town specified, . .	1	-	1	-	1
Blackstone.	4	1	5	16	21
In town specified, . .	4	-	4	11	15
Not in town specified, .	-	1	1	5	6
Blandford.	-	-	-	1	1
In town specified, . .	-	-	-	1	1
Not in town specified, .	-	-	-	-	-
Bolton	1	-	1	-	1
In town specified, . .	1	-	1	-	1
Not in town specified, .	-	-	-	-	-
BOSTON.	7,146	111	7,257	3,723	10,980
In city specified, . .	5,023	104	5,127	2,914	8,041
Not in city specified, . .	2,123	7	2,130	809	2,939
Bourne.	-	1	1	-	1
In town specified, . . .	-	1	1	-	1
Not in town specified, . .	-	-	-	-	-
Boxford.	-	-	-	1	1
In town specified, . . .	-	-	-	1	1
Not in town specified, . .	-	-	-	-	-

Towns and Cities in which Crimes were committed, classified by Nature of Crime, with Legal Residence — Continued.

TOWNS AND CITIES IN WHICH CRIMES WERE COMMITTED AND LEGAL RESIDENCE.	NATURE OF CRIME				
	Drunkenness	Liquor Offences	Total Drunkenness and Liquor Offences	Other Crimes	All Crimes
Boylston.	-	-	-	1	1
In town specified, . . .	-	-	-	-	-
Not in town specified, . .	-	-	-	1	1
Bradford.	3	-	3	4	7
In town specified, . . .	3	-	3	1	4
Not in town specified, . .	-	-	-	3	3
Braintree.	10	-	10	4	14
In town specified, . .	6	-	6	2	8
Not in town specified, .	4	-	4	2	6
Brewster.	-	-	-	2	2
In town specified, . .	-	-	-	1	1
Not in town specified, .	-	-	-	1	1
Bridgewater.	5	1	6	16	22
In town specified, . .	2	-	2	5	7
Not in town specified, .	3	1	4	11	15
Brimfield.	-	-	-	7	7
In town specified, . . .	-	-	-	4	4
Not in town specified, . .	-	-	-	3	3
BROCKTON.	191	14	205	91	296
In city specified, . . .	136	13	149	56	205
Not in city specified,. . .	55	1	56	35	91
Brookfield.	39	-	39	14	53
In town specified, . .	20	-	20	6	26
Not in town specified, .	19	-	19	8	27
Brookline.	28	1	29	35	64
In town specified, . .	11	1	12	16	28
Not in town specified, .	17	-	17	19	36
CAMBRIDGE.	741	10	751	304	1,055
In city specified, . . .	488	10	498	183	681
Not in city specified,. . .	253	-	253	121	374

Towns and Cities in which Crimes were committed, classified by Nature of Crime, with Legal Residence — Continued.

TOWNS AND CITIES IN WHICH CRIMES WERE COMMITTED AND LEGAL RESIDENCE.	NATURE OF CRIME				
	Drunkenness	Liquor Offences	Total Drunkenness and Liquor Offences	Other Crimes	All Crimes
Canton.	14	–	14	10	24
In town specified, . .	6	–	6	6	12
Not in town specified, .	8	–	8	4	12
Carver.	–	–	–	1	1
In town specified, . . .	–	–	–	–	–
Not in town specified, . .	–	–	–	1	1
Charlton.	1	2	3	–	3
In town specified, . .	1	2	3	–	3
Not in town specified, .	–	–	–	–	–
Chatham.	–	–	–	1	1
In town specified, . . .	–	–	–	–	–
Not in town specified, . .	–	–	–	1	1
Chelmsford.	–	–	–	1	1
In town specified, . .	–	–	–	–	–
Not in town specified, .	–	–	–	1	1
CHELSEA.	180	–	180	59	239
In city specified, . . .	108	–	108	41	149
Not in city specified, . . .	72	–	72	18	90
Cheshire.	–	–	–	2	2
In town specified, . . .	–	–	–	–	–
Not in town specified, . .	–	–	–	2	2
Chester.	4	–	4	8	12
In town specified, . .	3	–	3	3	6
Not in town specified, .	1	–	1	5	6
CHICOPEE.	122	–	122	48	170
In city specified, . . .	78	–	78	35	113
Not in city specified, . . .	44	–	44	13	57
Clinton.	57	1	58	20	78
In town specified, . . .	31	1	32	8	40
Not in town specified, . .	26	–	26	12	38

Towns and Cities in which Crimes were committed, classified by Nature of Crime, with Legal Residence — Continued.

TOWNS AND CITIES IN WHICH CRIMES WERE COMMITTED AND LEGAL RESIDENCE.	NATURE OF CRIME				
	Drunkenness	Liquor Offences	Total Drunkenness and Liquor Offences	Other Crimes	All Crimes
Cohasset.	1	-	1	-	1
In town specified, . . .	1	-	1	-	1
Not in town specified, . .	-	-	-	-	-
Concord.	1	-	1	13	14
In town specified, . . .	1	-	1	3	4
Not in town specified, . .	-	-	-	10	10
Conway.	1	-	1	-	1
In town specified, . .	1	-	1	-	1
Not in town specified, .	-	-	-	-	-
Cottage City.	1	-	1	1	2
In town specified, . . .	1	-	1	1	2
Not in town specified, . .	-	-	-	-	-
Cummington.	-	-	-	1	1
In town specified, . . .	-	-	-	1	1
Not in town specified, . .	-	-	-	-	-
Dalton.	1	-	1	6	7
In town specified, . . .	1	-	1	2	3
Not in town specified, . .	-	-	-	4	4
Dana.	-	-	-	1	1
In town specified, . . .	-	-	-	-	-
Not in town specified, . .	-	-.	-	1	1
Danvers.	9	1	10	8	18
In town specified, . . .	7	1	8	8	16
Not in town specified, . .	2	-	2	-	2
Dartmouth.	1	-	1	1	2
In town specified, . . .	-	-	-	-	-
Not in town specified, . .	1	-	1	1	2
Dedham.	62	1	63	19	82
In town specified, . . .	23	-	23	8	31
Not in town specified, . .	39	1	40	11	51

Towns and Cities in which Crimes were committed, classified by Nature of Crime, with Legal Residence — Continued.

TOWNS AND CITIES IN WHICH CRIMES WERE COMMITTED AND LEGAL RESIDENCE.	NATURE OF CRIME				
	Drunkenness	Liquor Offences	Total Drunkenness and Liquor Offences	Other Crimes	All Crimes
Deerfield.	1	–	1	4	5
In town specified, . . .	1	–	1	3	4
Not in town specified, . .	–	–	–	1	1
Dennis.	–	–	–	2	2
In town specified, .	–	–	–	2	2
Not in town specified, .	–	–	–	–	–
Dighton.	–	–	–	1	1
In town specified, . .	–	–	–	1	1
Not in town specified, .	–	–	–	–	–
Douglas.	–	1	1	5	6
In town specified, .	–	1	1	2	3
Not in town specified,	–	–	–	3	3
Dover.	–	–	–	1	1
In town specified, .	–	–	–	1	1
Not in town specified,	–	–	–	–	–
Dracut.	7	1	8	5	13
In town specified, . . .	1	1	2	3	5
Not in town specified, . .	6	–	6	2	8
Dudley.	2	–	2	1	3
In town specified, . . .	2	–	2	1	3
Not in town specified, . .	–	–	–	–	–
East Bridgewater.	1	–	1	2	3
In town specified, . . .	1	–	1	–	1
Not in town specified, . .	–	–	–	2	2
Eastham.	–	–	–	1	1
In town specified, . . .	–	–	–	–	–
Not in town specified, . .	–	–	–	1	1
Easthampton.	11	–	11	4	15
In town specified, . . .	2	–	2	3	5
Not in town specified, . .	9	–	9	1	10

*Towns and Cities in which Crimes were committed, classified by Nature of
Crime, with Legal Residence — Continued.*

TOWNS AND CITIES IN WHICH CRIMES WERE COMMITTED AND LEGAL RESIDENCE.	NATURE OF CRIME				
	Drunkenness	Liquor Offences	Total Drunkenness and Liquor Offences	Other Crimes	All Crimes
Easton.	9	2	11	6	17
In town specified, . . .	8	2	10	5	15
Not in town specified, . .	1	-	1	1	2
Edgartown.	-	-	-	2	2
In town specified, . . .	-	-	-	1	1
Not in town specified, . .	-	-	-	1	1
Egremont.	1	-	1	-	1
In town specified, . . .	-	-	-	-	-
Not in town specified, . .	1	-	1	-	1
Enfield.	-	-	-	1	1
In town specified, . . .	-	-	-	-	-
Not in town specified, . .	-	-	-	1	1
Erving.	-	-	-	1	1
In town specified, . . .	-	-	-	1	1
Not in town specified, . .	-	-	-	-	-
Essex.	-	-	-	2	2
In town specified, . . .	-	-	-	2	2
Not in town specified, . .	-	-	-	-	-
EVERETT.	126	-	126	36	162
In city specified, . . .	61	-	61	18	79
Not in city specified, . . .	65	-	65	18	83
Fairhaven.	2	-	2	3	5
In town specified, . . .	1	-	1	2	3
Not in town specified, . .	1	-	1	1	2
FALL RIVER.	325	9	334	440	774
In city specified, . . .	296	9	305	407	712
Not in city specified, . . .	29	-	29	33	62
Falmouth.	-	-	-	2	2
In town specified, . . .	-	-	-	-	-
Not in town specified, . .	-	-	-	2	2

Towns and Cities in which Crimes were committed, classified by Nature of Crime, with Legal Residence — Continued.

TOWNS AND CITIES IN WHICH CRIMES WERE COMMITTED AND LEGAL RESIDENCE.	NATURE OF CRIME				
	Drunkenness	Liquor Offences	Total Drunkenness and Liquor Offences	Other Crimes	All Crimes
FITCHBURG.	133	12	145	58	203
In city specified,	97	11	108	44	152
Not in city specified,	36	1	37	14	51
Florida.	–	–	–	1	1
In town specified,	–	–	–	1	1
Not in town specified,	–	–	–	–	–
Foxborough.	4	–	4	3	7
In town specified,	3	–	3	1	4
Not in town specified,	1	–	1	2	3
Framingham.	17	2	19	17	36
In town specified,	8	2	10	4	14
Not in town specified,	9	–	9	13	22
Franklin.	4	2	6	11	17
In town specified,	3	2	5	3	8
Not in town specified,	1	–	1	8	9
Freetown.	–	–	–	1	1
In town specified,	–	–	–	1	1
Not in town specified,	–	–	–	–	–
Gardner.	43	1	44	28	72
In town specified,	21	1	22	17	39
Not in town specified,	22	–	22	11	33
Gay Head.	–	–	–	2	2
In town specified,	–	–	–	–	–
Not in town specified,	–	–	–	2	2
Georgetown.	8	–	8	2	10
In town specified,	6	–	6	2	8
Not in town specified,	2	–	2	–	2
Gill.	–	–	–	1	1
In town specified,	–	–	–	–	–
Not in town specified,	–	–	–	1	1

Towns and Cities in which Crimes were committed, classified by Nature of Crime, with Legal Residence — Continued.

TOWNS AND CITIES IN WHICH CRIMES WERE COMMITTED AND LEGAL RESIDENCE.	NATURE OF CRIME				
	Drunkenness	Liquor Offences	Total Drunkenness and Liquor Offences	Other Crimes	All Crimes
GLOUCESTER.	89	3	92	59	151
In city specified, . . .	50	3	53	40	93
Not in city specified, . . .	39	–	39	19	58
Goshen.	–	–	–	3	3
In town specified, . . .	–	–	–	–	–
Not in town specified, . .	–	–	–	3	3
Grafton.	–	–	–	2	2
In town specified, . . .	–	–	–	2	2
Not in town specified, . .	–	–	–	–	–
Granville.	–	–	–	1	1
In town specified, . . .	–	–	–	–	–
Not in town specified, . .	–	–	–	1	1
Great Barrington.	13	–	13	20	33
In town specified, . . .	4	–	4	9	13
Not in town specified, . .	9	–	9	11	20
Greenfield.	14	–	14	15	29
In town specified, . .	6	–	6	7	13
Not in town specified, .	8	–	8	8	16
Greenwich.	–	–	–	4	4
In town specified, . . .	–	–	–	4	4
Not in town specified, . .	–	–	–	–	–
Hadley.	1	–	1	–	1
In town specified, . . .	1	–	1	–	1
Not in town specified, . .	–	–	–	–	–
Hamilton.	1	–	1	2	3
In town specified, . . .	–	–	–	–	–
Not in town specified, . .	1	–	1	2	3
Hardwick.	1	–	1	–	1
In town specified, . . .	1	–	1	–	1
Not in town specified, . .	–	–	–	–	–

Towns and Cities in which Crimes were committed, classified by Nature of Crime, with Legal Residence — Continued.

TOWNS AND CITIES IN WHICH CRIMES WERE COMMITTED AND LEGAL RESIDENCE.	NATURE OF CRIME				
	Drunkenness	Liquor Offences	Total Drunkenness and Liquor Offences	Other Crimes	All Crimes
Harvard.	2	1	3	–	3
In town specified,	–	1	1	–	1
Not in town specified,	2	–	2	–	2
Harwich.	–	1	1	3	4
In town specified,	–	1	1	3	4
Not in town specified,	–	–	–	–	–
HAVERHILL.	259	11	270	88	358
In city specified,	114	11	125	55	180
Not in city specified,	145	–	145	33	178
Hingham.	4	–	4	8	12
In town specified,	–	–	–	3	3
Not in town specified,	4	–	4	5	9
Hinsdale.	1	–	1	3	4
In town specified,	1	–	1	–	1
Not in town specified,	–	–	–	3	3
Holbrook.	4	–	4	2	6
In town specified,	3	–	3	–	3
Not in town specified,	1	–	1	2	3
Holden.	–	–	–	5	5
In town specified,	–	–	–	3	3
Not in town specified,	–	–	–	2	2
Holliston.	6	–	6	2	8
In town specified,	5	–	5	1	6
Not in town specified,	1	–	1	1	2
HOLYOKE.	417	–	417	138	555
In city specified,	325	–	325	111	436
Not in city specified,	92	–	92	27	119
Hopkinton.	2	–	2	11	13
In town specified,	2	–	2	5	7
Not in town specified,	–	–	–	6	6

Towns and Cities in which Crimes were committed, classified by Nature of Crime, with Legal Residence — Continued.

TOWNS AND CITIES IN WHICH CRIMES WERE COMMITTED AND LEGAL RESIDENCE.	NATURE OF CRIME				
	Drunkenness	Liquor Offences	Total Drunkenness and Liquor Offences	Other Crimes	All Crimes
Hubbardston.	2	-	2	3	5
In town specified, . .	1	-	1	3	4
Not in town specified, .	1	-	1	-	1
Hudson.	17	-	17	21	38
In town specified, . .	5	-	5	3	8
Not in town specified, .	12	-	12	18	30
Hull.	4	2	6	5	11
In town specified, . . .	-	2	2	2	4
Not in town specified, . .	4	-	4	3	7
Hyde Park.	29	1	30	37	67
In town specified, . . .	22	1	23	16	39
Not in town specified, . .	7	-	7	21	28
Ipswich.	8	-	8	6	14
In town specified, . .	3	-	3	4	7
Not in town specified, .	5	-	5	2	7
Lancaster.	1	-	1	-	1
In town specified, . .	-	-	-	-	-
Not in town specified, .	1	-	1	-	1
Lanesborough.	-	-	-	2	2
In town specified, . .	-	-	-	1	1
Not in town specified, .	-	-	-	1	1
LAWRENCE.	694	21	715	242	957
In city specified, . .	420	20	440	179	619
Not in city specified, . .	274	1	275	63	338
Lee.	11	-	11	14	25
In town specified, . . .	2	-	2	7	9
Not in town specified, . .	9	-	9	7	16
Leicester.	-	2	2	2	4
In town specified, . . .	-	2	2	1	3
Not in town specified, . .	-	-	-	1	1

Towns and Cities in which Crimes were committed, classified by Nature of Crime, with Legal Residence — Continued.

TOWNS AND CITIES IN WHICH CRIMES WERE COMMITTED AND LEGAL RESIDENCE.	NATURE OF CRIME				
	Drunkenness	Liquor Offences	Total Drunkenness and Liquor Offences	Other Crimes	All Crimes
Leominster.	19	2	21	6	27
In town specified, . . .	15	2	17	4	21
Not in town specified, . .	4	–	4	2	6
Leverett.	–	–	–	1	1
In town specified, . . .	–	–	–	1	1
Not in town specified, . .	–	–	–	–	–
Lexington.	7	–	7	8	15
In town specified, . . .	2	–	2	5	7
Not in town specified, . .	5	–	5	3	8
Lincoln.	–	–	–	1	1
In town specified, . .	–	–	–	–	–
Not in town specified, .	–	–	–	1	1
Littleton.	–	–	–	2	2
In town specified, . .	–	–	–	2	2
Not in town specified, .	–	–	–	–	–
LOWELL.	1,215	16	1,231	424	1,655
In city specified, . . .	855	16	871	351	1,222
Not in city specified, . . .	360	–	360	73	433
Lunenburg.	–	1	1	1	2
In town specified, . . .	–	1	1	1	2
Not in town specified, . .	–	–	–	–	–
LYNN.	474	11	485	116	601
In city specified, . . .	351	10	361	81	442
Not in city specified, . . .	123	1	124	35	159
MALDEN.	91	16	107	69	176
In city specified, . . .	43	16	59	42	101
Not in city specified, . . .	48	–	48	27	75
Manchester.	2	–	2	3	5
In town specified, . . .	–	–	–	1	1
Not in town specified, . .	2	–	2	2	4

Towns and Cities in which Crimes were committed, classified by Nature of Crime, with Legal Residence — Continued.

TOWNS AND CITIES IN WHICH CRIMES WERE COMMITTED AND LEGAL RESIDENCE.	Drunkenness	Liquor Offences	Total Drunkenness and Liquor Offences	Other Crimes	All Crimes
Mansfield.	–	–	–	29	29
In town specified, . . .	–	–	–	5	5
Not in town specified, . .	–	–	–	24	24
Marblehead.	26	3	29	10	39
In town specified, . . .	17	3	20	2	22
Not in town specified, . .	9	–	9	8	17
MARLBOROUGH.	138	1	139	29	168
In city specified, . . .	69	1	70	20	90
Not in city specified, . . .	69	–	69	9	78
Marshfield.	3	–	3	2	5
In town specified, . . .	2	–	2	2	4
Not in town specified, . .	1	–	1	–	1
Maynard.	2	1	3	3	6
In town specified, . . .	2	1	3	–	3
Not in town specified, . .	–	–	–	3	3
Medfield.	1	–	1	1	2
In town specified, . . .	1	–	1	1	2
Not in town specified, . .	–	–	–	–	–
MEDFORD.	91	–	91	33	124
In city specified, . . .	44	–	44	12	56
Not in city specified, . .	47	–	47	21	68
Medway.	7	–	7	13	20
In town specified, . . .	4	–	4	11	15
Not in town specified, . .	3	–	3	2	5
Melrose.	28	1	29	15	44
In town specified, . . .	14	1	15	10	25
Not in town specified, . .	14	–	14	5	19
Mendon.	–	–	–	4	4
In town specified, . . .	–	–	–	2	2
Not in town specified, . .	–	–	–	2	2

*Towns and Cities in which Crimes were committed, classified by Nature of
Crime, with Legal Residence — Continued.*

TOWNS AND CITIES IN WHICH CRIMES WERE COMMITTED AND LEGAL RESIDENCE.	NATURE OF CRIME				
	Drunkenness	Liquor Offences	Total Drunkenness and Liquor Offences	Other Crimes	All Crimes
Merrimac.	-	1	1	2	3
In town specified,	-	1	1	2	3
Not in town specified,	-	-	-	-	-
Methuen.	6	2	8	8	16
In town specified,	3	1	4	6	10
Not in town specified,	3	1	4	2	6
Middleborough.	2	-	2	6	8
In town specified,	2	-	2	-	2
Not in town specified,	-	-	-	6	6
Middleton.	-	-	-	2	2
In town specified,	-	-	-	-	-
Not in town specified,	-	-	-	2	2
Milford.	132	1	133	18	151
In town specified,	77	1	78	13	91
Not in town specified,	55	-	55	5	60
Millbury.	4	-	4	11	15
In town specified,	3	-	3	5	8
Not in town specified,	1	-	1	6	7
Millis.	2	-	2	1	3
In town specified,	1	-	1	-	1
Not in town specified,	1	-	1	1	2
Milton.	6	-	6	9	15
In town specified,	2	-	2	2	4
Not in town specified,	4	-	4	7	11
Monson.	-	-	-	17	17
In town specified,	-	-	-	16	16
Not in town specified,	-	-	-	1	1
Montague.	11	-	11	16	27
In town specified,	4	-	4	2	6
Not in town specified,	7	-	7	14	21

Towns and Cities in which Crimes were committed, classified by Nature of Crime, with Legal Residence — Continued.

TOWNS AND CITIES IN WHICH CRIMES WERE COMMITTED AND LEGAL RESIDENCE.	NATURE OF CRIME				
	Drunken-ness	Liquor Offences	Total Drunk-enness and Liquor Offences	Other Crimes	All Crimes
Nahant.	7	-	7	5	12
In town specified, . . .	-	-	-	-	-
Not in town specified. . .	7	-	7	5	12
Nantucket.	1	1	2	3	5
In town specified, . . .	1	1	2	3	5
Not in town specified, . .	-	-	-	-	-
Natick.	31	4	35	` 19	54
In town specified, . . .	26	4	30	14	44
Not in town specified, . .	5	-	5	5	10
Needham.	3	1	4	5	9
In town specified, . . .	3	1	4	2	6
Not in town specified, . .	-	-	-	3	3
NEW BEDFORD.	489	3	492	186	678
In city specified, . . .	351	3	354	156	510
Not in city specified, . . .	138	-	138	30	168
NEWBURYPORT.	161	2	163	57	220
In city specified, . . .	65	2	67	34	101
Not in city specified, . . .	96	-	96	23	119
New Marlborough.	-	-	-	2	2
In town specified, . . .	-	-	-	1	1
Not in town specified, . .	-	-	-	1	1
NEWTON.	37	2	39	52	91
In city specified, . . .	31	2	33	35	68
Not in city specified, . . .	6	-	6	17	23
Norfolk.	2	-	2	1	3
In town specified, . . .	1	-	1	-	1
Not in town specified, . .	1	-	1	1	2
NORTH ADAMS.	90	1	91	47	138
In city specified, . . .	36	1	37	20	57
Not in city specified, . . .	54	-	54	27	81

Towns and Cities in which Crimes were committed, classified by Nature of Crime, with Legal Residence — Continued.

TOWNS AND CITIES IN WHICH CRIMES WERE COMMITTED AND LEGAL RESIDENCE.	NATURE OF CRIME				
	Drunken-ness	Liquor Offences	Total Drunk-enness and Liquor Offences	Other Crimes	All Crimes
NORTHAMPTON.	161	-	161	28	189
In city specified, . .	76	-	76	10	86
Not in city specified,. .	85	-	85	18	103
North Andover.	1	-	1	1	2
In town specified, . . .	1	-	1	1	2
Not in town specified, . .	-	-	-	-	-
North Attleborough.	3	2	5	14	19
In town specified, . . .	3	2	5	8	13
Not in town specified, . .	-	-	-	6	6
Northborough.	1	-	1	-	1
In town specified, . .	-	-	-	-	-
Not in town specified, .	1	-	1	-	1
Northbridge.	3	3	6	4	10
In town specified, . .	3	3	6	3	9
Not in town specified, .	-	-	-	1	1
North Brookfield.	2	-	2	6	8
In town specified, . .	2	-	2	4	6
Not in town specified, .	-	-	-	2	2
Northfield.	-	-	-	2	2
In town specified, . . .	-	-	-	-	-
Not in town specified, . .	-	-	-	2	2
North Reading.	-	-	-	1	1
In town specified, . . .	-	-	-	-	-
Not in town specified, . .	-	-	-	1	1
Norwood.	14	-	14	11	25
In town specified, . . .	9	-	9	2	11
Not in town specified, . .	5	-	5	9	14
Orange.	5	-	5	5	10
In town specified, . . .	4	-	4	2	6
Not in town specified, . .	1	-	1	3	4

Towns and Cities in which Crimes were committed, classified by Nature of Crime, with Legal Residence — Continued.

TOWNS AND CITIES IN WHICH CRIMES WERE COMMITTED AND LEGAL RESIDENCE.	NATURE OF CRIME				
	Drunkenness	Liquor Offences	Total Drunkenness and Liquor Offences	Other Crimes	All Crimes
Otis.	-	-	-	1	1
In town specified,	-	-	-	-	-
Not in town specified,	-	-	-	1	1
Oxford.	-	-	-	4	4
In town specified,	-	-	-	3	3
Not in town specified,	-	-	-	1	1
Palmer.	35	-	35	15	50
In town specified,	11	-	11	4	15
Not in town specified,	24	-	24	11	35
Paxton.	-	-	-	1	1
In town specified,	-	-	-	-	-
Not in town specified,	-	-	-	1	1
Peabody.	37	4	41	26	67
In town specified,	23	4	27	20	47
Not in town specified,	14	-	14	6	20
Pepperell.	8	-	8	9	17
In town specified,	4	-	4	7	11
Not in town specified,	4	-	4	2	6
Petersham.	-	-	-	1	1
In town specified,	-	-	-	1	1
Not in town specified,	-	-	-	-	-
Phillipston.	-	1	1	1	2
In town specified,	-	1	1	1	2
Not in town specified,	-	-	-	-	-
PITTSFIELD.	62	5	67	48	115
In city specified,	31	5	36	20	56
Not in city specified,	31	-	31	28	59
Plymouth.	2	-	2	6	8
In town specified,	2	-	2	4	6
Not in town specified,	-	-	-	2	2

Towns and Cities in which Crimes were committed, classified by Nature of Crime, with Legal Residence — Continued.

TOWNS AND CITIES IN WHICH CRIMES WERE COMMITTED AND LEGAL RESIDENCE.	NATURE OF CRIME				
	Drunken-ness	Liquor Offences	Total Drunk-enness and Liquor Offences	Other Crimes	All Crimes
Princeton.	-	-	-	1	1
In town specified, .	-	-	-	-	-
Not in town specified, .	-	-	-	1	1
Provincetown.	1	-	1	3	4
In town specified, .	1	-	1	2	3
Not in town specified, .	-	-	-	1	1
QUINCY.	40	2	42	21	63
In city specified, .	24	2	26	5	31
Not in city specified, .	16	-	16	16	32
Randolph.	6	1	7	8	15
In town specified, . . .	6	1	7	6	13
Not in town specified, . .	-	-	-	2	2
Raynham.	5	-	5	4	9
In town specified, . . .	4	-	4	1	5
Not in town specified, . .	1	-	1	3	4
Reading.	5	-	5	-	5
In town specified, . . .	3	-	3	-	3
Not in town specified, . .	2	-	2	-	2
Rehoboth.	1	-	1	1	2
In town specified, .	-	-	-	-	-
Not in town specified, .	1	-	1	1	2
Revere.	21	2	23	12	35
In town specified, .	3	-	3	-	3
Not in town specified, .	18	2	20	12	32
Rochester.	-	-	-	1	1
In town specified, . . .	-	-	-	1	1
Not in town specified, . .	-	-	-	-	-
Rockland.	-	2	2	6	8
In town specified, . . .	-	2	2	6	8
Not in town specified, . .	-	-	-	-	-

Towns and Cities in which Crimes were committed, classified by Nature of Crime, with Legal Residence — Continued.

TOWNS AND CITIES IN WHICH CRIMES WERE COMMITTED AND LEGAL RESIDENCE.	Drunkenness	Liquor Offences	Total Drunkenness and Liquor Offences	Other Crimes	All Crimes
Rockport.	4	–	4	4	8
In town specified,	4	–	4	4	8
Not in town specified,	–	–	–	–	–
Rowe.	–	–	–	1	1
In town specified,	–	–	–	–	–
Not in town specified,	–	–	–	1	1
Russell.	1	–	1	–	1
In town specified,	1	–	1	–	1
Not in town specified,	–	–	–	–	–
Rutland.	–	–	–	1	1
In town specified,	–	–	–	–	–
Not in town specified,	–	–	–	1	1
SALEM.	245	15	260	62	322
In city specified,	137	13	150	44	194
Not in city specified,	108	2	110	18	128
Salisbury.	4	1	5	6	11
In town specified,	1	–	1	1	2
Not in town specified,	3	1	4	5	9
Sandwich.	1	1	2	3	5
In town specified,	1	1	2	2	4
Not in town specified,	–	–	–	1	1
Saugus.	–	2	2	2	4
In town specified,	–	1	1	2	3
Not in town specified,	–	1	1	–	1
Savoy.	–	–	–	1	1
In town specified,	–	–	–	1	1
Not in town specified,	–	–	–	–	–
Scituate.	1	–	1	–	1
In town specified,	1	–	1	–	1
Not in town specified,	–	–	–	–	–

Towns and Cities in which Crimes were committed, classified by Nature of Crime, with Legal Residence — Continued.

TOWNS AND CITIES IN WHICH CRIMES WERE COMMITTED AND LEGAL RESIDENCE.	NATURE OF CRIME				
	Drunkenness	Liquor Offences	Total Drunkenness and Liquor Offences	Other Crimes	All Crimes
Seekonk.	-	-	-	1	1
In town specified,	-	-	-	1	1
Not in town specified,	-	-	-	-	-
Sharon.	7	-	7	10	17
In town specified,	7	-	7	3	10
Not in town specified,	-	-	-	7	7
Sheffield.	3	-	3	14	17
In town specified,	3	-	3	6	9
Not in town specified,	-	-	-	8	8
Shelburne.	1	-	1	2	3
In town specified,	1	-	1	2	3
Not in town specified,	-	-	-	-	-
Sherborn.	-	1	1	3	4
In town specified,	-	1	1	1	2
Not in town specified,	-	-	-	2	2
Shirley.	4	-	4	2	6
In town specified,	2	-	2	2	4
Not in town specified,	2	-	2	-	2
Shrewsbury.	-	-	-	2	2
In town specified,	-	-	-	2	2
Not in town specified,	-	-	-	-	-
Shutesbury.	-	-	-	2	2
In town specified,	-	-	-	2	2
Not in town specified,	-	-	-	-	-
Somerset.	1	-	1	2	3
In town specified,	1	-	1	2	3
Not in town specified,	-	-	-	-	-
SOMERVILLE.	434	8	442	174	616
In city specified,	236	5	241	69	310
Not in city specified,	198	3	201	105	306

Towns and Cities in which Crimes were committed, classified by Nature of Crime, with Legal Residence — Continued.

TOWNS AND CITIES IN WHICH CRIMES WERE COMMITTED AND LEGAL RESIDENCE.	NATURE OF CRIME				
	Drunken-ness	Liquor Offences	Total Drunk-enness and Liquor Offences	Other Crimes	All Crimes
Southborough.	21	–	21	4	25
In town specified, . . .	7	–	7	2	9
Not in town specified, . .	14	–	14	2	16
Southbridge.	10	–	10	7	17
In town specified, . . .	4	–	4	3	7
Not in town specified, . .	6	–	6	4	10
South Hadley.	5	–	5	2	7
In town specified, . . .	3	–	3	2	5
Not in town specified, . .	2	–	2	–	2
Southwick.	1	–	1	1	2
In town specified, . . .	1	–	1	–	1
Not in town specified, . .	–	–	–	1	1
Spencer.	9	3	12	30	42
In town specified, . . .	6	3	9	13	22
Not in town specified, . .	3	–	3	17	20
SPRINGFIELD.	720	5	725	236	961
In city specified, . . .	490	4	494	128	622
Not in city specified, . . .	230	1	231	108	339
Sterling.	–	–	–	2	2
In town specified, . . .	–	–	–	2	2
Not in town specified, . .	–	–	–	–	–
Stockbridge.	1	–	1	4	5
In town specified, . . .	1	–	1	4	5
Not in town specified, . .	–	–	–	–	–
Stoneham.	28	–	28	6	34
In town specified, . . .	18	–	18	3	21
Not in town specified, . .	10	–	10	3	13
Stoughton.	12	3	15	10	25
In town specified, . . .	9	3	12	3	15
Not in town specified, . .	3	–	3	7	10

Towns and Cities in which Crimes were committed, classified by Nature of Crime, with Legal Residence — Continued.

TOWNS AND CITIES IN WHICH CRIMES WERE COMMITTED AND LEGAL RESIDENCE.	NATURE OF CRIME				
	Drunken-ness	Liquor Offences	Total Drunk-enness and Liquor Offences	Other Crimes	All Crimes
Stow.	-	-	-	1	1
In town specified,	-	-	-	-	-
Not in town specified,	-	-	-	1	1
Sturbridge.	6	1	7	5	12
In town specified,	4	1	5	1	6
Not in town specified,	2	-	2	4	6
Sudbury.	-	-	-	1	1
In town specified,	-	-	-	1	1
Not in town specified,	-	-	-	-	-
Sutton.	4	-	4	4	8
In town specified,	4	-	4	4	8
Not in town specified,	-	-	-	-	-
Swampscott.	2	-	2	1	3
In town specified,	1	-	1	-	1
Not in town specified,	1	-	1	1	2
TAUNTON.	193	1	194	43	237
In city specified,	110	1	111	23	134
Not in city specified,	83	-	83	20	103
Templeton.	2	-	2	2	4
In town specified,	1	-	1	2	3
Not in town specified,	1	-	1	-	1
Tewksbury.	1	-	1	6	7
In town specified,	-	-	-	1	1
Not in town specified,	1	-	1	5	6
Tolland.	-	-	-	3	3
In town specified,	-	-	-	3	3
Not in town specified,	-	-	-	-	-
Topsfield.	-	1	1	-	1
In town specified,	-	1	1	-	1
Not in town specified,	-	-	-	-	-

Towns and Cities in which Crimes were committed, classified by Nature of Crime, with Legal Residence — Continued.

TOWNS AND CITIES IN WHICH CRIMES WERE COMMITTED AND LEGAL RESIDENCE.	NATURE OF CRIME				
	Drunkenness	Liquor Offences	Total Drunkenness and Liquor Offences	Other Crimes	All Crimes
Townsend.	-	-	-	2	2
In town specified, . . .	-	-	-	1	1
Not in town specified, . .	-	-	-	1	1
Upton.	2	1	3	1	4
In town specified, . . .	1	-	1	1	2
Not in town specified, . .	1	1	2	-	2
Uxbridge.	-	1	1	4	5
In town specified, . . .	-	1	1	3	4
Not in town specified, . .	-	-	-	1	1
Wakefield.	19	-	19	9	28
In town specified, . . .	17	-	17	7	24
Not in town specified, . .	2	-	2	2	4
Wales.	-	-	-	1	1
In town specified, . . .	-	-	-	-	-
Not in town specified, . .	-	-	-	1	1
Walpole.	-	-	-	1	1
In town specified, . . .	-	-	-	-	-
Not in town specified, . .	-	-	-	1	1
WALTHAM.	171	-	171	62	233
In city specified, . . .	77	-	77	36	113
Not in city specified, . . .	94	-	94	26	120
Ware.	9	1	10	5	15
In town specified, . . .	3	1	4	3	7
Not in town specified, . .	6	-	6	2	8
Wareham.	1	2	3	2	5
In town specified, . .	1	-	1	1	2
Not in town specified, .	-	2	2	1	3
Warren.	1	1	2	1	3
In town specified, . . .	1	-	1	-	1
Not in town specified, . .	-	1	1	1	2

Towns and Cities in which Crimes were committed, classified by Nature of Crime, with Legal Residence — Continued.

TOWNS AND CITIES IN WHICH CRIMES WERE COMMITTED AND LEGAL RESIDENCE.	NATURE OF CRIME				
	Drunkenness	Liquor Offences	Total Drunkenness and Liquor Offences	Other Crimes	All Crimes
Warwick.	–	–	–	1	1
In town specified, . . .	–	–	–	1	1
Not in town specified, . .	–	–	–	–	–
Watertown.	5	–	5	8	13
In town specified, . . .	3	–	3	3	6
Not in town specified, . .	2	–	2	5	7
Wayland.	–	–	–	1	1
In town specified, . . .	–	–	–	1	1
Not in town specified, . .	–	–	–	–	–
Webster.	23	–	23	22	45
In town specified, . . .	13	–	13	11	24
Not in town specified, . .	10	–	10	11	21
Wellesley.	1	–	1	10	11
In town specified, . . .	–	–	–	–	–
Not in town specified, . .	1	–	1	10	11
Wendell.	1	–	1	3	4
In town specified, . . .	1	–	1	1	2
Not in town specified, . .	–	–	–	2	2
Westborough.	5	2	7	8	15
In town specified, . . .	4	2	6	2	8
Not in town specified, . .	1	–	1	6	7
West Boylston.	3	–	3	5	8
In town specified, . . .	3	–	3	3	6
Not in town specified, . .	–	–	–	2	2
West Brookfield.	5	–	5	4	9
In town specified, . . .	5	–	5	1	6
Not in town specified, . .	–	–	–	3	3
Westfield.	40	–	40	37	77
In town specified, . . .	21	–	21	17	38
Not in town specified, . .	19	–	19	20	39

Towns and Cities in which Crimes were committed, classified by Nature of Crime, with Legal Residence — Continued.

TOWNS AND CITIES IN WHICH CRIMES WERE COMMITTED AND LEGAL RESIDENCE.	NATURE OF CRIME				
	Drunken-ness	Liquor Offences	Total Drunk-enness and Liquor Offences	Other Crimes	All Crimes
Westford.	-	-	-	3	3
In town specified, . . .	-	-	-	2	2
Not in town specified, . .	-	-	-	1	1
Westminster.	1	-	1	-	1
In town specified, . . .	-	-	-	-	-
Not in town specified, . .	1	-	1	-	1
Weston.	-	-	-	1	1
In town specified, . . .	-	-	-	1	1
Not in town specified, . .	-	-	-	-	-
Westport.	-	-	-	2	2
In town specified, . . .	-	-	-	2	2
Not in town specified, . .	-	-	-	-	-
West Springfield.	7	-	7	2	9
In town specified, . . .	3	-	3	1	4
Not in town specified, . .	4	-	4	1	5
West Stockbridge.	1	-	1	6	7
In town specified, . . .	1	-	1	5	6
Not in town specified, . .	-	-	-	1	1
West Tisbury.	-	-	-	1	1
In town specified, . . .	-	-	-	1	1
Not in town specified, . .	-	-	-	-	-
Weymouth.	22	6	28	9	37
In town specified, . . .	19	5	24	8	32
Not in town specified, . .	3	1	4	1	5
Whately.	-	-	-	2	2
In town specified, . . .	-	-	-	1	1
Not in town specified, . .	-	-	-	1	1
Whitman.	1	1	2	11	13
In town specified, . . .	1	1	2	-	2
Not in town specified, . .	-	-	-	11	11

Towns and Cities in which Crimes were committed, classified by Nature of Crime, with Legal Residence — Concluded.

TOWNS AND CITIES IN WHICH CRIMES WERE COMMITTED AND LEGAL RESIDENCE.	NATURE OF CRIME				
	Drunken-ness	Liquor Offences	Total Drunk-enness and Liquor Offences	Other Crimes	All Crimes
Wilbraham.	-	-	-	1	1
In town specified,	-	-	-	1	1
Not in town specified,	-	-	-	-	-
Williamsburg.	-	-	-	1	1
In town specified,	-	-	-	1	1
Not in town specified,	-	-	-	-	-
Williamstown.	1	-	1	16	17
In town specified,	1	-	1	2	3
Not in town specified,	-	-	-	14	14
Winchendon.	10	2	12	5	17
In town specified,	4	2	6	3	9
Not in town specified,	6	-	6	2	8
Winchester.	46	-	46	8	54
In town specified,	21	-	21	4	25
Not in town specified,	25	-	25	4	29
WOBURN.	178	2	180	43	223
In city specified,	92	1	93	29	122
Not in city specified,.	86	1	87	14	101
WORCESTER.	766	7	773	328	1,101
In city specified,	505	7	512	239	751
Not in city specified,.	261	-	261	89	350
Wrentham.	1	1	2	4	6
In town specified,	-	1	1	1	2
Not in town specified,	1	-	1	3	4
Yarmouth.	-	-	-	3	3
In town specified,	-	-	-	2	2
Not in town specified,	-	-	-	1	1
THE STATE.	17,575	388	17,963	8,709	26,672
In city or town specified,	11,594	356	11,950	6,113	18,063
Not in city or town specified,	5,981	32	6,013	2,596	8,609

Referring to the recapitulation for the State, we note that out of the 26,672 convictions for all crimes, 18,063 were committed by residents of the city or town in which the crime occurred, while 8,609 were committed by non-residents. With respect to drunkenness, 11,594 convictions were due to cases of drunkenness by residents of the city or town in which the crime occurred, while 5,981 were residents of other cities or towns. With respect to crimes other than drunkenness and liquor offences, 6,113 were committed in towns or cities where the criminal had a legal residence, and 2,596 were committed in towns or cities in which the criminal did not have a legal residence. In the city of Boston, confining the comparison to drunkenness only, out of the 7,146 convictions, 5,023 were due to citizens of Boston, and 2,123 to citizens of other towns or cities. Boston for the full period of 12 months was under license. In Cambridge, which for the entire time has been under no license, out of 741 convictions for drunkenness, 488 were of residents of the city, and 253, of non-residents. Other comparisons can easily be made from the table.

The final table shows the number of convictions due to crimes committed in Massachusetts during the year and by non-residents of the State.

Crimes committed by Non-residents of Massachusetts.

NATURE OF CRIME.	Number of Crimes committed in Massachusetts	Number of Crimes committed by Non-residents of Massachusetts
THE STATE.	26,672	1,322
Abortion, ...	3	–
Abuse of female child, ...	6	–
Adultery, ...	86	5
Appropriating horse or horse and team, . . .	20	–
Assault or assault and battery, ...	1,652	50
Assault, felonious, ...	12	–
Assault on officer, ...	69	2
Assault with intent to commit rape, . . .	4	–
Assault with weapon, ...	61	3
Breaking and entering, ...	393	24
Breaking glass, ...	82	4
Burglars' tools, having, ...	2	–
Burning buildings, ...	8	–
Cheating, ...	11	–

Crimes committed by Non-residents of Massachusetts — Continued.

NATURE OF CRIME.	Number of Crimes committed in Massachusetts	Number of Crimes committed by Non-residents of Massachusetts
THE STATE — Con.		
Common nuisance, ...	15	–
Contempt, ...	21	1
Counterfeiting or uttering counterfeits, . . .	9	–
Cruelty, ...	45	–
Disorderly house, keeping, ...	56	2
Disturbing a meeting, ...	12	–
Disturbing the peace, ...	960	31
Drunkard, common, ...	75	–
Drunkenness, ...	17,500	668
Embezzlement, ...	79	4
Escape, ...	22	2
Evading carfare, ...	45	3
False pretences (defrauding), ...	101	12
Forgery, ...	27	1
Fornication, ...	379	10
Fraud, ...	14	2
Gaming laws, violating, ...	54	1
House of ill-fame, ...	12	–
Incest, ...	3	–
Indecent assault, ...	23	2
Indecent exposure, ...	34	–
Indecent language, ...	10	1
Larceny, ...	2,107	164
Lewdness, ...	49	1
Liquor carrying, ...	4	–
Liquor keeping, ...	98	1
Liquor nuisance, ...	66	–
Liquor selling, ...	220	4
Malicious mischief, ...	78	5
Malicious trespass, ...	57	2
Manslaughter, ...	17	–
Murder, ...	4	–
Neglect of family, ...	154	3
Nightwalker, common, ...	97	7
Nuisance, maintaining, ...	3	–
Peddling, ...	42	2
Perjury, ...	3	–
Polygamy, ...	15	–
Profanity, ...	18	3
Rape, ...	5	–
Receiving stolen goods (or money), ...	57	2
Rescue, ...	5	–

Crimes committed by Non-residents of Massachusetts — Concluded.

NATURE OF CRIME.	Number of Crimes committed in Massachusetts	Number of Crimes committed by Non-residents of Massachusetts
THE STATE — Con.		
Riot or riotous assault, ...	5	-
Robbery, ...	46	2
Stubborn children, ...	46	-
Sunday law, violating, ...	11	-
Threats, ...	37	-
Truancy, ...	1	-
Vagabonds and idle persons (tramps), . . .	957	213
Violation of probation, ...	1	-
Violation of school law, ...	3	-
Violating town or city by-laws (ordinances), . .	241	11
Walking on railroad track, ...	254	71
Other offences, ...	66	3

Out of the 26,672 convictions for all offences, 1,322 were of non-residents of the State. Referring to the liquor offences, we note that of the 17,500 persons convicted of drunkenness, 668 were non-residents. Four persons out of 220 convicted of liquor selling were non-residents, and one non-resident was convicted of liquor keeping out of 98 persons who were convicted of that offence.

INSANITY.

The tables relative to the insane are practically the same in form as those which have been presented respecting pauperism and crime. The first table shows the sex and political condition by age periods of the insane persons included in the investigation.

Insanity; Sex and Political Condition: By Age Periods.

SEX AND POLITICAL CONDITION.	AGE PERIODS			
	5-9	10-14	15-19	20-29
1 Males.	1	3	41	232
2 Citizen born, ...	1	1	31	136
3 Naturalized, ...	–	–	–	11
4 Alien, ...	–	2	10	83
5 Unknown, ...	–	▼	–	2
6 Females.	3	2	28	173
7 Citizen born, ...	2	1	18	89
8 Alien, ...	1	1	10	84
9 Unknown, ...	–	–	–	–
10 BOTH SEXES.	4	5	69	405
11 Citizen born, ...	3	2	49	225
12 Naturalized, ...	–	–	–	11
13 Alien, ...	1	3	20	167
14 Unknown, ...	–	–	–	2

The total number of cases is 1,836, the males numbering 974 and the females 862. The number who were citizen born is 1,002; naturalized, 107; alien, 718; the facts as to political condition being unknown in nine cases only. It will be seen, therefore, that the citizen born are in excess of those of foreign birth, as the naturalized and alien taken together number but 825. Out of the whole, only 78 were under 20 years of age;

Insanity; Parent Nativity: By Sex and Political Condition.

PARENT NATIVITY.	MALES.				
	Citizen Born	Naturalized	Alien	Unknown	Total
1 Both parents *native*, ...	315	1	6	–	322
2 Both parents *foreign*, ...	163	103	303	7	576
3 Both parents *unknown*, . . .	32	2	4	1	39
4 Father *native*, mother *foreign*, . .	20	–	1	–	21
5 Father *foreign*, mother *native*, . .	8	1	1	–	10
6 Father *native*, mother *unknown*, . .	5	–	–	–	5
7 Father *foreign*, mother *unknown*, .	–	–	–	–	–
8 Father *unknown*, mother *native*, .	1	–	–	–	1
9 Father *unknown*, mother *foreign*,	–	–	–	–	–
10 Totals, ...	544	107	315	8	974

Insanity ; Sex and Political Condition: By Age Periods.

		AGE PERIODS				Totals	
30-39	40-49	50-59	60-79	80+	Unknown		
239	188	127	127	14	2	974	1
138	99	62	63	12	1	544	2
20	31	15	28	1	1	107	3
81	56	48	34	1	-	315	4
-	2	2	2	-	-	8	5
218	184	108	127	16	3	862	6
129	103	43	60	12	1	458	7
89	81	65	67	4	1	403	8
-	-	-	-	-	1	1	9
457	372	235	254	30	5	1,836	10
267	202	105	123	24	2	1,002	11
20	31	15	28	1	1	107	12
170	137	113	101	5	1	718	13
-	2	2	2	-	1	9	14

the number between 20 and 29 being 405; between 30 and 39, 457; between 40 and 49, 372; between 50 and 59, 235; between 60 and 79, 254; while 30 persons were 80 years of age or over. The number of males and females in each of the age periods named does not greatly differ.

The parent nativity of the insane is shown in the following table :

Insanity; Parent Nativity: By Sex and Political Condition.

FEMALES				BOTH SEXES					
Citizen Born	Alien	Un-known	Total	Citizen Born	Natural-ized	Alien	Un-known	Totals	
252	1	-	253	567	1	7	-	575	1
130	381	-	511	293	103	684	7	1,087	2
39	17	1	57	71	2	21	2	96	3
12	1	-	13	32	-	2	-	34	4
21	2	-	23	29	1	3	-	33	5
2	-	-	2	7	-	-	-	7	6
-	-	-	-	-	-	-	-	-	7
1	-	-	1	2	-	-	-	2	8
1	1	-	2	1	-	1	-	2	9
458	403	1	862	1,002	107	718	9	1,836	10

Out of the whole number, 575 had both parents native, while 1,087 had both parents foreign; the others, excluding 105 for whom the facts as to parent nativity were unknown, had either father or mother foreign. While the preceding table showed that the number of citizen-born insane was in excess of the number of foreign born, this table indicates that the foreign-born strain, when parent nativity is taken into account, was largely in excess. Of the insane who had entirely native parentage, 322 were males and 253 females. Those of entirely foreign parentage included 576 males and 511 females.

The next table shows the town or city from which the insane were committed, and also indicates the general habit of the insane, as to the use of liquor, by sexes.

Town or City from which Sent, and Liquor Habits of Insane.

COUNTIES, CITIES, TOWNS, AND SEX.	Excessive Drinkers	Other Drinkers	Unknown	Total Abstainers	Number of Insane
BARNSTABLE.	1	1	4	9	15
Barnstable, ...	–	–	1	2	3
Males, ...	–	–	1	1	2
Females, ...	–	–	–	1	1
Bourne, ...	–	–	2	–	2
Males, ...	–	–	1	–	1
Females, ...	–	–	1	–	1
Chatham, ...	–	–	–	1	1
Males, ...	–	–	–	–	–
Females, ...	–	–	–	1	1
Mashpee, ...	–	–	–	1	1
Males, ...	–	–	–	–	–
Females, ...	–	–	–	1	1
Provincetown, ...	–	–	1	3	4
Males, ...	–	–	1	1	2
Females, ...	–	–	–	2	2
Sandwich, ...	–	1	–	1	2
Males, ...	–	1	–	–	1
Females, ...	–	–	–	1	1
Yarmouth, ...	1	–	–	1	2
Males, ...	1	–	–	–	1
Females, ...	–	–	–	1	1
BERKSHIRE.	7	9	13	16	45
Adams, ...	1	–	2	–	3
Males, ...	1	–	1	–	2
Females, ...	–	–	1	–	1

Town or City from which Sent, and Liquor Habits of Insane — Continued.

COUNTIES, CITIES, TOWNS, AND SEX.	Excessive Drinkers	Other Drinkers	Unknown	Total Abstainers	Number of Insane
BERKSHIRE — Con.					
Cheshire, ...	-	-	1	-	1
Males, ...	-	-	-	-	-
Females, ...	-	-	1	-	1
Clarksburg, ...	-	-	-	2	2
Males, ...	-	-	-	-	-
Females, ...	-	-	-	2	2
Dalton, ...	-	-	-	1	1
Males, ...	-	-	-	-	-
Females, ...	-	-	-	1	1
Great Barrington, . . .	-	-	-	4	4
Males, ...	-	-	-	2	2
Females, ...	-	-	-	2	2
Hinsdale, ...	-	-	2	-	2
Males, ...	-	-	1	-	1
Females, ...	-	-	1	-	1
Lee, ...	1	2	-	-	3
Males, ...	1	2	-	-	3
Females, ...	-	-	-	-	-
NORTH ADAMS, . . .	2	2	5	3	12
Males, ...	1	1	3	-	5
Females, ...	1	1	2	3	7
Peru, ...	1	-	1	-	2
Males, ...	1	-	-	-	1
Females, ...	-	-	1	-	1
PITTSFIELD, ...	2	2	2	4	10
Males, ...	2	1	-	-	3
Females, ...	-	1	2	4	7
Richmond, ...	-	1	-	-	1
Males, ...	-	1	-	-	1
Females, ...	-	-	-	-	-
Stockbridge, ...	-	1	-	-	1
Males, ...	-	-	-	-	-
Females, ...	-	1	-	-	1
West Stockbridge, . . .	-	-	-	1	1
Males, ...	-	-	-	-	-
Females, ...	-	-	-	1	1
Williamstown, ...	-	1	-	1	2
Males, ...	-	-	-	-	-
Females, ...	-	1	-	1	2
BRISTOL.	22	35	52	57	166
Attleborough, ...	-	1	3	3	7
Males, ...	-	-	2	1	3
Females, ...	-	1	1	2	4

Town or City from which Sent, and Liquor Habits of Insane — Continued.

COUNTIES, CITIES, TOWNS, AND SEX.	Excessive Drinkers	Other Drinkers	Unknown	Total Abstainers	Number of Insane
BRISTOL — Con.					
Berkley,	-	1	-	-	1
Males,	-	1	-	-	1
Females,	-	-	-	-	-
Dartmouth,	-	-	-	1	1
Males,	-	-	-	1	1
Females,	-	-	-	-	-
Easton,	-	-	1	2	3
Males,	-	-	1	1	2
Females,	-	-	-	1	1
Fairhaven,	2	-	-	1	3
Males,	2	-	-	-	2
Females,	-	-	-	1	1
FALL RIVER,	14	12	32	14	72
Males,	8	11	9	5	33
Females,	6	1	23	9	39
Mansfield,	-	1	-	-	1
Males,	-	1	-	-	1
Females,	-	-	-	-	-
NEW BEDFORD,	3	12	13	15	43
Males,	2	8	7	3	20
Females,	1	4	6	12	23
North Attleborough,	-	-	1	2	3
Males,	-	-	1	-	1
Females,	-	-	-	2	2
Norton,	-	2	-	-	2
Males,	-	2	-	-	2
Females,	-	-	-	-	-
Raynham,	-	-	-	1	1
Males,	-	-	-	-	-
Females,	-	-	-	1	1
Rehoboth,	-	-	-	1	1
Males,	-	-	-	-	-
Females,	-	-	-	1	1
Seekonk,	-	-	-	1	1
Males,	-	-	-	-	-
Females,	-	-	-	1	1
Somerset,	-	-	-	1	1
Males,	-	-	-	-	-
Females,	-	-	-	1	1
TAUNTON,	3	6	2	15	26
Males,	1	6	1	7	15
Females,	2	-	1	8	11

Town or City from which Sent, and Liquor Habits of Insane — Continued.

COUNTIES, CITIES, TOWNS, AND SEX.	Excessive Drinkers	Other Drinkers	Unknown	Total Abstainers	Number of Insane
DUKES.	-	-	-	3	3
Edgartown, ...	-	-	-	2	2
Males, ...	-	-	-	-	-
Females, ...	-	-	-	2	2
Tisbury, ...	-	-	-	1	1
Males, ...	-	-	-	-	-
Females, ...	-	-	-	1	1
ESSEX.	50	28	112	76	266
Amesbury, ...	-	2	-	2	4
Males, ...	-	1	-	1	2
Females, ...	-	1	-	1	2
Andover, ...	-	-	1	1	2
Males, ...	-	-	1	-	1
Females, ...	-	-	-	1	1
BEVERLY, ...	-	1	1	1	3
Males, ...	-	1	1	-	2
Females, ...	-	-	-	1	1
Boxford, ...	-	-	-	1	1
Males, ...	-	-	-	-	-
Females, ...	-	-	-	1	1
Bradford, ...	-	-	1	2	3
Males, ...	-	-	1	2	3
Females, ...	-	-	-	-	-
Danvers, ...	-	2	-	6	8
Males, ...	-	1	-	2	3
Females, ...	-	1	-	4	5
GLOUCESTER, ...	3	1	7	5	16
Males, ...	2	1	5	2	10
Females, ...	1	-	2	3	6
Groveland, ...	-	1	2	-	3
Males, ...	-	1	1	-	2
Females, ...	-	-	1	-	1
Hamilton, ...	-	-	2	-	2
Males, ...	-	-	2	-	2
Females, ...	-	-	-	-	-
HAVERHILL, ...	1	4	8	8	21
Males, ...	1	4	7	1	13
Females, ...	-	-	1	7	8
Ipswich, ...	1	-	2	1	4
Males, ...	1	-	1	-	2
Females, ...	-	-	1	1	2

Town or City from which Sent, and Liquor Habits of Insane — Continued.

COUNTIES, CITIES, TOWNS, AND SEX.	Excessive Drinkers	Other Drinkers	Unknown	Total Abstainers	Number of Insane
ESSEX — Con.					
LAWRENCE, . . .	10	6	24	15	55
Males, ...	7	6	10	3	26
Females, . . .	3	-	14	12	29
LYNN, ...	17	4	26	15	62
Males, ...	16	4	12	10	42
Females, ...	1	-	14	5	20
Manchester, ...	-	-	2	-	2
Males, ...	-	-	2	-	2
Females, ...	-	-	-	-	-
Marblehead, ...	-	-	1	2	3
Males, ...	-	-	-	-	-
Females, ...	-	-	1	2	3
Merrimac, ...	-	-	-	1	1
Males, ...	-	-	-	-	-
Females, ...	-	-	-	1	1
Methuen, ...	1	2	3	1	7
Males, ...	-	2	-	-	2
Females, ...	1	-	3	1	5
Middleton, ...	-	-	1	-	1
Males, ...	-	-	1	-	1
Females, ...	-	-	-	-	-
Newbury, ...	-	-	3	-	3
Males, ...	-	-	3	-	3
Females, ...	-	-	-	-	-
NEWBURYPORT, . . .	3	1	3	-	7
Males, ...	3	-	1	-	4
Females, ...	-	1	2	-	3
North Andover, . . .	1	-	-	-	1
Males, ...	1	-	-	-	1
Females, ...	-	-	-	-	-
Peabody, ...	4	1	2	1	8
Males, ...	3	1	2	1	7
Females, ...	1	-	-	-	1
Rockport, ...	-	-	1	1	2
Males, ...	-	-	1	-	1
Females, ...	-	-	-	1	1
Rowley, ...	-	-	-	1	1
Males, ...	-	-	-	1	1
Females, ...	-	-	-	-	-
SALEM, ...	9	3	17	8	37
Males, ...	7	3	13	4	27
Females, ...	2	-	4	4	10

Town or City from which Sent, and Liquor Habits of Insane — Continued.

COUNTIES, CITIES, TOWNS, AND SEX.	Excessive Drinkers	Other Drinkers	Unknown	Total Abstainers	Number of Insane
ESSEX — Con.					
Salisbury, ...	-	-	2	1	3
Males, ...	-	-	1	-	1
Females, ...	-	-	1	1	2
Saugus, ...	-	-	-	1	1
Males, ...	-	-	-	-	-
Females, ...	-	-	-	1	1
Swampscott, ...	-	-	2	1	3
Males, ...	-	-	2	-	2
Females, ...	-	-	-	1	1
Wenham, ...	-	-	1	1	2
Males, ...	-	-	1	-	1
Females, ...	-	-	-	1	1
FRANKLIN.	4	6	4	6	20
Bernardston, ...	-	-	1	-	1
Males, ...	-	-	1	-	1
Females, ...	-	-	-	-	-
Buckland, ...	-	1	-	-	1
Males, ...	-	1	-	-	1
Females, ...	-	-	-	-	-
Charlemont, ...	-	1	1	-	2
Males, ...	-	1	1	-	2
Females, ...	-	-	-	-	-
Colrain, ...	-	-	-	1	1
Males, ...	-	-	-	-	-
Females, ...	-	-	-	1	1
Deerfield, ...	1	1	-	2	4
Males, ...	1	1	-	-	2
Females, ...	-	-	-	2	2
Gill, ...	-	-	1	1	2
Males, ...	-	-	1	1	2
Females, ...	-	-	-	-	-
Greenfield, ...	1	1	-	1	3
Males, ...	1	1	-	1	3
Females, ...	-	-	-	-	-
New Salem, ...	-	-	-	1	1
Males, ...	-	-	-	1	1
Females, ...	-	-	-	-	-
Northfield, ...	2	-	-	-	2
Males, ...	2	-	-	-	2
Females, ...	-	-	-	-	-

Town or City from which Sent, and Liquor Habits of Insane — Continued.

COUNTIES, CITIES, TOWNS, AND SEX.	Excessive Drinkers	Other Drinkers	Unknown	Total Abstainers	Number of Insane
FRANKLIN — Con.					
Orange, ...	–	1	–	–	1
Males, ...	–	1	–	–	1
Females, ...	–	–	–	–	–
Shelburne, ...	–	–	1	–	1
Males, ...	–	–	1	–	1
Females, ...	–	–	–	–	–
Wendell, ...	–	1	–	–	1
Males, ...	–	1	–	–	1
Females, ...	–	–	–	–	–
HAMPDEN.	21	39	10	41	111
CHICOPEE, ...	3	2	–	2	7
Males, ...	2	1	–	1	4
Females, ...	1	1	–	1	3
East Longmeadow, . . .	–	1	–	–	1
Males, ...	–	–	–	–	–
Females, ...	–	1	–	–	1
HOLYOKE, ...	6	13	–	11	30
Males, ...	4	11	–	1	16
Females, ...	2	2	–	10	14
Monson, ...	1	1	–	–	2
Males, ...	1	–	–	–	1
Females, ...	–	1	–	–	1
Montgomery, ...	–	–	1	–	1
Males, ...	–	–	1	–	1
Females, ...	–	–	–	–	–
Palmer, ...	1	2	1	5	9
Males, ...	–	2	–	2	4
Females, ...	1	–	1	3	5
Russell, ...	1	1	–	–	2
Males, ...	1	1	–	–	2
Females, ...	–	–	–	–	–
Southwick, ...	–	–	2	–	2
Males, ...	–	–	2	–	2
Females, ...	–	–	–	–	–
SPRINGFIELD, ...	6	15	3	19	43
Males, ...	6	14	2	6	28
Females, ...	–	1	1	13	15
Tolland, ...	–	–	1	–	1
Males, ...	–	–	1	–	1
Females, ...	–	–	–	–	–

Town or City from which Sent, and Liquor Habits of Insane — Continued.

COUNTIES, CITIES, TOWNS, AND SEX.	Excessive Drinkers	Other Drinkers	Unknown	Total Abstainers	Number of Insane
HAMPDEN — Con.					
Westfield,	2	2	2	3	9
Males,	2	2	2	2	8
Females,	-	-	-	1	1
West Springfield,	1	-	-	1	2
Males,	1	-	-	-	1
Females,	-	-	-	1	1
Wilbraham,	-	2	-	-	2
Males,	-	2	-	-	2
Females,	-	-	-	-	-
HAMPSHIRE.	3	6	8	14	31
Amherst,	-	1	-	-	1
Males,	-	1	-	-	1
Females,	-	-	-	-	-
Belchertown,	-	1	-	-	1
Males,	-	1	-	-	1
Females,	-	-	-	-	-
Chesterfield,	-	-	-	1	1
Males,	-	-	-	-	-
Females,	-	-	-	1	1
Easthampton,	-	-	3	-	3
Males,	-	-	2	-	2
Females,	-	-	1	-	1
Goshen,	-	-	-	1	1
Males,	-	-	-	-	-
Females,	-	-	-	1	1
Hatfield,	-	-	1	-	1
Males,	-	-	-	-	-
Females,	-	-	1	-	1
Huntington,	-	-	-	1	1
Males,	-	-	-	-	-
Females,	-	-	-	1	1
NORTHAMPTON,	1	4	2	5	12
Males,	1	2	1	-	4
Females,	-	2	1	5	8
Southampton,	-	-	1	-	1
Males,	-	-	1	-	1
Females,	-	-	-	-	-
South Hadley,	2	-	-	3	5
Males,	2	-	-	-	2
Females,	-	-	-	3	3

Town or City from which Sent, and Liquor Habits of Insane — Continued.

COUNTIES, CITIES, TOWNS, AND SEX.	Excessive Drinkers	Other Drinkers	Unknown	Total Abstainers	Number of Insane
HAMPSHIRE — Con.					
Ware, ...	-	-	1	1	2
Males, ...	-	-	1	1	2
Females, ...	-	-	-	-	-
Williamsburg, ...	-	-	-	2	2
Males, ...	-	-	-	-	-
Females, ...	-	-	-	2	2
MIDDLESEX.	46	60	109	129	344
Acton, ...	-	-	1	-	1
Males, ...	-	-	1	-	1
Females, ...	-	-	-	-	-
Arlington, ...	-	1	1	1	3
Males, ...	-	1	-	1	2
Females, ...	-	-	1	-	1
Ayer, ...	-	-	2	-	2
Males, ...	-	-	1	-	1
Females, ...	-	-	1	-	1
Bedford, ...	-	-	1	-	1
Males, ...	-	-	-	-	-
Females, ...	-	-	1	-	1
Belmont, ...	-	-	-	1	1
Males, ...	-	-	-	-	-
Females, ...	-	-	-	1	1
CAMBRIDGE, ...	7	12	11	22	52
Males, ...	6	10	4	6	26
Females, ...	1	2	7	16	26
Concord, ...	-	-	-	1	1
Males, ...	-	-	-	-	-
Females, ...	-	-	-	1	1
EVERETT, ...	3	-	6	2	11
Males, ...	3	-	2	-	5
Females, ...	-	-	4	2	6
Framingham, ...	-	-	1	2	3
Males, ...	-	-	-	1	1
Females, ...	-	-	1	1	2
Groton, ...	-	-	1	1	2
Males, ...	-	-	-	-	-
Females, ...	-	-	1	1	2
Holliston, ...	-	1	2	2	5
Males, ...	-	1	1	1	3
Females, ...	-	-	1	1	2

Town or City from which Sent, and Liquor Habits of Insane — Continued.

COUNTIES, CITIES, TOWNS, AND SEX.	Excessive Drinkers	Other Drinkers	Unknown	Total Abstainers	Number of Insane
MIDDLESEX — Con.					
Hopkinton, ...	–	–	2	1	3
Males, ...	–	–	2	–	2
Females, ...	–	–	–	1	1
Hudson, ...	–	–	–	1	1
Males, ...	–	–	–	–	–
Females, ...	–	–	–	1	1
Lexington, ...	1	–	2	–	3
Males, ...	1	–	2	–	3
Females, ...	–	–	–	–	–
Littleton, ...	–	–	2	–	2
Males, ...	–	–	2	–	2
Females, ...	–	–	–	–	–
LOWELL, ...	7	9	23	14	53
Males, ...	7	6	13	3	29
Females, ...	–	3	10	11	24
MALDEN, ...	5	9	1	13	28
Males, ...	4	7	1	4	16
Females, ...	1	2	–	9	12
MARLBOROUGH, . . .	3	1	8	3	15
Males, ...	3	1	6	1	11
Females, ...	–	–	2	2	4
Maynard, ...	–	–	–	3	3
Males, ...	–	–	–	–	–
Females, ...	–	–	–	3	3
MEDFORD, ...	1	1	–	4	6
Males, ...	–	1	–	1	2
Females, ...	1	–	–	3	4
Melrose, ...	–	4	–	2	6
Males, ...	–	4	–	1	5
Females, ...	–	–	–	1	1
Natick, ...	1	–	5	–	6
Males, ...	1	–	2	–	3
Females, ...	–	–	3	–	3
NEWTON, ...	2	5	9	13	29
Males, ...	2	4	4	3	13
Females, ...	–	1	5	10	16
Pepperell, ...	–	–	3	2	5
Males, ...	–	–	3	–	3
Females, ...	–	–	–	2	2
Reading, ...	–	–	–	4	4
Males, ...	–	–	–	2	2
Females, ...	–	–	–	2	2

Town or City from which Sent, and Liquor Habits of Insane — Continued.

COUNTIES, CITIES, TOWNS, AND SEX.	Excessive Drinkers	Other Drinkers	Unknown	Total Abstainers	Number of Insane
MIDDLESEX — Con.					
Sherborn, ...	1	–	–	3	4
Males, ...	–	–	–	–	–
Females, ...	1	–	–	3	4
Shirley, ...	–	–	–	1	1
Males, ...	–	–	–	–	–
Females, ...	–	–	–	1	1
SOMERVILLE, ...	8	4	17	9	38
Males, ...	7	2	9	2	20
Females, ...	1	2	8	7	18
Stoneham, ...	–	2	–	2	4
Males, ...	–	2	–	–	2
Females, ...	–	–	–	2	2
Stow, ...	–	–	–	1	1
Males, ...	–	–	–	–	–
Females, ...	–	–	–	1	1
Tewksbury, ...	1	2	2	3	8
Males, ...	1	1	–	–	2
Females, ...	–	1	2	3	6
Townsend, ...	–	–	1	–	1
Males, ...	–	–	–	–	–
Females, ...	–	–	1	–	1
Tyngsborough, . . .	–	–	–	1	1
Males, ...	–	–	–	–	–
Females, ...	–	–	–	1	1
Wakefield, ...	–	1	–	4	5
Males, ...	–	1	–	–	1
Females, ...	–	–	–	4	4
WALTHAM, ...	2	3	3	4	12
Males, ...	2	3	2	3	10
Females, ...	–	–	1	1	2
Watertown, ...	–	–	3	–	3
Males, ...	–	–	3	–	3
Females, ...	–	–	–	–	–
Wilmington, ...	–	1	1	–	2
Males, ...	–	1	–	–	1
Females, ...	–	–	1	–	1
Winchester, ...	3	–	–	2	5
Males, ...	3	–	–	–	3
Females, ...	–	–	–	2	2
WOBURN, ...	1	4	1	7	13
Males, ...	1	2	1	1	5
Females, ...	–	2	–	6	8

Town or City from which Sent, and Liquor Habits of Insane — Continued.

COUNTIES, CITIES, TOWNS, AND SEX.	Excessive Drinkers	Other Drinkers	Unknown	Total Abstainers	Number of Insane
NANTUCKET.	1	–	1	1	3
Nantucket, ...	1	–	1	1	3
Males, ...	1	–	1	–	2
Females, ...	–	–	–	1	1
NORFOLK.	7	14	20	35	76
Bellingham, ...	–	–	1	–	1
Males, ...	–	–	–	–	–
Females, ...	–	–	1	–	1
Braintree, ...	–	–	2	2	4
Males, ...	–	–	1	1	2
Females, ...	–	–	1	1	2
Brookline, ...	1	1	–	1	3
Males, ...	1	1	–	–	2
Females, ...	–	–	–	1	1
Canton, ...	–	–	1	1	2
Males, ...	–	–	–	1	1
Females, ...	–	–	1	–	1
Cohasset, ...	–	–	–	1	1
Males, ...	–	–	–	–	–
Females, ...	–	–	–	1	1
Dedham, ...	2	2	–	2	6
Males, ...	2	2	–	–	4
Females, ...	–	–	–	2	2
Dover, ...	–	–	–	1	1
Males, ...	–	–	–	–	–
Females, ...	–	–	–	1	1
Foxborough, ...	2	–	–	1	3
Males, ...	2	–	–	–	2
Females, ...	–	–	–	1	1
Franklin, ...	–	–	1	1	2
Males, ...	–	–	1	–	1
Females, ...	–	–	–	1	1
Holbrook, ...	–	1	–	–	1
Males, ...	–	–	–	–	–
Females, ...	–	1	–	–	1
Hyde Park, ...	–	1	3	8	12
Males, ...	–	–	2	2	4
Females, ...	–	1	1	6	8
Medfield, ...	–	–	2	–	2
Males, ...	–	–	1	–	1
Females, ...	–	–	1	–	1

Town or City from which Sent, and Liquor Habits of Insane — Continued.

COUNTIES, CITIES, TOWNS, AND SEX.	Excessive Drinkers	Other Drinkers	Unknown	Total Abstainers	Number of Insane
NORFOLK — Con.					
Milton,	–	–	1	1	2
Males,	–	–	1	1	2
Females,	–	–	–	–	–
Needham,	–	–	1	1	2
Males,	–	–	1	1	2
Females,	–	–	–	–	–
Norwood,	–	1	–	1	2
Males,	–	–	–	–	–
Females,	–	1	–	1	2
QUINCY,	2	2	1	4	9
Males,	2	2	–	–	4
Females,	–	–	1	4	5
Randolph,	–	1	2	1	4
Males,	–	1	–	1	2
Females,	–	–	2	–	2
Walpole,	–	–	2	2	4
Males,	–	–	2	–	2
Females,	–	–	–	2	2
Wellesley,	–	2	–	2	4
Males,	–	2	–	–	2
Females,	–	–	–	2	2
Weymouth,	–	1	2	4	7
Males,	–	–	1	2	3
Females,	–	1	1	2	4
Wrentham,	–	2	1	1	4
Males,	–	2	–	–	2
Females,	–	–	1	1	2
PLYMOUTH.	14	8	17	26	65
Abington,	–	1	–	–	1
Males,	–	1	–	–	1
Females,	–	–	–	–	–
Bridgewater,	9	1	9	1	20
Males,	9	1	9	1	20
Females,	–	–	–	–	–
BROCKTON,	1	–	1	12	14
Males,	–	–	1	9	10
Females,	1	–	–	3	4
Duxbury,	–	–	–	3	3
Males,	–	–	–	1	1
Females,	–	–	–	2	2

Town or City from which Sent, and Liquor Habits of Insane — Continued

COUNTIES, CITIES, TOWNS, AND SEX.	Excessive Drinkers	Other Drinkers	Unknown	Total Abstainers	Number of Insane
PLYMOUTH — Con.					
Hanson,	-	-	2	-	2
Males,	-	-	1	-	1
Females,	-	-	1	-	1
Kingston,	-	-	-	1	1
Males,	-	-	-	-	-
Females,	-	-	-	1	1
Lakeville,	-	-	1	-	1
Males,	-	-	1	-	1
Females,	-	-	-	-	-
Marion,	-	-	-	1	1
Males,	-	-	-	1	1
Females,	-	-	-	-	-
Marshfield,	-	-	1	-	1
Males,	-	-	1	-	1
Females,	-	-	-	-	-
Middleborough,	-	1	-	2	3
Males,	-	1	-	2	3
Females,	-	-	-	-	-
Plymouth,	3	2	-	4	9
Males,	2	1	-	1	4
Females,	1	1	-	3	5
Rockland,	-	2	-	-	2
Males,	-	1	-	-	1
Females,	-	1	-	-	1
Scituate,	-	-	1	-	1
Males,	-	-	1	-	1
Females,	-	-	-	-	-
Wareham,	-	1	1	-	2
Males,	-	-	-	-	-
Females,	-	1	1	-	2
Whitman,	1	-	1	2	4
Males,	1	-	-	1	2
Females,	-	-	1	1	2
SUFFOLK.	94	137	59	175	465
BOSTON,	89	127	55	159	430
Males,	58	82	32	22	194
Females,	31	45	23	137	236
CHELSEA,	5	9	4	15	33
Males,	4	7	2	6	19
Females,	1	2	2	9	14

Town or City from which Sent, and Liquor Habits of Insane — Continued.

COUNTIES, CITIES, TOWNS, AND SEX.	Excessive Drinkers	Other Drinkers	Unknown	Total Abstainers	Number of Insane
SUFFOLK — Con.					
Revere, ...	-	-	-	1	1
Males, ...	-	-	-	1	1
Females, ...	-	-	-	-	-
Winthrop, ...	-	1	-	-	1
Males, ...	-	1	-	-	1
Females, ...	-	-	-	-	-
WORCESTER.	39	17	77	84	217
Ashburnham, ...	1	1	1	-	3
Males, ...	1	1	1	-	3
Females, ...	-	-	-	-	-
Athol, ...	-	-	1	2	3
Males, ...	-	-	-	-	-
Females, ...	-	-	1	2	3
Barre, ...	-	-	-	1	1
Males, ...	-	-	-	-	-
Females, ...	-	-	-	1	1
Blackstone, ...	1	-	5	1	7
Males, ...	1	-	1	-	2
Females, ...	-	-	4	1	5
Bolton, ...	-	1	-	-	1
Males, ...	-	-	-	-	-
Females, ...	-	1	-	-	1
Brookfield, ...	-	-	-	3	3
Males, ...	-	-	-	2	2
Females, ...	-	-	-	1	1
Clinton, ...	1	1	3	5	10
Males, ...	1	1	1	1	4
Females, ...	-	-	2	4	6
FITCHBURG, ...	-	-	6	2	8
Males, ...	-	-	5	-	5
Females, ...	-	-	1	2	3
Gardner, ...	-	-	-	2	2
Males, ...	-	-	-	2	2
Females, ...	-	-	-	-	-
Grafton, ...	-	-	2	2	4
Males, ...	-	-	-	2	2
Females, ...	-	-	2	-	2
Harvard, ...	-	-	-	1	1
Males, ...	-	-	-	-	-
Females, ...	-	-	-	1	1
Lancaster, ...	1	-	-	4	5
Males, ...	1	-	-	1	2
Females, ...	-	-	-	3	3

Town or City from which Sent, and Liquor Habits of Insane — Continued.

COUNTIES, CITIES, TOWNS, AND SEX.	Excessive Drinkers	Other Drinkers	Unknown	Total Abstainers	Number of Insane
WORCESTER — Con.					
Leominster,	–	–	–	3	3
Males,	–	–	–	2	2
Females,	–	–	–	1	1
Milford,	3	2	2	–	7
Males,	3	2	1	–	6
Females,	–	–	1	–	1
Millbury,	–	1	–	4	5
Males,	–	1	–	2	3
Females,	–	–	–	2	2
Northborough,	–	–	–	1	1
Males,	–	–	–	–	–
Females,	–	–	–	1	1
Northbridge,	–	–	1	2	3
Males,	–	–	–	1	1
Females,	–	–	1	1	2
North Brookfield,	–	–	–	2	2
Males,	–	–	–	–	–
Females,	–	–	–	2	2
Phillipston,	–	–	–	2	2
Males,	–	–	–	–	–
Females,	–	–	–	2	2
Southborough,	–	–	1	–	1
Males,	–	–	1	–	1
Females,	–	–	–	–	–
Southbridge,	2	–	–	5	7
Males,	2	–	–	2	4
Females,	–	–	–	3	3
Spencer,	2	–	5	–	7
Males,	2	–	4	–	6
Females,	–	–	1	–	1
Sterling,	–	–	–	1	1
Males,	–	–	–	–	–
Females,	–	–	–	1	1
Sturbridge,	–	–	–	1	1
Males,	–	–	–	–	–
Females,	–	–	–	1	1
Templeton,	–	1	1	–	2
Males,	–	–	1	–	1
Females,	–	1	–	–	1
Uxbridge,	–	–	–	1	1
Males,	–	–	–	–	–
Females,	–	–	–	1	1
Warren,	–	1	–	1	2
Males,	–	1	–	1	2
Females,	–	–	–	–	–

Town or City from which Sent, and Liquor Habits of Insane — Concluded.

COUNTIES, CITIES, TOWNS, AND SEX.	Excessive Drinkers	Other Drinkers	Unknown	Total Abstainers	Number of Insane
WORCESTER — Con.					
Webster, ...	2	-	-	7	9
Males, ...	2	-	-	4	6
Females, ...	-	-	-	3	3
Westborough, ...	-	1	2	3	6
Males, ...	-	1	2	1	4
Females, ...	-	-	-	2	2
West Boylston, ...	-	-	1	-	1
Males, ...	-	-	1	-	1
Females, ...	-	-	-	-	-
WORCESTER, ...	24	8	44	23	99
Males, ...	21	7	23	8	59
Females, ...	3	1	21	15	40
Not given, ...	2	-	2	5	9
Males, ...	2	-	1	3	6
Females, ...	-	-	1	2	3

RECAPITULATION.

COUNTIES, SEX, AND THE STATE.	Excessive Drinkers	Other Drinkers	Unknown	Total Abstainers	Number of Insane
BARNSTABLE.	1	1	4	9	15
Males, ...	1	1	3	2	7
Females, ...	-	-	1	7	8
BERKSHIRE.	7	9	13	16	45
Males, ...	6	5	5	2	18
Females, ...	1	4	8	14	27
BRISTOL.	22	35	52	57	166
Males, ...	13	29	21	18	81
Females, ...	9	6	31	39	85
DUKES.	-	-	-	3	3
Males, ...	-	-	-	-	-
Females, ...	-	-	-	3	3
ESSEX.	50	28	112	76	266
Males, ...	41	25	68	27	161
Females, ...	9	3	44	49	105

RECAPITULATION — Concluded.

COUNTIES, SEX, AND THE STATE.	Excessive Drinkers	Other Drinkers	Unknown	Total Abstainers	Number of Insane
FRANKLIN.	4	6	4	6	20
Males, ...	4	6	4	3	17
Females, ...	-	-	-	3	3
HAMPDEN.	21	39	10	41	111
Males, ...	17	33	8	12	70
Females, ...	4	6	2	29	41
HAMPSHIRE.	3	6	8	14	31
Males, ...	3	4	5	1	13
Females, ...	-	2	3	13	18
MIDDLESEX.	46	60	109	129	344
Males, ...	41	47	59	30	177
Females, ...	5	13	50	99	167
NANTUCKET.	1	-	1	1	3
Males, ...	1	-	1	-	2
Females, ...	-	-	-	1	1
NORFOLK.	7	14	20	35	76
Males, ...	7	10	10	9	36
Females, ...	-	4	10	26	40
PLYMOUTH.	14	8	17	26	65
Males, ...	12	5	14	16	47
Females, ...	2	3	3	10	18
SUFFOLK.	94	137	59	175	465
Males, ...	62	90	34	29	215
Females, ...	32	47	25	146	250
WORCESTER.	39	17	77	84	217
Males, ...	36	14	42	32	124
Females, ...	3	3	35	52	93
NOT GIVEN.	2	-	2	5	9
Males, ...	2	-	1	3	6
Females, ...	-	-	1	2	3
THE STATE.	311	360	488	677	1,836
Males, ...	246	269	275	184	974
Females, ...	65	91	213	493	862

For the State as a whole, the total number of insane being 1,836, the number of excessive drinkers was found to be 311; the number of other drinkers, that is, not excessive, 360; and the number of total abstainers, 677. Expressed in percentages, 16.94 per cent were excessive drinkers, 19.61 per cent drinkers of other degree, and 36.87 per cent total abstainers. But, as information upon the points covered by this table could not be ascertained in 488 cases, 26.58 per cent of the whole number, such a comparison is somewhat misleading. Disregarding the unknown cases, therefore, there remain 1,348 insane persons whose habits as to the use of liquor were ascertained. Of these, 699 were males and 649 females. Basing the comparison on these known cases, we find that 35.48 per cent of the males were excessive drinkers and 26.32 per cent total abstainers. Of the females, 10.02 per cent were excessive drinkers and 75.96 per cent total abstainers.

A similar table follows relating to the parents of the insane.

Town or City from which Sent, and Liquor Habits of Parents of Insane.

COUNTIES, CITIES, TOWNS, AND SEX.	One or Both Parents Intemperate	One or Both Parents Total Abstainers	Liquor Habits of Both Parents Unknown	Number of Insane
BARNSTABLE.	2	2	11	15
Barnstable, ...	–	1	2	3
Males, ...	–	1	1	2
Females, ...	–	–	1	1
Bourne, ...	–	–	2	2
Males, ...	–	–	1	1
Females, ...	–	–	1	1
Chatham, ...	–	1	–	1
Males, ...	–	–	–	–
Females, ...	–	1	–	1
Mashpee, ...	–	–	1	1
Males, ...	–	–	–	–
Females, ...	–	–	1	1
Provincetown, ...	1	–	3	4
Males, ...	1	–	1	2
Females, ...	–	–	2	2
Sandwich, ...	–	–	2	2
Males, ...	–	–	1	1
Females, ...	–	–	1	1
Yarmouth, ...	1	–	1	2
Males, ...	–	–	1	1
Females, ...	1	–	–	1

Town or City from which Sent, and Liquor Habits of Parents of Insane
— Continued.

COUNTIES, CITIES, TOWNS, AND SEX.	One or Both Parents Intemperate	One or Both Parents Total Abstainers	Liquor Habits of Both Parents Unknown	Number of Insane
BERKSHIRE.	14	10	21	45
Adams, ...	-	-	3	3
Males, ...	-	-	2	2
Females, ...	-	-	1	1
Cheshire, ...	1	-	-	1
Males, ...	-	-	-	-
Females, ...	1	-	-	1
Clarksburg, ...	2	-	-	2
Males, ...	-	-	-	-
Females, ...	2	-	-	2
Dalton, ...	1	-	-	1
Males, ...	-	-	-	-
Females, ...	1	-	-	1
Great Barrington, ...	-	-	4	4
Males, ...	-	-	2	2
Females, ...	-	-	2	2
Hinsdale, ...	-	-	2	2
Males, ...	-	-	1	1
Females, ...	-	-	1	1
Lee, ...	2	1	-	3
Males, ...	2	1	-	3
Females, ...	-	-	-	-
NORTH ADAMS, ...	3	2	7	12
Males, ...	1	-	4	5
Females, ...	2	2	3	7
Peru, ...	-	-	2	2
Males, ...	-	-	1	1
Females, ...	-	-	1	1
PITTSFIELD, ...	3	4	3	10
Males, ...	2	-	1	3
Females, ...	1	4	2	7
Richmond, ...	-	1	-	1
Males, ...	-	1	-	1
Females, ...	-	-	-	-
Stockbridge, ...	1	-	-	1
Males, ...	-	-	-	-
Females, ...	1	-	-	1
West Stockbridge, ...	1	-	-	1
Males, ...	-	-	-	-
Females, ...	1	-	-	1
Williamstown, ...	-	2	-	2
Males, ...	-	-	-	-
Females, ...	-	2	-	2

Town or City from which Sent, and Liquor Habits of Parents of Insane
— Continued.

COUNTIES, CITIES, TOWNS, AND SEX.	One or Both Parents Intemperate	One or Both Parents Total Abstainers	Liquor Habits of Both Parents Unknown	Number of Insane
BRISTOL.	43	38	85	166
Attleborough, ...	1	3	3	7
Males, ...	–	1	2	3
Females, ...	1	2	1	4
Berkley, ...	1	–	–	1
Males, ...	1	–	–	1
Females, ...	–	–	–	–
Dartmouth, ...	–	1	–	1
Males, ...	–	1	–	1
Females, ...	–	–	–	–
Easton, ...	1	1	1	3
Males, ...	–	1	1	2
Females, ...	1	–	–	1
Fairhaven, ...	1	–	2	3
Males, ...	1	–	1	2
Females, ...	–	–	1	1
FALL RIVER, ...	14	10	48	72
Males, ...	4	5	24	33
Females, ...	10	5	24	39
Mansfield, ...	1	–	–	1
Males, ...	1	–	–	1
Females, ...	–	–	–	–
NEW BEDFORD, ...	10	8	25	43
Males, ...	5	4	11	20
Females, ...	5	4	14	23
North Attleborough, . . .	1	1	1	3
Males, ...	1	–	–	1
Females, ...	–	1	1	2
Norton, ...	1	1	–	2
Males, ...	1	1	–	2
Females, ...	–	–	–	–
Raynham, ...	–	–	1	1
Males, ...	–	–	–	–
Females, ...	–	–	1	1
Rehoboth, ...	–	–	1	1
Males, ...	–	–	–	–
Females, ...	–	–	1	1
Seekonk, ...	–	–	1	1
Males, ...	–	–	–	–
Females, ...	–	–	1	1
Somerset, ...	–	1	–	1
Males, ...	–	–	–	–
Females, ...	–	1	–	1

Town or City from which Sent, and Liquor Habits of Parents of Insane
— Continued.

COUNTIES, CITIES, TOWNS, AND SEX.	One or Both Parents Intemperate	One or Both Parents Total Abstainers	Liquor Habits of Both Parents Unknown	Number of Insane
BRISTOL — Con.				
TAUNTON, ...	12	12	2	26
Males, ...	6	8	1	15
Females, ...	6	4	1	11
DUKES.	-	-	3	3
Edgartown, ...	-	-	2	2
Males, ...	-	-	-	-
Females, ...	-	-	2	2
Tisbury, ...	-	-	1	1
Males, ...	-	-	-	-
Females, ...	-	-	1	1
ESSEX.	17	15	234	266
Amesbury, ...	2	2	-	4
Males, ...	1	1	-	2
Females, ...	1	1	-	2
Andover, ...	-	-	2	2
Males, ...	-	-	1	1
Females, ...	-	-	1	1
BEVERLY, ...	-	1	2	3
Males, ...	-	-	2	2
Females, ...	-	1	-	1
Boxford, ...	-	-	1	1
Males, ...	-	-	-	-
Females, ...	-	-	1	1
Bradford, ...	-	-	3	3
Males, ...	-	-	3	3
Females, ...	-	-	-	-
Danvers, ...	1	4	3	8
Males, ...	1	-	2	3
Females, ...	-	4	1	5
GLOUCESTER, ...	1	-	15	16
Males, ...	-	-	10	10
Females, ...	1	-	5	6
Groveland, ...	-	-	3	3
Males, ...	-	-	2	2
Females, ...	-	-	1	1
Hamilton, ...	-	-	2	2
Males, ...	-	-	2	2
Females, ...	-	-	-	-
HAVERHILL, ...	2	-	19	21
Males, ...	1	-	12	13
Females, ...	1	-	7	8

Town or City from which Sent, and Liquor Habits of Parents of Insane
— Continued

COUNTIES, CITIES, TOWNS, AND SEX.	One or Both Parents Intemperate	One or Both Parents Total Abstainers	Liquor Habits of Both Parents Unknown	Number of Insane
ESSEX — Con.				
Ipswich, ...	-	-	4	4
Males, ...	-	-	2	2
Females, ...	-	-	2	2
LAWRENCE, ...	4	3	48	55
Males, ...	3	-	23	26
Females, ...	1	3	25	29
LYNN, ...	4	2	56	62
Males, ...	2	1	39	42
Females, ...	2	1	17	20
Manchester, ...	-	-	2	2
Males, ...	-	-	2	2
Females, ...	-	-	-	-
Marblehead, ...	-	-	3	3
Males, ...	-	-	-	-
Females, ...	-	-	3	3
Merrimac, ...	-	1	-	1
Males, ...	-	-	-	-
Females, ...	-	1	-	1
Methuen, ...	-	-	7	7
Males, ...	-	-	2	2
Females, ...	-	-	5	5
Middleton, ...	-	-	1	1
Males, ...	-	-	1	1
Females, ...	-	-	-	-
Newbury, ...	-	-	3	3
Males, ...	-	-	3	3
Females, ...	-	-	-	-
NEWBURYPORT, ...	-	-	7	7
Males, ...	-	-	4	4
Females, ...	-	-	3	3
North Andover, ...	-	-	1	1
Males, ...	-	-	1	1
Females, ...	-	-	-	-
Peabody, ...	1	-	7	8
Males, ...	1	-	6	7
Females, ...	-	-	1	1
Rockport, ...	-	-	2	2
Males, ...	-	-	1	1
Females, ...	-	-	1	1
Rowley, ...	-	1	-	1
Males, ...	-	1	-	1
Females, ...	-	-	-	-

Town or City from which Sent, and Liquor Habits of Parents of Insane
— Continued.

COUNTIES, CITIES, TOWNS, AND SEX.	One or Both Parents Intemperate	One or Both Parents Total Abstainers	Liquor Habits of Both Parents Unknown	Number of Insane
ESSEX — Con.				
SALEM, ...	1	1	35	37
Males, ...	1	1	25	27
Females, ...	-	-	10	10
Salisbury, ...	-	-	3	3
Males, ...	-	-	1	1
Females, ...	-	-	2	2
Saugus, ...	-	-	1	1
Males, ...	-	-	-	-
Females, ...	-	-	1	1
Swampscott, ...	1	-	2	3
Males, ...	-	-	2	2
Females, ...	1	-	-	1
Wenham, ...	-	-	2	2
Males, ...	-	-	1	1
Females, ...	-	-	1	1
FRANKLIN.	7	5	8	20
Bernardston, ...	-	-	1	1
Males, ...	-	-	1	1
Females, ...	-	-	-	-
Buckland, ...	1	-	-	1
Males, ...	1	-	-	1
Females, ...	-	-	-	-
Charlemont, ...	1	-	1	2
Males, ...	1	-	1	2
Females, ...	-	-	-	-
Colrain, ...	-	1	-	1
Males, ...	-	-	-	-
Females, ...	-	1	-	1
Deerfield, ...	1	3	-	4
Males, ...	-	2	-	2
Females, ...	1	1	-	2
Gill, ...	-	1	1	2
Males, ...	-	1	1	2
Females, ...	-	-	-	-
Greenfield, ...	2	-	1	3
Males, ...	2	-	1	3
Females, ...	-	-	-	-
New Salem, ...	-	-	1	1
Males, ...	-	-	1	1
Females, ...	-	-	-	-

Town or City from which Sent, and Liquor Habits of Parents of Insane
— Continued.

COUNTIES, CITIES, TOWNS, AND SEX.	One or Both Parents Intemperate	One or Both Parents Total Abstainers	Liquor Habits of Both Parents Unknown	Number of Insane
FRANKLIN — Con.				
Northfield, ...	-	-	2	2
Males, ...	-	-	2	2
Females, ...	-	-	-	-
Orange, ...	1	-	-	1
Males, ...	1	-	-	1
Females, ...	-	-	-	-
Shelburne, ...	-	-	1	1
Males, ...	-	-	1	1
Females, ...	-	-	-	-
Wendell, ...	1	-	-	1
Males, ...	1	-	-	1
Females, ...	-	-	-	-
HAMPDEN.	85	5	21	111
CHICOPEE, ...	7	-	-	7
Males, ...	4	-	-	4
Females, ...	3	-	-	3
East Longmeadow, . . .	1	-	-	1
Males, ...	-	-	-	-
Females, ...	1	-	-	1
HOLYOKE, ...	25	2	3	30
Males, ...	13	-	3	16
Females, ...	12	2	-	14
Monson, ...	2	-	-	2
Males, ...	1	-	-	1
Females, ...	1	-	-	1
Montgomery, ...	-	-	1	1
Males, ...	-	-	1	1
Females, ...	-	-	-	-
Palmer, ...	6	-	3	9
Males, ...	2	-	2	4
Females, ...	4	-	1	5
Russell, ...	2	-	-	2
Males, ...	2	-	-	2
Females, ...	-	-	-	-
Southwick, ...	-	-	2	2
Males, ...	-	-	2	2
Females, ...	-	-	-	-
SPRINGFIELD, ...	32	3	8	43
Males, ...	19	2	7	28
Females, ...	13	1	1	15

Town or City from which Sent, and Liquor Habits of Parents of Insane
— Continued.

COUNTIES, CITIES, TOWNS, AND SEX.	One or Both Parents Intemperate	One or Both Parents Total Abstainers	Liquor Habits of Both Parents Unknown	Number of Insane
HAMPDEN — Con.				
Tolland, ...	–	–	1	1
Males, ...	–	–	1	1
Females, ...	–	–	–	–
Westfield, ...	7	–	2	9
Males, ...	6	–	2	8
Females, ...	1	–	–	1
West Springfield, ...	1	–	1	2
Males, ...	–	–	1	1
Females, ...	1	–	–	1
Wilbraham, ...	2	–	'–	2
Males, ...	2	–	–	2
Females, ...	–	–	–	–
HAMPSHIRE.	17	5	9	31
Amherst, ...	–	1	–	1
Males, ...	–	1	–	1
Females, ...	–	–	–	–
Belchertown, ...	1	–	–	1
Males, ...	1	–	–	1
Females, ...	–	–	–	–
Chesterfield, ...	1	–	–	1
Males, ...	–	–	–	–
Females, ...	1	–	–	1
Easthampton, ...	–	–	3	3
Males, ...	–	–	2	2
Females, ...	–	–	1	1
Goshen, ...	–	1	–	1
Males, ...	–	–	–	–
Females, ...	–	1	–	1
Hatfield, ...	–	–	1	1
Males, ...	–	–	–	–
Females, ...	–	–	1	1
Huntington, ...	1	–	–	1
Males, ...	–	–	–	–
Females, ...	1	–	–	1
NORTHAMPTON, ...	9	1	2	12
Males, ...	3	–	1	4
Females, ...	6	1	1	8
Southampton, ...	–	–	1	1
Males, ...	–	–	1	1
Females, ...	–	–	–	–

Town or City from which Sent, and Liquor Habits of Parents of Insane
— Continued.

COUNTIES, CITIES, TOWNS, AND SEX.	One or Both Parents Intemperate	One or Both Parents Total Abstainers	Liquor Habits of Both Parents Unknown	Number of Insane
HAMPSHIRE — Con.				
South Hadley, ...	3	1	1	5
Males, ...	1	–	1	2
Females, ...	2	1	–	3
Ware, ...	1	–	1	2
Males, ...	1	–	1	2
Females, ...	–	–	–	–
Williamsburg, ...	1	1	–	2
Males, ...	–	–	–	–
Females, ...	1	1	–	2
MIDDLESEX.	123	39	182	344
Acton, ...	–	–	1	1
Males, ...	–	–	1	1
Females, ...	–	–	–	–
Arlington, ...	1	–	2	3
Males, ...	1	–	1	2
Females, ...	–	–	1	1
Ayer, ...	–	–	2	2
Males, ...	–	–	1	1
Females, ...	–	–	1	1
Bedford, ...	–	–	1	1
Males, ...	–	–	1	1
Females, ...	–	–	–	–
Belmont, ...	–	1	–	1
Males, ...	–	–	–	–
Females, ...	–	1	–	1
CAMBRIDGE, ...	24	8	20	52
Males, ...	14	4	8	26
Females, ...	10	4	12	26
Concord, ...	–	1	–	1
Males, ...	–	–	–	–
Females, ...	–	1	–	1
EVERETT, ...	1	–	10	11
Males, ...	–	–	5	5
Females, ...	1	–	5	6
Framingham, ...	–	–	3	3
Males, ...	–	–	1	1
Females, ...	–	–	2	2
Groton, ...	–	–	2	2
Males, ...	–	–	–	–
Females, ...	–	–	2	2

Town or City from which Sent, and Liquor Habits of Parents of Insane
— Continued.

COUNTIES, CITIES, TOWNS, AND SEX.	One or Both Parents Intemperate	One or Both Parents Total Abstainers	Liquor Habits of Both Parents Unknown	Number of Insane
MIDDLESEX — Con.				
Holliston, ...	1	-	4	5
Males, ...	1	-	2	3
Females, ...	-	-	2	2
Hopkinton, ...	-	-	3	3
Males, ...	-	-	2	2
Females, ...	-	-	1	1
Hudson, ...	-	-	1	1
Males, ...	-	-	-	-
Females, ...	-	-	1	1
Lexington, ...	1	-	2	3
Males, ...	1	-	2	3
Females, ...	-	-	-	-
Littleton, ...	-	-	2	2
Males, ...	-	-	2	2
Females, ...	-	-	-	-
LOWELL, ...	12	8	33	53
Males, ...	7	3	19	29
Females, ...	5	5	14	24
MALDEN, ...	23	2	3	28
Males, ...	12	1	3	16
Females, ...	11	1	-	12
MARLBOROUGH, ...	2	3	10	15
Males, ...	1	2	8	11
Females, ...	1	1	2	4
Maynard, ...	-	-	3	3
Males, ...	-	-	-	-
Females, ...	-	-	3	3
MEDFORD, ...	6	-	-	6
Males, ...	2	-	-	2
Females, ...	4	-	-	4
Melrose, ...	5	-	1	6
Males, ...	4	-	1	5
Females, ...	1	-	-	1
Natick, ...	1	-	5	6
Males, ...	1	-	2	3
Females, ...	-	-	3	3
NEWTON, ...	3	6	20	29
Males, ...	2	2	9	13
Females, ...	1	4	11	16
Pepperell, ...	-	-	5	5
Males, ...	-	-	3	3
Females, ...	-	-	2	2

Town or City from which Sent, and Liquor Habits of Parents of Insane
— Continued.

COUNTIES, CITIES, TOWNS, AND SEX.	One or Both Parents Intemperate	One or Both Parents Total Abstainers	Liquor Habits of Both Parents Unknown	Number of Insane
MIDDLESEX — Con.				
Reading,	3	1	–	4
Males,	1	1	–	2
Females,	2	–	-	2
Sherborn,	3	–	1	4
Males,	–	–	–	–
Females,	3	–	1	4
Shirley,	–	–	1	1
Males,	–	–	–	–
Females,	–	–	1	1
SOMERVILLE,	7	3	28	38
Males,	4	1	15	20
Females,	3	2	13	18
Stoneham,	2	–	–	2
Males,	2	–	–	2
Females,	–	–	–	–
Stoughton,	–	–	2	2
Males,	–	–	–	–
Females,	–	–	2	2
Stow,	–	–	1	1
Males,	–	–	–	–
Females,	–	–	1	1
Tewksbury,	4	–	4	8
Males,	1	–	1	2
Females,	3	–	3	6
Townsend,	-	–	1	1
Males,	–	–	–	–
Females,	–	–	1	1
Tyngsborough,	–	–	1	1
Males,	–	-	–	-
Females,	–	–	1	1
Wakefield,	3	–	2	5
Males,	1	–	–	1
Females,	2	–	2	4
WALTHAM,	5	4	3	12
Males,	5	3	2	10
Females,	–	1	1	2
Watertown,	–	–	3	3
Males,	–	–	3	3
Females,	–	–	–	–
Wilmington,	–	1	1	2
Males,	–	1	–	1
Females,	-	–	1	1

Town or City from which Sent, and Liquor Habits of Parents of Insane
— Continued.

COUNTIES, CITIES, TOWNS, AND SEX.	One or Both Parents Intemperate	One or Both Parents Total Abstainers	Liquor Habits of Both Parents Unknown	Number of Insane
MIDDLESEX — Con.				
Winchester, ...	5	-	-	5
Males, ...	3	-	-	3
Females, ...	2	-	-	2
WOBURN, ...	11	1	1	13
Males, ...	4	-	1	5
Females, ...	7	1	-	8
NANTUCKET.	2	-	1	3
Nantucket, ...	2	-	1`	3
Males, ...	2	-	-	2
Females, ...	-	-	1	1
NORFOLK.	28	17	31	76
Bellingham, ...	-	-	1	1
Males, ...	-	-	-	-
Females, ...	-	-	1	1
Braintree, ...	-	1	3	4
Males, ...	-	-	2	2
Females, ...	-	1	1	2
Brookline, ...	1	1	1	3
Males, ...	1	-	1	2
Females, ...	-	1	-	1
Canton, ...	-	1	1	2
Males, ...	-	1	-	1
Females, ...	-	-	1	1
Cohasset, ...	-	-	1	1
Males, ...	-	-	-	-
Females, ...	-	-	1	1
Dedham,.	5	-	1	6
Males, ...	4	-	-	4
Females, ...	1	-	1	2
Dover, ...	-	-	1	1
Males, ...	-	-	-	-
Females, ...	-	-	1	1
Foxborough, ...	2	1	-	3
Males, ...	1	1	-	2
Females, ...	1	-	-	1
Franklin, ...	-	1	1	2
Males, ...	-	-	1	1
Females, ...	-	1	-	1

Town or City from which Sent, and Liquor Habits of Parents of Insane
— Continued.

COUNTIES, CITIES, TOWNS, AND SEX.	One or Both Parents Intemperate	One or Both Parents Total Abstainers	Liquor Habits of Both Parents Unknown	Number of Insane
NORFOLK — Con.				
Holbrook, ...	-	1	-	1
Males, ...	-	-	-	-
Females, ...	-	1	-	1
Hyde Park, ...	5	3	4	12
Males, ...	1	1	2	4
Females, ...	4	2	2	8
Medfield, ...	-	-	1	1
Males, ...	-	-	1	1
Females, ...	-	-	-	-
Medway, ...	-	-	1	1
Males, ...	-	-	-	-
Females, ...	-	-	1	1
Milton, ...	-	1	1	2
Males, ...	-	1	1	2
Females, ...	-	-	-	-
Needham, ...	-	-	2	2
Males, ...	-	-	2	2
Females, ...	-	-	-	-
Norwood, ...	1	1	-	2
Males, ...	-	-	-	-
Females, ...	1	1	-	2
QUINCY, ...	3	2	4	9
Males, ...	1	1	2	4
Females, ...	2	1	2	5
Randolph, ...	3	-	1	4
Males, ...	2	-	-	2
Females, ...	1	-	1	2
Walpole, ...	1	1	2	4
Males, ...	-	-	2	2
Females, ...	1	1	-	2
Wellesley, ...	2	1	1	4
Males, ...	1	-	1	2
Females, ...	1	1	-	2
Weymouth, ...	2	2	3	7
Males, ...	1	-	2	· 3
Females, ...	1	2	1	4
Wrentham, ...	3	-	1	4
Males, ...	2	-	-	2
Females, ...	1	-	1	2

Town or City from which Sent, and Liquor Habits of Parents of Insane
— Continued.

COUNTIES, CITIES, TOWNS, AND SEX.	One or Both Parents Intemperate	One or Both Parents Total Abstainers	Liquor Habits of Both Parents Unknown	Number of Insane
PLYMOUTH.	12	10	43	65
Abington, ...	-	-	1	1
Males, ...	-	-	1	1
Females, ...	-	-	-	-
Bridgewater, ...	2	1	17	20
Males, ...	2	1	17	20
Females, ...	-	-	-	-
BROCKTON, ...	3	7	4	14
Males, ...	2	5	3	10
Females, ...	1	2	1	4
Duxbury, ...	3	-	-	3
Males, ...	1	-	-	1
Females, ...	2	-	-	2
Hanson, ...	-	-	1	1
Males, ...	-	-	1	1
Females, ...	-	-	-	-
Hanover, ...	-	-	1	1
Males, ...	-	-	-	-
Females, ...	-	-	1	1
Kingston, ...	-	-	1	1
Males, ...	-	-	-	-
Females, ...	-	-	1	1
Lakeville, ...	-	-	1	1
Males, ...	-	-	1	1
Females, ...	-	-	-	-
Marion, ...	-	-	1	1
Males, ...	-	-	1	1
Females, ...	-	-	-	-
Marshfield, ...	-	-	1	1
Males, ...	-	-	1	1
Females, ...	-	-	-	-
Middleborough, ...	-	-	3	3
Males, ...	-	-	3	3
Females, ...	-	-	-	-
Plymouth, ...	2	1	6	9
Males, ...	1	1	2	4
Females, ...	1	-	4	5
Rockland, ...	-	1	1	2
Males, ...	-	1	-	1
Females, ...	-	-	1	1

Town or City from which Sent, and Liquor Habits of Parents of Insane
— Continued.

COUNTIES, CITIES, TOWNS, AND SEX.	One or Both Parents Intemperate	One or Both Parents Total Abstainers	Liquor Habits of Both Parents Unknown	Number of Insane
PLYMOUTH — Con.				
Scituate, ...	–	–	1	1
Males, ...	–	–	1	1
Females, ...	–	–	–	–
Wareham, ...	1	–	1	2
Males, ...	–	–	–	–
Females, ...	1	–	1	2
Whitman, ...	1	–	3	4
Males, ...	1	–	1	2
Females, ...	–	–	2	2
SUFFOLK.	244	86	144	474
BOSTON, ...	231	78	130	439
Males, ...	106	33	60	199
Females, ...	125	45	70	240
CHELSEA, ...	12	7	14	33
Males, ...	7	4	8	19
Females, ...	5	3	6	14
Revere, ...	1	–	–	1
Males, ...	1	–	–	1
Females, ...	–	–	–	–
Winthrop, ...	–	1	–	1
Males, ...	–	1	–	1
Females, ...	–	–	–	–
WORCESTER.	20	48	140	208
Ashburnham, ...	–	–	3	3
Males, ...	–	–	3	3
Females, ...	–	–	–	–
Athol, ...	–	1	2	3
Males, ...	–	–	–	–
Females, ...	–	1	2	3
Barre, ...	–	–	1	1
Males, ...	–	–	–	–
Females, ...	–	–	1	1
Blackstone, ...	–	–	7	7
Males, ...	–	–	2	2
Females, ...	–	–	5	5
Bolton, ...	1	–	–	1
Males, ...	–	–	–	–
Females, ...	1	–	–	1

Town or City from which Sent, and Liquor Habits of Parents of Insane
— Continued.

COUNTIES, CITIES, TOWNS, AND SEX.	One or Both Parents Intemperate	One or Both Parents Total Abstainers	Liquor Habits of Both Parents Unknown	Number of Insane
WORCESTER — Con.				
Brookfield, ...	–	3	–	3
Males, ...	–	2	–	2
Females, ...	–	1	–	1
Clinton, ...	1	2	7	10
Males, ...	–	–	4	4
Females, ...	1	2	3	6
FITCHBURG, ...	–	–	8	8
Males, ...	–	–	5	5
Females, ...	–	–	3	3
Gardner, ...	–	2	–	2
Males, ...	–	2	–	2
Females, ...	–	–	–	–
Grafton, ...	–	2	2	4
Males, ...	–	2	–	2
Females, ...	–	–	2	2
Harvard, ...	1	–	–	1
Males, ...	–	–	–	–
Females, ...	1	–	–	1
Lancaster, ...	1	4	–	5
Males, ...	1	1	–	2
Females, ...	–	3	–	3
Leominster, ...	1	2	–	3
Males, ...	1	1	–	2
Females, ...	–	1	–	1
Milford, ...	1	–	6	7
Males, ...	1	–	5	6
Females, ...	–	–	1	1
Millbury, ...	2	3	–	5
Males, ...	1	2	–	3
Females, ...	1	1	–	2
Northborough, ...	–	–	1	1
Males, ...	–	–	–	–
Females, ...	–	–	1	1
Northbridge, ...	1	–	2	3
Males, ...	–	–	1	1
Females, ...	1	–	1	2
North Brookfield, ...	–	2	–	2
Males, ...	–	–	–	–
Females, ...	–	2	–	2
Phillipston, ...	–	–	2	2
Males, ...	–	–	–	–
Females, ...	–	–	2	2

Town or City from which Sent, and Liquor Habits of Parents of Insane
— Concluded.

COUNTIES, CITIES, TOWNS, AND SEX.	One or Both Parents Intemperate	One or Both Parents Total Abstainers	Liquor Habits of Both Parents Unknown	Number of Insane
WORCESTER — Con.				
Southborough, ...	–	–	1	1
Males, ...	–	–	1	1
Females, ...	–	–	–	–
Southbridge, ...	1	3	3	7
Males, ...	1	1	2	4
Females, ...	–	2	1	3
Spencer, ...	–	–	7	7
Males, ...	–	–	6	6
Females, ...	–	–	1	1
Sterling, ...	–	–	1	1
Males, ...	–	–	–	–
Females, ...	–	–	1	1
Sturbridge, ...	–	1	–	1
Males, ...	–	–	–	–
Females, ...	–	1	–	1
Templeton, ...	–	–	2	2
Males, ...	–	–	1	1
Females, ...	–	–	1	1
Uxbridge, ...	–	1	–	1
Males, ...	–	–	–	–
Females, ...	–	1	–	1
Warren, ...	2	–	–	2
Males, ...	2	–	–	2
Females, ...	–	–	–	–
Webster, ...	2	4	3	9
Males, ...	2	2	2	6
Females, ...	–	2	1	3
Westborough, ...	1	1	4	6
Males, ...	1	–	3	4
Females, ...	–	1	1	2
West Boylston, ...	–	–	1	1
Males, ...	–	–	1	1
Females, ...	–	–	–	–
WORCESTER, ...	5	17	77	99
Males, ...	4	11	44	59
Females, ...	1	6	33	40
Not given, ...	2	1	6	9
Males, ...	1	1	4	6
Females, ...	1	–	2	3

RECAPITULATION.

COUNTIES, SEX, AND THE STATE.	One or Both Parents Intemperate	One or Both Parents Total Abstainers	Liquor Habits of Both Parents Unknown	Number of Insane
BARNSTABLE.	2	2	11	15
Males, ...	1	1	5	7
Females, ...	1	1	6	8
BERKSHIRE.	14	10	21	45
Males, ...	5	2	11	18
Females, ...	9	8	10	27
BRISTOL.	43	38	85	166
Males, ...	20	21	40	81
Females, ...	23	17	45	85
DUKES.	-	-	3	3
Males, ...	-	-	-	-
Females, ...	-	-	3	3
ESSEX.	17	15	234	266
Males, ...	10	4	147	161
Females, ...	7	11	87	105
FRANKLIN.	7	5	8	20
Males, ...	6	3	8	17
Females, ...	1	2	-	3
HAMPDEN.	85	5	21	111
Males, ...	49	2	19	70
Females, ...	36	3	2	41
HAMPSHIRE.	17	5	9	31
Males, ...	6	1	6	13
Females, ...	11	4	3	18
MIDDLESEX.	123	39	182	344
Males, ...	67	18	93	178
Females, ...	56	21	89	166

RECAPITULATION — Concluded.

COUNTIES, SEX, AND THE STATE.	One or Both Parents Intemperate	One or Both Parents Total Abstainers	Liquor Habits of Both Parents Unknown	Number of Insane
NANTUCKET.	2	-	1	3
Males, ...	2	-	-	2
Females,.	-	-	1	1
NORFOLK.	28	17	31	76
Males, ...	14	5	17	36
Females,.	14	12	14	40
PLYMOUTH.	12	10	43	65
Males, ...	7	8	32	47
Females, ...	5	2	11	18
SUFFOLK.	244	86	144	474
Males, ...	114	38	68	220
Females,.	130	48	76	254
WORCESTER.	20	48	140	208
Males, ...	14	24	80	118
Females,.	6	24	60	90
NOT GIVEN.	2	1	6	9
Males, ...	1	1	4	6
Females,.	1	-	2	3
THE STATE.	616	281	939	1,836
Males, ...	316	128	530	974
Females,.	300	153	409	862

The information as to both of the parents of the insane could not be ascertained in 939 cases, or 51.14 per cent of the whole number. Of the others, in 616 cases, comprising 316 males and 300 females, one or both parents were intemperate. In 281 cases, comprising 128 males and 153 females, one or both parents were total abstainers.

The replies to the question, "Is the person's present condition of insanity due to the use or abuse of intoxicating liquors," are shown in the presentation which follows:

Is the Person's present Condition of Insanity due to the Use or Abuse of Intoxicating Liquors.

SEX AND POLITICAL CONDITION.	Yes	No	Not Ascertained	Totals
Males.	296	479	199	974
Citizen born, ...	145	287	112	544
Naturalized, ...	43	48	16	107
Alien, ...	106	139	70	315
Unknown, ...	2	5	1	8
Females.	87	644	131	862
Citizen born, ...	36	359	63	458
Alien, ...	51	285	67	403
Unknown, ...	–	–	1	1
BOTH SEXES.	383	1,123	330	1,836
Citizen born, ...	181	646	175	1,002
Naturalized, ...	43	48	16	107
Alien, ...	157	424	137	718
Unknown, ...	2	5	2	9

In this table the insane are classified by sex, and according to political condition. The number of instances in which the facts could not be ascertained was 330. Of the others, in 383 cases, including 296 males and 87 females, the replies indicated that the insanity was due to the liquor habit; but, on the other hand, in 1,123 cases, including 479 males and 644 females, the contrary fact appears. Expressed in percentages, these results are as follows: of the whole number of cases, the point was not ascertained as to 17.97 per cent; the reply was affirmative as to 20.86 per cent; and negative as to 61.17 per cent.

The next table contains the replies to the question, "Did the intemperate habits of one or both parents lead to the insanity of the person considered."

Did the Intemperate Habits of one or both Parents lead to the Insanity of the Person Considered.

SEX AND POLITICAL CONDITION.	Yes	No	Not Ascertained	Totals
Males.	6	455	513	974
Citizen born, ...	5	259	280	544
Naturalized, ...	–	60	47	107
Alien, ...	1	130	184	315
Unknown, ...	–	6	2	8
Females.	14	466	382	862
Citizen born, ...	7	253	198	458
Alien, ...	7	213	183	403
Unknown, ...	–	–	1	1
BOTH SEXES.	20	921	895	1,836
Citizen born, ...	12	512	478	1,002
Naturalized, ...	–	60	47	107
Alien, ...	8	343	367	718
Unknown, ...	–	6	3	9

In 895 cases the information could not be ascertained; in 20 cases the reply was "Yes," and in 921 cases, "No." Summarized in terms of percentage, the affirmative replies comprise 1.09 per cent of the whole number; the negative replies 50.16 per cent; and the non-ascertained cases 48.75 per cent. Of the cases in which the intemperate habits of parents led to insanity, six were males and 14 females.

The inquiry upon this point was carried back to the grandparents of the insane persons, wherever the information could be ascertained. The replies are presented in the next table.

Did the Intemperate Habits of the Grand-parents of the Person Considered lead to his (or her) state of Insanity.

SEX AND POLITICAL CONDITION.	Yes	No	Not Ascertained	Totals
Males.	101	87	786	974
Citizen born, ...	32	56	456	544
Naturalized, ...	20	7	80	107
Alien, ...	46	22	247	315
Unknown, ...	3	2	3	8

Did the Intemperate Habits of the Grand-parents of the Person Considered lead to his (or her) state of Insanity — Concluded.

SEX AND POLITICAL CONDITION.	Yes	No	Not Ascertained	Totals
Females.	83	83	696	862
Citizen born, ...	27	58	373	458
Alien, ...	56	25	322	403
Unknown, ...	–	–	1	1
BOTH SEXES.	184	170	1,482	1,836
Citizen born, ...	59	114	829	1,002
Naturalized, ...	20	7	80	107
Alien, ...	102	47	569	718
Unknown, ...	3	2	4	9

In the larger number of cases, for reasons which were stated in the introduction,* the information could not be ascertained respecting the grand-parents, the total number of such cases being 1,482 out of the aggregate number, 1,836. In 184 cases the information indicated that the insanity was attributable to the intemperance of the grand-parents, while in 170 cases the replies were in the negative. Under the affirmative replies are included 101 males and 83 females.

The final question upon this branch of the subject was, "Did the intemperate habits of others (neither parents nor grand-parents) lead to the insanity of the person considered." The next presentation contains the replies to this question.

Did the Intemperate Habits of Others (neither parents nor grand-parents) lead to the Insanity of the Person Considered.

SEX AND POLITICAL CONDITION.	Yes	No	Not Ascertained	Totals
Males.	82	353	539	974
Citizen born, ...	41	196	307	544
Naturalized, ...	15	44	48	107
Alien, ...	25	108	182	315
Unknown, ...	1	5	2	8
Females.	41	404	417	862
Citizen born, ...	17	218	223	458
Alien, ...	24	186	193	403
Unknown, ...	–	–	1	1

* See page 8 *ante.*

Did the Intemperate Habits of Others (neither parents nor grand-parents)
lead to the Insanity of the Person Considered — Concluded.

SEX AND POLITICAL CONDITION.	Yes	No	Not Ascertained	Totals
BOTH SEXES.	123	757	956	1,836
Citizen born, ...	58	414	530	1,002
Naturalized, ...	15	44	48	107
Alien, ...	49	294	375	718
Unknown, ...	1	5	3	9

In 956 cases the information could not be ascertained. In
123 cases the reply was "Yes," and in 757, "No." In terms
of percentage, the non-ascertained cases being 52.07 per cent
of the total number, 13.98 per cent of the replies were in the
affirmative, and 86.02 per cent in the negative.

Information was collected as to the use of tobacco and drugs
by the insane, and these facts are tabulated in the presentation
which follows.

Insanity; Use of Tobacco and Drugs by the Insane: By Sex, Political
Condition, and Age Periods.

AGE PERIOD: 5-9.

SEX AND POLITICAL CONDITION.	TOBACCO		Number of Insane	DRUGS		Number of Insane
	Users	Non-users		Users	Non-users	
Males.	–	1	1	–	1	1
Citizen born, . .	–	1	1	–	1	1
Females.	–	3	3	–	3	3
Citizen born, . . .	–	2	2	–	2	2
Alien, ...	–	1	1	–	1	1
BOTH SEXES.	–	4	4	–	4	4
Citizen born, . . .	–	3	3	–	3	3
Alien, ...	–	1	1	–	1	1

AGE PERIOD: 10-14.

Males.	1	2	3	–	3	3
Citizen born, . . .	1	–	1	–	1	1
Alien, ...	–	2	2	–	2	2

Insanity; Use of Tobacco and Drugs by the Insane: By Sex, Political Condition, and Age Periods — Continued.

AGE PERIOD: 10-14 — Concluded.

SEX AND POLITICAL CONDITION.	TOBACCO		Number of Insane	DRUGS		Number of Insane
	Users	Non-users		Users	Non-users	
Females.	–	2	2	–	2	2
Citizen born,	–	1	1	–	1	1
Alien, . .	–	1	1	–	1	1
BOTH SEXES.	1	4	5	–	5	5
Citizen born, . . .	1	1	2	–	2	2
Alien, ...	–	3	3	–	3	3

AGE PERIOD: 15-19.

Males.	19	22	41	–	41	41
Citizen born, . .	13	18	31	–	31	31
Alien, ...	6	4	10	–	10	10
Females.	–	28	28	–	28	28
Citizen born, . . .	–	18	18	–	18	18
Alien, ...	–	10	10	–	10	10
BOTH SEXES.	19	50	69	–	69	69
Citizen born, . . .	13	36	49	–	49	49
Alien, ...	6	14	20	–	20	20

AGE PERIOD: 20-29.

Males.	114	118	232	5	227	232
Citizen born, . . .	67	69	136	3	133	136
Naturalized, ...	6	5	11	–	11	11
Alien, ...	39	44	83	2	81	83
Unknown, ...	2	–	2	–	2	2
Females.	4	169	173	2	171	173
Citizen born, . . .	2	87	89	2	87	89
Alien, ...	2	82	84	–	84	84
BOTH SEXES.	118	287	405	7	398	405
Citizen born, . . .	69	156	225	5	220	225
Naturalized, ...	6	5	11	–	11	11
Alien, ...	41	126	167	2	165	167
Unknown, ...	2	–	2	–	2	2

Insanity; Use of Tobacco and Drugs by the Insane: By Sex, Political Condition, and Age Periods — Continued.

AGE PERIOD: 30–39.

SEX AND POLITICAL CONDITION.	TOBACCO		Number of Insane	DRUGS		Number of Insane
	Users	Non-users		Users	Non-users	
Males.	130	109	239	3	236	239
Citizen born, . . .	76	62	138	1	137	138
Naturalized, ...	12	8	20	1	19	20
Alien, ...	42	39	81	1	80	81
Females.	5	213	218	6	212	218
Citizen born, . . .	3	126	129	5	124	129
Alien, ...	2	87	89	1	88	89
BOTH SEXES.	135	322	457	9	448	457
Citizen born, . . .	79	188	267	6	261	267
Naturalized, . . .	12	8	20	1	19	20
Alien, ...	44	126	170	2	168	170

AGE PERIOD: 40–49.

	Users	Non-users	Number of Insane	Users	Non-users	Number of Insane
Males.	101	87	188	3	185	188
Citizen born, . . .	44	55	99	3	96	99
Naturalized, . . .	23	8	31	–	31	31
Alien, ...	33	23	56	–	56	56
Unknown, . . .	1	1	2	–	2	2
Females.	7	177	184	5	179	184
Citizen born, .	3	100	103	3	100	103
Alien, . . .	4	77	81	2	79	81
BOTH SEXES.	108	264	372	8	364	372
Citizen born, . . .	47	155	202	6	196	202
Naturalized, . . .	23	8	31	–	31	31
Alien, ...	37	100	137	2	135	137
Unknown, ...	1	1	2	–	2	2

AGE PERIOD: 50–59.

	Users	Non-users	Number of Insane	Users	Non-users	Number of Insane
Males.	61	66	127	2	125	127
Citizen born, . . .	24	38	62	1	61	62
Naturalized, . . .	7	8	15	–	15	15
Alien, ...	28	20	48	1	47	48
Unknown, . . .	2	–	2	–	2	2
Females.	6	102	108	4	104	108
Citizen born, . . .	1	42	43	–	43	43
Alien, ...	5	60	65	4	61	65

Insanity; Use of Tobacco and Drugs by the Insane : By Sex, Political Condition, and Age Periods — Continued.

AGE PERIOD : 50–59 — Concluded.

SEX AND POLITICAL CONDITION.	TOBACCO		Number of Insane	DRUGS		Number of Insane
	Users	Non-users		Users	Non-users	
BOTH SEXES.	67	168	235	6	229	235
Citizen born, . . .	25	80	105	1	104	105
Naturalized, ...	7	8	15	-	15	15
Alien, ...	33	80	113	5	108	113
Unknown, ...	2	-	2	-	2	2

AGE PERIOD : 60–79.

	TOBACCO		Number of Insane	DRUGS		Number of Insane
	Users	Non-users		Users	Non-users	
Males.	63	64	127	2	125	127
Citizen born, . . .	29	34	63	2	61	63
Naturalized, ...	18	10	28	-	28	28
Alien, ...	15	19	34	-	34	34
Unknown, ...	1	1	2	-	2	2
Females.	7	120	127	4	123	127
Citizen born, . . .	2	58	60	2	58	60
Alien, ...	5	62	67	2	65	67
BOTH SEXES.	70	184	254	6	248	254
Citizen born, . . .	31	92	123	4	119	123
Naturalized, ...	18	10	28	-	28	28
Alien, ...	20	81	101	2	99	101
Unknown, ...	1	1	2	-	2	2

AGE PERIOD : 80 +.

	TOBACCO		Number of Insane	DRUGS		Number of Insane
	Users	Non-users		Users	Non-users	
Males.	6	8	14	-	14	14
Citizen born, . . .	5	7	12	-	12	12
Naturalized, . . .	-	1	1	-	1	1
Alien, ...	1	-	1	-	1	1
Females.	2	14	16	1	15	16
Citizen born, . . .	1	11	12	1	11	12
Alien, ...	1	3	4	-	4	4
BOTH SEXES.	8	22	30	1	29	30
Citizen born, . . .	6	18	24	1	23	24
Naturalized, . . .	-	1	1	-	1	1
Alien, ...	2	3	5	-	5	5

Insanity; Use of Tobacco and Drugs by the Insane: By Sex, Political Condition, and Age Periods — Concluded.

AGE PERIOD: Unknown.

SEX AND POLITICAL CONDITION.	TOBACCO		Number of Insane	DRUGS		Number of Insane
	Users	Non-users		Users	Non-users	
Males.	–	2	2	–	2	2
Citizen born, . . .	–	1	1	–	1	1
Naturalized,. . . .	–	1	1	–	1	1
Females.	–	3	3	–	3	3
Citizen born, . . .	–	1	1	–	1	1
Alien, ...	–	1	1	–	1	1
Unknown, ...	–	1	1	–	1	1
BOTH SEXES.	–	5	5	–	5	5
Citizen born, . . .	–	2	2	–	2	2
Naturalized,. . . .	–	1	1	–	1	1
Alien, ...	–	1	1	–	1	1
Unknown, ...	–	1	1	–	1	1

RECAPITULATION.

SEX AND POLITICAL CONDITION.	TOBACCO		Number of Insane	DRUGS		Number of Insane
	Users	Non-users		Users	Non-users	
Males.	495	479	974	15	959	974
Citizen born, . . .	259	285	544	10	534	544
Naturalized,. . . .	66	41	107	1	106	107
Alien, ...	164	151	315	4	311	315
Unknown, ...	6	2	8	.	8	8
Females.	31	831	862	22	840	862
Citizen born, . . .	12	446	458	13	445	458
Alien, ...	19	384	403	9	394	403
Unknown, ...	–	1	1	–	1	1
BOTH SEXES.	526	1,310	1,836	37	1,799	1,836
Citizen born, . . .	271	731	1,002	23	979	1,002
Naturalized,. . . .	66	41	107	1	106	107
Alien, ...	183	535	718	13	705	718
Unknown, ...	6	3	9	–	9	9

RECAPITULATION: BY AGE PERIODS.

SEX AND AGE PERIODS.	TOBACCO		Number of Insane	DRUGS		Number of Insane
	Users	Non-users		Users	Non-users	
Males.	495	479	974	15	959	974
5–9, ...	-	1	1	-	1	1
10–14, ...	1	2	3	-	3	3
15–19, ...	19	22	41	-	41	41
20–29, ...	114	118	232	5	227	232
30–39, ...	130	109	239	3	236	239
40–49, ...	101	87	188	3	185	188
50–59, ...	61	66	127	2	125	127
60–79, ...	63	64	127	2	125	127
80 +, ...	6	8	14	-	14	14
Unknown, ...	-	2	2	-	2	2
Females.	31	831	862	22	840	862
5–9, ...	-	3	3	-	3	3
10–14, ...	-	2	2	-	2	2
15–19, ...	-	28	28	-	28	28
20–29, ...	4	169	173	2	171	173
30–39, ...	5	213	218	6	212	218
40–49, ...	7	177	184	5	179	184
50–59, ...	6	102	108	4	104	108
60–79, ...	7	120	127	4	123	127
80 +, ...	2	14	16	1	15	16
Unknown, ...	-	3	3	-	3	3
BOTH SEXES.	526	1,310	1,836	37	1,799	1,836
5–9, ...	-	4	4	-	4	4
10–14, ...	1	4	5	-	5	5
15–19, ...	19	50	69	-	69	69
20–29, ...	118	287	405	7	398	405
30–39, ...	135	322	457	9	448	457
40–49, ...	108	264	372	8	364	372
50–59, ...	67	168	235	6	229	235
60–79, ...	70	184	254	6	248	254
80 +, ...	8	22	30	1	29	30
Unknown, ...	-	5	5	-	5	5

Confining our analysis to the recapitulation for both sexes,
we note that the 1,836 insane cases considered included 526,
or 28.65 per cent, who were users of tobacco, and 37, or 2.02
per cent, who were users of drugs. The insignificant place
which the users of drugs hold in comparison with the total

number of insane persons conforms to information upon this
point obtained respecting the paupers and criminals. In this
table the users of tobacco and drugs are classified by sex and
by age periods. Of the females, 31 used tobacco, while 831
did not. Of the males, 495 used tobacco, while 479 did not.
The insane addicted to the use of drugs included 15 males
and 22 females. Of the persons under 20 years of age among
the males, only 20 used tobacco; while the females who were
addicted to its use are all above the age of 20. No minors of
either sex were found among the insane who used drugs. Of
the insane females who used tobacco, 19 were alien and 12
citizen born.

The following table exhibits the facts as to the use of tobacco
and drugs by the fathers of the insane persons.

*Insanity; Use of Tobacco and Drugs by Fathers of Insane Persons: By Sex,
Political Condition, and Age Periods.*

AGE PERIOD: 5–9.

SEX AND POLITICAL CONDITION.	TOBACCO		Number of Insane	DRUGS		Number of Insane
	Users	Non-users		Users	Non-users	
Males.	–	1	1	–	1	1
Citizen born, . .	–	1	1	–	1	1
Females.	1	2	3	–	3	3
Citizen born, . . .	1	1	2	–	2	2
Alien, ...	–	1	1	–	1	1
BOTH SEXES.	1	3	4	–	4	4
Citizen born, . . .	1	2	3	–	3	3
Alien, ...	–	1	1	–	1	1

AGE PERIOD: 10–14.

Males.	1	2	3	–	3	3
Citizen born, . . .	–	1	1	–	1	1
Alien, ...	1	1	2	–	2	2
Females.	1	1	2	–	2	2
Citizen born, . . .	–	1	1	–	1	1
Alien, ...	1	–	1	–	1	1

Insanity; Use of Tobacco and Drugs by Fathers of Insane Persons: By Sex, Political Condition, and Age Periods — Continued.

AGE PERIOD: 10-14 — Concluded.

SEX AND POLITICAL CONDITION.	TOBACCO		Number of Insane	DRUGS		Number of Insane
	Users	Non-users		Users	Non-users	
BOTH SEXES.	2	3	5	-	5	5
Citizen born, . . .	-	2	2	-	2	2
Alien, ...	2	1	3	-	3	3

AGE PERIOD: 15-19.

	TOBACCO		Number of Insane	DRUGS		Number of Insane
	Users	Non-users		Users	Non-users	
Males.	14	27	41	-	41	41
Citizen born, . .	11	20	31	-	31	31
Alien, ...	3	7	10	-	10	10
Females.	8	20	28	-	28	28
Citizen born, . . .	5	13	18	-	18	18
Alien, ...	3	7	10	-	10	10
BOTH SEXES.	22	47	69	-	69	69
Citizen born, . . .	16	33	49	-	49	49
Alien, ...	6	14	20	-	20	20

AGE PERIOD: 20-29.

	TOBACCO		Number of Insane	DRUGS		Number of Insane
	Users	Non-users		Users	Non-users	
Males.	71	161	232	1	231	232
Citizen born, .	42	94	136	-	136	136
Naturalized, . .	3	8	11	-	11	11
Alien, . . .	25	58	83	1	82	83
Unknown, . .	1	1	2	-	2	2
Females.	70	103	173	-	173	173
Citizen born, . .	36	53	89	-	89	89
Alien, . .	34	50	84	-	84	84
BOTH SEXES.	141	264	405	1	404	405
Citizen born, ...	78	147	225	-	225	225
Naturalized, ...	3	8	11	-	11	11
Alien, ...	59	108	167	1	166	167
Unknown, ...	1	1	2	-	2	2

*Insanity ; Use of Tobacco and Drugs by Fathers of Insane Persons : By Sex,
Political Condition, and Age Periods —* Continued.

AGE PERIOD : 30-39.

SEX AND POLITICAL CONDITION.	TOBACCO		Number of Insane	DRUGS		Number of Insane
	Users	Non-users		Users	Non-users	
Males.	67	172	239	–	239	239
Citizen born, . . .	41	97	138	–	138	138
Naturalized, ...	9	11	20	–	20	20
Alien, ...	17	64	81	–	81	81
Females.	76	142	218	–	218	218
Citizen born, . . .	45	84	129	–	129	129
Alien, ...	31	58	89	–	89	89
BOTH SEXES.	143	314	457	–	457	457
Citizen born, . . .	86	181	267	–	267	267
Naturalized, ...	9	11	20	–	20	20
Alien, ...	48	122	170	–	170	170

AGE PERIOD : 40-49.

	TOBACCO		Number of Insane	DRUGS		Number of Insane
	Users	Non-users		Users	Non-users	
Males.	55	133	188	–	188	188
Citizen born, . . .	21	78	99	–	99	99
Naturalized, ...	14	17	31	–	31	31
Alien, ...	20	36	56	–	56	56
Unknown, ...	–	2	2	–	2	2
Females.	67	117	184	–	184	184
Citizen born, . . .	39	64	103	–	103	103
Alien, ...	28	53	81	–	81	81
BOTH SEXES.	122	250	372	–	372	372
Citizen born, . . .	60	142	202	–	202	202
Naturalized, ...	14	17	31	–	31	31
Alien, ...	48	89	137	–	137	137
Unknown, ...	–	2	2	–	2	2

AGE PERIOD : 50-59.

	TOBACCO		Number of Insane	DRUGS		Number of Insane
	Users	Non-users		Users	Non-users	
Males.	47	80	127	–	127	127
Citizen born, . . .	20	42	62	–	62	62
Naturalized, ...	6	9	15	–	15	15
Alien, ...	19	29	48	–	48	48
Unknown, ...	2	–	2	–	2	2
Females.	34	74	108	–	108	108
Citizen born, . . .	.7	36	43	–	43	43
Alien, ...	27	38	65	–	65	65

*Insanity; Use of Tobacco and Drugs by Fathers of Insane Persons: By Sex,
Political Condition, and Age Periods* — Continued.

AGE PERIOD: 50–59 — Concluded.

SEX AND POLITICAL CONDITION.	TOBACCO		Number of Insane	DRUGS		Number of Insane
	Users	Non-users		Users	Non-users	
BOTH SEXES.	81	154	235	–	235	235
Citizen born, . . .	27	78	105	–	105	105
Naturalized, ...	6	9	15	–	15	15
Alien, ...	46	67	113	–	113	113
Unknown, ...	2	–	2	–	2	2

AGE PERIOD: 60–79.

Males.	35	92	127	–	127	127
Citizen born, . . .	17	46	63	–	63	63
Naturalized, ...	12	16	28	–	28	28
Alien, ...	6	28	34	–	34	34
Unknown, ...	–	2	2	–	2	2
Females.	39	88	127	–	127	127
Citizen born, . . .	13	47	60	–	60	60
Alien, ...	26	41	67	–	67	67
BOTH SEXES.	74	180	254	–	254	254
Citizen born, . . .	30	93	123	–	123	123
Naturalized, ...	12	16	28	–	28	28
Alien, ...	32	69	101	–	101	101
Unknown, ...	–	2	2	–	2	2

AGE PERIOD: 80 +.

Males.	4	10	14	–	14	14
Citizen born, . . .	3	9	12	–	12	12
Naturalized, ...	–	1	1	–	1	1
Alien, ...	1	–	1	–	1	1
Females.	7	9	16	–	16	16
Citizen born, . . .	4	8	12	–	12	12
Alien, ...	3	1	4	–	4	4
BOTH SEXES.	11	19	30	–	30	30
Citizen born, . . .	7	17	24	–	24	24
Naturalized, ...	–	1	1	–	1	1
Alien, ...	4	1	5	–	5	5

*Insanity ; Use of Tobacco and Drugs by Fathers of Insane Persons : By Sex,
Political Condition, and Age Periods — Concluded.*

AGE PERIOD: Unknown.

SEX AND POLITICAL CONDITION.	TOBACCO		Number of Insane	DRUGS		Number of Insane
	Users	Non-users		Users	Non-users	
Males.	–	2	2	–	2	2
Citizen born, . . .	–	1	1	–	1	1
Naturalized, ...	–	1	1	–	1	1
Females.	1	2	3	–	3	3
Citizen born, . . .	1	–	1	–	1	1
Alien, ...	–	1	1	–	1	1
Unknown, ...	–	1	1	–	1	1
BOTH SEXES.	1	4	5	–	5	5
Citizen born, . . .	1	1	2	–	2	2
Naturalized, ...	–	1	1	–	1	1
Alien, ...	–	1	1	–	1	1
Unknown, ...	–	1	1	–	1	1

RECAPITULATION.

SEX AND POLITICAL CONDITION.	TOBACCO		Number of Insane	DRUGS		Number of Insane
	Users	Non-users		Users	Non-users	
Males.	294	680	974	1	973	974
Citizen born, . . .	155	389	544	–	544	544
Naturalized, . . .	44	63	107	–	107	107
Alien, ...	92	223	315	1	314	315
Unknown, ...	3	5	8	–	8	8
Females.	304	558	862	–	862	862
Citizen born, . . .	151	307	458	–	458	458
Alien, ...	153	250	403	–	403	403
Unknown, ...	–	1	1	–	1	1
BOTH SEXES.	598	1,238	1,836	1	1,835	1,836
Citizen born, . . .	306	696	1,002	–	1,002	1,002
Naturalized, . . .	44	63	107	–	107	107
Alien, ...	245	473	718	1	717	718
Unknown, ...	3	6	9	–	9	9

RECAPITULATION: BY AGE PERIODS.

SEX AND AGE PERIODS.	TOBACCO		Number of Insane	DRUGS		Number of Insane
	Users	Non-users		Users	Non-users	
Males.	294	680	974	1	973	974
5-9, ...	-	1	1	-	1	1
10-14, ...	1	2	3	-	3	3
15-19, ...	14	27	41	-	41	41
20-29, ...	71	161	232	1	231	232
30-39, ...	67	172	239	-	239	239
40-49, ...	55	133	188	-	188	188
50-59, ...	47	80	127	-	127	127
60-79, ...	35	92	127	-	127	127
80+, ...	4	10	14	-	14	14
Unknown, . . .	-	2	2	-	2	2
Females.	304	558	862	-	862	862
5-9, ...	1	2	3	-	3	3
10-14, ...	1	1	2	-	2	2
15-19, ...	8	20	28	-	28	28
20-29, ...	70	103	173	-	173	173
30-39, ...	76	142	218	-	218	218
40-49, ...	67	117	184	-	184	184
50-59, ...	34	74	108	-	108	108
60-79, ...	39	88	127	-	127	127
80+, ...	7	9	16	-	16	16
Unknown, . . .	1	2	3	-	3	3
BOTH SEXES.	598	1,238	1,836	1	1,835	1,836
5-9, ...	1	3	4	-	4	4
10-14, ...	2	3	5	-	5	5
15-19, ...	22	47	69	-	69	69
20-29, ...	141	264	405	1	404	405
30-39, ...	143	314	457	-	457	457
40-49, ...	122	250	372	-	372	372
50-59, ...	81	154	235	-	235	235
60-79, ...	74	180	254	-	254	254
80+, ...	11	19	30	-	30	30
Unknown, . . .	1	4	5	-	5	5

The classification under political condition and by age periods is maintained in this table. Referring to the recapitulation, we find that out of 1,836 cases of insanity, 598, or 32.57 per cent, are cases in which the fathers used tobacco. There is also one case shown in which the father was addicted to the use of drugs.

Distributed by sex, the cases in which the fathers used tobacco included 294 males and 304 females.

A similar table relating to the mothers of the insane follows.

Insanity; Use of Tobacco and Drugs by Mothers of Insane Persons: By Sex, Political Condition, and Age Periods.

AGE PERIOD: 5-9.

SEX AND POLITICAL CONDITION.	TOBACCO		Number of Insane	DRUGS		Number of Insane
	Users	Non-users		Users	Non-users	
Males.	–	1	1	–	1	1
Citizen born, . . .	–	1	1	–	1	1
Females.	–	3	3	–	3	3
Citizen born, . . .	–	2	2	–	2	2
Alien, ...	–	1	1	–	1	1
BOTH SEXES.	–	4	4	–	4	4
Citizen born, . . .	–	3	3	–	3	3
Alien, ...	–	1	1	–	1	1

AGE PERIOD: 10-14.

SEX AND POLITICAL CONDITION.	TOBACCO		Number of Insane	DRUGS		Number of Insane
	Users	Non-users		Users	Non-users	
Males.	–	3	3	–	3	3
Citizen born, . . .	–	1	1	–	1	1
Alien, ...	–	2	2	–	2	2
Females.	–	2	2	–	2	2
Citizen born, . . .	–	1	1	–	1	1
Alien, ...	–	1	1	–	1	1
BOTH SEXES.	–	5	5	–	5	5
Citizen born, . . .	–	2	2	–	2	2
Alien, ...	–	3	3	–	3	3

AGE PERIOD: 15-19.

SEX AND POLITICAL CONDITION.	TOBACCO		Number of Insane	DRUGS		Number of Insane
	Users	Non-users		Users	Non-users	
Males.	–	41	41	–	41	41
Citizen born, . . .	–	31	31	–	31	31
Alien, ...	–	10	10	–	10	10

Insanity ; Use of Tobacco and Drugs by Mothers of Insane Persons : By Sex,
Political Condition, and Age Periods — Continued.

AGE PERIOD : 15-19 — Concluded.

SEX AND POLITICAL CONDITION.	TOBACCO		Number of Insane	DRUGS		Number of Insane
	Users	Non-users		Users	Non-users	
Females.	-	28	28	-	28	28
Citizen born, . . .	-	18	18	-	18	18
Alien, ...	-	10	10	-	10	10
BOTH SEXES.	-	69	69	-	69	69
Citizen born, . . .	-	49	49	-	49	49
Alien, ...	-	20	20	-	20	20

AGE PERIOD : 20-29.

Males.	-	232	232	-	232	232
Citizen born, . . .	-	136	136	-	136	136
Naturalized, ...	-	11	11	-	11	11
Alien, ...	-	83	83	-	83	83
Unknown, ...	-	2	2	-	2	2
Females.	3	170	173	-	173	173
Citizen born, . .	2	87	89	-	89	89
Alien, . . .	1	83	84	-	84	84
BOTH SEXES.	3	402	405	-	405	405
Citizen born, . . .	2	223	225	-	225	225
Naturalized, ...	-	11	11	-	11	11
Alien, ...	1	166	167	-	167	167
Unknown, ...	-	2	2	-	2	2

AGE PERIOD : 30-39.

Males.	-	239	239	-	239	239
Citizen born, . . .	-	138	138	-	138	138
Naturalized, ...	-	20	20	-	20	20
Alien, ...	-	81	81	-	81	81
Females.	1	217	218	-	218	218
Citizen born, . . .	-	129	129	-	129	129
Alien, ...	1	88	89	-	89	89

Insanity; Use of Tobacco and Drugs by Mothers of Insane Persons: By Sex,
Political Condition, and Age Periods — Continued.

AGE PERIOD: 30-39 — Concluded.

SEX AND POLITICAL CONDITION.	TOBACCO		Number of Insane	DRUGS		Number of Insane
	Users	Non-users		Users	Non-users	
BOTH SEXES.	1	456	457	–	457	457
Citizen born,	–	267	267	–	267	267
Naturalized,	–	20	20	–	20	20
Alien,	1	169	170	–	170	170

AGE PERIOD: 40-49.

Males.	–	188	188	–	188	188
Citizen born,	–	99	99	–	99	99
Naturalized,	–	31	31	–	31	31
Alien,	–	56	56	–	56	56
Unknown,	–	2	2	–	2	2
Females.	1	183	184	–	184	184
Citizen born,	1	102	103	–	103	103
Alien,	–	81	81	–	81	81
BOTH SEXES.	1	371	372	–	372	372
Citizen born,	1	201	202	–	202	202
Naturalized,	–	31	31	–	31	31
Alien,	–	137	137	–	137	137
Unknown,	–	2	2	–	2	2

AGE PERIOD: 50-59.

Males.	–	127	127	–	127	127
Citizen born,	–	62	62	–	62	62
Naturalized,	–	15	15	–	15	15
Alien,	–	48	48	–	48	48
Unknown,	–	2	2	–	2	2
Females.	1	107	108	–	108	108
Citizen born,	1	42	43	–	43	43
Alien,	–	65	65	–	65	65
BOTH SEXES.	1	234	235	–	235	235
Citizen born,	1	104	105	–	105	105
Naturalized,	–	15	15	–	15	15
Alien,	–	113	113	–	113	113
Unknown,	–	2	2	–	2	2

Insanity; Use of Tobacco and Drugs by Mothers of Insane Persons: By Sex, Political Condition, and Age Periods — Continued.

AGE PERIOD: 60–79.

SEX AND POLITICAL CONDITION.	TOBACCO		Number of Insane	DRUGS		Number of Insane
	Users	Non-users		Users	Non-users	
Males.	–	127	127	–	127	127
Citizen born, . . .	–	63	63	–	63	63
Naturalized, ...	–	28	28	–	28	28
Alien, ...	–	34	34	–	34	34
Unknown, ...	–	2	2	–	2	2
Females.	3	124	127	–	127	127
Citizen born, . .	2	58	60	–	60	60
Alien, ...	1	66	67	–	67	67
BOTH SEXES.	3	251	254	–	254	254
Citizen born, . . .	2	121	123	–	123	123
Naturalized, ...	–	28	28	–	28	28
Alien, ...	1	100	101	–	101	101
Unknown, ...	–	2	2	–	2	2

AGE PERIOD: 80 +.

SEX AND POLITICAL CONDITION.	TOBACCO		Number of Insane	DRUGS		Number of Insane
	Users	Non-users		Users	Non-users	
Males.	–	14	14	–	14	14
Citizen born, . . .	–	12	12	–	12	12
Naturalized, . . .	–	1	1	–	1	1
Alien, ...	–	1	1	–	1	1
Females.	–	16	16	–	16	16
Citizen born, . . .	–	12	12	–	12	12
Alien, ...	–	4	4	–	4	4
BOTH SEXES.	–	30	30	–	30	30
Citizen born, . . .	–	24	24	–	24	24
Naturalized, . . .	–	1	1	–	1	1
Alien, ...	–	5	5	–	5	5

Insanity; Use of Tobacco and Drugs by Mothers of Insane Persons: By Sex,
Political Condition, and Age Periods — Concluded.

AGE PERIOD: Unknown.

SEX AND POLITICAL CONDITION.	TOBACCO		Number of Insane	DRUGS		Number of Insane
	Users	Non-users		Users	Non-users	
Males.	–	2	2	–	2	2
Citizen born,	–	1	1	–	1	1
Naturalized, .	–	1	1	–	1	1
Females.	–	3	3	–	3	3
Citizen born,	–	1	1	–	1	1
Alien, . . .	–	1	1	–	1	1
Unknown, . .	–	1	1	–	1	1
BOTH SEXES.	–	5	5	–	5	5
Citizen born,	–	2	2	–	2	2
Naturalized, .	–	1	1	–	1	1
Alien, ...	–	1	1	–	1	1
Unknown, ...	–	1	1	–	1	1

RECAPITULATION.

SEX AND POLITICAL CONDITION.	TOBACCO		Number of Insane	DRUGS		Number of Insane
	Users	Non-users		Users	Non-users	
Males.	–	974	974	–	974	974
Citizen born,	–	544	544	–	544	544
Naturalized, .	–	107	107	–	107	107
Alien, ...	–	315	315	–	315	315
Unknown, . . .	–	8	8	–	8	8
Females.	9	853	862	–	862	862
Citizen born,	6	452	458	–	458	458
Alien, ...	3	400	403	–	403	403
Unknown, . . .	–	1	1	–	1	1
BOTH SEXES.	9	1,827	1,836	–	1,836	1,836
Citizen born,	6	996	1,002	–	1,002	1,002
Naturalized, .	–	107	107	–	107	107
Alien, ...	3	715	718	–	718	718
Unknown, . . .	–	9	9	–	9	9

RECAPITULATION: BY AGE PERIODS.

SEX AND AGE PERIODS.	TOBACCO		Number of Insane	DRUGS		Number of Insane
	Users	Non-users		Users	Non-users	
Males.	–	974	974	–	974	974
5–9, ...	–	1	1	–	1	1
10–14, ...	–	3	3	–	3	3
15–19, ...	–	41	41	–	41	41
20–29, ...	–	232	232	–	232	232
30–39, ...	–	239	239	–	239	239
40–49, ...	–	188	188	–	188	188
50–59, ...	–	127	127	–	127	127
60–79, ...	–	127	127	–	127	127
80 +, ...	–	14	14	–	14	14
Unknown, ...	–	2	2	–	2	2
Females.	9	853	862	–	862	862
5–9, ...	–	3	3	–	3	3
10–14, ...	–	2	2	–	2	2
15–19, ...	–	28	28	–	28	28
20–29, ...	3	170	173	–	173	173
30–39, ...	1	217	218	–	218	218
40–49, ...	1	183	184	–	184	184
50–59, ...	1	107	108	–	108	108
60–79, ...	3	124	127	–	127	127
80 +, ...	–	16	16	–	16	16
Unknown, ...	–	3	3	–	3	3
BOTH SEXES.	9	1,827	1,836	–	1,836	1,836
5 9, ...	–	4	4	–	4	4
10–14, ...	–	5	5	–	5	5
15–19, ...	–	69	69	–	69	69
20–29, ...	3	402	405	–	405	405
30–39, ...	1	456	457	–	457	457
40–49, ...	1	371	· 372	–	372	372
50–59, ...	1	234	235	–	235	235
60–79, ...	3	251	254	–	254	254
80 +, ...	–	30	30	–	30	30
Unknown, ...	–	5	5	–	5	5

There were very few cases in which the mothers of the insane
were addicted to the use of tobacco, only nine appearing out of
the aggregate number, 1,836. These nine insane persons whose
mothers used tobacco were all females. There were no instances

discovered in which the mothers of the insane were addicted to the use of drugs.

The next table shows the liquor habits of the insane in detail, by age periods, sex, and political condition.

Insanity; Sex, Political Condition, and Liquor Habits of the Insane: By Age Periods.

AGE PERIOD: 15-19.

SEX AND POLITICAL CONDITION.	Number addicted to the Use of Intoxicating Liquors	Excessive Drinkers	Social Drinkers	Home Drinkers	Periodical Drinkers	Occasional Drinkers	Aggregate Number of Drinking Conditions	Average Number of Drinking Conditions	Liquor Habits Unknown	Total Abstainers
Males.	12	1	11	3	-	11	26	2.17	5	24
Citizen born,	7	-	7	2	-	7	16	2.29	4	20
Alien,	5	1	4	1	-	4	10	2.00	1	4
Females.	-	-	-	-	-	-	-	-	6	22
Citizen born,	-	-	-	-	-	-	-	-	3	15
Alien,	-	-	-	-	-	-	-	-	3	7
BOTH SEXES.	12	1	11	3	-	11	26	2 17	11	46
Citizen born,	7	-	7	2	-	7	16	2.29	7	35
Alien,	5	1	4	1	-	4	10	2.00	4	11

AGE PERIOD: 20-29.

Males.	101	45	46	24	17	47	179	1.77	73	58
Citizen born,	54	25	25	7	12	23	92	1.70	41	41
Naturalized,	6	3	3	2	-	3	11	1.83	5	-
Alien,	39	17	18	15	5	19	74	1.89	27	17
Unknown,	2	-	-	-	-	2	2	1.00	-	-
Females.	24	10	10	8	4	11	43	1.79	44	105
Citizen born,	10	3	4	3	3	5	18	1.80	20	59
Alien,	14	7	6	5	1	6	25	1.79	24	46
BOTH SEXES.	125	55	56	32	21	58	222	1.78	117	163
Citizen born,	64	28	29	10	15	28	110	1.72	61	100
Naturalized,	6	3	3	2	-	3	11	1.83	5	-
Alien,	53	24	24	20	6	25	99	1.87	51	63
Unknown,	2	-	-	-	-	2	2	1.00	-	-

Insanity; Sex, Political Condition, and Liquor Habits of the Insane: By Age Periods — Continued.

AGE PERIOD: 30-39.

SEX AND POLITICAL CONDITION.	Number addicted to the Use of Intoxicating Liquors	Excessive Drinkers	Social Drinkers	Home Drinkers	Periodical Drinkers	Occasional Drinkers	Aggregate Number of Drinking Conditions	Average Number of Drinking Conditions	Liquor Habits Unknown	Total Abstainers
Males.	143	76	53	27	22	52	230	1.61	65	31
Citizen born,	80	41	29	13	15	28	126	1.58	37	21
Naturalized,	14	8	6	4	1	6	25	1.64	5	1
Alien,	49	27	18	10	6	18	79	1.61	23	9
Females.	43	21	16	13	6	16	72	1.67	50	125
Citizen born,	23	11	9	8	3	10	41	1 78	26	80
Alien,	20	10	7	5	3	6	31	1.55	24	45
BOTH SEXES.	186	97	69	40	28	68	302	1.62	115	156
Citizen born,	103	52	38	21	18	38	167	1.62	63	101
Naturalized,	14	8	6	4	1	6	25	1.79	5	1
Alien,	69	37	25	15	9	24	110	1.59	47	54

AGE PERIOD: 40-49.

SEX AND POLITICAL CONDITION.	Number addicted to the Use of Intoxicating Liquors	Excessive Drinkers	Social Drinkers	Home Drinkers	Periodical Drinkers	Occasional Drinkers	Aggregate Number of Drinking Conditions	Average Number of Drinking Conditions	Liquor Habits Unknown	Total Abstainers
Males.	115	64	44	26	9	44	187	1.63	48	25
Citizen born,	49	28	17	10	4	17	76	1 55	31	19
Naturalized,	27	19	8	5	-	8	40	1.48	3	1
Alien,	39	17	19	11	5	19	71	1.82	13	4
Unknown,	-	-	-	-	-	-	-	-	1	1
Females.	43	21	13	15	6	15	70	1.63	42	99
Citizen born,	15	8	4	4	3	3	22	1.47	21	67
Alien,	28	13	9	11	3	12	48	1.71	21	32
BOTH SEXES.	158	85	57	41	15	59	257	1.63	90	124
Citizen born,	64	36	21	14	7	20	98	1.53	52	86
Naturalized,	27	19	8	5	-	8	40	1.48	3	1
Alien,	67	30	28	22	8	31	119	1.78	34	36
Unknown,	-	-	-	-	-	-	-	-	1	1

AGE PERIOD: 50-59.

SEX AND POLITICAL CONDITION.	Number addicted to the Use of Intoxicating Liquors	Excessive Drinkers	Social Drinkers	Home Drinkers	Periodical Drinkers	Occasional Drinkers	Aggregate Number of Drinking Conditions	Average Number of Drinking Conditions	Liquor Habits Unknown	Total Abstainers
Males.	63	28	26	20	10	25	109	1.73	46	18
Citizen born,	19	8	7	5	3	8	31	1 63	30	13
Naturalized,	11	6	4	3	1	3	17	1.55	4	-
Alien,	31	13	14	11	5	14	57	1.84	12	5
Unknown,	2	1	1	1	1	-	4	2.00	-	-

Insanity; Sex, Political Condition, and Liquor Habits of the Insane: By Age Periods — Continued.

AGE PERIOD: 50-59 — Concluded.

SEX AND POLITICAL CONDITION.	Number addicted to the Use of Intoxicating Liquors	Excessive Drinkers	Social Drinkers	Home Drinkers	Periodical Drinkers	Occasional Drinkers	Aggregate Number of Drinking Conditions	Average Number of Drinking Conditions	Liquor Habits Unknown	Total Abstainers
Females.	24	12	6	9	2	8	37	1.54	30	54
Citizen born, .	5	3	–	1	–	2	6	1.20	15	23
Alien, . .	19	9	6	8	2	6	31	1.63	15	31
BOTH SEXES.	87	40	32	29	12	33	146	1.68	76	72
Citizen born, .	24	11	7	6	3	10	37	1.54	45	36
Naturalized, .	11	6	4	3	1	3	17	1.55	4	–
Alien, . .	50	22	20	19	7	20	88	1.76	27	36
Unknown, . .	2	1	1	1	1	–	4	2.00	–	–

AGE PERIOD: 60-79.

Males.	75	31	31	17	6	38	123	1.64	29	23
Citizen born, .	32	16	11	7	4	14	52	1.63	16	15
Naturalized, .	22	5	13	7	–	15	40	1.82	3	3
Alien, . .	20	10	6	2	2	8	28	1.40	10	4
Unknown, . .	1	–	1	1	–	1	3	3.00	–	1
Females.	20	1	11	11	5	14	42	2.10	36	71
Citizen born, .	3	–	1	1	–	3	5	1.67	17	40
Alien, . .	17	1	10	10	5	11	37	2.18	19	31
BOTH SEXES.	95	32	42	28	11	52	165	1.74	65	94
Citizen born, .	35	16	12	8	4	17	57	1.63	33	55
Naturalized, .	22	5	13	7	–	15	40	1.82	3	3
Alien, . .	37	11	16	12	7	19	65	1.76	29	35
Unknown, . .	1	–	1	1	–	1	3	3.00	–	1

AGE PERIOD: 80 +.

Males.	6	1	5	5	–	5	16	2.67	7	1
Citizen born, .	5	–	5	5	–	5	15	3.00	6	1
Naturalized, .	–	–	–	–	–	–	–	–	1	–
Alien, . .	1	1	–	–	–	–	1	1.00	–	–
Females.	2	–	2	2	–	2	6	3.00	4	10
Citizen born, .	–	–	–	–	–	–	–	–	3	9
Alien, . .	2	–	2	2	–	2	6	3.00	1	1

Insanity ; Sex, Political Condition, and Liquor Habits of the Insane : By Age Periods — Concluded.

AGE PERIOD : 80 + — Concluded.

SEX AND POLITICAL CONDITION.	Number addicted to the Use of Intoxicating Liquors	Excessive Drinkers	Social Drinkers	Home Drinkers	Periodical Drinkers	Occasional Drinkers	Aggregate Number of Drinking Conditions	Average Number of Drinking Conditions	Liquor Habits Unknown	Total Abstainers
BOTH SEXES.	8	1	7	7	-	7	22	2.75	11	11
Citizen born,	5	.-	5	5	-	5	15	3.00	9	10
Naturalized,	-	-	-	-	-	-	-	-	1	-
Alien,	3	1	2	2	-	2	7	2.33	1	1

AGE PERIOD : Unknown.

Males.	-	-	-	-	-	-	-	-	2	-
Citizen born,	-	-	-	-	-	-	-	ˑ -	1	-
Naturalized,	-	-	-	-	-	-	-	-	1	-
Females.	-	-	-	-	-	-	-	-	1	2
Citizen born,	-	-	-	-	-	-	-	-	-	1
Alien,	-	-	-	-	-	-	-	-	-	1
Unknown,	-	-	-	-	-	-	-	-	1	-
BOTH SEXES.	-	-	-	-	-	-	-	-	3	2
Citizen born,	-	-	-	-	-	-	-	-	1	1
Naturalized,	-	-	-	-	-	-	-	-	1	-
Alien,	-	-	-	-	-	-	-	-	-	1
Unknown,	-	-	-	-	-	-	-	-	1	-

RECAPITULATION.

SEX AND POLITICAL CONDITION.	Number addicted to the Use of Intoxicating Liquors	Excessive Drinkers	Social Drinkers	Home Drinkers	Periodical Drinkers	Occasional Drinkers	Aggregate Number of Drinking Conditions	Average Number of Drinking Conditions	Liquor Habits Unknown	Total Abstainers
Males.	515	246	216	122	64	222	870	1.69	275	180
Citizen born,	246	118	101	49	38	102	408	1.66	166	130
Naturalized,	80	41	34	21	2	35	133	1.66	22	5
Alien,	184	86	79	50	23	82	320	1.74	86	43
Unknown,	5	1	2	2	1	3	9	1.80	1	2
Females.	156	65	58	58	23	66	270	1.73	213	488
Citizen born,	56	25	18	17	9	23	92	1.64	105	294
Alien,	100	40	40	41	14	43	178	1.78	107	194
Unknown,	-	-	-	-	-	-	-	-	1	-

RECAPITULATION — Concluded.

SEX AND POLITICAL CONDITION.	Number addicted to the Use of Intoxicating Liquors	Excessive Drinkers	Social Drinkers	Home Drinkers	Periodical Drinkers	Occasional Drinkers	Aggregate Number of Drinking Conditions	Average Number of Drinking Conditions	Liquor Habits Unknown	Total Abstainers
BOTH SEXES.	671	311	274	180	87	288	1,140	1.70	488	668
Citizen born, .	302	143	119	66	47	125	500	1.66	271	424
Naturalized, .	80	41	34	21	2	35	133	1.66	22	5
Alien, . .	284	126	119	91	37	125	498	1.75	193	237
Unknown, . .	5	1	2	2	1	3	9	1.80	2	2

RECAPITULATION: BY AGE PERIODS.

SEX AND AGE PERIODS.	Number addicted to the Use of Intoxicating Liquors	Excessive Drinkers	Social Drinkers	Home Drinkers	Periodical Drinkers	Occasional Drinkers	Aggregate Number of Drinking Conditions	Average Number of Drinking Conditions	Liquor Habits Unknown	Total Abstainers
Males.	515	246	216	122	64	222	870	1.69	275	180
15–19, . .	12	1	11	3	–	11	26	2.17	5	24
20–29, . .	101	45	46	24	17	47	179	1.77	73	58
30–39, . .	143	76	53	27	22	52	230	1.61	65	31
40–49, . .	115	64	44	26	9	44	187	1.63	48	25
50–59, . .	63	28	26	20	10	25	109	1.73	46	18
60–79, . .	75	31	31	17	6	38	123	1.64	29	23
80+, . . .	6	1	5	5	–	5	16	2.67	7	1
Unknown, . .	–	–	–	–	–	–	–	–	2	–
Females.	156	65	58	58	23	66	270	1.73	213	488
15–19, . .	–	–	–	–	–	–	–	–	6	22
20–29, . .	24	10	10	8	4	11	43	1.79	44	105
30–39, . .	43	21	16	13	6	16	72	1.67	50	125
40–49, . .	43	21	13	15	6	15	70	1.63	42	99
50–59, . .	24	12	6	9	2	8	37	1.54	30	54
60–79, . .	20	1	11	11	5	14	42	2 10	36	71
80+, . . .	2	–	2	2	–	2	6	3.00	4	10
Unknown, . .	–	–	–	–	–	–	–	–	1	2
BOTH SEXES.	671	311	274	180	87	288	1,140	1.70	488	668
15–19, . .	12	1	11	3	–	11	26	2.17	11	46
20–29, . .	125	55	56	32	21	58	222	1.78	117	163
30–39, . .	186	97	69	40	28	68	302	1.62	115	156
40–49, . .	158	85	57	41	15	59	257	1.63	90	124
50–59, . .	87	40	32	29	12	33	146	1.68	76	72
60–79, . .	95	32	42	28	11	52	165	1.74	65	94
80+, . . .	8	1	7	7	–	7	22	2.75	11	11
Unknown, . .	–	–	–	–	–	–	–	–	3	2

This table shows a deficit of nine persons in the aggregate, including four males and five females. These nine persons were found in the age periods 5–9 and 10–14. As they were total abstainers, and there were no other facts reported for persons within age periods under 15, these were disregarded in tabulating the points covered by this table.

We refer in the analysis to the recapitulation. Of both sexes, there were 668 total abstainers and 488 persons for whom the information was not obtainable. The number addicted to the use of intoxicating liquors was 671, of whom 311 were found to be excessive drinkers. There were 274 who were properly included under the head of social drinkers; 180 home drinkers; 87 periodical drinkers; and 288 occasional drinkers. The excessive drinkers among the females numbered 65 out of 156, and among the males, 246 out of 515. In the classification of drinking conditions, the 156 females appear under 270 heads, an average of 1.73 to each person. The 515 males appear under 870 heads, an average of 1.69 to each person.

A similar table follows with reference to the fathers of the insane.

Insanity ; Sex, Political Condition, and Liquor Habits of Fathers of Insane Persons : By Age Periods.

AGE PERIOD: 5-9.

SEX AND POLITICAL CONDITION.	Number addicted to the Use of Intoxicating Liquors	Excessive Drinkers	Social Drinkers	Home Drinkers	Periodical Drinkers	Occasional Drinkers	Aggregate Number of Drinking Conditions	Average Number of Drinking Conditions	Liquor Habits Unknown	Total Abstainers
Males.	-	-	-	-	-	-	-	-	-	1
Citizen born,	-	-	-	-	-	-	-	-	-	1
Females.	2	1	1	1	-	1	4	2.00	1	-
Citizen born,	2	1	1	1	-	1	4	2.00	-	-
Alien,	-	-	-	-	-	-	-	-	1	-
BOTH SEXES.	2	1	1	1	-	1	4	2.00	1	1
Citizen born,	2	1	1	1	-	1	4	2.00	-	1
Alien,	-	-	-	-	-	-	-	-	1	-

AGE PERIOD: 10-14.

Males.	2	1	1	-	-	1	3	1.50	1	-
Citizen born,	1	-	1	-	-	1	2	2.00	-	-
Alien,	1	1	-	-	-	-	1	1.00	1	-

Insanity; Sex, Political Condition, and Liquor Habits of Fathers of Insane Persons: By Age Periods — Continued.

AGE PERIOD: 10-14 — Concluded.

SEX AND POLITICAL CONDITION.	Number addicted to the Use of Intoxicating Liquors	Excessive Drinkers	Social Drinkers	Home Drinkers	Periodical Drinkers	Occasional Drinkers	Aggregate Number of Drinking Conditions	Average Number of Drinking Conditions	Liquor Habits Unknown	Total Abstainers
Females.	1	1	-	-	-	-	1	1.00	1	-
Citizen born, .	-	-	-	-	-	-	-	-	1	-
Alien, . .	1	1	-	-	-	-	1	1.00	-	-
BOTH SEXES.	3	2	1	-	-	1	4	1.33	2	-
Citizen born, .	1	-	1	-	-	1	2	2.00	1	-
Alien, . .	2	2	-	-	-	-	2	1.00	1	-

AGE PERIOD: 15-19.

Males.	19	3	14	10	2	14	43	2.26	17	5
Citizen born, .	14	3	10	7	1	10	31	2.21	12	5
Alien, . .	5	-	4	3	1	4	12	2.40	5	-
Females.	10	2	7	7	1	8	25	2.50	14	4
Citizen born, .	5	2	3	3	-	3	11	2.20	10	3
Alien, . .	5	-	4	4	1	5	14	2.80	4	1
BOTH SEXES.	29	5	21	17	3	22	68	2.34	31	9
Citizen born, .	19	5	13	10	1	13	42	2.21	22	8
Alien, . .	10	-	8	7	2	9	26	2.60	9	1

AGE PERIOD: 20-29.

Males.	73	6	60	46	3	63	178	2.44	120	39
Citizen born, .	43	4	35	27	1	38	105	2.44	65	28
Naturalized, .	3	-	3	2	-	3	8	2.67	8	-
Alien, . .	26	2	21	16	2	21	62	2.38	47	10
Unknown, . .	1	-	1	1	-	1	3	3.00	-	1
Females.	74	4	61	55	4	67	191	2.58	77	22
Citizen born, .	37	2	31	27	3	34	97	2.62	38	14
Alien, . .	37	2	30	28	1	33	94	2.54	39	8
BOTH SEXES.	147	10	121	101	7	130	369	2.51	197	61
Citizen born, .	80	6	66	54	4	72	202	2.53	103	42
Naturalized, .	3	-	3	2	-	3	8	2.67	8	-
Alien, . .	63	4	51	44	3	54	156	2.48	86	18
Unknown, . .	1	-	1	1	-	1	3	3.00	-	1

Insanity; Sex, Political Condition, and Liquor Habits of Fathers of Insane Persons: By Age Periods — Continued.

AGE PERIOD: 30-39.

SEX AND POLITICAL CONDITION.	Number addicted to the Use of Intoxicating Liquors	Excessive Drinkers	Social Drinkers	Home Drinkers	Periodical Drinkers	Occasional Drinkers	Aggregate Number of Drinking Conditions	Average Number of Drinking Conditions	Liquor Habits Unknown	Total Abstainers
Males.	79	10	61	47	3	61	182	2.30	138	22
Citizen born, .	49	6	37	25	2	36	106	2.16	75	14
Naturalized, .	9	2	7	6	–	7	22	2.44	10	1
Alien, . .	21	2	17	16	1	18	54	2.57	53	7
Females.	72	9	50	43	3	60	165	2.29	100	46
Citizen born, .	42	5	27	25	3	35	95	2.26	55	32
Alien, . .	30	4	23	18	–	25	70	2.33	45	14
BOTH SEXES.	151	19	111	90	6	121	347	2.30	238	68
Citizen born, .	91	11	64	60	5	71	201	2.21	130	46
Naturalized, .	9	2	7	6	–	7	22	2.44	10	1
Alien, .	51	6	40	34	1	43	124	2.45	98	21

AGE PERIOD: 40-49.

Males.	64	5	52	43	1	57	158	2.47	104	20
Citizen born, .	28	3	20	18	1	23	65	2.32	58	13
Naturalized, .	17	1	14	9	–	16	40	2.35	13	1
Alien, . .	19	1	18	16	–	18	53	2.79	31	6
Unknown, . .	–	–	–	–	–	–	–	–	2	–
Females.	69	4	61	51	3	62	181	2.62	89	26
Citizen born, .	39	2	34	29	1	35	101	2.59	47	17
Alien, . .	30	2	27	22	2	27	80	2.67	42	9
BOTH SEXES.	133	9	113	94	4	119	339	2.55	193	46
Citizen born, .	67	5	54	47	2	58	166	2.44	105	30
Naturalized, .	17	1	14	9	–	16	40	2.35	13	1
Alien, . .	49	3	45	38	2	45	133	2.71	73	15
Unknown, . .	–	–	–	–	–	–	–	–	2	–

AGE PERIOD: 50-59.

Males.	38	2	32	26	2	35	97	2.55	74	15
Citizen born, .	13	1	12	10	2	12	37	2.85	41	8
Naturalized, .	7	–	7	5	–	7	19	2.71	7	1
Alien, . .	17	1	12	10	–	15	38	2.24	26	5
Unknown, . .	1	–	1	1	–	1	3	3.00	–	1

Insanity; Sex, Political Condition, and Liquor Habits of Fathers of Insane Persons: By Age Periods — Continued.

AGE PERIOD: 50–59 — Concluded.

SEX AND POLITICAL CONDITION.	Number addicted to the Use of Intoxicating Liquors	Excessive Drinkers	Social Drinkers	Home Drinkers	Periodical Drinkers	Occasional Drinkers	Aggregate Number of Drinking Conditions	Average Number of Drinking Conditions	Liquor Habits Unknown	Total Abstainers
Females.	31	2	27	23	1	26	79	2.55	53	24
Citizen born,	5	1	3	3	-	4	11	2.20	27	11
Alien,	26	1	24	20	1	22	68	2.62	26	13
BOTH SEXES.	69	4	59	49	3	61	176	2.55	127	39
Citizen born,	18	2	15	13	2	16	48	2.61	68	19
Naturalized,	7	-	7	5	-	7	19	2.71	7	1
Alien,	43	2	36	30	1	37	106	2.47	52	18
Unknown,	1	-	1	1	-	1	3	3.00	-	1

AGE PERIOD: 60–79.

SEX AND POLITICAL CONDITION.	Number addicted to the Use of Intoxicating Liquors	Excessive Drinkers	Social Drinkers	Home Drinkers	Periodical Drinkers	Occasional Drinkers	Aggregate Number of Drinking Conditions	Average Number of Drinking Conditions	Liquor Habits Unknown	Total Abstainers
Males.	37	2	32	28	-	35	97	2.62	64	26
Citizen born,	17	1	16	12	-	16	45	2.65	32	14
Naturalized,	12	-	10	11	-	11	32	2.67	9	7
Alien,	7	1	5	4	-	7	17	2.43	23	4
Unknown,	1	-	1	1	-	1	3	3.00	-	1
Females.	33	5	26	20	-	27	78	2.36	65	29
Citizen born,	13	2	9	8	-	11	30	2.31	29	18
Alien,	20	3	17	12	-	16	48	2.40	36	11
BOTH SEXES.	70	7	58	48	-	62	175	2.50	129	55
Citizen born,	30	3	25	20	-	27	75	2.50	61	32
Naturalized,	12	-	10	11	-	11	32	2.67	9	7
Alien,	27	4	22	16	-	23	65	2.41	59	15
Unknown,	1	-	1	1	-	1	3	3.00	-	1

AGE PERIOD: 80 +.

SEX AND POLITICAL CONDITION.	Number addicted to the Use of Intoxicating Liquors	Excessive Drinkers	Social Drinkers	Home Drinkers	Periodical Drinkers	Occasional Drinkers	Aggregate Number of Drinking Conditions	Average Number of Drinking Conditions	Liquor Habits Unknown	Total Abstainers
Males.	4	-	4	4	-	4	12	3.00	10	-
Citizen born,	3	-	3	3	-	3	9	3.00	9	-
Naturalized,	-	-	-	-	-	-	-	-	1	-
Alien,	1	-	1	1	-	1	3	3.00	-	-
Females.	7	-	6	5	-	7	18	2.57	8	1
Citizen born,	4	-	3	3	-	4	10	2.50	7	1
Alien,	3	-	3	2	-	3	8	2.67	1	-
BOTH SEXES.	11	-	10	9	-	11	30	2.72	18	1
Citizen born,	7	-	6	6	-	7	19	2.70	16	1
Naturalized,	-	-	-	-	-	-	-	-	1	-
Alien,	4	-	4	3	-	4	11	2.75	1	-

Insanity; Sex, Political Condition, and Liquor Habits of Fathers of Insane Persons: By Age Periods — Concluded.

AGE PERIOD: Unknown.

SEX AND POLITICAL CONDITION.	Number addicted to the Use of Intoxicating Liquors	Excessive Drinkers	Social Drinkers	Home Drinkers	Periodical Drinkers	Occasional Drinkers	Aggregate Number of Drinking Conditions	Average Number of Drinking Conditions	Liquor Habits Unknown	Total Abstainers
Males.	-	-	-	-	-	-	-	-	2	-
Citizen born,	-	-	-	-	-	-	-	-	1	-
Naturalized,	-	-	-	-	-	-	-	-	1	-
Females.	1	-	1	1	-	1	3	3.00	1	1
Citizen born,	1	-	1	1	-	1	3	3.00	-	-
Alien,	-	-	-	-	-	-	-	-	-	1
Unknown,	-	-	-	-	-	-	-	-	1	-
BOTH SEXES.	1	-	1	1	-	1	3	3.00	3	1
Citizen born,	1	-	1	1	-	1	3	3.00	1	-
Naturalized,	-	-	-	-	-	-	-	-	1	-
Alien,	-	-	-	-	-	-	-	-	-	1
Unknown,	-	-	-	-	-	-	-	-	1	-

RECAPITULATION.

SEX AND POLITICAL CONDITION.	Number addicted to the Use of Intoxicating Liquors	Excessive Drinkers	Social Drinkers	Home Drinkers	Periodical Drinkers	Occasional Drinkers	Aggregate Number of Drinking Conditions	Average Number of Drinking Conditions	Liquor Habits Unknown	Total Abstainers
Males.	316	29	256	204	11	270	770	2.44	530	128
Citizen born,	168	18	134	102	7	139	400	2.38	293	83
Naturalized,	48	3	41	33	-	44	121	2.52	49	10
Alien,	97	8	78	66	4	84	240	2.47	186	32
Unknown,	3	-	3	3	-	3	9	3.00	2	3
Females.	300	28	240	206	12	259	745	2.48	409	153
Citizen born,	148	15	112	100	7	128	362	2.45	214	96
Alien,	152	13	128	106	5	131	383	2.52	194	57
Unknown,	-	-	-	-	-	-	-	-	1	-
BOTH SEXES.	616	57	496	410	23	529	1,515	2.46	939	281
Citizen born,	316	33	246	202	14	267	762	2.41	507	179
Naturalized,	48	3	41	33	-	44	121	2.52	49	10
Alien,	249	21	206	172	9	215	623	2.50	380	89
Unknown,	3	-	3	3	-	3	9	3.00	3	3

RECAPITULATION: BY AGE PERIODS.

SEX AND AGE PERIODS.	Number addicted to the Use of Intoxicating Liquors	Excessive Drinkers	Social Drinkers	Home Drinkers	Periodical Drinkers	Occasional Drinkers	Aggregate Number of Drinking Conditions	Average Number of Drinking Conditions	Liquor Habits Unknown	Total Abstainers
Males.	316	29	256	204	11	270	770	2.44	530	128
5-9, . .	-	-	-	-	-	-	-	-	-	1
10-14, . .	2	1	1	-	-	1	3	1.50	1	-
15-19, . .	19	3	14	10	2	14	43	2.26	17	5
20-29, . .	73	6	60	46	3	63	178	2.44	120	39
30-39, . .	79	10	61	47	3	61	182	2.30	138	22
40-49, . .	64	5	52	43	1	57	158	2.47	104	20
50-59, . .	38	2	32	26	2	35	97	2.55	74	15
60-79, . .	37	2	32	28	-	35	97	2.62	64	26
80 +, . . .	4	-	4	4	-	4	12	3.00	10	-
Unknown, .	-	-	-	-	-	-	-	-	2	-
Females.	300	28	240	206	12	259	745	2.48	409	153
5-9, . .	2	1	1	1	-	1	4	2.00	1	-
10-14, . .	1	1	-	-	-	-	1	1.00	1	-
15-19, . .	10	2	7	7	1	8	25	2.50	14	4
20-29, . .	74	4	61	55	4	67	191	2.58	77	22
30-39, . .	72	9	50	43	3	60	165	2.29	100	46
40-49, . .	69	4	61	51	3	62	181	2.62	89	26
50-59, . .	31	2	27	23	1	26	79	2.55	53	24
60-79, . .	33	5	26	20	-	27	78	2.15	65	29
80 +, . . .	7	-	6	5	-	7	18	2.57	8	1
Unknown, .	1	-	1	1	-	1	3	3.00	1	1
BOTH SEXES.	616	57	496	410	23	529	1,515	2.46	939	281
5-9, . .	2	1	1	1	-	1	4	2.00	1	1
10-14, . .	3	2	1	-	-	1	4	1.33	2	-
15-19, . .	29	5	21	17	3	22	68	2.34	31	9
20-29, . .	147	10	121	101	7	130	369	2.51	197	61
30-39, . .	151	19	111	90	6	121	347	2.30	238	68
40-49, . .	133	9	113	94	4	119	339	2.53	193	46
50-59, . .	69	4	59	49	3	61	176	2.55	127	39
60-79, . .	70	7	58	48	-	62	175	2.50	129	55
80 +, . . .	11	-	10	9	-	11	30	2.72	18	1
Unknown, .	1	-	1	1	-	1	3	3.00	3	1

In this table the classification by age periods, sex, and political condition is maintained. In the case of 281 insane persons the fathers were total abstainers, and the facts as to 939 could not be ascertained. Excluding these, there remain 616 persons whose fathers were addicted to the use of intoxicating liquor, and among these fathers there were 57 excessive drinkers. Those included under the other different heads, respectively, are the following: social drinkers, 496; home drinkers, 410; periodical drinkers, 23; and occasional drinkers, 529. There were 316 male insane persons whose fathers were addicted to the use of intoxicating liquor, and of these fathers 29 were excessive drinkers. There were also 300 female insane persons whose fathers were addicted to liquor, 28 of these fathers being excessive drinkers.

A similar table for the mothers of the insane follows.

Insanity; Sex, Political Condition, and Liquor Habits of Mothers of Insane Persons: By Age Periods.

AGE PERIOD: 5-9.

SEX AND POLITICAL CONDITION.	Number addicted to the Use of Intoxicating Liquors	Excessive Drinkers	Social Drinkers	Home Drinkers	Periodical Drinkers	Occasional Drinkers	Aggregate Number of Drinking Conditions	Average Number of Drinking Conditions	Liquor Habits Unknown	Total Abstainers
Males.	-	-	-	-	-	-	-	-	-	1
Citizen born, .	-	-	-	-	-	-	-	-	-	1
Females.	1	-	1	1	-	1	3	3.00	2	-
Citizen born, .	1	-	1	1	-	1	3	3.00	1	-
Alien, . .	-	-	-	-	-	-	-	-	1	-
BOTH SEXES.	1	-	1	1	-	1	3	3.00	2	1
Citizen born, .	1	-	1	1	-	1	3	3.00	1	1
Alien, . .	-	-	-	-	-	-	-	-	1	-

AGE PERIOD: 10-14.

	Number addicted to the Use of Intoxicating Liquors	Excessive Drinkers	Social Drinkers	Home Drinkers	Periodical Drinkers	Occasional Drinkers	Aggregate Number of Drinking Conditions	Average Number of Drinking Conditions	Liquor Habits Unknown	Total Abstainers
Males.	2	1	1	1	-	1	4	2.00	1	-
Citizen born, .	1	1	-	-	-	-	1	1.00	-	-
Alien, . .	1	-	1	1	-	1	3	3.00	1	-
Females.	-	-	-	-	-	-	-	-	2	-
Citizen born, .	-	-	-	-	-	-	-	-	1	-
Alien, . .	-	-	-	-	-	-	-	-	1	-
BOTH SEXES.	2	1	1	1	-	1	4	2.00	3	-
Citizen born, .	1	1	-	-	-	-	1	1.00	1	-
Alien, . .	1	-	1	1	-	1	3	3.00	2	-

Insanity; Sex, Political Condition, and Liquor Habits of Mothers of Insane Persons: By Age Periods — Continued.

AGE PERIOD: 15-19.

SEX AND POLITICAL CONDITION.	Number addicted to the Use of Intoxicating Liquors	Excessive Drinkers	Social Drinkers	Home Drinkers	Periodical Drinkers	Occasional Drinkers	Aggregate Number of Drinking Conditions	Average Number of Drinking Conditions	Liquor Habits Unknown	Total Abstainers
Males.	3	–	1	3	–	2	6	2.00	17	21
Citizen born, .	1	–	–	1	–	1	2	2.00	12	18
Alien, . .	2	–	1	2	–	1	4	2.00	5	3
Females.	5	–	4	5	–	5	14	2.80	14	9
Citizen born, .	3	–	2	3	–	3	8	2.67	10	5
Alien, . .	2	–	2	2	–	2	6	3.00	4	4
BOTH SEXES.	8	–	5	8	–	7	20	2.50	31	30
Citizen born, .	4	–	2	4	–	4	10	2.50	22	23
Alien, . .	4	–	3	4	–	3	10	2.50	9	7

AGE PERIOD: 20-29.

SEX AND POLITICAL CONDITION.	Number addicted to the Use of Intoxicating Liquors	Excessive Drinkers	Social Drinkers	Home Drinkers	Periodical Drinkers	Occasional Drinkers	Aggregate Number of Drinking Conditions	Average Number of Drinking Conditions	Liquor Habits Unknown	Total Abstainers
Males.	24	1	16	20	–	19	56	2.33	124	84
Citizen born, .	9	1	6	8	–	5	20	2.22	68	59
Naturalized, .	1	–	1	1	–	1	3	3.00	8	2
Alien, . .	14	–	9	11	–	13	33	2.36	48	21
Unknown, . .	–	–	–	–	–	–	–	–	–	2
Females.	29	4	19	20	1	20	64	2.21	81	63
Citizen born, .	14	3	8	7	1	7	26	1.86	41	34
Alien, . .	15	1	11	13	–	13	38	2.53	40	29
BOTH SEXES.	53	5	35	40	1	39	120	2.26	205	147
Citizen born, .	23	4	14	15	1	12	46	2.00	109	93
Naturalized, .	1	–	1	1	–	1	3	3.00	8	2
Alien, . .	29	1	20	24	–	26	71	2.44	88	50
Unknown, . .	–	–	–	–	–	–	–	–	–	2

AGE PERIOD: 30-39.

SEX AND POLITICAL CONDITION.	Number addicted to the Use of Intoxicating Liquors	Excessive Drinkers	Social Drinkers	Home Drinkers	Periodical Drinkers	Occasional Drinkers	Aggregate Number of Drinking Conditions	Average Number of Drinking Conditions	Liquor Habits Unknown	Total Abstainers
Males.	30	1	20	26	–	27	74	2.47	143	66
Citizen born, .	15	1	8	11	–	13	33	2.20	77	46
Naturalized, .	6	–	5	6	–	6	17	2.83	11	3
Alien, . .	9	–	7	9	–	8	24	2.67	55	17

Insanity; Sex, Political Condition, and Liquor Habits of Mothers of Insane Persons: By Age Periods — Continued.

AGE PERIOD: 30-39 — Concluded.

SEX AND POLITICAL CONDITION.	Number addicted to the Use of Intoxicating Liquors	Excessive Drinkers	Social Drinkers	Home Drinkers	Periodical Drinkers	Occasional Drinkers	Aggregate Number of Drinking Conditions	Average Number of Drinking Conditions	Liquor Habits Unknown	Total Abstainers
Females.	28	5	20	19	-	21	65	2.32	104	86
Citizen born,	13	2	8	9	-	10	29	2.23	57	59
Alien,	15	3	12	10	-	11	36	2.40	47	27
BOTH SEXES.	58	6	40	45	-	48	139	2.40	247	152
Citizen born,	28	3	16	20	-	23	62	2.21	134	105
Naturalized,	6	-	5	6	-	6	17	2.83	11	3
Alien,	24	3	19	19	-	19	60	2.50	102	44

AGE PERIOD: 40-49.

Males.	24	1	20	20	-	22	63	2.63	105	59
Citizen born,	5	-	4	3	-	4	11	2.20	59	35
Naturalized,	7	-	5	6	-	7	18	2.57	13	11
Alien,	12	1	11	11	-	11	34	2.83	31	13
Unknown,	-	-	-	-	-	-	-	-	2	-
Females.	25	-	24	22	-	24	70	2.80	90	69
Citizen born,	6	-	6	6	-	6	18	3.00	48	49
Alien,	19	-	18	16	-	18	52	2.74	42	20
BOTH SEXES.	49	1	44	42	-	46	133	2.71	195	128
Citizen born,	11	-	10	9	-	10	29	2.64	107	84
Naturalized,	7	-	5	6	-	7	18	2.57	13	11
Alien,	31	1	29	27	-	29	86	2.77	73	33
Unknown,	-	-	-	-	-	-	-	-	2	-

AGE PERIOD: 50-59.

Males.	17	-	14	13	-	17	44	2.59	75	35
Citizen born,	2	-	2	2	-	2	6	3.00	42	18
Naturalized,	4	-	4	3	-	4	11	2.75	7	4
Alien,	11	-	8	8	-	11	27	2.45	26	11
Unknown,	-	-	-	-	-	-	-	-	-	2
Females.	9	-	9	8	-	9	26	2.89	54	45
Citizen born,	-	-	-	-	-	-	-	-	27	16
Alien,	9	-	9	8	-	9	26	2.89	27	29

Insanity ; Sex, Political Condition, and Liquor Habits of Mothers of Insane Persons: By Age Periods — Continued.

AGE PERIOD: 50–59 — Concluded.

SEX AND POLITICAL CONDITION.	Number addicted to the Use of Intoxicating Liquors	Excessive Drinkers	Social Drinkers	Home Drinkers	Periodical Drinkers	Occasional Drinkers	Aggregate Number of Drinking Conditions	Average Number of Drinking Conditions	Liquor Habits Unknown	Total Abstainers
BOTH SEXES.	26	–	23	21	–	26	70	2.69	129	80
Citizen born,	2	–	2	2	–	2	6	3.00	69	34
Naturalized,	4	–	4	3	–	4	11	2.75	7	4
Alien,	20	–	17	16	–	20	53	2.65	53	40
Unknown,	–	–	–	–	–	–	–	–	–	2

AGE PERIOD: 60–79.

Males.	12	–	9	11	–	12	32	2.67	65	50
Citizen born,	1	–	–	1	–	1	2	2.00	34	28
Naturalized,	5	–	3	4	–	5	12	2.40	8	15
Alien,	5	–	5	5	–	5	15	3.00	23	6
Unknown,	1	–	1	1	–	1	3	3.00	–	1
Females.	10	–	8	10	–	10	28	2.80	67	50
Citizen born,	1	–	1	1	–	1	3	3.00	31	28
Alien,	9	–	7	9	–	9	25	2.78	36	22
BOTH SEXES.	22	–	17	21	–	22	60	2.73	132	100
Citizen born,	2	–	1	2	–	2	5	2.50	65	56
Naturalized,	5	–	3	4	–	5	12	2.40	8	15
Alien,	14	–	12	14	–	14	40	2.86	59	28
Unknown,	1	–	1	1	–	1	3	3.00	–	1

AGE PERIOD: 80 +.

Males.	–	–	–	–	–	–	–	–	10	4
Citizen born,	–	–	–	–	–	–	–	–	9	3
Naturalized,	–	–	–	–	–	–	–	–	1	–
Alien,	–	–	–	–	–	–	–	–	–	1
Females.	1	–	1	1	–	1	3	3.00	8	7
Citizen born,	–	–	–	–	–	–	–	–	7	5
Alien,	1	–	1	1	–	1	3	3.00	1	2
BOTH SEXES.	1	–	1	1	–	1	3	3.00	18	11
Citizen born,	–	–	–	–	–	–	–	–	16	8
Naturalized,	–	–	–	–	–	–	–	–	1	–
Alien,	1	–	1	1	–	1	3	3.00	1	3

Insanity; Sex, Political Condition, and Liquor Habits of Mothers of Insane Persons: By Age Periods — Concluded.

AGE PERIOD: Unknown.

SEX AND POLITICAL CONDITION.	Number addicted to the Use of Intoxicating Liquors	Excessive Drinkers	Social Drinkers	Home Drinkers	Periodical Drinkers	Occasional Drinkers	Aggregate Number of Drinking Conditions	Average Number of Drinking Conditions	Liquor Habits Unknown	Total Abstainers
Males.	-	-	-	-	-	-	-	-	2	-
Citizen born,	-	-	-	-	-	-	-	-	1	-
Naturalized,	-	-	-	-	-	-	-	-	1	-
Females.	-	-	-	-	-	-	-	-	1	2
Citizen born,	-	-	-	-	-	-	-	-	-	1
Alien,	-	-	-	-	-	-	-	-	-	1
Unknown,	-	-	-	-	-	-	-	-	1	-
BOTH SEXES.	-	-	-	-	-	-	~	-	3	2
Citizen born,	-	-	-	-	-	-	-	-	1	1
Naturalized,	-	-	-	-	-	-	-	-	1	-
Alien,	-	-	-	-	-	-	-	-	-	1
Unknown,	-	-	-	-	-	-	-	-	1	-

RECAPITULATION.

SEX AND POLITICAL CONDITION.	Number addicted to the Use of Intoxicating Liquors	Excessive Drinkers	Social Drinkers	Home Drinkers	Periodical Drinkers	Occasional Drinkers	Aggregate Number of Drinking Conditions	Average Number of Drinking Conditions	Liquor Habits Unknown	Total Abstainers
Males.	112	4	81	94	-	100	279	2.49	542	320
Citizen born,	34	3	20	26	-	26	75	2.21	302	208
Naturalized,	23	-	18	20	-	23	61	2.65	49	35
Alien,	54	1	42	47	-	50	140	2.59	189	72
Unknown,	1	-	1	1	-	1	3	3.00	2	5
Females.	108	9	86	86	1	91	273	2.53	423	331
Citizen born,	38	5	26	27	1	28	87	2.29	223	197
Alien,	70	4	60	59	-	63	186	2.66	199	134
Unknown,	-	-	-	-	-	-	-	-	1	-
BOTH SEXES.	220	13	167	180	1	191	552	2.51	965	651
Citizen born,	72	8	46	53	1	54	162	2.25	525	405
Naturalized,	23	-	18	20	-	23	61	2.65	49	35
Alien,	124	5	102	106	-	113	326	2.63	388	206
Unknown,	1	-	1	1	-	1	3	3.00	3	5

RECAPITULATION: BY AGE PERIODS.

SEX AND AGE PERIODS.	Number addicted to the Use of Intoxicating Liquors	Excessive Drinkers	Social Drinkers	Home Drinkers	Periodical Drinkers	Occasional Drinkers	Aggregate Number of Drinking Conditions	Average Number of Drinking Conditions	Liquor Habits Unknown	Total Abstainers
Males.	112	4	81	94	–	100	279	2.49	542	320
5-9, . . .	–	–	–	–	–	–	–	–	–	1
10-14, . .	2	1	1	1	–	1	4	2.00	1	–
15-19, . .	3	–	1	3	–	2	6	2.00	17	21
20-29, . .	24	1	16	20	–	19	56	2.33	124	84
30-39, . .	30	1	20	26	–	27	74	2.47	143	66
40-49, . .	24	1	20	20	–	22	63	2.63	105	59
50-59, . .	17	–	14	13	–	17	44	2.59	75	35
60-79, . .	12	–	9	11	–	12	32	2.67	65	50
80 +, . . .	–	–	–	–	–	–	–	–	10	4
Unknown, . .	–	–	–	–	–	–	–	–	2	–
Females.	108	9	86	86	1	91	273	2.53	423	331
5-9, . . .	1	–	1	1	–	1	3	3.00	2	–
10-14, . .	–	–	–	–	–	–	–	–	2	–
15-19, . .	5	–	4	5	–	5	14	2.80	14	9
20-29, . .	29	4	19	20	1	20	64	2.21	81	63
30-39, . .	28	5	20	19	–	21	65	2.32	104	86
40-49, . .	25	–	24	22	–	24	70	2.80	90	69
50-59, . .	9	–	9	8	–	9	26	2.89	54	45
60-79, . .	10	–	8	10	–	10	28	2.80	67	50
80 +, . . .	1	–	1	1	–	1	3	3.00	8	7
Unknown, . .	–	–	–	–	–	–	–	–	1	2
BOTH SEXES.	220	13	167	180	1	191	552	2.51	965	651
5-9, . . .	1	–	1	1	–	1	3	3.00	2	1
10-14, . .	2	1	1	1	–	1	4	2.00	3	–
15-19, . .	8	–	5	8	–	7	20	2.50	31	30
20-29, . .	53	5	35	40	1	39	120	2.26	205	147
30-39, . .	58	6	40	45	–	48	139	2.40	247	152
40-49, . .	49	1	44	42	–	46	133	2.71	195	128
50-59, . .	26	–	23	21	–	26	70	2.69	129	80
60-79, . .	22	–	17	21	–	22	60	2.73	132	100
80 +, . . .	1	–	1	1	–	1	3	3.00	18	11
Unknown, . .	–	–	–	–	–	–	–	–	3	2

There were 651 insane persons whose mothers were total abstainers; there were also 965 for whom the facts as to mothers could not be ascertained. The number whose mothers were addicted to the use of intoxicating liquor was 220. In 13 instances the mothers were excessive drinkers; the classification under the other heads being as follows: social drinkers 167, home drinkers 180, periodical drinkers one, and occasional drinkers 191. There were 112 male insane persons whose mothers were addicted to the use of liquor, of whom four were excessive drinkers; and 108 female insane persons also had mothers addicted to the use of liquor, of whom nine were excessive drinkers.

We next present a series of three tables showing the kinds of liquor used by the insane and by the fathers and mothers of the insane. In each of these tables the insane are classified by age periods, sex, and political condition. The first table relates to the insane themselves. Nine persons, four males and five females, found in the age periods 5-9 and 10-14, being total abstainers, are excluded from consideration in this table for the reason given on page 353.

Insanity; Sex, Political Condition, and Kinds of Liquor Used by the Insane: By Age Periods.

AGE PERIOD: 15-19.

SEX AND POLITICAL CONDITION.	Number addicted to the Use of Intoxicating Liquors	Wines	Lager Beer	Malt Liquors	Distilled Liquors	Aggregate Number of Kinds of Liquor	Average Number of Kinds of Liquor	Particular Kinds of Liquor Unknown	Total Abstainers
Males.	12	-	9	5	4	18	1.50	5	24
Citizen born,	7	-	5	3	1	9	1.29	4	20
Alien,	5	-	4	2	3	9	1.80	1	4
Females.	-	-	-	-	-	-	-	6	22
Citizen born,	-	-	-	-	-	-	-	3	15
Alien,	-	-	-	-	-	-	-	3	7
BOTH SEXES.	12	-	9	5	4	18	1.50	11	46
Citizen born,	7	-	5	3	1	9	1.29	7	35
Alien,	5	-	4	2	3	9	1.80	4	11

AGE PERIOD: 20-29.

	Number addicted to the Use of Intoxicating Liquors	Wines	Lager Beer	Malt Liquors	Distilled Liquors	Aggregate Number of Kinds of Liquor	Average Number of Kinds of Liquor	Particular Kinds of Liquor Unknown	Total Abstainers
Males.	101	30	82	89	78	279	2.76	73	58
Citizen born,	54	16	47	49	40	152	2.81	41	41
Naturalized,	6	1	6	6	5	18	3.00	5	-
Alien,	39	13	27	32	33	105	2.67	27	17
Unknown,	2	-	2	2	-	4	2.00	-	-

Insanity; Sex, Political Condition, and Kinds of Liquor Used by the Insane:
By Age Periods — Continued.

AGE PERIOD: 20-29 — Concluded.

SEX AND POLITICAL CONDITION.	Number addicted to the Use of Intoxicating Liquors	Wines	Lager Beer	Malt Liquors	Distilled Liquors	Aggregate Number of Kinds of Liquor	Average Number of Kinds of Liquor	Particular Kinds of Liquor Unknown	Total Abstainers
Females.	24	10	18	14	15	57	2.38	44	105
Citizen born,	10	3	8	6	7	24	2.40	20	59
Alien, . . .	14	7	10	8	8	33	2.36	24	46
BOTH SEXES.	125	40	100	103	93	336	2.69	117	163
Citizen born,	64	19	55	55	47	176	2.75	61	100
Naturalized,	6	1	6	6	5	18	3.00	5	-
Alien, . . .	53	20	37	40	41	138	2.60	51	63
Unknown, . .	2	-	2	2	-	4	2.00	-	-

AGE PERIOD: 30-39.

Males.	143	50	130	126	121	427	2.99	65	31
Citizen born,	80	30	70	72	70	242	3.03	37	21
Naturalized,	14	7	14	12	13	46	3.29	5	1
Alien, . . .	49	13	46	42	38	139	2.84	23	9
Females.	43	11	33	32	33	109	2.53	50	125
Citizen born,	23	4	18	17	17	56	2.43	26	80
Alien, . . .	20	7	15	15	16	53	2.65	24	45
BOTH SEXES.	186	61	163	158	154	536	2.77	115	156
Citizen born,	103	34	88	89	87	298	2.89	63	101
Naturalized,	14	7	14	12	13	46	3.29	5	1
Alien, . . .	69	20	61	57	54	192	2.78	47	54

AGE PERIOD: 40-49.

Males.	115	39	101	97	96	333	2.87	48	25
Citizen born,	49	18	44	44	43	149	3.04	31	19
Naturalized,	27	10	23	23	24	80	2.96	3	1
Alien, . . .	39	11	34	30	29	104	2.60	13	4
Unknown, . .	-	-	-	-	-	-	-	1	1
Females.	43	17	34	34	32	117	2.72	42	99
Citizen born,	15	5	12	13	13	43	2.87	21	67
Alien, . . .	28	12	22	21	19	74	2.64	21	32

*Insanity; Sex, Political Condition, and Kinds of Liquor Used by the Insane:
By Age Periods — Continued.*

AGE PERIOD: 40–49 — Concluded.

SEX AND POLITICAL CONDITION.	Number addicted to the Use of Intoxicating Liquors	Wines	Lager Beer	Malt Liquors	Distilled Liquors	Aggregate Number of Kinds of Liquor	Average Number of Kinds of Liquor	Particular Kinds of Liquor Unknown	Total Abstainers
BOTH SEXES.	158	56	135	131	128	450	2.85	90	124
Citizen born, .	64	23	56	57	56	192	3.00	52	86
Naturalized, .	27	10	23	23	24	80	2.96	3	1
Alien, . . .	67	23	56	51	48	178	2.66	34	36
Unknown, . .	-	-	-	-	-	-	-	1	1

AGE PERIOD: 50–59.

Males.	63	17	51	46	51	165	2.62	46	18
Citizen born, .	19	5	13	12	15	45	2.37	30	13
Naturalized, .	11	3	11	10	7	31	2.82	4	-
Alien, . . .	31	9	25	22	27	83	2.68	12	5
Unknown, . .	2	-	2	2	2	6	3.00	-	-
Females.	24	6	16	21	19	62	2.58	30	54
Citizen born, .	5	2	2	3	5	12	2.40	15	23
Alien, . . .	19	4	14	18	14	50	2.63	15	31
BOTH SEXES.	87	23	67	67	70	227	2.61	76	72
Citizen born, .	24	7	15	15	20	57	2.38	45	36
Naturalized, .	11	3	11	10	7	31	2.82	4	-
Alien, . . .	50	13	39	40	41	133	2.60	27	36
Unknown, . .	2	-	2	2	2	6	3.00	-	-

AGE PERIOD: 60-79.

Males.	75	11	59	58	57	185	2.47	30	23
Citizen born, .	32	8	24	25	25	82	2.56	17	15
Naturalized, .	22	3	16	15	14	48	2 18	3	3
Alien, . . .	20	-	18	17	17	52	2.60	10	4
Unknown, . .	1	-	1	1	1	3	3.00	-	1
Females.	20	-	16	14	11	41	2.05	36	71
Citizen born, .	3	-	3	2	-	5	1.67	17	40
Alien, . . .	17	-	13	12	11	36	2.12	19	31

*Insanity; Sex, Political Condition, and Kinds of Liquor Used by the Insane:
By Age Periods — Concluded.*

AGE PERIOD: 60-79 — Concluded.

SEX AND POLITICAL CONDITION.	Number addicted to the Use of Intoxicating Liquors	Wines	Lager Beer	Malt Liquors	Distilled Liquors	Aggregate Number of Kinds of Liquor	Average Number of Kinds of Liquor	Particular Kinds of Liquor Unknown	Total Abstainers
BOTH SEXES.	95	11	75	72	68	226	2.38	66	94
Citizen born, .	35	8	27	27	25	87	2.49	34	55
Naturalized, -.	22	3	16	15	14	48	. 2.18	3	3
Alien, . . .	37	-	31	29	28	88	2.38	29	35
Unknown, . .	1	-	1	1	1	3	3.00	-	1

AGE PERIOD: 80+.

Males.	6	1	3	5	6	15	2.50	7	1
Citizen born, .	5	1	2	4	5	12	2.40	6	1
Naturalized, .	-	-	-	-	-	-	-	1	-
Alien, . . .	1	-	1	1	1	3	3.00	-	-
Females.	2	-	1	1	1	3	1.50	4	10
Citizen born, .	-	-	-	-	-	-	-	3	9
Alien, . . .	2	-	1	1	1	3	1.50	1	1
BOTH SEXES.	8	1	4	6	7	18	2.25	11	11
Citizen born, .	5	1	2	4	5	12	2.40	9	10
Naturalized, .	-	-	-	-	-	-	-	1	-
Alien, . . .	3	-	2	2	2	6	2.00	1	1

AGE PERIOD: Unknown.

Males.	-	-	-	-	-	-	-	2	-
Citizen born, .	-	-	-	-	-	-	-	1	-
Naturalized, .	-	-	-	-	-	-	-	1	-
Females.	-	-	-	-	-	-	-	1	2
Citizen born, .	-	-	-	-	-	-	-	-	1
Alien, . . .	-	-	-	-	-	-	-	-	1
Unknown, . .	-	-	-	-	-	-	-	1	-
BOTH SEXES.	-	-	-	-	-	-	-	3	2
Citizen born, .	-	-	-	-	-	-	-	1	1
Naturalized, .	-	-	-	-	-	-	-	1	-
Alien, . . .	-	-	-	-	-	-	-	-	1
Unknown, . .	-	-	-	-	-	-	-	1	-

RECAPITULATION.

SEX AND POLITICAL CONDITION.	Number addicted to the Use of Intoxicating Liquors	Wines	Lager Beer	Malt Liquors	Distilled Liquors	Aggregate Number of Kinds of Liquor	Average Number of Kinds of Liquor	Particular Kinds of Liquor Unknown	Total Abstainers
Males.	515	148	435	426	413	1,422	2.76	276	180
Citizen born, .	246	78	205	209	199	691	2.81	167	130
Naturalized, .	80	24	70	66	63	223	2.79	22	5
Alien, . . .	184	46	155	146	148	495	2.66	86	43
Unknown, . .	5	–	5	5	3	13	2.60	1	2
Females.	156	44	118	116	111	389	2.49	213	488
Citizen born, .	56	14	43	41	42	140	2.50	105	294
Alien, . . .	100	30	75	75	69	249	2.49	107	194
Unknown, . .	–	–	–	–	–	–	–	1	–
BOTH SEXES.	671	192	553	542	524	1,811	2.70	489	668
Citizen born, .	302	92	248	250	241	831	2.75	272	424
Naturalized, .	80	24	70	66	63	223	2.79	22	5
Alien, . . .	284	76	230	221	217	744	2.62	193	237
Unknown, . .	5	–	5	5	3	13	2.60	2	2

RECAPITULATION: BY AGE PERIODS.

SEX AND AGE PERIODS.	Number addicted to the Use of Intoxicating Liquors	Wines	Lager Beer	Malt Liquors	Distilled Liquors	Aggregate Number of Kinds of Liquor	Average Number of Kinds of Liquor	Particular Kinds of Liquor Unknown	Total Abstainers
Males.	515	148	435	426	413	1,422	2.76	276	180
15–19, . . .	12	–	9	5	4	18	1.50	5	24
20–29, . . .	101	30	82	89	78	279	2.76	73	58
30–39, . . .	143	50	130	126	121	427	2.99	65	31
40–49, . . .	115	39	101	97	96	333	2.87	48	25
50–59, . . .	63	17	51	46	51	165	2.62	46	18
60–79, . . .	75	11	59	58	57	185	2.47	30	23
80 +, . . .	6	1	3	5	6	15	2.50	7	1
Unknown, . .	–	–	–	–	–	–	–	2	–
Females.	156	44	118	116	111	389	2.49	213	488
15–19, . . .	–	–	–	–	–	–	–	6	22
20–29, . . .	24	10	18	14	15	57	2.38	44	105
30–39, . . .	43	11	33	32	33	109	2.53	50	125
40–49, . . .	43	17	34	34	32	117	2.72	42	99
50–59, . . .	24	6	16	21	19	62	2.58	30	54
60–79, . . .	20	–	16	14	11	41	2.05	36	71
80 +, . . .	2	–	1	1	1	3	1.50	4	10
Unknown, . .	...	–	–	–	–	–	–	1	2

RECAPITULATION: BY AGE PERIODS — Concluded.

SEX AND AGE PERIODS.	Number addicted to the Use of Intoxicating Liquors	Wines	Lager Beer	Malt Liquors	Distilled Liquors	Aggregate Number of Kinds of Liquor	Average Number of Kinds of Liquor	Particular Kinds of Liquor Unknown	Total Abstainers
BOTH SEXES.	671	192	553	542	524	1,811	2.70	489	668
15-19, . . .	12	–	9	5	4	18	1.50	11	46
20-29, . . .	125	40	100	103	93	336	2.69	117	163
30-39, . . .	186	61	163	158	154	536	2.77	115	156
40-49, . . .	158	56	135	131	128	450	2.85	90	124
50-59, . . .	87	23	67	67	70	227	2.61	76	72
60-79, . . .	95	11	75	72	68	226	2.38	66	94
80 +, . . .	8	1	4	6	7	18	2.25	11	11
Unknown, . .	–	–	–	–	–	–	–	3	2

There were 668 total abstainers, and 489 others for whom the information contained in this table could not be ascertained. Disregarding these persons, there remain 671 insane persons addicted to the use of intoxicating liquors, of whom 192 used wines; 553 lager beer; 542 malt liquors; and 524 distilled liquors; the average number of kinds of liquor used by each person being 2.70. For each sex the proportions using the different kinds of liquor are substantially the same as those indicated for both sexes.

The next table shows the kinds of liquor used by the fathers of the insane.

Insanity; Sex, Political Condition, and Kinds of Liquor Used by Fathers of Insane Persons: By Age Periods.

AGE PERIOD: 5-9.

SEX AND POLITICAL CONDITION.	Number addicted to the Use of Intoxicating Liquors	Wines	Lager Beer	Malt Liquors	Distilled Liquors	Aggregate Number of Kinds of Liquor	Average Number of Kinds of Liquor	Particular Kinds of Liquor Unknown	Total Abstainers
Males.	–	–	–	–	–	–	–	–	1
Citizen born, .	–	–	–	–	–	–	–	–	1
Females.	2	–	2	1	1	4	2.00	1	–
Citizen born, .	2	–	2	1	1	4	2.00	–	–
Alien, . . .	–	–	–	–	–	–	–	1	–
BOTH SEXES.	2	–	2	1	1	4	2.00	1	1
Citizen born, .	2	–	2	1	1	4	2.00	–	1
Alien, . . .	–	–	–	–	–	–	–	1	–

Insanity; Sex, Political Condition, and Kinds of Liquor Used by Fathers of Insane Persons: By Age Periods — Continued.

AGE PERIOD: 10–14.

SEX AND POLITICAL CONDITION.	Number addicted to the Use of Intoxieating Liquors	Wines	Lager Beer	Malt Liquors	Distilled Liquors	Aggregate Number of Kinds of Liquor	Average Number of Kinds of Liquor	Particular Kinds of Liquor Unknown	Total Abstainers
Males.	2	1	–	–	2	3	1.50	1	–
Citizen born,	1	–	–	–	1	1	1.00	–	–
Alien, . . .	1	1	–	–	1	2	2.00	1	–
Females.	1	–	1	1	1	3	3.00	1	–
Citizen born,	–	–	–	–	–	–	–	1	–
Alien, . . .	1	–	1	1	1	3	3.00	–	–
BOTH SEXES.	3	1	1	1	3	6	2.00	2	–
Citizen born,	1	–	–	–	1	1	1.00	1	–
Alien, . . .	2	1	1	1	2	5	2.50	1	–

AGE PERIOD: 15–19.

SEX AND POLITICAL CONDITION.	Number addicted	Wines	Lager Beer	Malt Liquors	Distilled Liquors	Aggregate	Average	Particular Unknown	Total Abstainers
Males	19	2	13	12	13	40	2.11	18	5
Citizen born,	14	2	9	8	9	28	2.00	13	5
Alien, . . .	5	–	4	4	4	12	2.40	5	–
Females.	10	2	8	6	5	21	2.10	14	4
Citizen born,	5	–	5	5	4	14	2.80	10	3
Alien, . . .	5	2	3	1	1	7	1.40	4	1
BOTH SEXES.	29	4	21	18	18	61	2.10	32	9
Citizen born,	19	2	14	13	13	42	2.21	23	8
Alien, . . .	10	2	7	5	5	19	1.90	9	1

AGE PERIOD: 20–29.

SEX AND POLITICAL CONDITION.	Number addicted	Wines	Lager Beer	Malt Liquors	Distilled Liquors	Aggregate	Average	Particular Unknown	Total Abstainers
Males.	73	11	44	55	58	168	2.30	120	39
Citizen born,	43	3	29	34	34	100	2.33	65	28
Naturalized,	3	1	3	3	3	10	3.33	8	–
Alien, . . .	26	7	12	17	20	56	2.15	47	10
Unknown, . .	1	–	–	1	1	2	2.00	–	1
Females.	74	13	39	55	51	158	2.14	77	22
Citizen born,	37	4	22	28	28	82	2.22	38	14
Alien, . . .	37	9	17	27	23	76	2.05	39	8
BOTH SEXES.	147	24	83	110	109	326	2.22	197	61
Citizen born,	80	7	51	62	62	182	2.28	103	42
Naturalized,	3	1	3	3	3	10	3.33	8	–
Alien, . . .	63	16	29	44	43	132	2.10	86	18
Unknown, . .	1	–	–	1	1	2	2.00	–	1

Insanity; Sex, Political Condition, and Kinds of Liquor Used by Fathers of Insane Persons: By Age Periods — Continued.

AGE PERIOD: 30-39

SEX AND POLITICAL CONDITION.	Number addicted to the Use of Intoxicating Liquors	Wines	Lager Beer	Malt Liquors	Distilled Liquors	Aggregate Number of Kinds of Liquor	Average Number of Kinds of Liquor	Particular Kinds of Liquor Unknown	Total Abstainers
Males.	79	14	50	58	63	185	2.34	138	22
Citizen born,	49	8	33	38	39	118	2.41	75	14
Naturalized,	9	2	4	8	7	21	2.33	10	1
Alien, . . .	21	4	13	12	17	46	2.19	53	7
Females.	72	9	36	53	56	154	2.14	100	46
Citizen born,	42	3	25	33	34	95	2.26	55	32
Alien, . .	30	6	11	20	22	59	1.97	45	14
BOTH SEXES.	151	23	86	111	119	339	2.25	238	68
Citizen born,	91	11	58	71	73	213	2.34	130	46
Naturalized,	9	2	4	8	7	21	2.33	10	1
Alien, . . .	51	10	24	32	39	105	2.06	98	21

AGE PERIOD: 40-49.

Males.	64	14	39	45	47	145	2.27	104	20
Citizen born,	28	7	19	22	23	71	2.54	58	13
Naturalized,	17	2	9	12	13	36	2.12	13	1
Alien, . . .	19	5	11	11	11	38	2.00	31	6
Unknown, . .	-	-	-	-	-	-	-	2	-
Females.	69	10	26	46	58	140	2.03	89	26
Citizen born,	39	7	16	24	33	80	2.05	47	17
Alien, . . .	30	3	10	22	25	60	2.00	42	9
BOTH SEXES.	133	24	65	91	105	285	2.14	193	46
Citizen born,	67	14	35	46	56	151	2.25	105	30
Naturalized,	17	2	9	12	13	36	2.12	13	1
Alien, . . .	49	8	21	33	36	98	2.00	73	15
Unknown, . .	-	-	-	-	-	-	-	2	-

AGE PERIOD: 50-59.

Males.	38	8	16	29	29	82	2.16	74	15
Citizen born,	13	3	7	13	12	35	2.69	41	8
Naturalized,	7	2	3	5	6	16	2.29	7	1
Alien, . . .	17	3	5	10	10	28	1.65	26	5
Unknown, . .	1	-	1	1	1	3	3.00	-	1
Females.	31	-	10	24	27	61	1.97	53	24
Citizen born,	5	-	1	2	5	8	1.60	27	11
Alien, . . .	26	-	9	22	22	53	2.04	26	13

Insanity ; Sex, Political Condition, and Kinds of Liquor Used by Fathers of Insane Persons: By Age Periods — Continued.

AGE PERIOD : 50-59 — Concluded.

SEX AND POLITICAL CONDITION.	Number addicted to the Use of Intoxicating Liquors	Wines	Lager Beer	Malt Liquors	Distilled Liquors	Aggregate Number of Kinds of Liquor	Average Number of Kinds of Liquor	Particular Kinds of Liquor Unknown	Total Abstainers
BOTH SEXES.	69	8	26	53	56	143	2.07	127	39
Citizen born, .	18	3	8	15	17	43	2.39	68	19
Naturalized, .	7	2	3	5	6	16	2.29	7	1
Alien, . . .	43	3	14	32	32	81	1.88	52	18
Unknown, . .	1	-	1	1	1	3	3.00	-	1

AGE PERIOD : 60-79.

	Number addicted	Wines	Lager Beer	Malt Liquors	Distilled Liquors	Aggregate Number	Average Number	Particular Kinds Unknown	Total Abstainers
Males.	37	6	12	28	29	75	2.03	64	26
Citizen born, .	17	4	5	13	15	37	2.18	32	14
Naturalized, .	12	1	5	9	8	23	1.92	9	7
Alien, . . .	7	-	1	6	6	13	1.86	23	4
Unknown, . .	1	1	1	-	-	2	2.00	-	1
Females.	33	2	13	21	29	65	1.97	65	29
Citizen born, .	13	1	4	6	12	23	1.77	29	18
Alien, . . .	20	1	9	15	17	42	2.10	36	11
BOTH SEXES.	70	8	25	49	58	140	2.00	129	55
Citizen born, .	30	5	9	19	27	60	2.00	61	32
Naturalized, .	12	1	5	9	8	23	1.92	9	7
Alien, . . .	27	1	10	21	23	55	2.04	59	15
Unknown, . .	1	1	1	-	-	2	2.00	-	1

AGE PERIOD : 80 +.

	Number addicted	Wines	Lager Beer	Malt Liquors	Distilled Liquors	Aggregate Number	Average Number	Particular Kinds Unknown	Total Abstainers
Males.	4	1	-	3	4	8	2.00	10	-
Citizen born, .	3	1	-	2	3	6	2.00	9	-
Naturalized, .	-	-	-	-	-	-	-	1	-
Alien, . . .	1	-	-	1	1	2	2.00	-	-
Females.	7	1	2	7	7	17	2.43	8	1
Citizen born, .	4	1	2	4	4	11	2.75	7	1
Alien, . . .	3	-	-	3	3	6	2.00	1	-
BOTH SEXES.	11	2	2	10	11	25	2.27	18	1
Citizen born, .	7	2	2	6	7	17	2.43	16	1
Naturalized, .	-	-	-	-	-	-	-	1	-
Alien, . . .	4	-	-	4	4	8	2.00	1	-

Insanity; Sex, Political Condition, and Kinds of Liquor Used by Fathers of Insane Persons: By Age Periods — Concluded.

AGE PERIOD: Unknown.

SEX AND POLITICAL CONDITION.	Number addicted to the Use of Intoxicating Liquors	Wines	Lager Beer	Malt Liquors	Distilled Liquors	Aggregate Number of Kinds of Liquor	Average Number of Kinds of Liquor	Particular Kinds of Liquor Unknown	Total Abstainers
Males.	-	-	-	-	-	-	-	2	-
Citizen born,	-	-	-	-	-	-	-	1	-
Naturalized,	-	-	-	-	-	-	-	1	-
Females.	1	-	1	1	1	3	3.00	1	1
Citizen born,	1	-	1	1	1	3	3.00	-	-
Alien, . .	-	-	-	-	-	-	-	-	1
Unknown, .	-	-	-	-	-	-	-	1	-
BOTH SEXES.	1	-	1	1	1	3	3.00	3	1
Citizen born,	1	-	1	1	1	3	3.00	1	-
Naturalized,	-	-	-	-	-	-	-	1	-
Alien, . .	-	-	-	-	-	-	-	-	1
Unknown, .	-	-	-	-	-	-	-	1	-

RECAPITULATION.

SEX AND POLITICAL CONDITION.	Number addicted to the Use of Intoxicating Liquors	Wines	Lager Beer	Malt Liquors	Distilled Liquors	Aggregate Number of Kinds of Liquor	Average Number of Kinds of Liquor	Particular Kinds of Liquor Unknown	Total Abstainers
Males.	316	57	174	230	245	706	2.23	531	123
Citizen born,	168	28	102	130	136	396	2.54	294	83
Naturalized,	48	8	24	37	37	106	2.21	49	10
Alien, . .	97	20	46	61	70	197	2.03	186	32
Unknown, .	3	1	2	2	2	7	2.33	2	3
Females.	300	37	138	215	236	626	2.09	409	153
Citizen born,	148	16	78	104	122	320	2.16	214	96
Alien, . .	152	21	60	111	114	306	2.01	194	57
Unknown, .	-	-	-	-	-	-	-	1	-
BOTH SEXES.	616	94	312	445	481	1,332	2.16	940	281
Citizen born,	316	44	180	234	258	716	2.27	508	179
Naturalized,	48	8	24	37	37	106	2.21	49	10
Alien, . .	249	41	106	172	184	503	2.02	380	89
Unknown, .	3	1	2	2	2	7	2.33	3	3

RECAPITULATION: BY AGE PERIODS.

SEX AND AGE PERIODS.	Number addicted to the Use of Intoxicating Liquors	Wines	Lager Beer	Malt Liquors	Distilled Liquors	Aggregate Number of Kinds of Liquor	Average Number of Kinds of Liquor	Particular Kinds of Liquor Unknown	Total Abstainers
Males.	316	57	174	230	245	706	2.23	531	128
5-9, . . .	-	-	-	-	-	-	-	-	1
10-14, . . .	2	1	-	-	2	3	1.50	1	-
15-19, . . .	19	2	13	12	13	40	2.11	18	5
20-29, . . .	73	11	44	55	58	168	2.30	120	39
30-39, . . .	79	14	50	58	63	185	2.34	138	22
40-49, . . .	64	14	39	45	47	145	2.27	104	20
50-59, . . .	38	8	16	29	29	82	2.16	74	15
60-79, . . .	37	6	12	28	29	75	2.03	64	26
80 +, . . .	4	1	-	3	4	8	2.00	10	-
Unknown, . .	-	-	-	-	-	-	-	2	-
Females.	300	37	138	215	236	626	2.09	409	153
5-9, . . .	2	-	2	1	1	4	2.00	1	-
10-14, . . .	1	-	1	1	1	3	3.00	1	-
15-19, . . .	10	2	8	6	5	21	2.10	14	4
20-29, . . .	74	13	39	55	51	158	2.14	77	22
30-39, . . .	72	9	36	53	56	154	2.14	100	46
40-49, . . .	69	10	26	46	58	140	2.03	89	26
50-59, . . .	31	-	10	24	27	61	1.97	53	24
60-79, . . .	33	2	13	21	29	65	1.97	65	29
80 +, . . .	7	1	2	7	7	17	2.43	8	1
Unknown, . .	1	-	1	1	1	3	3.00	1	1
BOTH SEXES.	616	94	312	445	481	1,332	2 16	940	281
5-9, . . .	2	-	2	1	1	4	2.00	1	1
10-14, . . .	3	1	1	1	3	6	2.00	2	-
15-19, . . .	29	4	21	18	18	61	2.10	32	9
20-29, . . .	147	24	83	110	109	326	2.22	197	61
30-39, . . .	151	23	86	111	119	339	2.25	238	68
40-49, . . .	133	24	65	91	105	285	2.14	193	46
50-59, . . .	69	8	26	53	56	143	2.07	127	39
60-79, . . .	70	8	25	49	58	140	2.00	129	55
80 +, . . .	11	2	2	10	11	25	2.27	18	1
Unknown, . .	1	-	1	1	1	3	3.00	3	1

Referring to the recapitulation, we find, among the fathers, 281 total abstainers, and 940 others for whom the facts considered in the table were unknown. The information contained in the table is complete as to 616 fathers of insane persons, who were addicted to the use of intoxicating liquor, these including 94 who used wines, 312 lager beer, 445 malt liquors, and 481 distilled liquors, the average number of kinds of liquor used by the fathers being 2.16.

The next table relates to the kinds of liquor used by the mothers of the insane.

Insanity; Sex, Political Condition, and Kinds of Liquor Used by Mothers of Insane Persons: By Age Periods.

AGE PERIOD: 5–9.

SEX AND POLITICAL CONDITION.	Number addicted to the Use of Intoxicating Liquors	Wines	Lager Beer	Malt Liquors	Distilled Liquors	Aggregate Number of Kinds of Liquor	Average Number of Kinds of Liquor	Particular Kinds of Liquor Unknown	Total Abstainers
Males.	-	-	-	-	-	-	-	-	1
Citizen born,	-	-	-	-	-	-	-	-	1
Females.	1	-	1	-	-	1	1.00	2	-
Citizen born,	1	-	1	-	-	1	1.00	1	-
Alien, . . .	-	-	-	-	-	-	-	1	-
BOTH SEXES.	1	-	1	-	-	1	1.00	2	1
Citizen born,	1	-	1	-	-	1	1.00	1	1
Alien, . . .	-	-	-	-	-	-	-	1	-

AGE PERIOD: 10–14.

SEX AND POLITICAL CONDITION.	Number addicted to the Use of Intoxicating Liquors	Wines	Lager Beer	Malt Liquors	Distilled Liquors	Aggregate Number of Kinds of Liquor	Average Number of Kinds of Liquor	Particular Kinds of Liquor Unknown	Total Abstainers
Males.	2	1	-	-	1	2	1.00	1	-
Citizen born,	1	-	-	-	1	1	1.00	-	-
Alien, . . .	1	1	-	-	-	1	1.00	1	-
Females.	-	-	-	-	-	-	-	2	-
Citizen born,	-	-	-	-	-	-	-	1	-
Alien, . . .	-	-	-	-	-	-	-	1	-
BOTH SEXES.	2	1	-	-	1	2	1.00	3	-
Citizen born,	1	-	-	-	1	1	1.00	1	-
Alien, . . .	1	1	-	-	-	1	1.00	2	-

AGE PERIOD: 15–19.

SEX AND POLITICAL CONDITION.	Number addicted to the Use of Intoxicating Liquors	Wines	Lager Beer	Malt Liquors	Distilled Liquors	Aggregate Number of Kinds of Liquor	Average Number of Kinds of Liquor	Particular Kinds of Liquor Unknown	Total Abstainers
Males.	3	-	1	2	1	4	1.33	17	21
Citizen born,	1	-	-	1	-	1	1.00	12	18
Alien, . . .	2	-	1	1	1	3	1.50	5	3

Insanity; Sex, Political Condition, and Kinds of Liquor Used by Mothers of Insane Persons: By Age Periods — Continued.

AGE PERIOD: 15-19 — Concluded.

SEX AND POLITICAL CONDITION.	Number addicted to the Use of Intoxicating Liquors	Wines	Lager Beer	Malt Liquors	Distilled Liquors	Aggregate Number of Kinds of Liquor	Average Number of Kinds of Liquor	Particular Kinds of Liquor Unknown	Total Abstainers
Females.	5	1	3	3	2	9	1.80	14	9
Citizen born,	3	-	2	3	2	7	2.33	10	5
Alien, . . .	2	1	1	-	-	2	1.00	4	4
BOTH SEXES.	8	1	4	5	3	13	1.63	31	30
Citizen born,	4	-	2	4	2	8	2.00	22	23
Alien, . . .	4	1	2	1	1	5	1.25	9	7

AGE PERIOD: 20-29.

Males.	24	7	13	16	14	50	2.08	124	84
Citizen born,	9	-	6	9	6	21	2.33	68	59
Naturalized,	1	1	1	1	1	4	4.00	8	2
Alien, . . .	14	6	6	6	7	25	1.79	48	21
Unknown, . .	-	-	-	-	-	-	-	-	2
Females.	29	9	14	18	13	54	1.86	81	63
Citizen born,	14	4	9	9	7	29	2.07	41	34
Alien, . . .	15	5	5	9	6	25	1.67	40	29
BOTH SEXES.	53	16	27	34	27	104	1.96	205	147
Citizen born,	23	4	15	18	13	50	2.17	109	93
Naturalized,	1	1	1	1	1	4	4.00	8	2
Alien, . . .	29	11	11	15	13	50	1.72	88	50
Unknown, . .	-	-	-	-	-	-	-	-	2

AGE PERIOD: 30-39.

Males.	30	5	17	19	18	59	1.97	143	66
Citizen born,	15	3	10	12	10	35	2.33	77	46
Naturalized,	6	1	2	3	4	10	1.67	11	3
Alien, . . .	9	1	5	4	4	14	1.56	55	17
Females.	28	1	13	22	19	55	1.96	104	86
Citizen born,	13	-	8	11	8	27	2.08	57	59
Alien, . . .	15	1	5	11	11	28	1.87	47	27
BOTH SEXES.	58	6	30	41	37	114	1.97	247	152
Citizen born,	28	3	18	23	18	62	2.21	134	105
Naturalized,	6	1	2	3	4	10	1.67	11	3
Alien, . . .	24	2	10	15	15	42	1.75	102	44

Insanity ; Sex, Political Condition, and Kinds of Liquor Used by Mothers of Insane Persons: By Age Periods — Continued.

AGE PERIOD : 40–49.

SEX AND POLITICAL CONDITION.	Number addicted to the Use of Intoxicating Liquors	Wines	Lager Beer	Malt Liquors	Distilled Liquors	Aggregate Number of Kinds of Liquor	Average Number of Kinds of Liquor	Particular Kinds of Liquor Unknown	Total Abstainers
Males.	24	7	16	14	11	48	2.00	105	59
Citizen born,	5	1	4	4	3	12	2.40	59	35
Naturalized,	7	1	5	5	5	16	2.29	13	11
Alien, . . .	12	5	7	5	3	20	1.67	31	13
Unknown,	-	-	-	-	-	-	-	2	-
Females.	25	3	12	19	17	51	2.04	90	69
Citizen born,	6	-	4	5	4	13	2.17	48	49
Alien, . . .	19	3	8	14	13	38	2.00	42	20
BOTH SEXES.	49	10	28	33	28	99	2.02	195	128
Citizen born,	11	1	8	9	7	25	2.27	107	84
Naturalized,	7	1	5	5	5	16	2.29	13	11
Alien, . . .	31	8	15	19	16	58	1.87	73	33
Unknown, . .	-	-	-	-	-	-	-	2	-

AGE PERIOD : 50-59.

Males.	17	3	3	8	10	24	1.41	75	35
Citizen born,	2	-	-	-	2	2	1.00	42	18
Naturalized,	4	1	2	2	2	7	1.75	7	4
Alien, . . .	11	2	1	6	6	15	1.36	26	11
Unknown, . .	-	-	-	-	-	-	-	-	2
Females.	9	-	4	7	5	16	1.78	54	45
Citizen born,	-	-	-	-	-	-	-	27	16
Alien, . . .	9	-	4	7	5	16	1.78	27	29
BOTH SEXES.	26	3	7	15	15	40	1.54	129	80
Citizen born,	2	-	-	-	2	2	1.00	69	34
Naturalized,	4	1	2	2	2	7	1.75	7	4
Alien, . . .	20	2	5	13	11	31	1.55	53	40
Unknown, . .	-	-	-	-	-	-	-	-	2

AGE PERIOD : 60-79.

Males.	12	3	3	8	4	18	1.50	65	50
Citizen born,	1	1	-	-	-	1	1.00	34	28
Naturalized,	5	1	1	3	1	6	1.20	8	15

Insanity; Sex, Political Condition, and Kinds of Liquor Used by Mothers of Insane Persons: By Age Periods — Continued.

AGE PERIOD: 60-79 — Concluded.

SEX AND POLITICAL CONDITION.	Number addicted to the Use of Intoxicating Liquors	Wines	Lager Beer	Malt Liquors	Distilled Liquors	Aggregate Number of Kinds of Liquor	Average Number of Kinds of Liquor	Particular Kinds of Liquor Unknown	Total Abstainers
Males — Con.									
Alien, . . .	5	-	1	5	3	9	1.80	23	6
Unknown, . .	1	1	1	-	-	2	2.00	-	1
Females.	10	-	4	6	7	17	1.70	67	50
Citizen born, .	1	-	1	1	-	2	2.00	31	28
Alien, . . .	9	-	3	5	7	15	1.67	36	22
BOTH SEXES.	22	3	7	14	11	35	1.59	132	100
Citizen born, .	2	1	1	1	-	3	1.50	65	56
Naturalized, .	5	1	1	3	1	6	1.20	8	15
Alien, . . .	14	-	4	10	10	24	1.71	59	28
Unknown, . .	1	1	1	-	-	2	2.00	-	1

AGE PERIOD: 80 +.

Males.	-	-	-	-	-	-	-	10	4
Citizen born, .	-	-	-	-	-	-	-	9	3
Naturalized, .	-	-	-	-	-	-	-	1	-
Alien, . . .	-	-	-	-	-	-	-	-	1
Females.	1	-	-	1	-	1	1.00	8	7
Citizen born, .	-	-	-	-	-	-	-	7	5
Alien, . . .	1	-	-	1	-	1	1.00	1	2
BOTH SEXES.	1	-	-	1	-	1	1.00	18	11
Citizen born, .	-	-	-	-	-	-	-	16	8
Naturalized, .	-	-	-	-	-	-	-	1	-
Alien, . . .	1	-	-	1	-	1	1.00	1	3

AGE PERIOD: Unknown.

Males.	-	-	-	-	-	-	-	2	-
Citizen born, .	-	-	-	-	-	-	-	1	-
Naturalized, .	-	-	-	-	-	-	-	1	-
Females.	-	-	-	-	-	-	-	1	2
Citizen born, .	-	-	-	-	-	-	-	-	1
Alien, . . .	-	-	-	-	-	-	-	-	1
Unknown, . .	-	-	-	-	-	-	-	1	-

Insanity; Sex, Political Condition, and Kinds of Liquor Used by Mothers of Insane Persons: By Age Periods — Concluded.

AGE PERIOD: Unknown — Concluded.

SEX AND POLITICAL CONDITION.	Number addicted to the Use of Intoxicating Liquors	Wines	Lager Beer	Malt Liquors	Distilled Liquors	Aggregate Number of Kinds of Liquor	Average Number of Kinds of Liquor	Particular Kinds of Liquor Unknown	Total Abstainers
BOTH SEXES.	–	–	–	–	–	–	–	3	2
Citizen born,	–	–	–	–	–	–	–	1	1
Naturalized,	–	–	–	–	–	–	–	1	–
Alien,	–	–	–	–	–	–	–	–	1
Unknown,	–	–	–	–	–	–	–	1	–

RECAPITULATION.

SEX AND POLITICAL CONDITION.	Number addicted to the Use of Intoxicating Liquors	Wines	Lager Beer	Malt Liquors	Distilled Liquors	Aggregate Number of Kinds of Liquor	Average Number of Kinds of Liquor	Particular Kinds of Liquor Unknown	Total Abstainers
Males.	112	26	53	67	59	205	1.83	542	320
Citizen born,	34	5	20	26	22	73	2.15	302	208
Naturalized,	23	5	11	14	13	43	1.87	49	35
Alien,	54	15	21	27	24	87	1.61	189	72
Unknown,	1	1	1	–	–	2	2.00	2	5
Females.	108	14	51	76	63	204	1.89	423	331
Citizen born,	38	4	25	29	21	79	2.08	223	197
Alien,	70	10	26	47	42	125	1.79	199	134
Unknown,	–	–	–	–	–	–	–	1	–
BOTH SEXES.	220	40	104	143	122	409	1.86	965	651
Citizen born,	72	9	45	55	43	152	2.11	525	405
Naturalized,	23	5	11	14	13	43	1.87	49	35
Alien,	124	25	47	74	66	212	1.71	388	206
Unknown,	1	1	1	–	–	2	2.00	3	5

RECAPITULATION: BY AGE PERIODS.

SEX AND AGE PERIODS.	Number addicted to the Use of Intoxicating Liquors	Wines	Lager Beer	Malt Liquors	Distilled Liquors	Aggregate Number of Kinds of Liquor	Average Number of Kinds of Liquor	Particular Kinds of Liquor Unknown	Total Abstainers
Males.	112	26	53	67	59	205	1.83	542	320
5–9,	–	–	–	–	–	–	–	–	1
10–14,	2	1	–	–	1	2	1.00	1	–
15–19,	3	–	1	2	1	4	1.33	17	21

RECAPITULATION: BY AGE PERIODS — Concluded.

Sex and Age Periods.	Number addicted to the Use of Intoxicating Liquors	Wines	Lager Beer	Malt Liquors	Distilled Liquors	Aggregate Number of Kinds of Liquor	Average Number of Kinds of Liquor	Particular Kinds of Liquor Unknown	Total Abstainers
Males — Con.									
20-29, . . .	24	7	13	16	14	50	2.08	124	84
30-39, . . .	30	5	17	19	18	59	1.97	143	66
40-49, . . .	24	7	16	14	11	48	2.00	105	59
50-59, . . .	17	3	3	8	10	24	1.41	75	35
60-79, . . .	12	3	3	8	4	18	1.50	65	50
80 +, . . .	-	-	-	-	-	-	-	10	4
Unknown, . .	-	-	-	-	-	-	-	2	-
Females.	108	14	51	76	63	204	1.89	423	331
5-9, . . .	1	-	1	-	-	1	1.00	2	-
10-14, . . .	-	-	-	-	-	-	-	2	-
15-19, . . .	5	1	3	3	2	9	1.80	14	9
20-29, . . .	29	0	14	18	13	54	1.86	81	63
30-39, . . .	28	1	13	22	19	55	1.96	104	86
40-49, . . .	25	3	12	19	17	51	2.04	90	69
50-59, . . .	9	-	4	7	5	16	1.78	54	45
60-79, . . .	10	-	4	6	7	17	1.70	67	50
80 +, . . .	1	-	-	1	-	1	1.00	8	7
Unknown, . .	-	-	-	-	-	-	-	1	2
Both Sexes.	220	40	104	143	122	409	1.86	965	651
5-0, . . .	1	-	1	-	-	1	1.00	2	1
10-14, . . .	2	1	-	-	1	2	1.00	3	-
15-19, . . .	8	1	4	5	3	13	1.63	31	39
20-29, . . .	53	16	27	34	27	104	1.96	205	147
30-39, . . .	58	6	30	41	37	114	1.97	247	152
40-49, . . .	49	10	28	33	28	99	2.02	195	128
50-59, . . .	26	3	7	15	15	40	1.54	129	80
60-79, . . .	22	3	7	14	11	35	1.59	132	100
80 +, . . .	1	-	-	1	-	1	1.00	18	11
Unknown, . .	-	-	-	-	-	-	-	3	2

Among the mothers, there were 651 total abstainers, and 965 others for whom the points considered could not be ascertained. Of the 220 mothers who were addicted to the use of liquor, 40 used wines, 104 lager beer, 143 malt liquors, and 122 distilled liquors, the average number of kinds of liquor used by the mothers being 1.86.

In the next table the leading points relating to the use of liquor are summarized in connection with a classification showing the occupations of the insane.

RECAPITULATION.— *Relation of the Liquor Traffic to Insanity: By Sex and Occupations.*

	SEX AND OCCUPATIONS.	Number of Insane	Is the person's present condition of Insanity due to the use or abuse of Intoxicating Liquors			LIQUOR HABITS OF INSANE			
			Yes	No	Not Ascertained	Excessive Drinkers	Other Drinkers	Unknown	Total Abstainers
1	*Males.*	974	296	479	199	246	269	275	184
2	Agents, canvassers, collectors, etc., ...	14	5	8	1	3	7	2	2
3	Blacksmiths and wheelwrights, ...	7	1	4	2	1	5	-	1
4	Bookbinders, . . .	2	-	2	-	-	-	1	1
5	Bookkeepers, . . .	10	2	7	1	2	3	4	1
6	Boot and shoemakers, . .	70	19	29	22	17	12	26	15
7	Brickmakers, . . .	1	-	-	1	-	-	1	-
8	Building trades, . . .	24	6	14	4	3	9	6	6
9	Carpenters, ...	35	8	25	2	7	8	7	13
10	Carriage makers, . . .	1	-	1	-	-	-	-	1
11	Cigar makers, . . .	6	2	3	1	2	2	1	1
12	Clerks and salesmen, . .	27	7	15	5	5	10	6	6
13	Dealers, traders, peddlers (all kinds), . . .	53	17	28	8	17	14	7	15
14	Domestic service, . .	5	-	3	2	-	3	2	-
15	Electricians, . . .	2	-	1	1	-	1	1	-
16	Factory operatives, . .	85	24	41	20	21	21	27	16
17	Farmers and farm laborers,	59	15	30	14	11	14	28	6
18	Furniture makers and finishers, ...	7	2	3	2	1	2	2	2
19	Government service, . .	5	1	3	1	1	2	-	2
20	Hat makers and finishers, .	1	-	1	-	-	1	-	-
21	Hotel and boarding-house proprietors, . . .	3	1	1	1	1	1	1	-
22	Laborers, ...	202	80	69	53	63	62	64	13
23	Leather makers and workers,	18	7	9	2	6	5	3	4
24	Machinists, ...	14	5	8	1	4	6	2	2
25	Manufacturers, . . .	10	2	6	2	3	1	5	1
26	Mariners and fishermen, .	15	6	6	3	4	4	4	3
27	Mechanics, ...	10	2	5	3	1	7	2	-
28	Messengers, ...	5	-	5	-	-	4	-	1
29	Metal workers, . . .	32	12	16	4	11	11	6	4
30	Painters, ...	16	6	6	4	5	6	4	1
31	Paper makers, . . .	1	1	-	-	1	-	-	-
32	Personal service, . . .	33	13	13	7	13	6	7	7
33	Printers, ...	11	3	8	-	1	5	2	3
34	Professional service, . .	19	4	13	2	3	6	4	6

RECAPITULATION. — *Relation of the Liquor Traffic to Insanity: By Sex and Occupations.*

KINDS OF LIQUOR						TOBACCO		DRUGS		
Wines only	Lager Beer and Malt Liquors only	Distilled Liquors only	Two or All Kinds	Unknown	Inapplicable*	Users	Non-users	Users	Non-users	
4	84	26	400	276	184	495	479	15	959	1
-	2	-	8	2	2	10	4	1	13	2
-	2	1	3	-	1	4	3	-	7	3
-	-	-	-	1	1	-	2	-	2	4
-	-	-	5	4	1	6	4	-	10	5
-	4	1	24	26	15	26	44	3	67	6
-	-	-	-	1	-	-	1	-	1	7
-	2	1	9	6	6	14	10	-	24	8
-	2	2	11	7	13	16	19	-	35	9
-	-	-	-	-	1	-	1	-	1	10
-	-	-	4	1	1	4	2	-	6	11
-	3	-	12	6	6	18	9	-	27	12
1	6	1	23	7	15	27	26	2	51	13
1	-	-	2	2	-	2	3	1	4	14
-	-	-	1	1	-	1	1	-	2	15
-	9	3	30	27	16	34	51	1	84	16
-	2	2	20	29	6	24	35	1	58	17
-	2	-	1	2	2	3	4	-	7	18
-	1	-	2	-	2	4	1	-	5	19
-	-	-	1	-	-	1	-	-	1	20
-	-	-	2	1	-	1	2	-	3	21
1	20	5	99	64	13	113	89	-	202	22
-	1	-	10	3	4	12	6	-	18	23
-	2	-	8	2	2	10	4	-	14	24
-	1	1	2	5	1	5	5	1	9	25
-	1	-	7	4	3	6	9	-	15	26
-	1	-	7	2	-	6	4	1	9	27
-	2	-	2	-	1	4	1	-	5	28
-	3	-	19	6	4	19	13	1	31	29
-	2	1	8	4	1	11	5	1	15	30
-	-	-	1	-	-	1	-	-	1	31
-	1	-	18	7	7	20	13	-	33	32
-	2	1	3	2	3	9	2	-	11	33
-	1	1	7	4	6	9	10	2	17	34

* Total Abstainers.

RECAPITULATION. — *Relation of the Liquor Traffic to Insanity : By Sex and Occupations* — Concluded.

	SEX AND OCCUPATIONS.	Number of Insane	Is the person's present condition of **Insanity** due to the use or abuse of **Intoxicating Liquors**			LIQUOR HABITS OF INSANE			
			Yes	No	Not Ascertained	Excessive Drinkers	Other Drinkers	Unknown	Total Abstainers
	Males — Con.								
1	Stable keepers, . . .	11	5	1	5	4	1	6	–
2	Stone cutters, . . .	8	3	3	2	2	5	–	1
3	Students, ...	7	–	7	–	–	–	2	5
4	Tailors and seamstresses (all kinds), . . .	11	5	5	1	3	2	3	3
5	Transportation, teamsters, expressmen, etc., . .	36	16	15	5	14	11	6	5
6	Woodworkers, . . .	5	–	3	2	1	1	1	2
7	Other occupations, . .	15	4	8	3	4	4	5	2
8	Not stated, ...	78	12	54	12	11	7	27	33
9	*Females.*	862	87	644	131	65	91	213	493
10	At home, ...	14	–	9	5	–	1	5	8
11	Bookbinders, . . .	2	1	1	–	1	1	–	–
12	Bookkeepers, . . .	2	–	2	–	–	–	1	1
13	Boot and shoemakers,. .	4	–	4	–	–	–	–	4
14	Button makers, . . .	1	–	1	–	–	–	–	1
15	Clerks and saleswomen, .	4	–	4	–	–	1	–	3
16	Dealers, traders, peddlers (all kinds), . . .	1	–	1	–	–	–	–	1
17	Domestic service, . .	146	22	96	28	16	18	38	74
18	Dressmakers, . . .	18	2	15	1	–	5	3	10
19	Factory operatives, . .	59	7	40	12	5	7	22	25
20	Furniture makers and finishers, ...	1	1	–	–	1	–	–	–
21	Hat makers and finishers, .	3	–	3	–	–	1	–	2
22	Hotel and boarding-house proprietors, . . .	5	–	5	–	–	2	1	2
23	Housekeepers, . . .	88	7	63	18	4	9	26	49
24	Housewives, . . .	292	34	222	36	28	31	65	168
25	Housework, ...	26	3	18	5	2	1	7	16
26	Personal service, . . .	18	2	14	2	2	3	1	12
27	Printers, ...	2	–	2	–	–	–	–	2
28	Professional service, . .	13	–	13	–	–	–	1	12
29	Students, ...	2	–	2	–	–	–	1	1
30	Tailoresses and seamstresses (all kinds), . . .	18	1	17	–	1	2	2	13
31	Other occupations, . .	1	–	1	–	–	–	1	–
32	Not stated, ...	142	7	111	24	5	9	39	89

RECAPITULATION. — *Relation of the Liquor Traffic to Insanity: By Sex and Occupations* — Concluded.

KINDS OF LIQUOR						TOBACCO		DRUGS		
Wines only	Lager Beer and Malt Liquors only	Distilled Liquors only	Two or All Kinds	Un-known	Inappli-cable*	Users	Non-users	Users	Non-users	
-	1	1	3	6	-	3	8	-	11	1
-	1	2	4	-	1	5	3	-	8	2
-	-	-	-	2	5	1	6	-	7	3
-	-	-	5	3	3	5	6	-	11	4
-	5	1	19	6	5	26	10	-	36	5
-	-	1	1	1	2	1	4	-	5	6
-	1	1	6	5	2	9	6	-	15	7
1	4	-	13	27	33	25	53	-	78	8
6	35	10	105	213	493	31	831	22	840	9
-	-	-	1	5	8	-	14	-	14	10
-	-	-	2	-	-	-	2	-	2	11
-	-	-	-	1	1	-	2	-	2	12
-	-	-	-	-	4	-	4	-	4	13
-	-	-	-	-	1	-	1	-	1	14
-	1	-	-	-	3	2	2	-	4	15
-	-	-	-	-	1	-	1	-	1	16
3	5	1	25	38	74	7	139	1	145	17
1	1	-	3	3	10	-	18	1	17	18
-	4	2	6	22	25	-	59	2	57	19
-	-	-	1	-	-	-	1	-	1	20
-	-	-	1	-	2	-	3	-	3	21
-	-	-	2	1	2	1	4	-	5	22
-	5	-	8	26	49	5	83	3	85	23
2	11	6	40	65	168	11	281	12	280	24
-	1	-	2	7	16	1	25	1	25	25
-	1	-	4	1	12	-	18	-	18	26
-	-	-	-	-	2	-	2	-	2	27
-	-	-	-	1	12	-	13	1	12	28
-	-	-	-	1	1	-	2	-	2	29
-	2	-	1	2	13	-	18	-	18	30
-	-	-	-	1	-	-	1	-	1	31
-	4	1	9	30	89	4	138	1	141	32

* Total Abstainers.

The summary shows that in the case of 296 males out of the 974, the insanity was due to the use of intoxicating liquors. As to 479, however, the contrary is true. In 199 instances the information was not ascertained. The 974 males include 246 excessive drinkers and 269 other drinkers; information upon this point being unknown in 275 cases, and 184 being total abstainers. Wines only were used by four of these males, while 84 used lager beer and malt liquors only; 26 distilled liquors only; and 400 two or all kinds of liquor. In 276 cases, information as to the kinds of liquor used was unknown. The users of tobacco numbered 495 and the non-users, 479; the users of drugs, 15; and the non-users, 959. As regards the occupations of these insane males, the most numerous class includes the laborers, who numbered 202. The factory operatives numbered 85; boot and shoemakers, 70; farmers and farm laborers, 59; dealers, traders, and peddlers of all kinds, 53; no other single class shown in the table containing more than 50 persons.

As to the females, in 87 cases out of the 862, the insanity

RECAPITULATION. — *Relation of the Liquor Traffic to Insanity : By Sex and Political Condition.*

	SEX AND POLITICAL CONDITION.	Number of Insane	Is the person's present condition of Insanity due to the use or abuse of Intoxicating Liquors			LIQUOR HABITS OF INSANE			
			Yes	No	Not Ascertained	Excessive Drinkers	Other Drinkers	Unknown	Total Abstainers
1	*Males.*	974	296	479	199	246	269	275	184
2	Citizen born, . . .	544	145	287	112	118	128	166	132
3	Naturalized or alien, . .	422	149	187	86	127	137	108	50
4	Unknown, ...	8	2	5	1	1	4	1	2
5	*Females.*	862	87	644	131	65	91	213	493
6	Citizen born, . . .	458	36	359	63	25	31	105	297
7	Naturalized or alien, . .	403	51	285	67	40	60	107	196
8	Unknown, ...	1	-	-	1	-	-	1	-
9	BOTH SEXES.	1,836	383	1,123	330	311	360	488	677
10	Citizen born, . . .	1,002	181	646	175	143	159	271	429
11	Naturalized or alien, . .	825	200	472	153	167	197	215	246
12	Unknown, ...	9	2	5	2	1	4	2	2

was due to the use of intoxicating liquors; but in 644 cases it was due to other causes; information as to 131 being not ascertained. Excessive drinkers among the females numbered 65, the other drinkers 91, total abstainers 493, and as to 213, information upon this point was not ascertained. Six used wines only, 35 lager beer and malt liquors only, 10 distilled liquors only, and 105 used two or all kinds of liquor; the facts as to the kinds of liquor used being unknown in 213 cases. Of the women, 31 used tobacco, and 22 used drugs. The most numerous class as regards occupations is housewives, numbering 292, while domestic servants numbered 146, housekeepers 88, and factory operatives 59. No other single class represented in the table contained more than 25 persons, except persons engaged in housework (neither domestic servants, housekeepers, nor housewives), who numbered 26.

The final recapitulation brings the leading facts under a classification showing place of birth, sex, and political condition. The first section of this table classifies the insane by sex, under citizen born and naturalized or alien.

RECAPITULATION. — *Relation of the Liquor Traffic to Insanity: By Sex and Political Condition.*

			KINDS OF LIQUOR				TOBACCO		DRUGS		
Wines only	Lager Beer and Malt Liquors only	Distilled Liquors only	Two or All Kinds	Un- known	Inappli- cable *	Users	Non- users	Users	Non- users	
4	84	26	400	276	184	495	479	15	959	1
1	42	14	188	167	132	259	285	10	534	2
3	40	12	209	108	50	230	192	5	417	3
-	2	-	3	1	2	6	2	-	8	4
6	35	10	105	213	493	31	831	22	840	5
-	13	3	40	105	297	12	446	13	445	6
6	22	7	65	107	196	19	384	9	394	7
-	-	-	-	1	-	-	1	-	1	8
10	119	36	505	489	677	526	1,310	37	1,799	9
1	55	17	228	272	429	271	731	23	979	10
9	62	19	274	215	246	249	576	14	811	11
-	2	-	3	2	2	6	3	-	9	12

* Total Abstainers.

RECAPITULATION. — *Relation of the Liquor Traffic to Insanity: By Sex,*
Political Condition, and Place of Birth.

	SEX, POLITICAL CONDITION, AND PLACE OF BIRTH.	Number of Insane	Is the person's present condition of **Insanity** due to the use or abuse of **Intoxicating Liquors**			LIQUOR HABITS OF INSANE			
			Yes	No	Not Ascertained	Excessive Drinkers	Other Drinkers	Unknown	Total Abstainers
1	MALES.	974	296	479	199	246	269	275	184
2	*Citizen Born.*	544	145	287	112	118	128	166	132
3	Alabama, ...	1	1	–	–	1	–	–	–
4	California, ...	2	–	1	1	–	1	1	–
5	Connecticut, . . .	11	4	6	1	4	5	1	1
6	District of Columbia, . .	1	–	1	–	–	–	–	1
7	Georgia, ...	2	–	1	1	–	–	2	–
8	Illinois, ...	2	1	1	–	–	1	1	–
9	Kentucky, ...	3	2	1	–	2	–	1	–
10	Maine, ...	35	10	17	8	10	7	9	9
11	Maryland, ...	2	1	1	–	1	1	–	–
12	Massachusetts, . . .	394	106	206	82	85	93	123	93
13	Michigan, ...	2	2	–	–	2	–	–	–
14	New Hampshire, . . .	25	2	18	5	1	6	9	9
15	New Jersey, . . .	4	2	2	–	2	–	–	2
16	New York, ...	13	3	5	5	2	3	6	2
17	North Carolina, . . .	3	–	1	2	–	1	2	–
18	Ohio, ...	1	–	1	–	–	–	–	1
19	Oregon, ...	1	1	–	–	1	–	–	–
20	Pennsylvania, . . .	2	1	1	–	–	1	–	1
21	Rhode Island, . . .	17	7	10	–	6	5	2	4
22	Vermont, ...	18	1	12	5	1	3	7	7
23	Virginia, ...	4	–	2	2	–	–	2	2
24	United States (not specified),	1	1	–	–	–	1	–	–
25	*Naturalized or Alien.*	422	149	187	86	127	137	108	50
26	Austria (Bohemia), . .	1	–	1	–	–	–	–	1
27	Austria (Hungary), . .	4	–	2	2	–	2	2	–
28	Austria (not specified), .	3	1	2	–	1	1	–	1
29	Belgium, ...	1	–	1	–	–	–	–	1
30	Born at sea, ...	1	–	–	–	–	1	–	–
31	Canada, ...	49	15	22	12	13	8	18	10
32	China, ...	3	–	2	1	–	2	1	–
33	Denmark, ...	1	–	–	1	–	–	1	–
34	England, ...	43	14	25	4	12	13	10	8
35	France, ...	1	–	–	1	–	–	1	–
36	Germany (Prussia), . .	2	1	1	–	1	–	1	–
37	Germany (not specified), .	30	5	19	6	6	19	5	–

RECAPITULATION.— *Relation of the Liquor Traffic to Insanity : By Sex, Political Condition, and Place of Birth.*

	KINDS OF LIQUOR						TOBACCO		DRUGS		
Wines only	Lager Beer and Malt Liquors only	Distilled Liquors only	Two or All Kinds	Un-known	Inapplicable *	Users	Non-users	Users	Non-users	
4	84	26	400	276	184	495	479	15	959	1
1	42	14	188	167	132	259	285	10	534	2
-	-	-	1	-	-	1	-	-	1	3
-	-	-	1	1	-	1	1	1	1	4
-	4	-	5	1	1	8	3	-	11	5
-	-	-	-	-	1	1	-	-	1	6
-	-	-	-	2	-	-	2	-	2	7
-	-	-	1	1	-	1	1	-	2	8
-	-	-	2	1	-	2	1	-	3	9
-	3	2	12	9	9	19	16	2	33	10
-	-	-	2	-	-	2	-	-	2	11
1	34	10	132	124	93	184	210	7	387	12
-	-	-	2	-	-	2	-	-	2	13
-	-	1	6	9	9	9	16	-	25	14
-	-	-	2	-	2	3	1	-	4	15
-	-	-	5	6	2	5	8	-	13	16
-	-	-	1	2	-	1	2	-	3	17
-	-	-	-	-	1	-	1	-	1	18
-	-	-	1	-	-	1	-	-	1	19
-	-	1	-	-	1	1	1	-	2	20
-	1	-	10	2	4	10	7	-	17	21
-	-	-	4	7	7	7	11	-	18	22
-	-	-	-	2	2	-	4	-	4	23
-	-	-	1	-	-	1	-	-	1	24
3	40	12	209	108	50	230	192	5	417	25
-	-	-	-	-	1	-	1	-	1	26
-	1	1	-	2	-	2	2	-	4	27
-	-	-	2	-	1	1	2	-	3	28
-	-	-	-	-	1	1	-	-	1	29
-	-	-	1	-	-	-	1	-	1	30
-	5	-	16	18	10	18	31	-	49	31
1	-	-	1	1	-	1	2	1	2	32
-	-	-	-	1	-	-	1	-	1	33
-	4	1	20	10	8	21	22	-	43	34
-	-	-	-	1	-	-	1	-	1	35
-	-	-	1	1	-	1	1	-	2	36
-	10	-	15	5	-	19	11	-	30	37

* Total Abstainers.

RECAPITULATION. — *Relation of the Liquor Traffic to Insanity: By Sex, Political Condition, and Place of Birth —* Continued.

	SEX, POLITICAL CONDITION, AND PLACE OF BIRTH.	Number of Insane	Is the person's present condition of **Insanity** due to the use or abuse of **Intoxicating Liquors**			LIQUOR HABITS OF INSANE			
			Yes	No	Not Ascertained	Excessive Drinkers	Other Drinkers	Unknown	Total Abstainers
	MALES — Con.								
	Naturalized or Alien — Con.								
1	Greece, ...	1	–	–	1	–	–	1	–
2	Holland, ...	2	–	1	1	–	1	1	–
3	Ireland, ...	180	98	57	25	82	52	33	13
4	Italy, ...	9	1	4	4	–	6	2	1
5	New Brunswick, . . .	11	1	9	1	–	7	2	2
6	Newfoundland, . . .	3	1	1	1	2	1	–	–
7	Norway, ...	1	–	1	–	–	–	–	1
8	Nova Scotia, . . .	21	4	12	5	3	8	7	3
9	Poland, ...	9	–	4	5	–	1	7	1
10	Portugal (Western Islands),	1	–	–	1	–	–	1	–
11	Portugal (not specified), .	2	–	1	1	–	–	1	1
12	Prince Edward Island, .	7	2	3	2	2	3	1	1
13	Russia, ...	14	1	7	6	1	5	6	2
14	Scotland, ...	9	2	5	2	1	5	3	–
15	Sweden, ...	11	1	6	4	2	1	4	4
16	Switzerland, . . .	1	1	–	–	1	–	–	–
17	West Indies, . . .	1	–	1	–	–	1	–	–
18	*Unknown.*	8	2	5	1	1	4	1	2
19	England, ...	2	–	2	–	–	–	–	2
20	Germany, ...	1	–	1	–	–	1	–	–
21	Ireland, ...	3	2	1	–	1	2	–	–
22	New Brunswick, . . .	1	–	1	–	–	1	–	–
23	Not stated, . . .	1	–	–	1	–	–	1	–
24	FEMALES.	862	87	644	131	65	91	213	493
25	*Citizen Born.*	458	36	359	63	25	31	105	297
26	Connecticut, ...	10	–	8	2	–	–	2	8
27	Indiana, ...	1	–	–	1	–	–	1	–
28	Iowa, ...	4	–	4	–	–	–	–	4
29	Louisiana, . . .	1	1	–	–	1	–	–	–
30	Maine, ...	50	1	41	8	1	1	16	32
31	Maryland, ...	1	–	1	–	–	–	–	1
32	Massachusetts, . . .	310	30	236	44	21	24	70	195
33	Michigan, ...	2	–	2	–	–	–	1	1
34	Minnesota, . . .	1	–	1	–	–	–	–	1

RECAPITULATION. — *Relation of the Liquor Traffic to Insanity : By Sex, Political Condition, and Place of Birth* — Continued.

| | KINDS OF LIQUOR | | | | | TOBACCO | | DRUGS | | |
Wines only	Lager Beer and Malt Liquors only	Distilled Liquors only	Two or All Kinds	Un-known	Inappli-cable*	Users	Non-users	Users	Non-users	
-	-	-	-	1	-	-	1	-	1	1
-	1	-	-	1	-	1	1	-	2	2
-	8	7	119	33	13	120	60	3	177	3
1	-	-	5	2	1	4	5	-	9	4
-	3	1	3	2	2	7	4	-	11	5
-	-	1	2	-	-	3	-	1	2	6
-	-	-	-	-	1	-	1	-	1	7
-	4	-	7	7	3	10	11	-	21	8
-	-	-	1	7	1	1	8	-	9	9
-	-	-	-	1	-	-	1	-	1	10
-	-	-	-	1	1	1	1	-	2	11
-	1	-	4	1	1	5	2	-	7	12
1	1	-	4	6	2	4	10	-	14	13
-	1	1	4	3	-	6	3	-	9	14
-	1	-	2	4	4	3	8	-	11	15
-	-	-	1	-	-	-	1	-	1	16
-	-	-	1	-	-	1	-	-	1	17
-	2	-	3	1	2	6	2	-	8	18
-	-	-	-	-	2	1	1	-	2	19
-	-	-	1	-	-	1	-	-	1	20
-	1	-	2	-	-	3	-	-	3	21
-	1	-	-	-	-	1	-	-	1	22
-	-	-	-	1	-	-	1	-	1	23
6	35	10	105	213	493	31	831	22	840	24
-	13	3	40	105	297	12	446	13	445	25
-	-	-	-	2	8	-	10	-	10	26
-	-	-	-	1	-	-	1	-	1	27
-	-	-	-	-	4	-	4	-	4	28
-	-	-	1	-	-	1	-	-	1	29
-	1	-	1	16	32	2	48	3	47	30
-	-	-	-	-	1	-	1	-	1	31
-	11	2	32	70	195	8	302	6	304	32
-	-	-	-	1	1	-	2	-	2	33
-	-	-	-	-	1	-	1	-	1	34

* Total Abstainers.

RECAPITULATION. — *Relation of the Liquor Traffic to Insanity : By Sex, Political Condition, and Place of Birth* — Continued.

	SEX, POLITICAL CONDITION, AND PLACE OF BIRTH.	Number of insane	Is the person's present condition of **Insanity** due to the use or abuse of **Intoxicating Liquors**			LIQUOR HABITS OF INSANE			
			Yes	No	Not Ascertained	Excessive Drinkers	Other Drinkers	Unknown	Total Abstainers
	FEMALES — Con.								
	Citizen Born — Con.								
1	Missouri,	1	-	1	-	-	-	-	1
2	New Hampshire,	19	-	19	-	-	1	2	16
3	New Jersey,	2	-	2	-	-	-	-	2
4	New York,	23	1	17	5	1	2	5	15
5	Pennsylvania,	3	-	3	-	-	-	1	2
6	Rhode Island,	6	1	5	-	-	2	-	4
7	South Carolina,	1	-	1	-	-	-	-	1
8	Vermont,	17	2	12	3	1	1	7	8
9	Virginia,	4	-	4	-	-	-	-	4
10	West Virginia,	1	-	1	-	-	-	-	1
11	United States(not specified),	1	-	1	-	-	-	-	1
12	*Naturalized or Alien.*	403	51	285	67	40	60	107	196
13	Africa,	1	-	1	-	-	-	-	1
14	Austria (Bohemia),	1	-	1	-	-	-	-	1
15	Austria (not specified),	3	-	2	1	-	-	1	2
16	Born at sea,	1	1	-	-	-	1	-	-
17	Canada,	34	1	25	8	1	3	12	18
18	Denmark,	2	-	-	2	-	-	2	-
19	England,	39	2	34	3	2	8	6	23
20	France,	2	-	1	1	-	-	1	1
21	Germany,	15	1	10	4	1	4	5	5
22	Ireland,	195	41	122	32	29	32	50	84
23	Italy,	2	-	2	-	-	2	-	-
24	New Brunswick,	19	-	18	1	-	3	2	14
25	Newfoundland,	8	1	5	2	1	-	3	4
26	Norway,	1	-	-	1	-	-	1	-
27	Nova Scotia,	22	3	17	2	4	1	5	12
28	Poland,	2	-	1	1	-	1	1	-
29	Portugal (Western Islands),	4	-	4	-	-	-	1	3
30	Prince Edward Island,	8	1	7	-	1	1	1	5
31	Russia,	6	-	5	1	-	2	-	4
32	Scotland,	18	-	14	4	1	2	9	6
33	Sweden,	16	-	13	3	-	-	5	11
34	Switzerland,	1	-	1	-	-	-	-	1
35	Wales,	1	-	1	-	-	-	1	-
36	West Indies,	2	-	1	1	-	-	1	1

RECAPITULATION. — *Relation of the Liquor Traffic to Insanity : By Sex, Political Condition; and Place of Birth* — Continued.

	KINDS OF LIQUOR						TOBACCO		DRUGS		
Wines only	Lager Beer and Malt Liquors only	Distilled Liquors only	Two or All Kinds	Un-known	Inappli-cable *		Users	Non-users	Users	Non-users	
-	-	-	-	-	1		-	1	-	1	1
-	-	-	1	2	16		-	19	-	19	2
-	-	-	-	-	2		-	2	1	1	3
-	-	-	3	5	15		1	22	1	22	4
-	-	-	-	1	2		-	3	-	3	5
-	1	-	1	-	4		-	6	1	5	6
-	-	-	-	-	1		-	1	-	1	7
-	-	1	1	7	8		-	17	1	16	8
-	-	-	-	-	4		-	4	-	4	9
-	-	-	-	-	1		-	1	-	1	10
-	-	-	-	-	1		-	1	-	1	11
6	22	7	65	107	196		19	384	9	394	12
-	-	-	-	-	1		-	1	-	1	13
-	-	-	-	-	1		-	1	-	1	14
-	-	-	-	1	2		-	3	-	3	15
-	-	-	1	-	-		-	1	-	1	16
1	1	-	2	12	18		-	34	1	33	17
-	-	-	-	2	-		-	2	-	2	18
1	3	2	4	6	23		1	38	-	39	19
-	-	-	-	1	1		-	2	-	2	20
-	3	-	2	5	5		2	13	-	15	21
1	9	3	50	48	84		11	184	5	190	22
1	-	-	1	-	-		-	2	-	2	23
-	1	2	-	2	14		-	19	1	18	24
-	-	-	1	3	4		-	8	-	8	25
-	-	-	-	1	-		-	1	-	1	26
-	1	-	4	5	12		3	19	2	20	27
-	1	-	-	1	-		-	2	-	2	28
-	-	-	-	1	3		-	4	-	4	29
-	-	-	2	1	5		-	8	-	8	30
2	-	-	-	-	4		-	6	-	6	31
-	3	-	-	9	6		2	16	-	18	32
-	-	-	-	5	11		-	16	-	16	33
-	-	-	-	-	1		-	1	-	1	34
-	-	-	-	1	-		-	1	-	1	35
-	-	-	-	1	1		-	2	-	2	36

* Total Abstainers.

RECAPITULATION.— *Relation of the Liquor Traffic to Insanity: By Sex, Political Condition, and Place of Birth* — Continued.

	Sex, Political Condition, and Place of Birth.	Number of Insane	Is the person's present condition of **Insanity** due to the use or abuse of **Intoxicating Liquors**			Liquor Habits of Insane			
			Yes	No	Not Ascertained	Excessive Drinkers	Other Drinkers	Unknown	Total Abstainers
	FEMALES — Con.								
1	Unknown.	1	-	-	1	-	-	1	-
2	Not stated, .	1	-	-	1	-	-	1	-
3	BOTH SEXES.	1,836	383	1,123	330	311	360	488	677
4	Citizen Born.	1,002	181	646	175	143	159	271	429
5	Alabama, ...	1	1	-	-	1	-	-	-
6	California, ...	2	-	1	1	-	1	1	-
7	Connecticut, . . .	21	4	14	3	4	5	3	9
8	District of Columbia, .	1	-	1	-	-	-	-	1
9	Georgia, ...	2	-	1	1	-	-	2	-
10	Illinois, ...	2	1	1	-	-	1	1	-
11	Indiana, ...	1	-	-	1	-	-	1	-
12	Iowa, ...	4	-	4	-	-	-	-	4
13	Kentucky, ...	3	2	1	-	2	-	1	-
14	Louisiana, ...	1	1	-	-	1	-	-	-
15	Maine, ...	85	11	58	16	11	8	25	41
16	Maryland, ...	3	1	2	-	1	1	-	1
17	Massachusetts, . . .	704	136	442	126	106	117	193	288
18	Michigan, ...	4	2	2	-	2	-	1	1
19	Minnesota, ...	1	-	1	-	-	-	-	1
20	Missouri, ...	1	-	1	-	-	-	-	1
21	New Hampshire, . . .	44	2	37	5	1	7	11	25
22	New Jersey, . . .	6	2	4	-	2	-	-	4
23	New York, ...	36	4	22	10	3	5	11	17
24	North Carolina, . . .	3	-	1	2	-	1	2	-
25	Ohio, ...	1	-	1	-	-	-	-	1
26	Oregon, ...	1	1	-	-	1	-	-	-
27	Pennsylvania, . . .	5	1	4	-	-	1	1	3
28	Rhode Island, . . .	23	8	15	-	6	7	2	8
29	South Carolina, . . .	1	-	1	-	-	-	-	1
30	Vermont, ...	35	3	24	8	2	4	14	15
31	Virginia, ...	8	-	6	2	-	-	2	6
32	West Virginia, . . .	1	-	1	-	-	-	-	1
33	United States (not specified),	2	1	1	-	-	1	-	1
34	Naturalized or Alien.	825	200	472	153	167	197	215	246
35	Africa, ...	1	-	1	-	-	-	-	1
36	Austria (Bohemia), . .	2	-	2	-	-	-	-	2

RECAPITULATION. — *Relation of the Liquor Traffic to Insanity: By Sex, Political Condition, and Place of Birth* — Continued.

Wines only	Lager Beer and Malt Liquors only	Distilled Liquors only	Two or All Kinds	Un-known	Inappli-cable *	Users	Non-users	Users	Non-users	
			KINDS OF LIQUOR			TOBACCO		DRUGS		
-	-	-	-	1	-	-	1	-	1	1
-	-	-	-	1	-	-	1	-	1	2
10	119	36	505	489	677	526	1,310	37	1,799	3
1	55	17	228	272	429	271	731	23	979	4
-	-	-	1	-	-	1	-	-	1	5
-	-	-	1	1	-	1	1	1	1	6
-	4	-	5	3	9	8	13	-	21	7
-	-	-	-	-	1	1	-	-	1	8
-	-	-	-	2	-	-	2	-	2	9
-	-	-	1	1	-	1	1	-	2	10
-	-	-	-	1	-	-	1	-	1	11
-	-	-	-	-	4	-	4	-	4	12
-	-	-	2	1	-	2	1	-	3	13
-	-	-	1	-	-	1	-	-	1	14
-	4	2	13	25	41	21	64	5	80	15
-	-	-	2	-	1	2	1	-	3	16
1	45	12	164	194	288	192	512	13	691	17
-	-	-	2	1	1	2	2	-	4	18
-	-	-	-	-	1	-	1	-	1	19
-	-	-	-	-	1	-	1	-	1	20
-	-	1	7	11	25	9	35	-	44	21
-	-	-	2	-	4	3	3	1	5	22
-	-	-	8	11	17	6	30	1	35	23
-	-	-	1	2	-	1	2	-	3	24
-	-	-	-	-	1	-	1	-	1	25
-	-	-	1	-	-	1	-	-	1	26
-	-	1	-	1	3	1	4	-	5	27
-	2	-	11	2	8	10	13	1	22	28
-	-	-	-	-	1	-	1	-	1	29
-	-	1	5	14	15	7	28	1	34	30
-	-	-	-	2	6	-	8	-	8	31
-	-	-	-	-	1	-	1	-	1	32
-	-	-	1	-	1	1	1	-	2	33
9	62	19	274	215	246	249	576	14	811	34
-	-	-	-	-	1	-	1	-	1	35
-	-	-	-	-	2	-	2	-	2	36

* Total Abstainers.

RECAPITULATION. — *Relation of the Liquor Traffic to Insanity: By Sex, Political Condition, and Place of Birth* — Concluded.

	SEX, POLITICAL CONDITION, AND PLACE OF BIRTH.	Number of Insane	Is the person's present condition of Insanity due to the use or abuse of Intoxicating Liquors			LIQUOR HABITS OF INSANE			
			Yes	No	Not Ascertained	Excessive Drinkers	Other Drinkers	Unknown	Total Abstainers
	BOTH SEXES — Con.								
	Naturalized or Alien — Con.								
1	Austria (Hungary), . .	4	-	2	2	-	2	2	-
2	Austria (not specified), .	6	1	4	1	1	1	1	3
3	Belgium, ...	1	-	1	-	-	-	-	1
4	Born at sea, ...	2	2	-	-	-	2	-	-
5	Canada, ...	83	16	47	20	14	11	30	28
6	China, ...	3	-	2	1	-	2	1	-
7	Denmark, ...	3	-	-	3	-	-	3	-
8	England, ...	82	16	59	7	14	21	16	31
9	France, ...	3	-	1	2	-	-	2	1
10	Germany (Prussia), . .	2	1	1	-	1	-	1	-
11	Germany (not specified), .	45	6	29	10	7	23	10	5
12	Greece, ...	1	-	-	1	-	-	1	-
13	Holland, ...	2	-	1	1	-	1	1	-
14	Ireland, ...	375	139	179	57	111	84	83	97
15	Italy, ...	11	1	6	4	-	8	2	1
16	New Brunswick, . . .	30	1	27	2	-	10	4	16
17	Newfoundland, . . .	11	2	6	3	3	1	3	4
18	Norway, ...	2	-	1	1	-	-	1	1
19	Nova Scotia, . . .	43	7	29	7	7	9	12	15
20	Poland, ...	11	-	5	6	-	2	8	1
21	Portugal (Western Islands),	5	-	4	1	-	-	2	3
22	Portugal (not specified), .	2	-	1	1	-	-	1	1
23	Prince Edward Island, .	15	3	10	2	3	4	2	6
24	Russia, ...	20	1	12	7	1	7	6	6
25	Scotland, ...	27	2	19	6	2	7	12	6
26	Sweden, ...	27	1	19	7	2	1	9	15
27	Switzerland, . . .	2	1	1	-	1	-	-	1
28	Wales, ...	1	-	1	-	-	-	1	-
29	West Indies, . . .	3	-	2	1	-	1	1	1
30	*Unknown.*	9	2	5	2	1	4	2	2
31	Not stated, ...	9	2	5	2	1	4	2	2

Of the total number, 1,836, the citizen born numbered 1,002, including 181 whose insanity was due to the use of liquor. The naturalized or alien numbered 825, including 200 whose in-

RECAPITULATION. — *Relation of the Liquor Traffic to Insanity : By Sex, Political Condition, and Place of Birth* — Concluded.

Kinds of Liquor						Tobacco		Drugs		
Wines only	Lager Beer and Malt Liquors only	Distilled Liquors only	Two or All Kinds	Unknown	Inapplicable *	Users	Non-users	Users	Non-users	
-	1	1	-	2	-	2	2	-	4	1
-	-	-	2	1	3	1	6	-	6	2
-	-	-	-	-	1	1	-	-	1	3
-	-	-	2	-	-	-	2	-	2	4
1	6	-	18	30	28	18	65	1	82	5
1	-	-	1	1	-	1	2	1	2	6
-	-	-	-	3	-	-	3	-	3	7
1	7	3	24	16	31	22	60	-	82	8
-	-	-	-	2	1	-	3	-	3	9
-	-	-	1	1	-	1	1	-	2	10
-	13	-	17	10	5	21	24	-	45	11
-	-	-	-	1	-	-	1	-	1	12
-	1	-	-	1	-	1	1	-	2	13
1	17	10	167	83	97	131	244	8	367	14
2	-	-	6	2	1	4	7	-	11	15
-	4	3	3	4	16	7	23	1	29	16
-	-	1	3	3	4	3	8	1	10	17
-	-	-	-	1	1	-	2	-	2	18
-	5	-	11	12	15	13	30	2	41	19
-	1	-	1	8	1	1	10	-	11	20
-	-	-	-	2	3	-	5	-	5	21
-	-	-	-	1	1	1	1	-	2	22
-	1	-	6	2	6	5	10	-	15	23
3	1	-	4	6	6	4	16	-	20	24
-	4	1	4	12	6	8	19	-	27	25
-	1	-	2	9	15	3	24	-	27	26
-	-	-	1	-	1	-	2	-	2	27
-	-	-	-	1	-	-	1	-	1	28
-	-	-	1	1	1	1	2	-	3	29
-	2	-	3	2	2	6	3	-	9	30
-	2	-	3	2	2	6	3	-	9	31

* Total Abstainers.

sanity was due to the use of liquor. Information as to political condition was unknown as to nine, two of whom were insane on account of the use of liquor. The excessive drinkers among the citizen born numbered 143 ; other drinkers, 159 ; total abstainers, 429 ; the facts as to liquor habits being unknown as to 271. The naturalized or alien include 167 excessive drinkers, 197 other drinkers, 246 total abstainers ; information upon this point being unknown as to 215. One of the citizen born used wines only ; 55 lager beer and malt liquors only ; 17 distilled liquors only ; and 228 two or all kinds of liquor ; information as to the kinds of liquor being unknown in 272 cases. Among the naturalized or alien, there were nine who used wines only ; 62 lager beer and malt liquors only ; 19 distilled liquors only ; and 274 who used two or all kinds ; information upon this point being unknown in 215 cases. The citizen born include 271 users of tobacco, and the naturalized or alien include 249 users of tobacco. There were 23 users of drugs among the citizen born, and 14 among the naturalized or alien. Of the 544 citizen-born male insane persons, 394 were born in Massachusetts, of whom 106 were insane on account of the use of liquor, the number of excessive drinkers being 85. Of the naturalized or alien males, who numbered 422, 180 were born in Ireland ; of these, 98 were insane on account of the use of liquor, and 82 were excessive drinkers. The birthplaces of the others are distributed among various foreign countries, 49 being born in Canada, 43 in England, 30 in Germany, and 21 in Nova Scotia.

The 862 female insane persons include 458 citizen born, of whom 310 were born in Massachusetts, 30 being insane from the use of liquor, and 21 being excessive drinkers. Of the 403 naturalized or alien female insane persons, 195 were born in Ireland ; of these, 41 were insane on account of the use of liquor, and 29 were excessive drinkers. The number born in England was 39, while 34 were born in Canada, 22 in Nova Scotia, 18 in Scotland, 16 in Sweden, and 15 in Germany ; the others being distributed among various other foreign countries.

FACTS CONCERNING INMATES OF OTHER STATE INSTITUTIONS.

There are a few institutions in the State, which, from their nature, have not been included among the sources of information from which the statistics in the preceding tables have been derived. These are the Massachusetts Hospital for Dipsomaniacs, at Foxborough; the Lyman School for Boys; Lancaster State Industrial School for Females; Monson State Primary School; Massachusetts School for the Feeble-minded, at Waltham; and the Hospital Cottages for Children, at Baldwinville. It will be seen that these institutions do not exactly fall into the penal or pauper classes, and the information derived from them will now be summarized in text.

In the Massachusetts Hospital for Dipsomaniacs, at Foxborough, information was obtained for 202 inmates, all of whom were males. Of these, 145 were citizen born, 40 naturalized, and 16 alien, while the political condition of one was not ascertained. Of the whole number, 63 had both parents native and 126 both parents foreign, while the parent nativity of the others was either unknown, or one parent was foreign. Of course, owing to the nature of the institution, the condition of the inmates was due to the intemperate use of liquor. Only eight of the inmates considered that the intemperate habits of their parents led to their own intemperance, while 157 returned an unqualified negative to this inquiry, the information as to 37 not being ascertained. None of the inmates considered that the intemperate habits of guardians other than their parents led to their present condition. To the question "Did the intemperate habits of others (neither parents nor guardians) lead to the present condition of the person considered," the replies were mainly in the negative, except so far as the influence of associates was contributory. Of the inmates, 192 used tobacco, while nine were addicted to the intemperate use of drugs. The number who reported that their fathers used tobacco was 136, while four inmates stated that their mothers used tobacco. Among the fathers of the inmates, 13 were excessive drinkers, while only one reported that his mother was an excessive drinker. To sum up the information derived from this source, we may say that of the 202 inmates, all of whom were there on account of the use of intoxicating liquors, 155 were excessive drinkers, 12 used lager beer and malt liquors only, 17 distilled liquors only, while the others used two or all kinds of liquors.

These facts are summarized in tabular form in the following presentation.

	SEX AND POLITICAL CONDITION.	Number of Inmates	Is the person's present **Condition** due to the use or abuse of **Intoxicating Liquors**			Liquor Habits of Inmates			
			Yes	No	Not Ascertained	Excessive Drinkers	Other Drinkers	Unknown	Total Abstainers
1	*Males*	202	202	–	–	155	47	–	–
2	Citizen born, . . .	145	145	–	–	112	33	–	–
3	Naturalized or alien, . .	56	56	–	–	42	14	–	–
4	Unknown, ...	1	1	–	–	1	–	–	–

In the Lyman School for Boys, the facts as to 158 inmates were obtained, 126 being citizen born and 32 aliens. Of the whole number, 31 had both parents native, 85 both parents foreign, and the others had either one parent foreign, or the facts as to parentage were unknown. Only one inmate was thought to be in the institution on account of the use or abuse of intoxicating liquors, but 46 ascribed their condition to the intemperate habits of one or both parents; the facts upon this point being unascertained in 37 cases. There was one other inmate who deemed his present condition due to the intem-

	SEX AND POLITICAL CONDITION.	Number of Inmates	Is the person's present **Condition** due to the use or abuse of **Intoxicating Liquors**			Liquor Habits of Inmates			
			Yes	No	Not Ascertained	Excessive Drinkers	Other Drinkers	Unknown	Total Abstainers
1	*Males.*	158	1	156	1	–	15	–	143
2	Citizen born, . . .	126	1	125	–	–	10	–	116
3	Naturalized or alien, . .	32	–	31	1	–	5	–	27

In the Lancaster State Industrial School, 74 inmates were canvassed, all of whom were females; the citizen born numbering 54, the alien 18, while the nativity of two was unknown. The number who had both parents native was 11, while 27 had both parents foreign; the others either having one parent foreign or the facts as to parentage were unknown. The inmates of this institution were all under 20 years of age, and

Wines only	Lager Beer and Malt Liquors only	Distilled Liquors only	Two or All Kinds	Un-known	Inappli-cable *	Users	Non-users	Users	Non-users	
KINDS OF LIQUOR						TOBACCO		DRUGS		
-	12	17	173	-	-	192	10	9	193	1
-	9	13	123	-	-	139	6	8	137	2
-	3	4	49	-	-	52	4	1	55	3
-	-	-	1	-	-	1	-	-	1	4

* Total Abstainers.

perate habits of his guardians other than parents, while three
replied that the intemperate habits of others (neither parents
nor guardians) led to their present condition. Tobacco was
used by 141 of the inmates, all of whom, it should be stated,
were under 20 years of age. Of the fathers of the inmates,
114 were addicted to the use of liquor, 31 being excessive
drinkers. Of the mothers, 57 used liquor, 14 using it excessively.

The following table shows a summary of the facts derived
from this institution.

Wines only	Lager Beer and Malt Liquors only	Distilled Liquors only	Two or All Kinds	Unknown	Inappli-cable *	Users	Non-users	
KINDS OF LIQUOR						TOBACCO		
2	7	-	6	-	143	141	17	1
1	4	-	5	-	116	111	15	2
1	3	-	1	-	27	30	2	3

* Total Abstainers.

16 of them reported their present condition to be due to the
intemperate use of intoxicating liquors, while 22 reported
that the intemperate habits of one or both parents led to their
condition, and two others stated that the intemperance of
guardians other than parents was the impelling cause. There
were also five who stated that the intemperate habits of others
(neither parents nor guardians) led to their present condition.

Twenty-one of the inmates used liquor, three being excessive drinkers. Only one of the inmates was reported as a user of tobacco, while 36 reported that their fathers used it, and one that it was used by the mother. Liquor was used by the

	SEX AND POLITICAL CONDITION.	Number of Inmates	Is the person's present **Condition** due to the use or abuse of **Intoxicating Liquors**			LIQUOR HABITS OF INMATES			
			Yes	No	Not Ascertained	Excessive Drinkers	Other Drinkers	Unknown	Total Abstainers
1	*Females.*	74	16	52	6	3	18	9	44
2	Citizen born, . . .	54	14	37	3	2	14	6	32
3	Naturalized or alien, . .	18	2	13	3	1	4	3	10
4	Unknown, ...	2	–	2	–	–	–	–	2

The inmates of the Monson State Primary School were of both sexes, and during the time covered by the investigation numbered 67, all of whom were under the age of 15 years, and none of whom were addicted to the use of intoxicating liquors. There were 39, however, who reported that the intemperate habits of their parents led to their condition, and three others that the intemperate habits of guardians other than parents were responsible. There were 14 who used tobacco, while tobacco was used by the fathers of 36, and by

	SEX AND POLITICAL CONDITION.	Number of Inmates	Is the person's present **Condition** due to the use or abuse of **Intoxicating Liquors**			LIQUOR HABITS OF INMATES			
			Yes	No	Not Ascertained	Excessive Drinkers	Other Drinkers	Unknown	Total Abstainers
1	*Males.*	51	–	50	1	–	1	2	48
2	Citizen born, . . .	42	–	41	1	–	1	1	40
3	Naturalized or alien, . .	9	–	9	–	–	–	1	8
4	*Females.*	16	–	16	–	–	–	–	16
5	Citizen born, . . .	15	–	15	–	–	–	–	15
6	Naturalized or alien, . .	1	–	1	–	–	–	–	1
7	BOTH SEXES.	67	–	66	1	–	1	2	64
8	Citizen born, . . .	57	–	56	1	–	1	1	55
9	Naturalized or alien, . .	10	–	10	–	–	–	1	9

fathers of 42 of the inmates, and by the mothers of 19. Of the fathers 14 were excessive drinkers, of the mothers five.

The following table gives a summary of the information derived from this institution.

| | KINDS OF LIQUOR | | | | | | TOBACCO | | |
Wines only	Lager Beer and Malt Liquors only	Distilled Liquors only	Two or All Kinds	Unknown	Inappli- cable *	Users	Non- users		
3	11	-	7	9	44	1	73	1
2	8	-	6	6	32	1	53	2
1	3	-	1	3	10	-	18	3
-	-	-	-	-	2	-	2	4

* Total Abstainers.

the mothers of two. Of the inmates of this institution, 14 had both parents native, 24 both parents foreign, and the others had either one parent foreign, or the facts as to parent nativity were unknown. Of the fathers of these persons, 45 were addicted to the use of liquor, while 32 were excessive drinkers. On the other hand, 26 had mothers who were addicted to the use of liquor, 13 of these mothers being excessive drinkers.

A summary showing the leading facts as to the inmates follows.

| | KINDS OF LIQUOR | | | | | | TOBACCO | | |
Wines only	Lager Beer and Malt Liquors only	Distilled Liquors only	Two or All Kinds	Unknown	Inappli- cable *	Users	Non- users		
-	1	-	-	2	48	14	37	1
-	1	-	-	1	40	11	31	2
-	-	-	-	1	8	3	6	3
-	-	-	-	-	16	-	16	4
-	-	-	-	-	15	-	15	5
-	-	-	-	-	1	-	1	6
-	1	-	-	2	64	14	53	7
-	1	-	-	1	55	11	46	8
-	-	-	-	1	9	3	7	9

* Total Abstainers.

The inmates of the Massachusetts School for Feeble-minded who were canvassed in the investigation numbered 53, of whom 38 were males and 15 females. The parentage was wholly native in 24 cases, wholly foreign in nine, the others having either one parent foreign or the facts upon this point were unknown. The ages of the inmates did not exceed 30 years, the majority being between five and fifteen years. The personal use of intoxicating liquors did not appear to be responsible for the condition of any of them, but the intemperance of parents in two cases was said to be responsible, and the

	SEX AND POLITICAL CONDITION.	Number of Inmates	Is the person's present Condition due to the use or abuse of Intoxicating Liquors			Liquor Habits of Inmates			
			Yes	No	Not Ascertained	Excessive Drinkers	Other Drinkers	Unknown	Total Abstainers
1	*Males.*	38	–	38	–	–	–	–	38
2	Citizen born, . . .	33	–	33	–	–	–	–	33
3	Naturalized or alien, . .	3	–	3	–	–	–	–	3
4	Unknown, ...	2	–	2	–	–	–	–	2
5	*Females.*	15	–	15	–	–	–	–	15
6	Citizen born, . . .	12	–	12	–	–	–	–	12
7	Naturalized or alien, .	3	–	3	–	–	–	–	3
8	Both Sexes.	53	–	53	–	–	–	–	53
9	Citizen born, . . .	45	–	45	–	–	–	–	45
10	Naturalized or alien, . .	6	–	6	–	–	–	–	6
11	Unknown, ...	2	–	2	–	–	–	–	2

At the Hospital Cottages, at Baldwinville, 70 inmates were found, nearly all of whom were minors, and the personal use of liquor was not considered influential in causing the condition of the inmates. The intemperate habits of one or both parents, however, was said to be the cause in five cases. No tobacco was used either by the inmates or by their mothers; it was said to be used by the fathers in 22 cases. Of the inmates, 29 had both parents native, 28 both parents foreign,

intemperate habits of guardians other than parents in one other case. None of the inmates used tobacco, although it was used by 18 of their fathers, but not by their mothers, so far as ascertained. As to the fathers, 13 were addicted to the use of intoxicating liquors, one being reported as an excessive drinker. Of the mothers, six were reported as addicted to the use of liquor, three being excessive drinkers.

The following table presents a recapitulation of the leading facts.

KINDS OF LIQUOR						TOBACCO		
Wines only	Lager Beer and Malt Liquors only	Distilled Liquors only	Two or All Kinds	Unknown	Inappli- cable*	Users	Non- users	
–	–	–	–	–	38	–	38	1
–	–	–	–	–	33	–	33	2
–	–	–	–	–	3	–	3	3
–	–	–	–	–	2	–	2	4
–	–	–	–	–	15	–	15	5
–	–	–	–	–	12	–	12	6
–	–	–	–	–	3	–	3	7
–	–	–	–	–	53	–	53	8
–	–	–	–	–	45	–	45	9
–	–	–	–	–	6	–	6	10
–	–	–	–	–	2	–	2	11

* Total Abstainers.

while the parent nativity of the others was either unknown, or else one of the parents at least was foreign. Among the fathers of these inmates, 26 were addicted to the use of intoxicating liquors, while six were reported as excessive drinkers. Among the mothers, five were addicted to the use of liquor; none, however, being excessive drinkers.

The following summary gives a recapitulation of the leading facts as to the inmates.

	SEX AND POLITICAL CONDITION.	Number of Inmates	Is the person's present **Condition** due to the use or abuse of **Intoxicating Liquors**			Liquor Habits of Inmates			
			Yes	No	Not Ascertained	Excessive Drinkers	Other Drinkers	Unknown	Total Abstainers
1	*Males.*	39	–	36	3	–	–	4	35
2	Citizen born, . . .	34	–	31	3	–	–	4	30
3	Naturalized or alien, . .	4	–	4	–	–	–	–	4
4	Unknown, ...	1	–	1	–	–	–	–	1
5	*Females.*	31	–	26	5	–	–	5	26
6	Citizen born, . . .	25	–	21	4	–	–	4	21
7	Naturalized or alien, . .	3	–	3	–	–	–	–	3
8	Unknown, ...	3	–	2	1	–	–	1	2
9	Both Sexes.	70	–	62	8	–	–	9	61
10	Citizen born, . . .	59	–	52	7	–	–	8	51
11	Naturalized or alien, . .	7	–	7	–	–	–	–	7
12	Unknown, ...	4	–	3	1	–	–	1	3

SUMMARY OF CONCLUSIONS.

The following summary presents in condensed form some of the main points derived from the investigation.

PAUPERISM.

Out of 3,230 paupers, this being the total number found in the State institutions during 12 consecutive months, 2,108, or about 65 in every 100 (65.26 per cent), were addicted to the use of liquor. The excessive drinkers numbered 505, or about 16 in every 100 (15.63 per cent), of all the paupers. The total abstainers numbered 866, or about 27 in every 100 (26.81 per cent), of all the paupers.

Of the total abstainers, however, 429 were minors; 281 being under 10 years of age. There were also 31 minors addicted to the use of liquor. Excluding all the minors, whether total abstainers or not, we have 2,752 paupers of adult years, of whom 2,077, or about 75 in every 100 (75.47 per cent), were addicted to the use of liquor, including 504 excessive drinkers and 1,573 drinkers not classed as excessive.

Wines only	Lager Beer and Malt Liquors only	Distilled Liquors only	Two or All Kinds	Unknown	Inapplicable*	Users	Non-users	
KINDS OF LIQUOR						TOBACCO		
-	-	-	-	4	35	-	39	1
-	-	-	-	4	30	-	34	2
-	-	-	-	-	4	-	4	3
-	-	-	-	-	1	-	1	4
-	-	-	-	5	26	-	31	5
-	-	-	-	4	21	-	25	6
-	-	-	-	-	3	-	3	7
-	-	-	-	1	2	-	3	8
-	-	-	-	9	61	-	70	9
-	-	-	-	8	51	-	59	10
-	-	-	-	-	7	-	7	11
-	-	-	-	1	3	-	4	12

* Total Abstainers.

Of the whole number of paupers, 47.74 per cent, or nearly 48 in every 100, had one or both parents intemperate.

Of the whole number, 39.44 per cent, or about 39 in every 100, attributed their pauperism to their own intemperate habits; about five in every 100 considered their pauperism due to the intemperance of their parents, one or both; and about one in every 100 attributed their pauperism to the intemperance of those upon whom they were dependent, other than parents.

Of the whole number addicted to the use of liquor, namely 2,108, there were 25, or about one in every 100, who used wines only; 417, or about 20 in every 100, who used lager beer or malt liquors only; 38, or not quite two in every 100, who used distilled liquors only; and 1,628, or about 77 in every 100, more than three-fourths of the whole number, who used all kinds or at least two kinds of liquor.

Of the whole number of paupers (without discriminating as to sex) 2,005, or about 62 in every 100, used tobacco. Of

the males (no discrimination being made as to ages) nearly
75 in every 100, used tobacco. Only three paupers were found
among the whole number who used drugs intemperately.

Of the whole number of paupers (3,230) 1,019, or about 32
in every 100 (31.55 per cent), were citizen born; 320, or
about 10 in every 100 (9.91 per cent), were naturalized; and
1,867, or about 58 in every 100 (57.80 per cent), were alien.
The number having both parents native was 305, or about nine
in every 100 (9.44 per cent), while 2,652, or about 82 in
every 100 (82.11 per cent), had both parents foreign. The
others were either of wholly or partly unknown parentage, or
had father or mother foreign.

CRIME.

Out of 26,672 convictions for various offences during 12
consecutive months, 17,575, or about 66 in every 100 (65.89
per cent), were convictions for drunkenness; and 657, or
about two in every 100 (2.46 per cent), for drunkenness in
combination with other offences. Hence 18,232 convictions,
or about 68 in every 100 (68.36 per cent), included drunkenness either wholly or in part.

In 21,863 cases, about 82 in every 100 (81.97 per cent), the
offender was in liquor at the time the offence was committed.

In 8,440 cases in which drunkenness did not form part of
the offence, that is, in which the offender was convicted of a
crime other than drunkenness, 3,640, or about 43 in every
100 (43.13 per cent), were cases in which the offender was in
liquor at the time the offence was committed. Of these 8,440
cases, 4,852, or about 57 in every 100 (57.49 per cent), were
cases in which the offender was in liquor at the time the intent
was formed to commit the offence.

Out of the whole number of cases, namely 26,672, there
were 22,514 in which the intemperate habits of the offender
led to a condition which induced the crime. These constitute
about 84 in every 100, or 84.41 per cent, of the whole number
of cases. Disregarding convictions connected with drunken-

ness there remain 4,294 convictions for other crimes, committed under conditions created by the intemperate habits of the criminal. These constitute 50.88 per cent, or nearly 51 in every 100, of the total number of convictions for crimes other than drunkenness.

In 16,115 cases, 60.42 per cent of the whole number, or about 60 in every 100, the intemperate habits of persons other than the offender were said to have been influential in the commitment of the offence, and 3,611, or 42.78 per cent, about 43 in every 100, of the total convictions for crimes other than drunkenness were of this class.

Of the whole number of convictions, namely 26,672, the number of offenders addicted to the use of liquor (no discrimination being made as to sex) was 25,137, or about 94 in every 100 (94.24 per cent). The excessive drinkers numbered 4,516, about 17 in every 100 (16.93 per cent), and the total abstainers numbered 1,535, about six in every 100 (5.76 per cent).

Of the total abstainers, however, 632 were minors. There were also 680 minors addicted to the use of liquor. Excluding all the minors, whether total abstainers or not, we have 25,360 offenders of adult years, of whom 24,457, or about 96 in every 100 (96.44 per cent), were addicted to the use of liquor, including 4,482 excessive drinkers and 19,975 drinkers not classed as excessive.

Of the whole number of offenders 57.89 per cent, or nearly 58 in every 100, had fathers who were addicted to the use of liquor, while 20.49 per cent, or about 20 in every 100, had mothers addicted to the use of liquor.

Of the whole number of offenders addicted to the use of liquor, namely 25,137, there were 126, or less than one in every 100, who used wines only; 4,293, or about 17 in every 100, who used lager beer or malt liquors only; 728, or about three in every 100, who used distilled liquors only; and

19,990, or about 80 in every 100, nearly eight-tenths of the whole number, who used all kinds or at least two kinds of liquor.

Of the whole number of offenders (without discriminating as to sex), 22,738, or about 85 in every 100, used tobacco. Of the males (no discrimination being made as to ages), nearly 94 in every 100 used tobacco.

Of the whole number of offenders (26,672) 14,131 or about 53 in every 100 (52.98 per cent), were citizen born; 3,726, or about 14 in every 100 (13.97 per cent), were naturalized; and 8,815, or about 33 in every 100 (33.05 per cent), were alien. The number having both parents native was 4,089, or about 15 in every 100 (15.33 per cent), while 21,204, or about 80 in every 100 (79.50 per cent), had both parents foreign. The others were either of wholly or partly unknown parentage or had father or mother foreign.

During the twelve months covered by the investigation, the arrests in the State for all offences numbered about 41 (41.41) to each 1,000 of the population. In cities such arrests numbered about 55 (55.01), and in towns about 16 (15.67) to each 1,000 of the population. The arrests for drunkenness only numbered about 25 (24.59) in the State at large, about 34 (33.73) in the cities, and about seven (7.29) in the towns, to each 1,000 of the population.

There were 35 towns which changed their policy with respect to license during the 12 months covered by the investigation. Of these, 14 show a larger average number of arrests per month under no license than under license, but the number in either case is quite small in these towns. In 19 of the towns which changed their policy during the year, the average number of arrests per month for drunkenness was larger, and usually considerably larger, under license than under no license. In five small towns there were no arrests for drunkenness under either system. In one town there was one arrest for drunkenness during four months of license, and two during eight months of no license.

There were five cities which changed their policy with respect to license during the 12 months. The average number of arrests per month for drunkenness was less in all of these cities under no license than under license, as shown in the following table :

CITIES.	NUMBER OF MONTHS		AVERAGE NUMBER OF ARRESTS PER MONTH FOR DRUNKENNESS	
	License	No License	License	No License
Haverhill, ...	8	4	81.63	26.50
Lynn, ...	4	8	315.00	117.63
Medford, ...	8	4	20.12	13.25
Pittsfield, ...	4	8	93.25	36.75
Salem, ...	4	8	140.50	29.63

INSANITY.

Out of 1,836 cases of insanity, this being the total number found in the institutions canvassed during 12 consecutive months, there were found 671 instances, or about 37 in every 100 (36.55 per cent), in which the person was addicted to the use of liquor. The excessive drinkers numbered 311, or about 17 in every 100 (16.94 per cent), of all the insane. The total abstainers numbered 677, or about 37 in every 100 (36.87 per cent), of all the insane. Information as to the drinking habits of 488, or 26.58 per cent, of the whole number could not be ascertained.

Of the total abstainers 55 were minors, nine being under 15 years of age. There were also 12 minors addicted to the use of liquor. Excluding all the minors, whether total abstainers or not, and also excluding the adults for whom the facts as to the use of liquor could not be ascertained, we have 1,281 adult insane persons, of whom 659, or about 51 in every 100 (51.44 per cent), were addicted to the use of liquor, including 311 excessive drinkers and 348 drinkers not classed as excessive.

Of the whole number of insane persons, 33.55 per cent, or nearly 34 in every 100, were known to have one or both parents who were intemperate. This point could not be ascertained in 51.14 per cent of the whole number of cases however. Of the cases in which the facts could be determined, namely 897, there were 616, about 69 in every 100 (68.67 per cent), in which one or both parents were intemperate.

As to the direct influence of the use of liquor upon insanity the following facts appear: of the whole number (1,836) the investigation indicated that in 383 instances, about 21 in every 100 (20.86 per cent), the intemperance of the person led to his insanity. There were however 330 cases as to which this point could not be ascertained. Of the cases in which the point was fully determined, namely 1,506, there were therefore 383, or about 25 in every 100 (25.43 per cent), in which the intemperate habits of the person were considered the cause of insanity.

Only about one person in every 100 (1.09 per cent) of the entire number of the insane, was considered to be insane on account of the intemperance of his parents. Disregarding the cases in which the facts were unknown we have remaining 941 as to which this point was fully ascertained. Of these only 20, about two in every 100 (2.13 per cent), were thought to be insane on account of the intemperate habits of parents, either father or mother. As to grand-parents the facts could not be ascertained in 1,482 cases. Forming our conclusion upon the 354 cases in which the facts as to grand-parents were ascertained, we find 184, or about 52 in every 100 (51.98 per cent), in which the intemperance of grand-parents was considered to have led to the insanity of the person.

The intemperance of others, neither parents nor grand-parents, was considered the cause of the insanity of the person in 123 out of 880 cases, about 14 in every 100 (13.98 per cent). In this class there were 956 cases as to which the point could not be ascertained. These have therefore been disregarded in this statement.

Of the whole number of insane persons addicted to the use of liquor, namely 671, there were 10, or about one in every

100, who used wines only; 119, or about 18 in every 100, who used lager beer or malt liquors only; 36, or about five in every 100, who used distilled liquors only; and 505, or about 75 in every 100, three-fourths of the whole number, who used all kinds or at least two kinds of liquor.

Of the whole number of insane (without discriminating as to sex), 526, or about 29 in every 100, used tobacco. Of the males (no discrimination being made as to ages) nearly 51 in every 100 used tobacco. Only 37 insane persons out of the whole number, about two in every 100, used drugs intemperately.

Of the whole number of insane persons (1,836) 1,002 or about 55 in every 100 (54.58 per cent), were citizen born; 107, or about six in every 100 (5.83 per cent), were naturalized; and 718, or about 39 in every 100 (39.11 per cent), were alien.

The number having both parents native was 575 or about 31 in every 100 (31.32 per cent), while 1,087, or about 59 in every 100 (59.20 per cent), had both parents foreign. The others were either of wholly or partly unknown parentage, or had father or mother foreign.

VIOLATIONS OF THE LIQUOR LAW.

The figures relating to convictions and sentences, on pages 220 and 221, classify the crimes under three heads, namely, drunkenness, drunkenness and other crimes, and other crimes only. The convictions tabulated under the head of other crimes only, include the convictions for violations of the liquor law. In order to enable the reader to note the number of convictions for violations of the liquor law alone, with the sentences imposed for such convictions, a separate tabulation has been made of such offences, and the results are presented in the table which follows. The violations of the liquor law are classed under four heads, namely, liquor carrying, liquor keeping, maintaining a liquor nuisance, and liquor selling. In the table the convictions under each of these heads are separately presented, and the table also shows the number of convictions by sex and in the aggregate.

SEX AND LIQUOR OFFENCES.	FINES ONLY			IMPRISONMENT ONLY		
	Number	Aggregate Fines	Average Fine	Number	Aggregate Time (Days)	Average Time (Days)
1 *Males.*	191	$14,458.23	$75.70	28	2,370	85
2 Liquor carrying, . .	2	175.00	87.50	–	–	–
3 Liquor keeping, . .	58	4,785.00	82.50	5	330	66
4 Liquor nuisance, . .	25	2,228.54	89.14	9	810	90
5 Liquor selling, . . .	106	7,269.69	68.58	14	1,230	88
6 *Females.*	55	3,552.02	64.58	5	420	84
7 Liquor keeping, . .	12	866.00	72.17	1	120	120
8 Liquor nuisance, . .	5	400.00	80.00	2	150	75
9 Liquor selling, . . .	38	2,286.02	60.16	2	150	75
10 BOTH SEXES.	246	18,010.25	73.21	33	2,790	85
11 Liquor carrying, . .	2	175.00	87.50	–	–	–
12 Liquor keeping, . .	70	5,651.00	80.73	6	450	75
13 Liquor nuisance, . .	30	2,628.54	87.62	11	960	87
14 Liquor selling, . . .	144	9,555.71	66.36	16	1,380	86

Confining our analysis of the table to the figures for both sexes, we note that there were, in the 12 months covered by the investigation, 246 convictions for violations of the liquor law which were punished by fines only, the aggregate amount of fines in these cases being $18,010.25, or an average fine in each case of $73.21. Besides these, there were 33 convictions which were punished by imprisonment only, the aggregate time of imprisonment being 2,790 days, or an average of 85 days' imprisonment in each case. There were also 96 convictions punished by fine and imprisonment. In these cases the aggregate amount of fines imposed was $9,851.00, and the aggregate time of imprisonment amounted to 9,010 days, this being an average fine of $102.61, and an average imprisonment of 94 days in each case. There were 13 cases in which an alternative sentence was imposed of fine or imprisonment. The aggregate amount of fines imposed in these cases was $890.00, and the aggregate imprisonment amounted to 1,050 days, being an average of $68.46 fine and 81 days' imprisonment in each case. The total number of convictions for violations of the liquor law, without discriminating as to the nature

	FINES AND IMPRISONMENT					FINES OR IMPRISONMENT				
Num-ber	AGGREGATE		AVERAGE		Num-ber	AGGREGATE		AVERAGE		
	Fines	Time (Days)	Fine	Time (Days)		Fines	Time (Days)	Fine	Time (Days)	
73	$7,791.00	6,460	$106.73	88	12	$840.00	960	$70.00	80	1
2	250.00	180	125.00	90	-	-	-	-	-	2
12	1,150.00	970	95.83	81	3	225.00	360	75.00	120	3
18	1,780.00	2,010	98.89	112	1	100.00	90	100.00	90	4
41	4,611.00	3,300	112.46	80	8	515.00	510	64.38	64	5
23	2,060.00	2,550	89.56	111	1	50.00	90	50.00	90	6
7	575.00	780	82.14	111	-	-	-	-	-	7
5	460.00	690	92.00	138	1	50.00	90	50.00	90	8
11	1,025.00	1,080	93.18	98	-	-	-	-	-	9
96	9,851.00	9,010	102.61	94	13	890.00	1,050	68.46	81	10
2	250.00	180	125.00	90	-	-	-	-	-	11
19	1,725.00	1,750	90.79	92	3	225.00	360	75.00	120	12
23	2,240.00	2,700	97.39	117	2	150.00	180	75.00	90	13
52	5,636.00	4,380	108.38	84	8	515.00	510	64.38	64	14

of the sentence or as to the particular nature of the offence, was 388. Distributed under the heads shown in the table, the aggregate number of convictions is as follows : liquor carrying, 4 ; liquor keeping, 98 ; liquor nuisance, 66 ; liquor selling, 220.

It is perhaps unnecessary to state in closing, that it is not the province of this Bureau to draw deductions from the results of this investigation, to discuss the evil of intemperance in the light of these facts, or to apply the evidence presented to the support of any theory of the regulation or prohibition of the liquor traffic.

The facts reported are exhaustive within the field covered, and they are of great importance. Our duty is confined to the careful collection and accurate presentation of these facts, with such an analysis of the tables as seems necessary to render them intelligible. In this work neither theory nor bias has place. Our end is reached if the figures tell their story so plainly that its meaning is unobscured.

It is of course true that no investigation of this kind can deal with the psychological aspects of the drinking problem, or with the social conditions which have an important influence upon it.   It may be determined, for example, as we have shown, that the use of liquor is a direct cause of a given number of cases of pauperism, crime, or insanity.   It may be shown that the drinking habit once formed transmits itself from parent to offspring, and that the sins of the father are visited upon the children, not merely in fastening the appetite upon the child, but in subjecting him to pauperism, crime, or insanity.   The converse proposition is perhaps often true, namely, that pauperism and other evils, to say nothing of peculiar mental states, or inherited peculiarities of constitution, lead, in the first instance, to intemperance ; and the facts upon this point are neither clear nor easily obtainable.

Many of the paupers canvassed in this investigation were deficient in mental stamina, and while this is by no means so largely true with respect to the criminals, it is impossible to determine what peculiarities of brain exist among them, until criminal pathology has progressed much farther than at present. How far the use of liquor is directly responsible for the present condition of numbers of these persons may be-shown by the statistical method.   How far the mental and physical deficiencies of the individual may have led to his use of liquor is another question, and this can hardly be shown by statistics. The causes which lie back of the drinking habit are equally as important as the results of the habit itself, but their determination is obviously outside the limits of such an investigation as this.